Sixth Edition

Writing Themes About Literature

EDGAR V. ROBERTS

*Lehman College
of
The City University of New York*

PRENTICE HALL   *Englewood Cliffs, New Jersey 07632*

Library of Congress Cataloging-in-Publication Data

ROBERTS, EDGAR V.
　Writing themes about literature.

　Includes index.
　1. English language—Rhetoric.　2. Literature—
Study and teaching.　I. Title.
PE1408.R593 1988　　　808'.0668　　　87-17401
ISBN　0-13-970757-3

for Nanette

Editorial/production supervision: Lisa A. Domínguez
Cover design: Ben Santora
Manufacturing buyer: Ray Keating

Printed in the United States of America
10　9　8　7　6　5　4　3　2

ISBN 0-13-970757-3　　01

PRENTICE-HALL INTERNATIONAL (UK) LIMITED, *London*
PRENTICE-HALL OF AUSTRALIA PTY. LIMITED, *Sydney*
PRENTICE-HALL CANADA INC., *Toronto*
PRENTICE-HALL HISPANOAMERICANA, S. A., *Mexico*
PRENTICE-HALL OF INDIA PRIVATE LIMITED, *New Delhi*
PRENTICE-HALL OF JAPAN, INC., *Tokyo*
SIMON & SCHUSTER ASIA PTE. LTD., *Singapore*
EDITORA PRENTICE-HALL DO BRASIL, LTDA., *Rio de Janeiro*

Contents

Chapter 14   Writing About Tone: The Writer's Control over Attitudes and Feelings   167

Literary Tone and Speaking Tone of Voice, 167   Tone as Shown by Characters Within a Work, 168   Tone and the Author's Attitude Toward Readers, 168   Laughter, Comedy, and Farce, 169   Irony, 171   Writing About Tone, 173   *Sample Themes*, 175, 178   Commentaries on the Themes, 177, 180

Chapter 15   Writing Three Themes on Prosody: Rhythm, Segments, and Rhyme   181

I. THE RHYTHM OF POETRY: BEAT, METER, AND SCANSION, 181   Things to Consider in Studying Rhythm, 182   Cadence Groups, 182   Syllables, 184   Stress, Meter, Feet, Beat, and Metrical Scansion, 184   Metrical Feet, 185   The Caesura, or Pause, 191   Emphasis by Formal Substitution, 192   Emphasis by Rhetorical Variation, 193   Writing About Rhythm in Poetry, 194   *Sample Theme*, 197   Commentary on the Theme, 199   II. SOUNDS AND SEGMENTS, 200   Vowel Sounds, 200   Consonant Sounds, 201   Distinguishing Sounds from Spelling, 201   Segmental Poetic Devices, 201   Euphony and Cacophony, 203   Writing About Sounds and Segments in Poetry, 204   *Sample Theme*, 206   Commentary on the Theme, 210   III. RHYME, 210   Rhyme and Poetic Quality, 211   Rules and Variants in Rhyme, 211   Rhyme and Rhythm, 212   Describing Rhymes, 213   Rhyme Schemes, 213   Writing About Rhyme, 215   *Sample Theme*, 217   Commentary on the Theme, 219

Chapter 16   Writing Two Themes Based on a Close Reading: I. General Content and II. Style   221

Studying Your Passage, 221   Types of Close-Reading Themes, 223   I. THE GENERAL CONTENT OF A PASSAGE, 223   General Purposes of the Close-Reading Theme, 224   Writing About General Content in a Passage, 225   Numbers for Easy Reference, 226   *Sample Theme*, 226   Commentary on the Theme, 227   II. THE STYLE OF A PASSAGE, 228   Examples of Style and Its Relation to Character, 229   Two Major Approaches to Style, 230   Diction: Choice of Words, 230   Rhetoric, 234   Writing About the Style of a Passage, 237   *Sample Theme*, 239   Commentary on the Theme, 241

Chapter 17   Writing About Film   243

Film and Stage Plays, 243   The Painter, the Photographer, and the Filmmaker, 244   Techniques, 245   Editing or Montage: The Heart of the Filmmaker's Craft, 246   Visual Techniques, 247   Action and the Human Body, 249   Sound, 250   Writing About Film, 251   *Sample Theme*, 252   Commentary on the Theme, 255

Chapter 18   Writing the Research Theme   257

Selecting a Topic, 258   Setting Up a Bibliography, 260   Taking Notes and Paraphrasing Material, 261   Writing the Research Theme, 272   *Sample Research Essay*, 274   Commentary on the Theme, 281

To the Instructor

In submitting the sixth edition of *Writing Themes About Literature*, I have kept and strengthened those features which so many of you have valued over the years. As always, I base my approach not on genres, from which essay assignments are to be somehow determined, but rather on specific topics for full-length themes on texts in any genre (though in addition the topics work for shorter and paragraph-length assignments). The chapters may also be used as starting points for study and discussion. The result is that the sixth edition offers great scope and variety, either for a one-semester course or for a two- or three-semester sequence, with the possibility of complete or close-to-complete use.

As in each past edition of *Writing Themes About Literature*, the chapters consist of two parts. The first is a discussion of a literary approach, and the second is a sample theme (or two or, in one chapter, three) showing how the problems may be treated in a theme.

A major characteristic preserved in this edition is that the chapters are arranged in order of increasing difficulty. With the précis theme in Chapter 2, students begin with the simplest writing about any of the genres. The third chapter, now containing two topics, is also basic and essential; the fourth is concerned with the responses of liking and disliking. The next four chapters introduce analytical techniques important in both narrative and drama, although point of view and idea may also be studied in poetry. Chapters 9, 10, and 11 are usually aimed at poetry, but Chapter 11, Symbolism and Allegory, works for any genre. The twelfth-chapter theme, on comparison-contrast, illustrates in its two parts the ways in which the earlier techniques may be focused on topics from any of the genres. In addition, the theme of extended comparison may serve as a longer assignment for a one-semester course.

From Chapters 13 to 18, the topics are increasingly technical and sophisticated. The later chapters combine and build on the various techniques of analysis presented in the earlier chapters. As in the past, I have kept and strengthened the chapter on film because films and VCR screenings are now a norm in many courses.

Although you might assign the chapters in sequence throughout your course, you may choose them according to need and objective. One instructor, for example, might pass over the earlier, more general chapters and go directly to the later, more technical ones. Another might omit the longer comparison-contrast theme while repeating the shorter one for separate assignments such as comparative studies of imagery, structure, character, personal likes, and point of view. Still another might use just a few of the chapters, assigning them two or more times until students have overcome initial difficulties. No matter how the chapters are used, the two parts—discussion and illustration—should enable students to improve the quality of their analytical writing.

The illustrative sample themes are presented in the belief that the word *imitation* need not be preceded by adjectives like *slavish* or *mere*. Their purpose is to show what *might* be done—not what *must* be done—on particular assignments. Without examples, students must add the task of creating their own thematic form to the already complex task of understanding new concepts and new works of literature. Some students may follow the samples closely, while others may adapt them or use them as a point of departure. My assumption is that students will become more free to go their own ways as they become more experienced.

Because the sample themes are guides, they represent a full treatment of each of the various topics. Nevertheless, in this edition they have been kept within the approximate lengths of most assignments. If students are writing outside of class, they can readily create themes as full as the samples. Even though the samples treat an average of three aspects of particular topics, there is nothing to prevent assigning only one aspect, either for an impromptu or an outside-class theme. For example, using the chapter on setting, you might assign a paragraph about the use of setting in only the first scene of a story, or a paragraph about interior settings, colors, or shades of light.

Following each sample essay is a commentary—a feature new in the fourth edition and continued in the fifth and sixth—presented to help students connect the precepts in the first part of the chapter to the example in the second.

I have designed all changes in the sixth edition of *Writing Themes About Literature*, as in earlier editions, to guide and help students in reading, studying, thinking, planning, drafting, organizing, and writing. Many chapters are extensively revised; some are almost entirely rewritten. Readers who have become familiar with *Literature: An Introduction to Reading and Writing* (1986) and its companion, *Fiction: An Introduction to Reading and Writing* (1987), in which I was joined by the late Henry Jacobs, may see the strong use made there of *Writing Themes About Literature*. Now there is complementary cross-fertilization. My revisions here have been deeply affected by my work on these other books, particularly in Chapters 3, 6, 9, 10, 14, 15, and 18, but also elsewhere in greater or lesser degrees.

Users of past editions will find the greatest changes in Chapters 3 (Writing About Plot and Structure), 9 (Writing About Imagery), 10 (Writing About Metaphor and Simile), 11 (Writing About Symbolism and Allegory), and 17 (Writing About Film). In making these modifications, together with all the other many revisions, alterations, repositionings, and additions (and subtractions), I have tried to improve, sharpen, and freshen the underlying information and examples. With all these changes, the sixth edition of *Writing Themes About Literature* is comprehensive for composition courses in which literature is introduced, and also for literature courses at any level.

A major change needs special mention, and this is the increased number of works in Appendix C. At one time I believed that clarifying references could be drawn from a pool of works commonly known by advanced high school and college students, and I therefore thought that no reference anthology was necessary. I presented a small number of works in the second edition, keyed to some but not all of the sample themes, but reviewers recommended against it for the next editions. Recent commentary, however, has emphasized that references to unknown works, even complete and self-explanatory ones, do not fully explain and clarify. Therefore, in the fifth edition, and now almost fully in the sixth, I have made the book more self-contained by augmenting Appendix C (in two chapters, however, I have continued to assume acquaintance with Shakespeare's *Hamlet*). The result is that references and sample themes may be easily verified by a reading of the accompanying works. Thus, the student preparing a theme of comparison-contrast can compare the sample themes on that topic with the complete text of Frank O'Connor's "First Confession." This story is also a subject in the sample theme on character developed extensively in Chapter 1, Preliminary, and in the first part of Chapter 16, in addition to the references made to it elsewhere in the text. The other included works are used similarly. I believe that the unity and coherence provided by these works give students great help in understanding their own assignments.

Another innovation in the sixth edition is the glossary based on the terms set in boldface in the text. The increasing number of students taking entrance examinations and GREs has prompted this change. Now, a student may consult the list, which contains definitions and page numbers for further reference, and thereby develop full and systematic knowledge of important concepts in the text.

The sixth edition brings into focus something that has been true of *Writing Themes About Literature* since its first appearance in 1964. The book is to be used in the classroom as a practical guide for writing; the stress throughout is on writing. This emphasis is made to help students not only in composition and literature, but in most of their classes. In other subjects like psychology, economics, sociology, biology, and political science, instructors use texts and ask students to develop raw data, and they assign writing on this basis. Writing is on external, written materials, not on descriptions of the student's own experiences or on opinions. Writing is about reading.

Yet we instructors of composition face the problems we have always faced. On the one hand, the needs of other departments, recently thrown into renewed focus by studies about writing across the curriculum, cause wide diversification of subject matter, straining the general knowledge of the staff and also creating a certain topical and thematic disunity. On the other hand, programs stressing internalized subject matter, such as personal experiences or occasional topic materials, have little bearing on writing for other courses. We as English faculty, with a background in literature, have the task of meeting the service needs of the institution without compromising our own disciplinary commitment.

The approach in this book is aimed at these dilemmas. Teachers can work with their own discipline—literature—while also fulfilling their primary and often required responsibility of teaching writing that is externally, not internally, directed. The book thus keeps the following issues in perspective:

The requirement of the institution for composition.

The need of students to develop writing skills based on written texts.

The responsibility of the English faculty to teach writing while still working within their own expertise.

It is therefore gratifying to claim that the approach in *Writing Themes About Literature* has been tested for many years. It is no longer new, but it is still novel. It works. It gives coherence to the sometimes fragmented composition course. It also provides for adaptation and, as I have stressed, variety. Using the book, you can develop a virtually endless number of new topics for themes. One obvious benefit is the possibility of entirely eliminating not only the traditional, infamous "theme barrels" in fraternity and sorority houses, but also the newer interference from business enterprises that provide themes to order.

While *Writing Themes About Literature* is designed, as I have said in the past, as a rhetoric of practical criticism for students, it is based on profoundly held convictions. I believe that true liberation in a liberal arts curriculum is achieved only through clearly defined goals. Just to make assignments and let students do with them what they can is to encourage frustration and mental enslavement. But if students develop a deep knowledge of specific approaches to subject material, they can begin to develop some of that expertise that is essential to freedom. As Pope said:

> True ease in writing comes from art, not chance,
> As those move easiest who have learned to dance.

It is almost axiomatic that the development of writing skill in one area—in this instance, the interpretation of literature—has an enabling effect on skill in other areas. The search for information with a particular goal in mind; the asking of pointed questions; the testing, rephrasing, and developing of ideas—all these and more are transferable skills for students to build on throughout their college years and beyond.

I have one concluding article of faith. Those of us whose careers have been established in the study of literature have made commitments to our belief in its value. The study of literature is valid in and for itself. But literature as an art form employs techniques and creates problems for readers that can be dealt with only through analysis, and analysis means work. Thus the immediate aim of *Writing Themes About Literature* is to help students read and write about individual literary works. But the ultimate objective (in the past I wrote *"primary* objective") is to promote the pleasurable study and, finally, the love of literature.

ACKNOWLEDGMENTS

As I complete my preparation of the Sixth Edition of *Writing Themes About Literature* I express my deepest thanks to those who have been loyal to the previous editions. Your approval of the book not only has merited thanks, but it has also challenged me to create an acceptable new edition.

The changes in the following pages are based on my own experiences and thought, and also on my continued work with my students at Lehman College. As I acknowledge these sources, I am reminded of how much my book has been influenced by the collective wisdom of many, many other people. Specific help has come from a number of reviewers whose suggestions for changes have been invaluable to me in all stages of my revisions. They are Professors Sybil M. Patterson of Hillsborough Community College, Robbie C. Pinter of Belmont College, Beverly Slaughter of Brevard Community College, Ralph F. Voss of the University of Alabama, and Arthur A. Wagner of Macomb Community College. In addition, conversations and discussions with others have influenced my changes in innumerable and immeasurable ways. Of particular importance was my work with the late Henry Jacobs, of the University of Alabama, with whom I collaborated on two books for Prentice Hall. He was a hard worker, a brilliant writer, an honest and firm critic, and a kind man.

In addition, I am grateful to Phil Miller of Prentice Hall, who has given me firm and friendly support over a number of years. I should also like to thank Jane Baumann of Prentice Hall for her great courtesy and helpfulness, and Carol Carter of Prentice Hall for her uplifting enthusiasm. Extra thanks go to Lisa Domínguez, the production editor of the sixth edition, for her skill, patience, helpfulness, and hard work. Special thanks are due to Nancy Velthaus, who copyedited the manuscript. She caught many mistakes, and offered many improvements.

EDGAR V. ROBERTS

chapter 1

Preliminary

THE PROCESS OF WRITING THEMES
ABOUT LITERATURE

The following chapters are theme, or essay, assignments based on a number of analytical approaches important in the study of literature. The assignments are designed to fulfill two goals of composition and English courses: (1) to write good themes, and (2) to assimilate great works of literature into the imagination. On the negative side, the chapters aim to help you avoid themes that do no more than retell a story, state an undeveloped opinion, or describe the life of the author. On the positive side, the book aims to help you improve your writing skills through the use of literature as subject matter. Integral to your writing is your standard of literary judgment and the knowledge you acquire to separate good literature from bad. The book encourages the development of these skills by requiring you to apply, in well-prepared essays, specific approaches to good reading.

No educational process is complete until you have applied what you study. That is, you have not learned something—really *learned* it—until you talk or write about it or until you apply it to a question or problem. The need for application requires you to recognize where your learning is incomplete so that you may strengthen your knowledge. Thus, it is easy for you to read the chapter on point of view (the position from which details are seen, described, and considered), and it is also easy to read, say, Frank O'Connor's story "First Confession." But your grasp of point of view as a concept will not be complete—nor will your appreciation of at least one aspect of the technical artistry of "First Confession" be complete—until you have written about the technique itself as it is employed in the story (see Chapter 6). As you write, you will need to reread parts of the work, study your notes on it, and compare them with what you understand about the problem itself. In writing, you must check facts, grasp their relationship to your topic, develop insights into the value and artistry of the work, and express your understanding in a well-organized and well-substantiated theme. After you have finished a number of such essays, you should be able to approach other literary works with more confidence and skill. The more you know and the more you can apply, the more expert and demanding you will be.

What Is Literature?

This question is not easily answered. Whole books have been devoted to the topic, and no single definition will satisfy everyone. Furthermore, once a definition has been made, the limits it imposes make it inadequate for at least some writing that some people may want to call *literature*. Nevertheless, there are many things that may be said to assist an understanding of what is included in the category.

Technically, anything spoken or written may be called literature, including everything from a grocery list to Shakespeare's sonnets. It is clear, however, that a grocery list, though written, should be excluded because it does not do those things that we expect from a literary work. That is, it does not interest, entertain, stimulate, broaden, or ennoble the reader. Even though it may be organized according to the places in a supermarket (dairy areas, frozen food areas, produce areas, and so on), just as a Shakespearean sonnet is structured by 3 four-line stanzas and a concluding set of two lines, it is not designed to engage the imagination or stimulate the emotions of readers. A grocery list, in short, is simply useful; it is not literature. It is to works like Shakespeare's sonnets, which invite our emotional and intellectual involvement, that we confine our definition.

Except for the chapter on film (Chapter 17), the literature we are concerned with here is in a written form. The form offers advantages, although they may not seem immediately clear in this age of video cassette recorders. The first is flexibility. You can choose to read a work according to your mood at any time you wish, and you may read and reread for your own comprehension and appreciation. You can stop at a word, should you wish, and you can go back to look at an earlier sentence. All you need to do is turn a page and fix your eyes on the desired spot; there is no machinery to adjust. By contrast, when using a VCR, should you wish to go back to a previous part of a show, you need to operate machinery, and you can never stop at any particular point and still get motion or sound, because all you will have is a stationary picture. On the other hand, with a book you can see a number of words at a glance and comprehend them at the same time. If you are studying, you may underline words, and may write your responses and ideas in the margin for reinforcement of your understanding.

Also, when you read, you depend only on your own effort and imagination. There are no actors, no settings, no photographic or musical techniques to supersede your own reconstruction of the author's ideas. Some might consider this aspect of reading a weakness, but remember that the spectacle of a performance, while graphic and stimulating, is also limiting. If your goal is intellectual independence, you can achieve it more readily by genuinely savoring the written word, even though reading may be more difficult and demanding than just looking at a television or movie screen. With reading you can take the time to reflect and digest: You can stop reading and think for a while about what you have just read. Or you can get up to do something else if you need to. When you return you can pick up your book and continue reading just where you left off. The book will always wait for you and will not change during the time you are gone. You can carry the book with you from room to room in your home or at school, and you can browse in it during private moments or when riding public transportation.

This is not to belittle the "warmer" media of television and film—there is a definite place for these—but only to contrast them with written literature. All literature, in whatever form, has many things to offer, and the final word on the value of literary study has not been written. Often, in fact, people read books and poems without explaining, even to themselves, why they enjoy them, because goals and ideals are not easily articulated. There are, however, areas of general agreement about some of the things that reading great literature can do.

Literature helps us grow, both personally and intellectually; it provides an objective base for our knowledge and understanding; it helps us connect ourselves to the broader cultural, philosophic, and religious world of which we are a part; it enables us to recognize human dreams and struggles in different places and times that we would never otherwise know; it helps us develop mature sensibility and compassion for the condition of all living things—human, animal, and vegetable; it gives us the knowledge and perception needed to appreciate the beauty of order and arrangement, just as a well-structured song or a beautifully done painting can; it provides the comparative basis from which we can see worthiness in the aims of all people, therefore helping us see beauty in the world around us; it exercises our emotions through interest, concern, tension, excitement, hope, fear, regret, laughter, and sympathy. Through cumulative experience in reading, great literature shapes our goals and values by helping us clarify our own identities, both positively, through acceptance of the admirable in human beings, and negatively, through rejection of the sinister. It helps us shape our judgments through the comparison of the good and the bad. Both in our everyday activities and in the decisions we make as individuals and as citizens, it enables us to develop a perspective on the events that occur around us and in the world at large, thereby enabling us to gain understanding and control. It encourages us to assist creative, talented people who need recognition and support. It is one of the shaping influences of life. It helps to make us human.

TYPES OF LITERARURE: THE GENRES

In practice, and for convenience, literature may be classified into four categories or *genres*: (1) narrative, (2) poetry, (3) drama, and (4) nonfiction prose. All these forms have many common characteristics. While the major purpose of nonfiction prose, for example, is to inform, the other genres also provide information (although informing is incidental to the others). All are art forms, each with its own internal requirements of structure and style. In varying degrees, all the forms are dramatic and imaginative. That is, they have at least some degree of action, or are based at least in part in a dramatic situation. Usually, however, the first three categories are considered *imaginative* literature, and are separated from nonfiction prose, or essays. The idea is that nonfiction prose is designed to deal with facts, interpretations, and conclusions. By contrast, imaginative literature, while related to truths of the earth and the universe, may be based upon postulated situations that in fact never occurred or may never occur. This is not to say that imaginative literature is not truthful, but rather that its truth is truth to life and human nature, not necessarily to the detailed world of historical facts in which we all live.

Narrative Fiction

A narrative is an account of a series of events, usually fictional, although sometimes events in fiction may also be historical. The two kinds of narrative fiction you will read most often are *short stories* and *novels*. *Myths*, *parables*, *romances*, and *epics* are also part of the genre. A short story is usually about one or two characters undergoing difficulty or facing a problem. The characters may go uphill or downhill, but they almost never remain the same, for even staying the same may be interpreted as downhill or uphill. Although the characters interact with each other and with circumstances, these relationships are described briefly, for the shortened form of the story does not permit leisurely or extensive development of gradual changes in character. The novel, on the other hand, permits the full and sometimes exhaustive development of these interactions, for it is a deliberately longer form. Like the short story, the novel usually focuses on a small number of characters, although in a novel the cast of secondary characters is often large and the number of incidents is multiplied.

Poetry

Poetry is a broad term that includes many subtypes, such as *sonnet*, *lyric*, *pastoral*, *ballad*, *song*, *ode*, *drama* (which may be in either prose or poetry), *epic*, *mock epic*, and *dramatic monologue*. Poetry is a compressed, and often deeply emotional, form. Each word counts for more than in prose, and the basic arrangement is separate lines rather than paragraphs, although *stanzas* correspond to paragraphs, and *cantos* sometimes correspond to chapters. Poetry relies more heavily than prose on *imagery* and *figurative language*, that is, on comparative, allusive, suggestive forms of expression that are applicable to a wide number of human situations. It is this compactness of expression, combined with the broadness of application, that makes poetry unique. Because poetry is so compact, the *rhythms* of poetic speech become as vital as the emotions and ideas. Sometimes these rhythms are called the *music* of poetry. Some poetic forms are free and open, particularly since the time of the American poet Walt Whitman. Other forms are carefully arranged and measured into definite, countable units, and often employ *rhymes* to impress the minds and fix the memories of readers and listeners.

The topics of poetry can be anything that concerns human beings. For this reason poetry is more like an essay than either of the other forms, for often the poet explores a topic in much the same way as the writer of an essay might do. Love, personal tributes, meditations, psychological studies, reviews of folklore, attacks on conspicuous consumption, religious worship, friendship, funerary occasions, celebrations of the seasons or the time of day, observations on life in the streets or in the home—these are just a few of the innumerable topics poetry can deal with. While writers of narrative and drama confine themselves exclusively to their respective forms, the poet is free to select any form he or she wishes. Thus some of the best poetry is dramatic (for example, Shakespeare's plays) and narrative (Milton's epic poem *Paradise Lost*).

Drama

A drama or play is designed to be performed on a stage by living actors. It therefore consists of *dialogue* together with directions for action. Like narrative fiction, it usually focuses on a single character or a small number of characters. Drama does not rely on narration, however, but presents speech and action which render the interactions that cause change in the characters and resolve the conflicts among the characters. Drama *shows* people doing things and talking themselves alive; by contrast, narrative *tells* you about these activities. (To the degree that short stories and novels include speech or dialogue, they use the technique of drama.) A *film script* is like drama, although films often require much unspoken action (*visuals*), together with special effects of sight and sound. It is often difficult to read a dramatic text because you miss a good deal of what real actors could bring to their parts by way of helpful interpretation. Reading a play or film script therefore requires energetic imaginative reconstruction.

The dramatic types are *tragedy*, *comedy*, and *farce*. In the face of human disasters, tragedy attempts to elevate human values and therefore to show the most admirable qualities of human beings. Comedy treats people as they are, laughing at them or sympathizing with them, but showing them to be loving and successful nevertheless. Farce exaggerates human foolishness, gets the characters into improbable and lunatic situations, and laughs at everyone in sight.

Nonfiction Prose

This is a broad term including short forms like *essays* and *articles* and also longer nonfictional and nondramatic works. The essay or article is a form for ideas, interpretations, and descriptions. The topics are unlimited; they may be on social, political, artistic, scientific, and other subjects, In an essay, an author focuses on one topic, such as the influence of diet on health, or the contrast between envy and ambition. The writer develops a single topic fully but not exhaustively. When exhaustiveness is the goal, the writer expands the essay into a book, which retains the same focus as the essay, but permits a wide examination and application of the entire subject.

The *article* is closely related to the essay. It explores and draws conclusions from facts, and sometimes is exclusively factual. Therefore the article is used in scholarly areas such as economics, chemistry, physics, geology, anthropology, and history. When an article is used exclusively to report research findings, it is distant from the essay in style, but when a writer combines factual material with conclusions and interpretations, the article approaches the essay. When the article is enlarged, it becomes a book.

READING AND STUDYING LITERATURE

Sometimes there is a confusion between reading and studying. We read many things in the course of daily life, but we do not perform the same actions each time we read. For example, looking at a menu, at a comic page, at a news article, or at an editorial requires differing responses and involvement. The menu requires a decision about what food to order; the comic page requires a coordination of picture and the balloon-enclosed speeches. The article requires that we assimilate details and begin to form some kind of response. Reading an editorial requires that we understand the information being discussed, that we recognize the reasonableness of the editorial position taken, and that we determine to agree or disagree with the position. All these reading tasks require different amounts of time and thought.

The actual study of a work requires more action and thought than the simple reading of it, yet many students expect that reading alone is a sufficient form of study. One can *read* a work without being able to say much about the lives of the characters or about the ideas, without being able to describe the form of the work, and without being able to say that anything was learned from it. This sort of reading is casual, and, although a person doing such reading might truthfully say that he or she has "covered the material," there is no way to support a further claim that a job of *studying* has been done.

No, studying is something else. The situation envisioned for you as a reader of this book is that you are going to study, and that you will be doing so in preparation for classroom discussion and writing. There is a widely accepted assumption in college that you should spend two hours of study out of class for every period you spend in class. This number may be arbitrary, but if you devote that much time, on average, over your student career, you will experience profound growth as a *disciplined* rather than a casual reader.

The things you need to do in the process of study are not particularly difficult or unusual. Your objective should be to learn an assigned work and to develop as complete an understanding of it as possible. If you have particular methods that have worked for you, keep following those. In one way or another, however, most study methods follow somewhat similar patterns: First, read the work through to get an overview of it; in other words, just a simple reading is acceptable as a beginning. Then, on a following reading and on as many readings as you can develop time for, use a pencil or pen to mark out interesting and noteworthy passages, and spend time thinking directly about the content of these places. As a set of general procedures, from this point on you should do the following:

1. Write down and try to remember words that are new or not totally familiar. Wherever you run across a passage that you do not quickly understand, decide whether the problem arises from any words you cannot define. Use your dictionary and write down meanings in a notebook, but be sure to compare the definitions with the passage containing the words, so that your understanding of the context is clear.

2. Consider your thoughts and responses as you read. Did you laugh, smile, worry, get scared, feel a thrill, learn a great deal, feel proud, find a lot to think about? In your notebook, try to describe how the various parts of the work caused your reactions.

3. Make notes on interesting characterizations, events, techniques, and ideas. If you like a character, try to describe what you like. If you dislike an idea, try to put your reasons for dislike into your own words.

4. Try to see patterns developing. Make an outline or scheme for the story or main idea. What are the conflicts in the work? How does the author resolve them? Is one force, idea, or side the winner? Why? How do you respond to the winner or loser?

5. Is there anything you do not understand? Make a note of the difficulty so that you can ask your instructor about it the next time you are in class.

6. For further study, make use of your marks and underlinings. Write some of the passages on cards, and carry the cards with you. When you are riding or walking to class, or at other times, try to memorize phrases, sentences, or lines of poetry.

7. Make a practice of writing a paragraph, or several paragraphs, describing your thoughts and responses after reading and considering the work. If you are reading the work in preparation for writing a specific type of essay, your paragraphs may become useful to you later, for they may be directly transferable to the essay. Even if you are making only a general preparation, however, try to continue the practice of always committing your thoughts to paper.

Trying to Develop Perspective on Your Reading

One of the major reading problems is that people find it difficult to develop a perspective on a particular work. They see only what is there, and have difficulty answering questions about how something is done because they do not have a sufficiently large basis of comparison. Thus, their understanding and appreciation are limited. If you try to recreate, at least to some degree, the choices an author had when dealing with the subject matter of the work in front of you, however, you can begin to develop the perspectives necessary to increase your comprehension of the nature and achievement of that work.

Such a development of perspective requires an exertion of imagination, for seeing what *could be* in relation to what *is* requires you to think of other possibilities, other treatments. It requires you to determine what the work is like as a finished product, and to see it as a developing product that the author brings into being as a result of many conscious artistic choices. The task is difficult, but you can help yourself by answering questions like these as you study: How else could this topic be handled? What would be the possible effects of some other method? What other works do I know in which the same topic is treated, and what are these other works like? In what way or ways is the treatment in the work I am studying different from and/or superior to these other ways? In answering questions like these, you are developing the objectivity necessary to evaluate works, while preserving your sense of the work that is actually there.

WRITING FOCUSED THEMES ON LITERARY TOPICS

Writing is the sharpened, focused expression of thought and study. As you develop your writing skills, you also improve your perceptions and increase your critical faculties. One can truthfully say that you never reach a point where you master the art of writing. Although everyone must fall short of such a state, the attempt is worthwhile, and everyone can improve their writing to the best of their ability.

The topic matter in this book is designed to help you along your way as a thinker and writer. The subject is literature: studying it, asking questions about it, and, above all, writing about it. The assumption is that the development of your ability to write about literature will also prepare you to handle topics in other activities and disciplines. Literature itself contains the subject material, though not in a systematic way, of philosophy, religion, psychology, sociology, and politics. Learning to analyze literature and to write about it will also improve your perception of these various disciplines. Developing the capacity for analysis will enable you to bring the same skill, at some future time which none of us can now predict, to a problem that at first may seem difficult, if not impossible.

Writing begins with the development of an idea. Not all ideas are equal; some are better than others. Setting good ideas is not a right that you have from birth, but an acquisition, a development of skill as a thinker and writer. You will discover that your thinking will improve the longer you engage in the analysis of literature (or the analysis of any topic). In the same way, the quality of your ideas will improve as you go through the process of originating ideas, seeing the flaws in some of your thinking processes, proposing new avenues of development, securing new data to support ideas, and creating new aspects of an idea in the course of diligent and applied thought. Your objective always will be to persuade a person reading your essays that your considerations have been based on facts and that your conclusions are correct and worthwhile.

Writing is not like ordinary conversation and classroom discussion because writing must stick with great determination to a specific point of development. Ordinary conversation is usually random and disorganized;

it shifts frequently—sometimes without clear cause—from topic to topic, and it is sometimes needlessly repetitive. Classroom discussion is more like writing because it is a form of organized talk, but there may be digressions that are sometimes not relevant. Thus classroom discussion, while formal, is free and spontaneous. Writing, by contrast, is the most concise and highly organized form of expression that will ever be required of you.

What Is a Theme, or Essay?

It needs to be emphasized again and again that writing demands tight organization and control. The first requirement of the finished theme—although it is not the first requirement in the writing *process*—is that it have a *central idea*. We will consider a *theme* or *essay* as a developed set of paragraphs all related systematically to a central idea. Everything in the essay should be directly connected to the idea or should contribute to the reader's understanding of the idea.

Let us consider this thought as it relates to essays about literature. A successful essay should be a brief but thorough examination, not an exhaustive treatment, of a particular subject. It might be a character study, an analysis of the point of view of a story or poem, or a comparison-contrast. The thoroughness is achieved by consistent references to the central idea throughout the essay. That is, typical central ideas might be (1) that a character is strong and tenacious (De Maupassant's "The Necklace," pp. 324–29), (2) that the point of view makes the action seem "up close and personal" (O'Connor's "First Confession," pp. 325–31), or (3) that one work is different from or better than another. Everything in essays with these central ideas is to be related to these ideas. Thus, it is a fact that Mathilde Loisel (in "The Necklace") spends ten years working almost like a slave to repay a debt. This fact is not relevant to an essay on character unless you show that the hard work reveals Mathilde's strength and tenacity. Similarly, it is not important in an essay about point of view to say tht Jackie and Nora speak to each other (though it is essential in "First Confession" itself) unless you relate their conversations to the personal quality of the story resulting from the first-person point of view. By the same token, any attempt to show that "First Confession" reveals more about character than "The Necklace" must be introduced as part of an argument that O'Connor's story is different from or superior to De Maupassant's, at least as regards the development of character.

In the finished essay, all these principles should hold. When planning and writing your essay, you should have them as your goal. Here they are again:

1. The essay should cover the assigned topic (for example, character, point of view, etc.).

2. The essay should have a central idea that governs its development.
3. The essay should be organized so that every part contributes something to the reader's understanding of the central idea.

"Writer's Block"

Themes do not organize themselves magically as they are written. When students look at a finished, polished, well-formed essay written by someone else, they may at first believe that it was perfect as it flowed from the writer's pen, typewriter, or word processor. Realizing that their own work does not come out so well, they despair and go into "writer's block." That is, they may sit for hours facing blank sheets of paper, waiting for the perfect theme to "arrive." Because it does not, they are able to write nothing at all. They are blocked.

This cause of writer's block—the assumption that the theme must be perfect the first time—is false. The truth is that everyone works hard to produce a good piece of writing. If you could see the early drafts of writing you admire, you would be surprised—and encouraged—to see how messy, uncertain, and incomplete they are. In final drafts, early ideas are discarded and others added; new facts are introduced; early paragraphs are cut in half and assembled elsewhere with parts of other early paragraphs; words are changed and misspellings corrected; sentences are revised or completely rewritten, and new writing is added to flesh out the reassembled materials.

All this is normal. In fact, for your own purposes, you should use the finished theme not as something to begin with, but rather as something to achieve—a goal or ideal. How you reach your goal is up to you, because everyone has unique work habits. But you should always remember that writing is a process—a process in which you try to overcome not only the difficulties of reading and interpreting the literary work, but also the natural resistance of your own mind. Many people find their minds wandering when they try to write. They think about something else, look out the window, turn on a radio or TV set, go to sleep, get something to eat, call someone on the phone, drum their fingers, go out to find a little action, or do anything else to delay the moment of composition.

Many of these difficulties can be overcome by the realization that writing cannot be perfect the first time. It is important to start writing, no matter how bad the first products seem, to create a beginning, an engagement with the materials. You are not committed to anything you first put down on paper or on your screen. You may throw it out and write something else, or you may write over it, or move it around, as you wish. But if you keep your ideas locked in your mind by not beginning to write anything at all, you will have nothing to work with, and then your frustration will be justified.

The Process of Writing a Theme

Despite all this, there are a number of things you can do systematically as you write a theme about literature. These have been entitled *invention* and *prewriting*. Invention is the process of discovering things to say. Prewriting is the process of studying, thinking, raising and answering questions, planning, developing tentative ideas and first drafts, crossing out, erasing, changing, rearranging, and adding. In a way, prewriting and invention are different words for the process of planning and thinking. They both acknowledge the mysterious and uncertain ways in which minds work, as well as the fact that ideas are not always known and shaped until they are written. *Writing, at any stage, should always be considered a process of discovery as well as creation.*

The following description of the writing process is presented as an approximation of planning and writing. You may change the order as you wish, and may leap over any of the steps if you are able. In the entire process, however, you will probably not vary the stages widely.

Not every step in the writing process can be detailed here. There is not enough space to show the development of separate drafts before the final draft. If you compare the original notes (to follow) with early drafts of observations and paragraphs, however, you may see that many changes take place and that the steps ultimately merge.

1. *Read the work through at least once for general understanding.* It is important to have general knowledge of the work before you develop materials for your theme. Be sure, in this first reading, to follow all the general principles of studying as listed above (pp. 7–8).

2. *Take notes with your specific assignment in mind.* If you are writing about a character, for example, take notes on things done by, said by, thought by, said about, and thought about the character. The same applies if your assignment is on metaphor, or ideas, and so on. By focusing your notes in this way, and by excluding other approaches to the work, you are already concentrating on your writing assignment.

3. *Use a pen, pencil, typewriter, or word processor as an extension of your thought.* Writing, together with actually *seeing* and *reflecting about* the things written, is for most people a vital part of thinking. Therefore, it is essential to get thoughts into a visible form so that you can develop them further. For many people, the hand is a psychological necessity in this process. For others, thoughts may proceed through the fingers into a typewriter or a word processor.

A special word seems in order about word processors. More and more, they occupy an important niche in the composing process. Once you master the keyboard—the same as for a typewriter—the word processor can help you in developing ideas, for you can eliminate unworkable thoughts almost as quickly as you write them. You may also move sentences and paragraphs tentatively into new places, test out how they look, and move them somewhere else if you do not like them. If you see questionable spellings, you can check them out with a dictionary and make corrections right on the screen (I cannot recommend the various spelling-check programs for students, at least during their student days). At any moment, you are only a step away from perfect final copy, so the word processor creates constant encouragement for you to improve and to keep improving, right up until the moment of printing the final draft.

No matter what method of writing you use, however, the important thing to realize is that unwritten thought is still incomplete thought. Get your ideas written onto a page or a screen, where you can look at them and work with them to make improvements.

In addition, at some advanced step in your composing process, prepare a complete draft. Even with a word processor, you cannot lay everything out in front of you at once, but can see only a small part on your screen. A clean, readable draft permits you to see everything together and to make even more improvements. Sight is vital.

4. *Use the questions in the chapter on which the assignment is based.* Your answers to these questions, together with your notes and ideas, can often be the basis for parts of a theme.

5. *For all your preliminary materials, use cards or only one side of the paper.* In this way, you can spread out everything and get an overview as you plan and write. Do not write on both sides of the paper, for ideas that are out of sight are often out of mind.

6. *Once your have put everything together in this way, try to develop a central idea.* This will serve as the focus of your planning and writing.

Finding a Central Idea or a Thesis

You cannot find a central idea in a hat. It comes about as a result of the steps just described. In a way, you might think of discovering a central idea as a major goal in prewriting. Once you have the idea, you have a guide for accepting some of your materials, rejecting others, rearranging, changing, and rewording. It is therefore necessary to see how the central idea can be developed and how it can be used.

MAKING NOTES.   Let us assume that your assignment is a theme about the character Jackie in O'Connor's story "First Confession." (To read the complete story, see p. 325.) The following is a collection of notes and observations that you might write when reading the story. Notice that page numbers are noted so you can easily go back to the story at any time to refresh your memory on any details.

> Jackie blames others, mainly his grandmother, for his troubles. He hates her bare feet and her eating and drinking habits. He dislikes his sister,

Nora, for "sucking up" to the grandmother. Also, Nora tells on him. He is ashamed to bring a friend home to play because of grandmother. (p. 326)

He likes money rather than Mrs. Ryan's talk of hell.

He is shocked by the story about the "fellow" who "made a bad confession." (pp. 326–27)

After learning to examine his conscience, he believes that he has broken all ten commandments because of the grandmother.

He lies about a toothache to avoid confession. A kid's lie. (p. 327)

He believes his sister is a "raging malicious devil." He remembers her "throwing" him through the church door. (p. 328)

Very imaginative. Believes that he will make a "bad confession and then die in the night and be continually coming back and burning people's furniture."

This is funny, and also childish. He thinks women are hypocrites. (p. 328)

He is frightened by the dark confessional. (p. 328)

Curious and adventurous. He gets up on the shelf and kneels.

He is also frightened by the tone of the priest's voice. He falls out on the church floor and gets whacked by his sister. (p. 329)

Note: All the things about Jackie as a child are told by Jackie as an older person. The man is sort of telling a joke on himself.

Jackie is smart, can think about himself as a sinner once the priest gives him a clue. He likes the kind words of the priest, is impressed with him.

He begins reacting against the words of Mrs. Ryan and Nora, calling them "cackling." (p. 329)

He has sympathy for his mother. Calls her "poor soul." Seems to fear his father, who has given him the "flaking." (p. 326)

Note: Jackie is a child, and easily swayed. He says some things that are particularly childish and cute, such as coming back to burn furniture. His fears show that he is childish and naive. He is gullible. His memory of his anger against his sister shows a typical attitude of brother and sister.

WRITING OBSERVATIONS FROM YOUR NOTES: "BRAINSTORMING." Once you have notes like these, your job is to make something out of them. The notes do not make up a theme; they are disorganized and unfocused. However, they represent a starting point from which ideas may be organized and developed. Since the imaginary assignment we are discussing concerns character (rather than plot, imagery, symbolism, or the like), you should go back over your notes and extract single-sentence observations that relate specifically to character traits and development. Care must be taken to ensure that these sentences focus on the subject at hand—character—and do not lead toward plot summary or digressions. Such a reformulated list of sentences about Jackie's character might look like this:

Jackie likes thinking about money (the half crown) rather than hell. Is he irreligious, or does this show his childish nature?

He seems to be older when he is telling the story.

He has a dislike for his sister that seems to be normal brother-and-sister rivalry.

He tells a fib about the toothache, but he tells everything else to the priest. He is not a liar.

He blames his gran for his troubles. Is he irresponsible? No, he is just behaving like a child.

He is curious and adventurous, as much as a seven-year-old can be.

He is easily scared and impressed (see his response to the bad confession story, and his first response to the priest).

He says cute things, the sort of things a child would say (the old man in the pew, coming back to burn the furniture). He seems real as a child.

These are all observations that might or might not turn out to be worth much in your theme. It is not possible to tell until you do some further thinking about them. These basic ideas, however, are worth working up further, along with additional substantiating details.

DEVELOPING YOUR OBSERVATIONS AS PARAGRAPHS. As you develop these basic ideas, you should be consulting the original set of notes and also looking at the text to get the details straight. As you write, you should bring in any new details that seem relevant. Here are paragraphs that expand some of the observations presented above. You might consider this paragraph-writing phase a "second step" in the brainstorming needed for the theme:

1. Jackie comes to life. He seems real. His experiences are those that a child might have, and his reactions are lifelike. All brothers and sisters fight. All kids are "heart scalded" when they get a "flaking."

2. Jackie shows a great amount of anger. He kicks his grandmother on the shin and won't eat her cooking. He is mad at Nora for the penny that she gets from grandmother, and he "lashes out" at Nora with the bread knife. He blames his troubles on his grandmother. He talks about the "hypocrisy of women." He thinks that the stories of Mrs. Ryan and the religion of his sister are the "cackle of old women and girls." (p. 329)

3. Everything about Jackie as a child that we get in the story is told by Jackie when he is older, probably a grown man. The story is comic, and part of the comedy comes because the man is telling a jokelike story about himself.

4. Jackie's main characteristic is that he is a child and does many childish things. He remembers his anger with his sister. He also remembers being shocked by Mrs. Ryan's stories about hell. He crawls onto the

ledge in the confessional. He is so impressed with the bad confession story that he says twice that he fears burning furniture. Some of these things are charming and cute, such as the observation about the old man having a grandmother and his thinking about the money when Mrs. Ryan offers the coin to the first boy who holds his finger in the candle flame.

DETERMINING YOUR CENTRAL IDEA.   Once you have reached this stage in your thinking, you are ready to pull the materials together and form a central idea or a thesis. To do this, look for a common thread or term that runs through many of your observations. In the notes, sentences, and paragraphs developed in the hypothetical assignment on character in "First Confession," one common thread is the term "childish." The anger, the sibling rivalry, the attraction to the coin, the fear of burning someone's furniture, the fib about the toothache—all these can be seen as childish signs. Once you have found this common thread (and it could easily have been some other point, such as Jackie's anger, or his attitude toward the females around him), it can be used as the central idea in an evolving theme.

Because the central idea is so vital in shaping a theme, it should be formed as carefully as possible in a complete sentence. Just the word "childishness" would not give us as much as any of the following sentences:

1.   The main trait of Jackie is his childishness.
2.   Jackie is bright and sensitive, but above all childlike.
3.   Jackie is no more than a typical child.
4.   Jackie is above all a child, with all the beauties of childhood.

Each of these ideas would guide a different kind of theme. The first would show that Jackie's actions and thoughts are childish. The third would do much the same thing but would also stress Jackie's limitations as a child. The second would show Jackie's better qualities and would show how they are limited by his age. The fourth might emphasize the charm and "cuteness" that were pointed out in some of the notes and observations.

You might phrase the central idea several different ways before you choose the one that will yield the most focused theme. Once you have a central idea (let us use the first one), you will be able to use it to bring your observations and conclusions into focus.

Let's take paragraph 2 in the brainstorming phase, the one about Jackie's anger. With childishness as our central idea, we can use the topic of anger as a way of illustrating Jackie's childish character. Is his anger adult or childish? Is it normal or psychotic? Is it sudden or deliberate? In the light of these questions, we may conclude that all the examples of angry action and thought can be seen as the normal responses or reflections of a child. With the material thus "arranged" in this way, we can reshape the second paragraph as follows:

Original Paragraph	Reshaped Paragraph
Jackie shows a great amount of anger. He kicks his grandmother on the shin and won't eat her cooking. He is mad at Nora for the penny that she gets from grandmother, and he "lashes out" at Nora with the bread knife. He blames his troubles on his grandmother. He talks about the "hypocrisy of women." He thinks the stories of Mrs. Ryan and the religion of his sister are the "cackle of old women and girls." (p. 329)	Jackie's great amount of anger is childish. Kicking his grandmother, refusing to eat her cooking, and lashing out at Nora with the bread knife are instances of childish anger. His jealousy of Nora and his distrust of women (as hypocrites) are the results of immature and childish thought. His anger at religion, evident in his claim that the fears of Mrs. Ryan and Nora are the "cackle of old women and girls" (p. 329), is also childish.

Notice here that the materials in each paragraph are substantially the same but that the central idea has shaped the right-hand paragraph. The left-hand column describes Jackie's anger, while the one on the right makes the claim that all the examples of angry action and thought are childish and immature. Once our paragraph has been shaped in this way, it is almost ready for placement into the emerging theme.

The Thesis Sentence

Using the central idea as a guide, we can now go back to the earlier materials for arrangement. The goal is to establish a number of points to be developed as paragraphs in support of the central idea. The paragraphs written as the second step of brainstorming will serve us well. Paragraph 2, the one we have just "shaped," discusses childish anger. Paragraph 3 has material that could be used in an introduction (since it does not directly discuss any precise characteristics but instead describes how the reader gets the information about Jackie). Paragraph 1 has material that might be good in a conclusion. Paragraph 4 has two topics (it is not a unified paragraph), which may be labeled "responses" and "outlook." We may put these points into a list:

1. Responses
2. Outlook
3. Anger

Once we have established this list, we may use it as the basic order for the development of our theme.

For the benefit of the reader, however, we should also use this ordering for the writing of our **thesis sentence**. This sentence is the operative sentence in the first part of the following general plan for most themes:

Tell what you are going to say.
Say it.
Tell what you've said.

The thesis sentence tells your reader what to expect. It is a plan for your theme: It connects the central idea and the list of topics in the order in which you plan to present them. Thus, if we put the central idea at the left and our list of topics at the right, we have the shape of a thesis sentence:

Central Idea	Topics
The main trait of Jackie is his childishness.	1. Responses 2. Outlook 3. Anger

From this arrangement we can write the following thesis sentence, which should usually be the concluding sentence before the body of the theme (that section in which you "say it," that is, in which you develop your central idea):

The childishness is emphasized in his responses, outlook, and anger.

With any changes made necessary by the context of your final theme, this thesis sentence and your central idea can go directly into your introduction. The central idea, as we have seen, is the glue. The thesis sentence shows the parts that are to be fastened together, that is, the topics in which the central idea will be demonstrated.

The Body of the Theme: Topic Sentences

The term regularly used in this book for the development of the central idea is **body**. The body is the section where you present the materials you have been working up in your planning. You may rearrange or even reject some of what you have developed, as you wish, as long as you change your thesis sentence to account for the changes. Since the thesis sentence we have generated contains three topics, we will use these to form the theme.

Just as the organization of the entire theme is based on the thesis sentence, the organization of each paragraph is based on its **topic sentence**. The topic sentence is made up of one of the topics listed in the thesis sentence, combined with an assertion about how the topic will support the central idea. The first topic in our example is Jackie's responses, and the topic sentence should show how these responses illustrate a phase of Jackie's childishness. Suppose we choose the phase of the child's gullibility or impressionability. We can put together the topic and the phase, to get the following topic sentence:

Jackie's responses show childish impressionability.

The details that will be used to develop the paragraph will then show how Jackie's responses illustrate the impressionability and gullibility associated with children.

You should follow the same process in forming the other topic sentences, so that when you finish them you can use them in your essay.

The Outline

All along we have actually been developing an **outline** to shape and organize the essay. Some writers never use a formal outline at all, whereas others find one to be quite helpful to them as they write. Still other writers insist that they cannot produce an outline until they have finished their theme. All these views can be reconciled if you realize that finished themes should have a tight structure. At some point, therefore, you should create an outline as a guide. It may be early in your prewriting, or it may be late. What is important is that your final theme follow an outline form.

The kind of outline we have been developing here is the "analytical sentence outline." This type is easier to create than it sounds, for it is nothing more than a graphic form, a skeleton, of your theme. It consists of the following:

1. Title
2. Introduction
   a. Central idea
   b. Thesis sentence
3. Body
   a.
   b. } points announced in the thesis sentence
   c. etc.
4. Conclusion

The conclusion is optional in this scheme. Because the topic of the conclusion is a separate item, it is technically independent of the body, but it is part of the thematic organization and hence should be closely tied to the central idea. It may be a summary of the main points in the theme ("tell what you've said"). It may also be an evaluation of the ideas, or it may suggest further points of analysis that you did not write about in the body. Each of the following chapters offers suggestions to help you develop materials for your conclusions.

Remember that your outline should be a guide for organizing thoughts and already completed paragraphs. Throughout the discussion of the writing process, we have seen that writing is discovery. At the right point, your outline can help you in this discovery. That is, the need to make your theme conform to the plan of the outline may help you to reshape, reposition, and reword some of your ideas.

When completed, the outline should have the following appearance (using the character study of Jackie in "First Confession"):

1. Title: "Jackie's Childish Character in O'Connor's 'First Confession' "
2. Introduction
   a. Central idea: The main trait of Jackie is his childishness.
   b. Thesis sentence: This childishness is emphasized in his responses, outlook, and anger.
3. Body: Topic sentences.
   a. Jackie's responses show childish impressionability.
   b. His outlook reflects the simplicity of a child.
   c. His anger is also that of a child.
4. Conclusion.
   Topic sentence: Jackie seems real as a child.

By the time you have created an outline like this one, you will have been planning and drafting your theme for quite some time. The outline will thus be a guide for *finishing* and *polishing* your theme, not for actually developing it. Usually you will have already completed the main parts of the body and will use the outline for the introduction and conclusion.

Briefly, here is the way to use the outline:

1. Include both the central idea and the thesis sentence in your introduction. (Some instructors require a fusion of the two in the final draft. Therefore, make sure you know what your instructor expects.) Use the suggestions in the chapter assignment to determine what else might be included in the introduction.
2. Include the various topic sentences at the beginning of your paragraphs, changing them as necessary to provide transitions or qualifications. Throughout this book the various topics are confined to separate paragraphs. However, it is also acceptable to divide the topic into two or more paragraphs, particularly if the topic is difficult or highly detailed. Should you make this division, your topic then is really a *section*, and your second and third paragraphs should each have their own topic sentences.

In paragraphs designed to demonstrate the validity of an assertion, the topic sentence usually begins the paragraph. The details then illustrate the truth of the assertion in the topic sentence. (Details about the use of evidence will follow below, pp. 24–29.) It is also acceptable to have the topic sentence elsewhere in the paragraph, particularly if your paragraph is a "thought paragraph," in which you use details to lead up to your topic idea.

Throughout this book, for illustrative purposes, all the central ideas, thesis sentences, and topic sentences are underlined so that you may distinguish them clearly as guides for your own writing.

THE SAMPLE THEME

The following theme is a sample of the finished product of the process we have been illustrating. You will recognize the various organizing sentences because they are underlined. These are the sentences from the outline, with changes made to incorporate them into the theme and to provide transitions from paragraph to paragraph. You will also see that some of the paragraphs and thoughts have been taken from the prewriting stages, with necessary changes to bring them into tune with the central idea. (See the illustration of this change on p. 17)

In each of the chapters in this book there are similar sample themes. It would be impossible to show the complete writing process for each of these, but you may assume that each was completed more or less like the one illustrated here. There were many good starts, and many false ones. Much was changed and rearranged, and much was redone once the outline for the theme was established. The materials for each theme were developed in the light of the issues introduced and exemplified in the first parts of each of the chapters. The plan for each theme corresponds to an outline, and its length is within the limits of many of the themes you will be assigned to write.

Sample Theme

Jackie's Childish Character in O'Connor's "First Confession"[*]

---

[1] Jackie, the main character in O'Connor's "First Confession," is a child at the time of the action. All the things we learn about him, however, are told by him as an older person. The story is funny, and part of the humor is produced because the narrator is telling what amounts to a joke on himself. For this reason he brings out his own childhood childishness. That is, if Jackie were

[*]See p. 325 for this story.

[1] mature, the joke would not work because so much depends on his being young, powerless, and gullible. The main thing about Jackie, then, is his childishness.° This quality is emphasized in his responses, outlook, and anger.□

[2] Jackie's responses show the ease with which a child may be impressed. His grandmother embarrasses him with her drinking, eating, and unpleasant habits. He is so "shocked" by the story about the bad confession that twice he states his fear of saying a bad confession and coming back to burn furniture. He is quickly impressed by the priest and is able to change his mind about his sins (to his own favor) after no more than a few words with this man.

[3] His outlook above all reflects the limitations and the simplicity of a child. He is not old enough to know anything about the outside world, and therefore he supposes that the old man next to him at confession has also had problems with a grandmother. This same limited view causes him to think only about the half crown when Mrs. Ryan talks about punishment. It is just like a child to see everything in personal terms, without the detached, broad views of an experienced adult.

[4] His anger is also that of a child, although an intelligent one. Kicking his grandmother and lashing out against Nora with the bread knife are the reflexive actions of childish anger. He also has anger that he thinks about. His jealousy of Nora and his claim that women are hypocrites are the results of thought, even though this thought is immature and childish. His thinking about religion after first speaking to the priest makes him claim that the fears of Mrs. Ryan and Nora are the "cackle of old women and girls" (p. 348). He is intelligent, but he is also childish.

[5] Jackie therefore seems real as a child. His reactions are the right ones for a child to have. All brothers and sisters fight, and all children are "heart scalded" when they get a "flaking." The end of life and eternal punishment are remote for a child, whose first concern is the pleasure that money can buy. Therefore, Jackie's thoughts about the half crown are truly those of a child, as are all his thoughts and actions. The strength of "First Confession" is the reality and consistency of Jackie as a child.

Theme Commentaries

Throughout this book, short commentaries follow each sample theme. Each discussion points out how the assignment is handled and how the instruction provided in the first part of the chapter is incorporated into the theme. For themes in which several approaches are suggested, the commentary points out which one is employed. When a sample theme uses two or more approaches, the commentary makes this fact clear. It is hoped that the commentaries will help you develop the insight necessary to use the sample themes as aids in your own study and writing.

° Central idea
□ Thesis sentence

SOME COMMON PROBLEMS IN WRITING THEMES

The fact that you understand the early stages of the composition process and can apply the principles of developing a central idea and organizing with an outline and thesis sentence does not mean that you will have no problems in writing well. It is not hard to recognize good writing when you see it, but it can be difficult to explain why it is superior.

The most difficult and perplexing questions you will ask as you write are: (1) "How can I improve my writing?" (2) "If I got a C on my last essay, why wasn't the grade a B or an A? How can I get higher grades?" These are really the same question, but each has a different emphasis. Another way to ask this question is: "When I first read a work, I have a hard time following it. Yet when my instructor explains it, my understanding is greatly increased. How can I develop the ability to understand the work and write about it well without my instructor's help? How can I become an independent, confident reader and writer?"

The theme assignments in this book are designed to help you do just that. One of the major flaws in many themes about literature is that, despite the writer's best intentions and plans, they do no more than retell a story or describe an idea. Retelling the story shows only that you have read the work, not that you have thought about it. Writing a good theme, however, shows that you have digested the material and arranged it into a pattern of thought. In only one of the following chapters are you asked to retell a story or rephrase factual material. This is the **précis theme** (Chapter 2), and even here a major purpose is to help you make the distinction between retelling a story and making an analysis. All other chapters require and illustrate analytical processes that show your thought and understanding.

Establishing an Order in Making References

There are a number of ways in which you may set up patterns of development to show your understanding. One is to refer to events or passages in an order that you yourself establish. You need not present them in the order in which they occurred, but can change them around to make them fit into your own thematic plans. Rarely, if ever, should you begin your theme by describing the opening of the work; it is better to talk about the conclusion or the middle first. Beginning the body of your theme by referring to later parts of the work will almost force you to discuss your own central idea rather than to retell a story. If you look back at paragraph 3 of the sample theme on "First Confession," you will see that this technique has been used. The two references there are presented in reverse order from the story. This reversal shows the writer's own organization, not the organization of the work being analyzed.

Your Mythical Reader: A Student Who Has Read but Not Thought

Consider the audience, or "mythical reader" for whom you are writing. Imagine that you are writing to other students. They have read the assigned work, just as you have, but they have not thought about it. It is easy to imagine how to write for such mythical readers. They know the events or have followed the thread of the argument. They know who says what and when it is said. As a result, you do not need to tell these readers about everything in the work, but should think of your role as that of an *explainer* or *interpreter*. Tell them what things mean in relationship to your central idea. *Do not, however, just retell the story.*

To look at the situation in still another way, you may have read stories about Sherlock Holmes and Dr. Watson. Holmes always points out to Watson that all the facts are available to both of them, but that, though Watson *sees*, he does not *observe*. Your role is like that of Holmes, explaining and interpreting facts, and drawing conclusions that your audience of mythical readers, like Watson, cannot draw for themselves even though they see the same things that you do. If you look back at the sample theme on "First Confession," you will notice that everywhere *the assumption has been made that the reader has read the story already.* References to the story are thus made primarily to remind the reader of something he or she already knows, but *the principal emphasis of the theme is to draw conclusions and develop arguments.*

Using Literary Material as Evidence

The comparison with Sherlock Holmes should remind you that whenever you write on any topic, you are like a detective using clues as evidence for building a case, or a lawyer using evidence as support for arguments. If you argued in favor of securing a greater voice for students in college government, for example, you would introduce such evidence as past successes with student government, increased maturity of modern-day students, the constitutional amendment granting eighteen-year-olds the right to vote, and so on.

Writing about literature requires evidence as well. For practical purposes only, when you are writing a theme, you may conveniently regard the work assigned as evidence for your arguments. You should make references to the work only as a part of the logical development of your discourse. Your objective is to convince your reader of your own knowledge and reasonableness, just as lawyers attempt to convince a jury of the reasonableness of their arguments.

The whole question of the use of evidence is a far-reaching one. Students of law spend years studying proper uses of evidence. Logicians have devised the system of syllogisms and inductive reasoning to regulate the use of evidence. It would not be logical, for example, to conclude from Shakespeare's play *Macbeth* that Macbeth behaves like a true friend and great king. His murders, his rages, and his pangs of guilty conscience form evidence that makes this conclusion absurd.

To see how material from the work may become supporting evidence in a theme, let us refer again to the sample theme on "First Confession." The fourth paragraph is about Jackie's anger being an aspect of his childlike nature. Four separate details from the story are introduced in support. If you also look again at how this paragraph was first developed in the light of the central idea (p. 22), you will see that the details are not introduced to tell the story. Two of them specifically show the reflexive nature of childhood anger, and the other two show Jackie's immature, childish thought, despite his obvious intelligence. Use this way of introducing detail as a model for your own themes.

It is vital to use evidence correctly in order for your reader to follow your idea. Let us look briefly at two examples to see how writing may be made better by the evidential use of details. These are from themes on the character of Smirnov, the major male character in Chekhov's play *The Bear* (see pp. 359–68 for the text of this play):

A major trait of Smirnov is his uncontrolled impetuosity. He insults Luka when he first enters. Then he demands immediate payment of the 2400 rubles that the dead Popov owed him, when he first meets Mrs. Popov. He insists on the money, in fact, that very day. He then declares that he will wait a week, or even a year, until he is paid. When Mrs. Popov goes out, he threatens his own servant outside, who has gotten the reins of his horse tangled up. In telling his own story, Popov indicates his past passions, having fought three duels over women, and having been involved in twenty-one love affairs, all now over. He does not control his own strength, but breaks two chairs when he grips them too firmly. The high point of his action is his challenge to

A major trait of Smirnov is his uncontrolled impetuosity. It is clear that he acts and speaks first, and thinks only afterward. His entering insults of Luka, for example, and his request for immediate payment from Mrs. Popov, even though she has no cash on hand to pay her dead husband's debt, both show a person of great impetuosity. This trait is also shown in his confession to the audience about his past affairs. We may conclude that his love life would have been different if he had entered his relationships with greater care and understanding. The most remarkable and also most amusing illustrations of his impetuousness are his sudden challenge to Mrs. Popov and his more sudden discovery and declaration of love for her. In every action, Smirnov is shown as

Mrs. Popov after she talks back to him. Then he almost immediately falls in love with her because of her angry acceptance of his challenge. His final actions are his declaration of love for Mrs. Popov and his kissing her.

a person unable to control his temper and his impulses.

Although the first example has more words than the second (172 to 142), it is not adequate, for in it the writer simply restates things that the audience already knows. The paragraph is cluttered with details, and even though it begins with a good point (the same as in the second paragraph), its observations and conclusions are minimal. If you judge it for what you might learn about Cheknov's actual use of Smirnov's actions in *The Bear*, you cannot avoid concluding that it gives you no help at all in understanding the play. The writer did not have to think much in order to write the paragraph.

On the other hand, the second paragraph is responsive to the declared topic, and it required a good deal of thought to write. Phrases like "It is clear that" and "The most remarkable and also most amusing illustrations" show that the writer of paragraph 2 has assumed that the audience knows the story and now wants help in interpretation. Paragraph 2 therefore guides readers by connecting five major actions to the topic as stated in the first sentence: It uses these details only as evidence, not as a recounting of actions. By contrast, paragraph 1 recounts eleven separate actions from the play, and does not tie these to the topic. More details could have been added to paragraph 2, but these are excluded because they are unnecessary, if not irrelevant. While both paragraphs begin with the same topic, paragraph 2 supports the point, while paragraph 1 does not.

The answer to that difficult question of how to turn C writing into an A is to be found in the comparison of the two passages. Close comparison shows that superior writers always allow their minds to play on the materials. They try to give readers the results of their thoughts. They dare to trust their responses and are not afraid to make judgments about the literary work they are considering. Their principal aim in referring to actions, scenes, and characters in a work is to develop their own thematic pattern. Observe this quality again by contrasting two passages dealing with the same facts of the story:

He insults Luka when he first enters. Then he demands immediate payment of the 2400 rubles that the dead Popov owed him, when he first meets Mrs. Popov. He insists on the money, in fact, that very day. He then declares that he will wait a week, or even a year, until he is paid.

His entering insults of Luka, for example, and his request for immediate payment from Mrs. Popov, even though she has no cash on hand to pay her dead husband's debt, both show a person of great impetuosity.

Passage 1 is detailed and accurate, but no more. Passage 2, by contrast, links the essential parts of the details to the announced trait of impetuosity. The words "for example" and "both show" indicate the writer's thoughtful use of evidence in support of argument. There are many things that make good writing good, but one of the most important is the way in which a writer uses facts as evidence in an original pattern of thought. Always try to achieve this quality in your writing.

KEEPING TO YOUR POINT

Whenever you write a theme about literature, then, you must pay great attention to the proper organization and proper use of references to the work assigned. As you write, you should try constantly to keep your material unified, for should you go off on a tangent, you are following the material rather than leading it. It is all too easy to start with your point but then wander off into a retelling of a story. Once again, resist the tendency to be a narrator rather than an interpreter.

Let us look at another example. The following paragraph is drawn from an essay on "The Theme of Death and Life in Chekhov's *The Bear*." In this paragraph the writer discusses the theme as shown in the character of Mrs. Popov. The idea is to assert that her real feelings point her toward life rather than death, as represented by her allegiance to her dead husband:

> Mrs. Popov's allegiance to death is not real or human, but rather formal. In the seven months since her husband died, she has shut herself away from the world, and has worn black widow's weeds according to custom. She recalls her husband's fine appearance while riding, and hence she orders extra oats for Toby, his horse, as a special act of love. She even observes an "anniversary" of his death on the same day each month. All this she does while she continues to powder her nose, and she also recalls the loneliness of those days when her husband left her at home, the humiliation of his open courtship of other women, and the painful discovery of a desk full of love letters from the women with whom he had affairs.

This paragraph shows how easily writers may be diverted from their objective in writing. The first sentence is actually an effective topic sentence, suggesting that the writer begins with a good plan. The remaining part, however, does not follow through. The flaw is that the material of the paragraph, while an accurate account of what happens in the story itself, does not get tied to the topic in any way. Once the second sentence is underway, the paragraph gets lost in a retelling of events, and the fine opening sentence is almost forgotten. The material may be relevant to the topic—in fact, it is—but the writer does not point out its relevance. From the example of this paragraph, we may conclude that writers should not rely on detail alone to make meanings clear. Instead, they must make the connections of detail and conclusions needed to make all relationships *explicitly* clear.

Let us see how this problem of focusing detail may be addressed. If the ideal paragraph could be schematized with line drawings, we might say that the paragraph's topic should be a straight line, moving toward and reaching a specific goal (explicit meaning), with an exemplifying line moving away from the straight line briefly in order to bring in evidence, but returning to the line after each new fact in order to demonstrate the relevance of this fact. Thus, the ideal scheme would look like this:

Notice that the exemplifying line, or the example or the documenting line, always returns to the topic line. A scheme for the above paragraph on *The Bear*, however, would look like this:

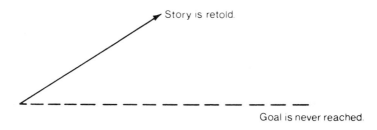

How might this paragraph be improved? The best way is to reintroduce the topic again and again throughout the paragraph to keep reminding the reader of the relevance of the exemplifying material. Each time you mention the topic you bring yourself back to the line, and this practice should prevail no matter what the topic. If you are analyzing point of view, for example, you should keep pointing out the relevance of your material to the point of view of the work; the same applies to character or whatever aspect of literature you are studying. According to this principle, we might revise the paragraph on *The Bear* as follows, keeping as much of the original wording as we can. (Parts of sentences stressing the relationship of the examples to the topic of the paragraph are underlined.)

> Mrs. Popov's allegiance to death is not real or human, but rather formal. <u>She does all the expected and even the "right" things, but her real feelings seem to be lying in wait to get her back into life.</u> It is true that in the seven months since her husband died, she has worn black widow's weeds according to custom. <u>It is also true that</u> she recalls her husband's

fine appearance while riding, and hence that she orders extra oats for Toby, his horse, as a special act of love. It even true that she observes his death as an "anniversary" on the same day each month. But the fragility of her allegiance is shown by stronger realities. Her use of powder, for example, is formally unnecessary, but it shows that she wants to be alluring. Her real feelings are shown in her recollections of the loneliness of those days when her husband left her alone at home. Open anger at him is suggested by her memory of the humiliation of his open courtship of other women, and also by her painful discovery of a desk full of love letters from the women with whom he had affairs. These indications of her real feelings, not her formal observances, mark her as one more strongly inclined to life than death.

The paragraph has been improved so that now it reaches the goal promised in the topic sentence. While it has also been lengthened, the length has been caused not by inessential detail, but by phrases and sentences that give the paragraph form and direction. You might object that if you lengthened all your paragraphs in this way, your themes would grow too bulky. The answer to this objection is that you should reduce the total number of major points and paragraphs in your essays, on the theory that *it is better to develop a few topics pointedly than many pointlessly.* Revision done to strengthen central and topic ideas requires that you throw out some topics or else incorporate them as subpoints in the topics you keep. This process can result only in improvement.

INSIGHT, NEWNESS, GROWTH

Sticking to a point is therefore one of the first requirements of a good essay, for you will not be successful unless you have thoroughly exemplifed and supported your central idea. Another of the important qualities of excellence, however, is not only to be well organized, but also to make the central idea expand and grow. The word *growth* is a metaphor for development, the creation of new insights, the disclosure of ideas that were not at first noticeable, the expression of new, fresh, and original interpretations.

An obvious response to this ideal description of excellence is that it is difficult to be original when you are writing about someone else's work. "The author has said everything," might go the argument, "and therefore I can do little more than follow the story (poem, or play)." This claim assumes that you have no choice in selecting material for a theme, and no opportunity to make individual thoughts and original contributions. But you have. The author has presented the work to you, and you can, if you look hard, find layer upon layer of meaning. One obvious area where you can exert your power of originality is in the development and formulation of the central idea for your theme. For example, a first thought about Chekhov's comedy *The Bear* might be that it is "about love." Just this topic does not go very far, however, and an additional idea might be developed from the observation that the love is "sudden." This idea is regrettably not very original either. But a more original insight can be provided if the topic is related directly to the anger of the major characters. Then an idea might be that "love is so strong a force that it emerges even against the apparently conscious wills of those falling in love." With this idea it is possible to do more in creating a fresh, original essay analyzing the improbable events and dialogue of the play than the simple topic "love" could ever do.

You can also develop your ability to treat your subject freshly and originally if you plan the body of the essay to build up to what you think is your most important, incisive, and well conceived idea. As an example of such planning, the following arrangement of topics for paragraphs illustrates how a central idea may be widened. Let us assume the central idea to be "that the farcical humor in *The Bear* is grounded in a realistic view of life." The following paragraphs are presented not as a finished theme, but rather as a set of thoughts in a rising order of importance to show, with titles, how the exemplification of a central idea may also allow for originality and growth:

1. *The Bear* as a Funny Play

The Bear is funny not only because the characters behave foolishly, but also because they are recognizably human, no matter how they are exaggerated. Mrs. Popov's devotion to her dead husband is real, though overblown, while Smirnov's outbursts against women disguise his continuing capacity for infatuation. Once the two come into conflict, humor is a natural result, as their poses are shown to be both foolish and untenable. Also, their real wishes to love and be loved win out over their previous resolutions, and the incongruousness of their "conversions" underscores the comic nature of the play.

2. *The Bear* and the Power of Emotion over Resolution

Funny as *The Bear* is, however, it could not cause laughter if it did not speak truth. People may make many resolutions about their personal lives—this is what the play seems to say—but love, like friendship, takes place independently, regardless of their conscious decisions. The major improbability of the love between Mrs. Popov and Smirnov is thus not that they fall in love, but only that they fall in love so quickly. Granted their characters, with Mrs. Popov's fidelity and Smirnov's desire for abiding love with women, it is natural that they would begin loving each other in the heightened emotion of their anger. Both characters are representative in this respect, because they are tuned to their deeply felt needs to love rather than to their deliberate decisions to lead solitary and unsatisfying lives.

3. *The Bear* and Its Larger Implications

Even above the power of inclination over deliberation, *The Bear* has larger symbolic significance. The extreme positions held by both Mrs. Popov and Smirnov are, in the play, simply personal. But both characters share the human, societal, and national quality of steering into extremes of conduct and policy that have more serious results. Thus, it is funny that Mrs. Popov should declare eternal loyalty to her dead husband, but the results are not funny when a nation follows monomaniacal leaders who are committed to dead and destructive ideas. In *The Bear*, things end happily as the threatened duel is shown to be unnecessary, impossible, and ridiculous. While symbolically many countries, like many people, should fall in love, like Mrs. Popov and Smirnov, the fact is that they do not. That they fail only too often, and begin fighting, highlights the improbability of *The Bear*. One may wish that real-life resolutions of crises would all be like the one in Chekhov's play. We could use more laughter and less war.

These examples outline a pattern of growth from personal, to social, to national. A finished essay along these lines would try to show that Chekhov's amusing farce is also an example of larger human wishes and needs. The subject is thus not just illustrated, but enlarged. Details from *The Bear*, as shown in the examples, are included as a part of this developing pattern of growth; in no way are they introduced simply to retell the major events of the play. The pattern shows how two primary standards of excellence in writing—organization and growth—can be met. Without these qualities, there is no totally successful writing, just as there is no successful thinking.

It should be clear that whenever you write, an important goal should be the development of your central idea. You should try to go somewhere with your idea, to give your readers insights about the literary materials that they did not have before they started reading. To the degree that you can learn to develop your ideas, you will receive recognition for increasingly superior writing achievements.

Admittedly, in a short theme you will be able to move only a short distance with an idea, but you should never be satisfied to leave the idea exactly where you found it. Nurture it and make it grow. Constantly adhere to and develop your topic.

USING ACCURATE AND FORCEFUL LANGUAGE

The best writing has the qualities of accuracy, force, and insight. Quite often the first products of our minds are rather weak, and they need to be rethought, recast, and reworded. Sometimes this process cannot be carried out immediately, for it may take days or even weeks for us to gain objectivity about what we say. As a student, you usually do not have that kind of time, and thus you must acquire the habit of challenging your own statements almost as soon as you write them. Ask yourself whether they really mean what you want, or if you can make a stronger statement than you have.

As an example, consider the following statement, put forward as a central idea about *The Bear*:

> The central idea in this play is about how Mrs. Popov and Smirnov fall suddenly in love.

This sentence could not carry a writer very far in the development of a theme on the subject. Because it promises nothing more than a simple retelling of the play's events, it needs further thought and rephrasing. Here are two possible new central ideas, developed from this first sentence, that would be more productive as a basis for a theme:

> In the play Chekhov dramatizes the idea that inner forces of character are stronger than conscious decisions.

> Chekhov makes the outcome of the play a celebration of good nature and love.

Although both these sentences might produce similar themes, the first would probably explore the contrast between the open declarations of the characters, and would examine their less obvious qualities. The second sentence, however, points toward an essay that might pass over the open declarations, while examining the loving nature of the characters. This sentence, since it includes the word *celebration*, might emphasize the ways in which the play is built around the force of love. In any event, either of the two sentences would be more helpful as a statement of a central idea than the first one.

Sometimes, in seeking to say something, we wind up saying nothing. For example, consider these two sentences from themes about Robert Frost's poem "Desert Places" (see pp. 355–56 for the poem):

> 1. It seems as though the author's anticipation of meeting his own desert places causes him to respond as he does in the poem.
> 2. This incident, although it may seem trivial or unimportant, has substantial significance in the creation of his poem; by this I mean the incident that occurred is essentially what the poem is all about.

The vagueness of sentences like these must be resisted. A sentence should not end up in limbo the way these do. The first sentence is satisfactory up to the verb "causes," but then it falls apart. If Frost has created a response for the speaker in the poem, it is best to describe *what* that response is rather than to state vaguely that there *is* a response. A more forceful restatement of the first sentence may thus be, "It seems as though the author's anticipation of meeting his own 'desert places' causes him to consider that personal needs are more pressing than cosmic." With this revision, the writer could go on to consider the meaning of Frost's final stanza and could relate the idea there to the events and ideas described in the first part of the poem. Without the revision, it is not clear where the writer would go.

The second sentence is so vague that it confuses rather than informs. Such sentences hint at an idea and claim importance for it, but they never directly define what that idea is. If we adopt the principle that it is better to name the specific things we are talking about, the second sentence could be rewritten as follows:

> Although the falling of winter snow may seem trivial or common, the incident causes the speaker to meditate on the emptiness of his own spirit; the significance of the poem thus grows from one of the most common of seasonal events.

When you write your own sentences, you might test them in a similar way. Are you referring to an idea? State the idea directly. Are you mentioning a response or impression? Do not say simply, "The poem left me with a definite impression," but describe the impression: "The poem left me with an impression of sympathy," or "of understanding the hard lot of the migrant farmer." Similarly, do not rest with a statement such as "I found this story interesting," but try to describe what was interesting and why it was interesting. If you always confront your impressions and responses by trying to name them and to pin them down, your sentences should take on exactness and force. Naturally, your instructor will probably tell you whatever you have accomplished or failed to accomplish. Good writing habits that you develop from these criticisms of your work, and from discussions with your instructor, will help you to write more forcefully and accurately.

Whenever you write a theme, then, keep these ideas in mind: Return to the point you wish to make; regard the material in the work you have read as evidence to support your argument, not as story to be retold or as idea to be summarized. Demonstrate that all exemplifying detail is relevant to your main point. Constantly try to develop your topic; make it bigger than it was when you began writing. Constantly try to make your statements accurate, complete, and forceful. If you observe these precepts, you should be well on the way toward successfully handling any of the themes described in this book.

chapter 2

Writing a Précis, or Abridgment

A précis is a shortening, in your own words, of the text of a written work. The words *précis* and *precise* are closely related, and this connection is helpful in enabling an understanding of the nature of a précis—namely, a cutting down of a story, play, or long poem into its *precise,* essential parts. The object is to make a short encapsulation of a work. Other words describing the précis are *abridgment, paraphrase, abstract, condensation,* and *epitome. Epitome* is particularly helpful as a description for a précis, for an epitome is a cutting away of inessentials, so that only the important, most vital parts remain.

USES OF THE PRÉCIS

The précis is important in the service of study, research, and speaking and writing. One of the best ways to study any work is to write a précis of it, for by so doing you force yourself to grasp each of the parts. Writing a précis can be used in note-taking, preparation for exams, establishment and clarification of facts for any body of discourse, study for classroom discussion, and the reinforcement of things learned in the past. The object of a précis should not be to tell everything, but only as much as will give the highlights, so that any reader would know the main points of the work about which the précis has been written.

When you do research (see Chapter 18, pp. 257–283), you must take notes on the material you find. Here the ability to shorten and paraphrase is essential, for it is impossible to reproduce everything in your notes. The better you are able to write a précis, the better will be your research.

In discussions, you will improve your arguments if you refer briefly but accurately to sections of the work being discussed. When you are writing an essay, particularly a longer one, it is often necessary to remind your reader of the events or facts in the work. Here the need is not to tell everything, but just enough so that your conclusions will be self-sustaining. In an argumentative or persuasive speech or essay, when you are trying to convince your listeners or readers, it is necessary to present a common understanding of the facts so that you can eliminate possible objections that may be raised about your use of detail.

For all these occasions you will profit from the technique of paraphrasing or abstracting. Although you may sometimes need to condense an entire plot or epitomize an entire argument, most often you will refer to no more than parts of works, because your arguments will depend on a number of separate interpretations. No matter what your future needs are, however, your ability to write a précis will be helpful.

GUIDELINES

The guidelines to follow in the development of a précis are these:

1. **SELECTION.** Only essential details belong in a précis. For example, at the opening of the story "The Necklace" (for the text of this story, see Appendix C, pp. 314–19), De Maupassant describes the pleasing daydreams of the major character, Mathilde Loisel. She is preoccupied with visions of the pleasures of wealth, such as large anterooms, tapestries, lamps, valets, silks, end tables, expensive bric-a-brac, private rooms, and elegant and exotic meals. Including references to all these, however, would needlessly lengthen a précis of "The Necklace." Instead, it is sufficient to say something like "Mathilde daydreams about wealth," because this description gets at the vital facts about her dissatisfaction with her life and her longing for a wealthier one.

The concentration on essentials enables the shortening required of a précis. Thus, a 5000-word story might be epitomized in 100, 200, or 400 words. It is clear that more details might be selected for inclusion in a longer précis than in shorter ones. Whatever the length of the final précis, however, selection of detail is to be based on the importance of the material in the work being considered.

2. **ACCURACY.** All details in your précis should be both correct and accurate. There is a problem not just of factual misstatement, but also of using words that might give a misleading impression of the original. Thus,

in "The Necklace," Mathilde cooperates with her husband for ten long years to repay their 18,000-franc debt. In a précis about this detail it would be easy, and correct, to say that she "works" during this time. The word "works" is misleading, however, for it may be interpreted to mean that Mathilde gets paid for outside employment. In fact, she does not. What De Maupassant tells us is that Mathilde gives up her servant girl and then does all the heavy housework herself as a part of her general economizing in her *own* household, not in the houses of others.

In the same way, the need to condense long sections of a work necessarily produces the need for comprehensive words that accurately account for sections of the story, play, or narrative poem. Thus, in "The Necklace," Loisel needs 36,000 francs to replace the lost necklace. He is far short of this sum, and he therefore borrows 18,000 francs to make it up. Just to say "he borrows money," however (even the exact sum), does not accurately account for the outrageous interest rates set by the lenders and loan sharks with whom he deals. To be accurate, a précis description must also refer to these desperate promises to pay. Thus, a clause like "he accepts almost ruinous interest rates to get the needed loans" covers not only the borrowing, but also the way in which Loisel mortgages the future. For any précis, word choices should be made with comprehensive accuracy.

3. DICTION. The précis is to be an original essay, to be judged as original, and therefore it should be written in your own words, not those from the work you are abridging. The best way to ensure original wording is to read the work, record the major events, and then put the work out of sight during the writing process. That way, you can avoid the temptation to borrow words directly.

However, if a number of words from the text find their way into the précis even after you have tried conscientiously to be original, then it is important to put these words into quotation marks. As long as direct quotations are kept at a minimum, they are acceptable. Too many quoted words, however, indicate that the précis is not really original writing.

4. OBJECTIVITY. A précis should be scrupulously factual. It is therefore necessary to avoid explanatory or introductory material unless it is a true part of the story. As much effort should be made to avoid conclusions in a précis as is exerted to include them in other kinds of writing about literature. Here is a comparative example of what to do and what to avoid:

What To Do	What To Avoid
Mathilde Loisel, a French housewife married to a minor clerk, is unhappy with her poor household possessions. She daydreams about wealth and is	De Maupassant opens the story by introducing the dissatisfaction that ultimately will propel Mathilde Loisel and her husband to their ten-year disaster.

even more dissatisfied after visiting Jeanne Forrestier, a rich woman who is a former schoolmate. One day Loisel, Mathilde's husband, brings home an invitation to an exclusive dinner dance. Mathilde angrily claims that she has nothing to wear, but Loisel gives her all his savings to buy a party dress.

Mathilde's unhappiness with her own household possessions, and her dreams about wealth, lead her naturally to reproach her husband when he brings home the invitation to the dinner at the Ministry of Education. It is clear that her unhappiness leads her to spend beyond their means for a special party dress.

The right-hand column contains a guiding topic sentence, to which the following sentences adhere. Such writing is commendable everywhere else, but not in a précis. The left-hand column is better writing *as a précis*, for it presents a selection of details only as they appear in the story, without introductory sentences, because in the story there are no such introductions.

5. SENTENCES. Because of the concise and factual nature of the précis, it is tempting to write sentences that are comparable to short bursts of machine-gun fire. Sentences of this kind are often called "choppy" or "bumpy." Here is an example of choppy sentences:

> Mathilde gives up her nice apartment. She works hard for ten years. She climbs stairs. She cleans the floors. She uses big buckets of water. She gets coarse and loud. She haggles with shopkeepers. She is no longer young and beautiful.

An entire essay consisting of sentences like these might make readers feel as though they actually have been machine-gunned. The problem is to include detail but also to remember to shape and organize sentences. Here is a more acceptable set of sentences revised to contain the same information:

> She gives up her nice apartment and devotes herself to hard work for the entire ten years. At home, she climbs many stairs and throws buckets of water to clean the floors. When marketing, she haggles with shopkeepers for bargains. At the end of the time, this hard work has made her loud and coarse, and her youthful beauty is gone.

This revision blends the shorter sentences together and attempts to make a contrast between the second and third sentences. Even though sentences in a précis are to be almost rigidly factual, there is a need to make them as graceful as possible.

WRITING A PRÉCIS

Your writing task is to make a reduction of the original with the least possible distortion. Thus it is necessary to keep intact the arrangement and sequence of the original. For example, let us suppose that a work has a surprise ending, like that in "The Necklace." In a précis, it is important to keep the same order and withhold the conclusion until the very end. It is proper, however, to introduce essential details of circumstance, such as names and places, at the beginning of the précis, even though these details are not brought out immediately in the story. For example, De Maupassant does not name Mathilde right away, and he never says that she is French, but a précis of "The Necklace" would be obscure if these details were withheld.

If your assignment is to write a very short précis, say 100 to 150 words, you might confine everything to only one paragraph. For a longer précis, the normal principle of devoting a separate paragraph to each topic applies. If each major division, episode, scene, action, or section of the story or play is considered a topic, then the précis may be divided into paragraphs devoted to each of the divisions.

Sometimes the author may number these divisions or scenes, or sometimes, as in De Maupassant's "The Necklace," the author may use spaces on the page to separate the parts or scenes of the work. The paragraphing in the sample theme recognizes these divisions, although for brevity some of the spaced sections are combined into one paragraph. The first paragraph, for example, includes the the first three spaced divisions, leading up to the dinner dance. The last paragraph follows the last spaced division exactly. Sometimes stories have no such divisions, but seem to run continuously. For these you may need to create your own topics, such as (1) the events leading up to the main action, (2) the action itself, and (3) the consequences of the action. Or you may be able to determine sections for paragraphing according to the entrances or exits of some of the characters. Always, you must use your own judgment about paragraphing, and the best way is to let the work itself be your guide.

Sample Theme

A Précis of De Maupassant's "The Necklace"[*]

---

[1]
Mathilde Loisel, a Parisian housewife married to a minor clerk, is unhappy with her poor household possessions. She daydreams about wealth, and is even more dissatisfied after visiting Jeanne Forrestier, a rich woman who is a former schoolmate. One day Loisel, Mathilde's husband, brings home an invitation to an exclusive dinner dance. Mathilde angrily claims that she has nothing to wear, but Loisel gives her all his money to buy a party dress. With no jewelry to match, she is ready to give up the affair, but at Loisel's suggestion she borrows a beautiful necklace from Jeanne.

[*] For the text of this story, please see Appendix C, pp. 314–19.

[2] At the party, Mathilde is a huge success, but afterward she and Loisel hurry away because she is ashamed to be seen in her everyday shawl. Upon arriving home, she is horrified to discover that she has lost the necklace.

[3] In desperation, Loisel and she spend a week looking for the necklace. Unable to find it, Loisel buys another for 36,000 francs. He uses his entire inheritance for half of this sum, and borrows the rest wherever he can, accepting almost ruinous interest rates to get the needed loans.

[4] For the next ten years Mathilde and Loisel make sacrifices to pay back both principal and interest. She gives up her nice apartment and devotes herself to hard work for the entire ten years. At home, she climbs many stairs and throws buckets of water to clean the floors. When marketing, she haggles with shopkeepers for bargains. At the end of the time, this hard work has made her loud and coarse, and her youthful beauty is gone.

[5] One Sunday she takes a walk in the fashionable Champs-Elysées and sees Jeanne, who does not recognize her at first because of her changed appearance. Mathilde tells Jeanne of her ten years of sacrifice. Sympathetically, Jeanne responds by explaining that the original necklace had been false, and worth no more than 500 francs.

COMMENTARY ON THE THEME

This précis, about 300 words long, illustrates the selection of major actions and the omission of interesting but inessential detail. Thus, the clause "she daydreams about wealth" contains four words, but it condenses more than 150 words of detailed description in the story. The next clause about the rich friend, Jeanne Forrestier, is longer, but it condenses a relatively short passage in the story. The clause is important, however, because it relates Mathilde's increased dissatisfaction upon seeing Jeanne, and Jeanne is doubly important, for she is the owner of the false necklace that is the cause of the Loisel family downfall. The principle here is this: The selection of what to include in a précis depends not so much upon the length as upon the significance of parts in the original.

Each of the five paragraphs in the précis is devoted to a comparable episode of "The Necklace." Paragraph 1 describes the story up to the party; paragraph 2 the events of the party leading up to the discovery of the loss. The third and fourth paragraphs deal with the borrowing of money to restore the necklace, and with the ten-year sacrifice to pay back the loans. The last paragraph contains the scene in which Mathilde learns that the sacrifice was unnecessary.

The basis in the précis for determining the appropriateness of episodes to paragraphs is not time but unity. Thus, paragraph 1 is unified by Mathilde's dissatisfaction, which leads her to accept her husband's savings for her dress and also to borrow the seemingly expensive necklace for the party. Paragraph 2 describes an episode that takes place within a few hours, but the unifying element is the party and the discovery of the loss immediately after it. The events of paragraph 4, on the other hand, take ten years, and the unifying principle is the coarsening of Mathilde's character under the effects of her long and hard labors.

chapter 3

Writing About Plot and Structure:
The Organization of Narratives and Drama

I. PLOT

Fictional people or characters are derived from life, and so are the things they do. These things are the **actions** or **incidents,** which occur in sequence or in chronological order. Once we have established the **narrative** or sequential order, however, there is still more to be considered. This is **plot,** or the plan of development of the actions.

WHAT IS PLOT?

Without a plot, we do not have a story or drama. A plot is a plan or groundwork of human motivations, with the actions resulting from believable and realistic human responses. In a well-plotted work, nothing is irrelevant; everything is related. The British novelist E. M. Forster, in *Aspects of the Novel*, presents a memorable illustration of plot. As a bare-minimum narration of actions in contrast to a story with a plot, he uses the following: "The king died, and then the queen died." This sentence describes a sequence, a chronological order, but no more. To have a plot, a sequence must be integrated with human motivation. Thus, Forster's following sentence contains a plot: "The king died, and then the queen died of grief." Once the narrative introduces the operative element "of grief," which shows that one thing (grief over the king's death) produces or overcomes another (the normal human desire to live), there is a plot. Thus, stories and plays take place in chronological order, but time is important not simply because one thing happens *after* another, but because one thing happens *because of* another. It is response, interaction, causation, and conflict that make a plot out of a simple series of actions.

CONFLICT.   **Conflict,** the last word on this list, is the most significant element of plot. In fact, it is the essence of plot, because in conflict, human responses are brought out to their highest degree. In its most elemental form, a conflict is the opposition of two people. They may fight, argue, enlist help against each other, and otherwise carry on their opposition. Conflicts may also exist between larger groups of people, although in imaginative literature, conflicts between individuals are more identifiable and therefore more interesting. Conflict may also exist between an individual and larger forces, such as natural objects, ideas, modes of behavior, public opinion, and the like. The existence of difficult **choices** that a character must make may also be presented as a conflict, or **dilemma.** In addition, the conflict may occur not necessarily as direct opposition, but rather as contrasting ideas or values. In short, there are many ways to bring out a conflict in fictional works.

CONFLICT, DOUBT, TENSION, AND INTEREST.   The reason conflict is the major ingredient in a plot is that once two forces are in opposition, there is doubt about the outcome. If the reader becomes interested in and engaged with the characters, this doubt produces curiosity and tension. The same concern is the lifeblood of athletic competition. For just a moment, consider which kind of football game is more interesting: (1) one in which the score goes back and forth and there is doubt about the outcome right up to the last second, or (2) one in which one of the teams gets so far ahead in the first quarter that there is no more doubt about the winner. The interest that a highly contested game provides is also generated by a conflict in a story. The conflict should be a genuine contest, an engagement between characters or forces of approximately equal strength. It should never be a walkaway, mismatch, rout, or "laugher," as the terminology from the sports world goes. Unless there is doubt there is no tension, and unless there is tension there is no interest.

CONFLICT IN PLOT.   To see a plot in operation, let us build on Forster's description. Here is a bare plot for a story: "John and Jane meet, fall in love, and get married." This plot has no apparent conflict and therefore only minimal interest, and it probably would draw very few readers. Let us, however, try the same essential narrative of "boy meets girl" and introduce some conflicting elements:

> John and Jane meet at school and fall in love. They go together for two years, and they plan to marry, but a problem arises. Jane wants

to develop a career first, and after marriage she wants to be an equal contributor to the family. John understands Jane's desire for a career, but he wants to marry first and let her continue her studies afterward in preparation for her goal. Jane believes that this solution will not work, insisting instead that it is a trap from which she will never escape. This conflict interrupts their plans, and they part in regret and anger. They go in different ways even though they still love each other; both marry other people and build separate lives and careers. Neither is completely happy even though they like and respect their spouses. Many years later, after having children and grandchildren, they meet again. John is now a widower and Jane has divorced. Their earlier conflict no longer a barrier, they marry and live successfully together. During their marriage, however, even their new happiness is tinged with reproach and regret because of their earlier conflict, their increasing age, and the lost years they might have spent with each other.

Here we have a true plot because our story contains a conflict that takes a number of shapes. The (1) initial difference in plans and hopes is resolved by (2) a parting of the characters, leading them to separate lives that are (3) not totally happy. The final marriage produces (4) not unqualified happiness, but a note of regret and (5) a sense of time lost that cannot be restored. It is the establishment of these contrasting or conflicting situations and responses that produces the interest our short-short story contains. The situation is lifelike; the conflict stems from realistic values; the outcome is true to life. The imposition of the various conflicts and contrasts has made an interesting plot out of what could have been a common "boy meets girl" sequence.

WRITING ABOUT PLOT

A theme about plot is a description and analysis of the conflict and the developments and routes it takes. A straightforward chronological listing, as in the précis theme (See Chapter 2), is not the goal. The organization of a theme about plot is not based on parts of the story or principal events, because these would invite a chronological summary. Instead, the organization is to be developed out of the important elements of the conflict or conflicts.

Introduction

The things to be brought out in the introduction are brief references to the principal characters, circumstances, and issues of the plot; also, as a central idea for the theme, there should be a sentence describing the plot or principal conflict. The thesis sentence contains the topics to be developed in the body.

Body

The body focuses on the major elements of the plot, brought out to emphasize the plan of conflict in the story or play. Who is the main character? What qualities of this character are important in the conflict? What strengths and weaknesses does the character have? What is the conflict? How is it embodied in the work? What person or persons are the antagonists, and how do their characteristics and interests involve them in the conflict? If the conflict stems out of contrasting ideas or values, what are these and how are they brought out? Does the major character face a difficult decision of any sort? (In our model short-short story, for example, Jane faces the decision of choosing a career and losing John, or accepting John on his terms and losing her career.) Are the effects of any decision the intended ones? In terms of success by personal, occupational, or political standards, does the conflict make the principal character successful or unsuccessful, happy or dissatisfied? Does the character emerge from the conflict in triumph, defeat, or somewhere in the middle? Answers to questions like these form the basis of the body of the essay.

Because a description of elements in a plot can grow too long, it is necessary to be selective and also to decide on a particular approach. Rather than detailing everything point by point, for example, it is preferable to stress the major character and his or her involvement in the conflict. Such a theme on Eudora Welty's "A Worn Path" might emphasize Phoenix as she encounters the various obstacles that she must meet and overcome. Similarly, an essay about the plot of De Maupassant's "The Necklace" might emphasize the major character, Mathilde, as she changes from a rather spoiled and petulant woman because of her frustration about not being rich, to one who becomes coarse and loud because of her ten years of hardship and sacrifice.

When there is a conflict between two major characters, the most obvious approach is to focus equally on both. For brevity, however, it is also possible to stress just one of them. Thus, in Chekhov's *The Bear*, Mrs. Popov, whose conflict is between loyalty to her dead husband and love for the very alive Smirnov, might be emphasized in the discussion, even though Smirnov is equally major and important.

In addition, the plot may be analyzed more broadly in terms of things such as impulses, goals, ideas, values, issues, and historical perspectives. Thus, it might be possible to emphasize the elements of chance that seem to work against Mathilde, in contrast to her dreams and wishes for wealth that are never realized. A discussion of the plot of "First Confession" might stress the youth and childishness of the major character, Jackie, inasmuch as the plot could not develop without his immaturity. In short, when you sketch out your ideas for the body, you have liberty of choice in what to include and develop.

Conclusion

The conclusion may contain a brief summary of the points in the body. Often, a study of plot necessarily leaves out one of the most important reasons for reading, and that is the *impact* of the plot. The conclusion is a fitting location for a brief consideration of effect. Additional comments might concentrate on an evaluation of the plot, such as whether the author has contrived it in any way to tip the balance toward one side or the other, or whether it is realistic, true to life, fair, and impartial.

Sample Theme

*The Plot of Eudora Welty's "A Worn Path"**

[1]   At first, the complexity of Eudora Welty's plot in "A Worn Path" is not clear. The main character is Phoenix Jackson, an old, poor, and frail black woman; the story seems to be no more than a record of her walk to Natchez through the woods from her rural home. By the story's end, however, the plot is clear: It consists of the brave attempts of a courageous, valiant woman to carry on normally despite overwhelming negative forces.° It is the gap between her determination and the odds against her that gives the story its impact. The powers she opposes in the story are environment, poverty, and old age.□

[2]   Environment is shown, during that portion of the story when Phoenix walks to town, as almost an active opponent. Thus she must contend against a long hill, a thorn bush, a log across a creek that poses a threat of falling, and a barbed-wire fence. Also a part of the force against her is the dog that attacks her. Against these obstacles, Phoenix asserts her determination by carrying on a cheerful monologue. She prevails, for the moment at least, because she finally reaches her destination, the city of Natchez.

[3]   The poverty against which Phoenix must contend is evident not in any one spot, but is shown throughout. She cannot take her trip to town by car, for example, but must walk alone on the long "worn path" wearing only tennis shoes. She has no money, and keeps the nickel dropped by the hunter; at the medical office she asks for and gets another nickel. She is the recipient of charity, and is given the "soothing syrup" for her grandson as a free service. Despite the boy's obvious need for advanced medical care, she does not have the means to provide it, and the story therefore shows that her guardianship is doomed.

[4]   Old age as an opponent is shown in signs of Phoenix's increasing senility. Not her mind but her feet tell her where to find the medical office in Natchez. Despite her quiet inner strength, she is unable to tell the nursing attendant why she is there. Instead she sits dumbly and unknowingly for a time. Against

*For the text of this story, please see Appendix C, pp. 331–37.
° Central idea
□ Thesis sentence

[4]   the power of advancing age, Phoenix is slowly losing. The implication is that she soon will lose entirely.

[5]   This brief description of the elements of conflict in the plot can only hint at the final power of the story. Phoenix is strong and admirable, but with everything against her, she can never win. The story itself is layered to bring out the full range of the conditions against her. Welty saves the most hopeless fact, the condition of the invalid grandson, to the very end. It is this delayed final revelation of the plot that creates almost overwhelming sympathy for Phoenix. The plot is powerful because it is so real, and Phoenix is a pathetic but memorable protagonist struggling against overwhelming odds.

COMMENTARY ON THE THEME

In this theme on plot, emphasis is given to the major aspects of the conflict in "A Worn Path." The plot involves the protagonist, Phoenix, who is opposed not by any person, for the other persons in the story are nice to her, but by environment, poverty, and old age. The introduction points out how these forces cumulatively account for the story's impact. Paragraph 2 details the environmental obstacles of the conflict, the sheer physical difficulties she must experience. Paragraph 3 examines Phoenix's poverty, and the fourth paragraph considers her old age. The concluding paragraph introduces one other major conflict—the invalid condition of the grandson—as another of the conflicting forces. This paragraph also points out that in this set of conflicts the protagonist cannot win, except as she lives out her duty and her devotion to help her grandson. Continuing the theme of the introduction, the last paragraph also accounts for the power of the plot: By building up to Phoenix's personal affirmation against unbeatable forces, the story evokes both strong sympathy and great admiration.

II. STRUCTURE

Structure describes the arrangement and placement of materials within a narrative or drama. While *plot* describes the conflict or conflicts, *structure* concerns the way in which the work is laid out and given form or shape to bring out the conflict. The word belongs to a whole family of common words that are concerned with spreading and ordering, including *instruct*, *construct*, *street*, *stratagem*, and, pleasantly, *streusel* (a layering of dough in a pastry).

       The study of structure in fiction and drama is about the causes and reasons (*stratagem* here is the most helpful related word) behind matters such as placement, balance, recurring themes, juxtapositions, true and misleading conclusions, suspense, and the imitation of models or forms like letters, conversations, confessions, and the like. Thus, a story may be divided into parts, or it might develop according to a pattern of movement from countryside to city, or a play might be arranged according to the developing relationships between two people from their first introduction to their falling in love. The study of structure is about these arrangements and the purposes for which they are made.

Formal Categories of Structure

Many aspects of structure are common to all genres of literature. Particularly for drama and narratives, however, the following aspects form the backbone, skeleton, or pattern of development.

1. EXPOSITION. Exposition is the laying out, the putting forth, of the materials in the work: the main characters, their backgrounds, characteristics, basic assumptions about life, goals, limitations, and potentials. Exposition presents everything that is going to be important in the pattern of actions. It may not be limited to the beginning of the work, however, where it is most expected, but it may be found anywhere. Thus, there may be intricacies, twists, turns, false leads, blind alleys, surprises, and other quirks introduced in order to perplex, intrigue, please, and otherwise interest readers. Whenever something new arises, to the degree that it is new it is a part of exposition. Eventually, however, the introduction of new materials must cease and the story must proceed to a conclusion using only those elements of exposition that have already been included.

2. COMPLICATION. The complication marks the onset of the major conflict in the story—the onset of the plot. The participants are the **protagonist** and the **antagonist,** together with whatever ideas and values they represent, such as good and evil, individualism and collectivization, childhood and age, love and hate, intelligence and stupidity, knowledge and ignorance, freedom and slavery, desire and resistance, and the like.

3. CRISIS. The crisis is the turning point, the separation between what has gone before and what will come after. In practice, the crisis is usually a decision or action undertaken to resolve the conflict. It is important to stress, however, that the crisis, though a result of operating forces and decisions, may not produce the intended results. That situation is the next part of the formal structure, the climax.

4. CLIMAX. The climax (a Greek word meaning *ladder*) is the *high point* in the action, in which the conflict and the consequent tension are brought out to the fullest extent. Another way to think of climax is to define it as the point when all the rest of the action becomes firmly set —the point of inevitability and no return. For example, in Chekhov's play *The Bear*, (please see Appendix C, pp. 359–68), the climax occurs when Smirnov begins instructing Mrs. Popov in the use of her dueling pistol, with which she wants to shoot Smirnov himself. This action begins in anger, but once Smirnov begins touching Mrs. Popov to show her the proper techniques of holding, aiming, and shooting the gun, his feelings turn to desire and then to love. Her feelings change, too. Thus this climactic action makes the concluding events, improbable and contradictory as they are, absolutely certain.

5. RESOLUTION OR DÉNOUEMENT.   The resolution (a releasing or un-tying) or dénouement (untying) is the set of actions bringing the story to its conclusion. The resolution of *The Bear* is the increasing recognition by both Smirnov and Mrs. Popov that their anger has turned to love, leading them to their final embrace. Once the "untying" has been done, the author usually concludes the story as quickly as possible. Chekhov ends *The Bear* by having his characters embrace and kiss as the servants enter dumb-foundedly. The endings of Welty's "A Worn Path," O'Connor's "First Confession," and Collier's "The Chaser" all describe characters walking away. The major actions of these works are all completed, and this final action, the walking, underscores the note of finality.

Formal and Actual Structure

The formal structure just described is an ideal one, a pattern that takes place in straightforward, chronological order; it is almost identical to the plot. In practice, however, most narratives and dramas vary the ideal structure, even though all the elements are present. Mystery stories, for example, postpone climaxes until the last moment, and also necessarily delay crucial exposition, inasmuch as the goal is to mystify. In a story where the exposition allows readers to know who a wrongdoer is, by contrast, the goal of the story is often to create suspense about whether the protagonist can maintain life while seeking the wrongdoer out.

More realistic, less artificial stories might also embody structural varia-tions. For example, in Welty's "A Worn Path," a memorable variation is produced by the information introduced at the very end. During most of the story, the complication seems to be that Phoenix Jackson's major prob-lem or conflict is with (1) her age and (2) the natural environment. At the end, however, we learn the additional detail that she is the sole guardian and caretaker of an invalid grandson. Thus, even at the end, we get exposi-tion and complication, so much so that our previous understanding of the conflict must be rethought and revised. The anguish of our response is made more acute, for Phoenix's antagonist is not just age and environ-ment, but also hopeless illness. The *structure* of the story, in other words, is designed to withhold an essential detail to maximize impact. The resolution of the story, coming as it does at the same moment as this crucial complication, points toward the final, inevitable defeat of Phoenix, while it also demonstrates her valiant character.

Other variants in structure are almost as numerous as the works you will encounter. There might be a **flashback** method, for example: The moment at which the flashback is introduced may be a part of the resolution of the plot, and the flashback might lead you into a moment of climax, but then might go from there to develop the details that are more properly part of the exposition. Let us again consider our brief plot about John and Jane, and develop a flashback way of structuring the story.

> Jane is now old, and a noise outside causes her to think of the argument that forced her to part with John many years before. Then she thinks of the years she and John have spent happily together after they married. She then contrasts her happiness with her earlier, less happy marriage, and from there she reflects on her years of courtship with John before their conflict over career plans developed. Then she looks over at John, reading in a chair, and smiles. John smiles back, and the story ends.

This structure is only one way of telling the story. There might be others. Let us suppose that John is in a sickbed at the time Jane thinks about their past, or he might be dead in his coffin. These variations would produce different stories. Additionally, let us suppose that Jane is a widow of many years, either thinking about her past or giving advice to a son or daughter. Then, too, she might be looking back as a divorcee from her first marriage, having just met John again, with the final action being their wedding. The years of happiness might then be introduced as anticipation, or as a resolution described by a narrator, who might have heard about things later from a friend. In short, the possibilities of structuring our little story are great. Using a flashback method such as the one demonstrated here, we would necessarily bring out all the formal elements of plot, but the actual arrangement—the real structure—would be unique.

There are of course many other ways to structure narratives and plays. A plot might be developed by a group of persons, each one knowing only a part of the details. By the time all finish making their contributions, all the necessary complications and resolutions would be clear. If a story or play is structured as though it is a dream, elements of exposition and complication might appear not in chronological but in illogical order. Glaspell's *Trifles*, while not a dream, develops from the chance discoveries that Mrs. Peters and Mrs. Hale make in Mrs. Wright's kitchen, as their husbands wander through the rest of the house searching for other clues. Additionally, parts of a story might be arranged in fragments of conversation, as in "A Worn Path," or a ceremony witnessed by a major character, as in "Young Goodman Brown," or as an announcement of a party, as in "The Necklace." Another work might develop mostly with narration and selectively with dialogue, as in "The Lottery," and still another might be almost totally dialogue, as in "The Chaser."

Questions for the Study of Structure

In the determination of the structure of any work, however, there are a number of recurrent questions that might be asked. What does the reader need to know in order to understand the actions? Are all these things actually included? How are they arranged? Do they come at a point when they might be expected, in light of the plot? What comes first, and why? What comes afterward, and why? If the second and following actions preceded the first action, how would the story be different? How does the present ordering of actions, scenes, speeches, and narration contribute to the completion of the story? How are these placements influential in the effect produced by the story?

WRITING ABOUT STRUCTURE

Your theme about structure is to be concerned with arrangement and shape. In form, the theme should not follow the pattern of the narrative or play part by part. Rather, it explains why things are where they are: "Why is this here and not there?" is the fundamental question to be answered. Thus, it is possible to begin with a consideration of the crisis of the work, and in explaining the position of the crisis to consider how the author's manipulation of the exposition and complication have built up to it. Some vital piece of information, for example, might have been withheld in the earlier exposition (as in "A Worn Path"), and presented at the crisis; thus, the crisis might be heightened because there would have been less suspense if the detail had been introduced earlier. Another thing to consider is the effect or impact of the work, and then to analyze how the structuring produced this effect.

Introduction

The introduction first presents a general overview of the work, and then centers on the aspect or aspects of structure to be emphasized in the body of the theme. The central idea is a succinct statement about the structure, such as that it is built up to reveal the desperate nature of a character's situation, or that it is designed to create surprise, or that it is arranged to bring out maximum humor. The thesis sentence points out the various main headings of the body.

Body

The body is best developed in concert or agreement with what the work contains. Thus, a story may contain a number of separate scenes or settings, such as the countryside, city, and building in "A Worn Path." An essay based on the structural importance of these locations would explain the relationship of each to the development of the plot. Similarly, in both "Miss Brill" and "Young Goodman Brown," both major characters have taken a short trip away from home, and then they are affected powerfully and severely by events that occur within a forest and public park. A structural study of these stories might stem out of these locations and their relationship to the resolution of the plot.

Other ways to consider structure would also necessarily be developed from noteworthy characteristics of the story. In "A Worn Path," a vital piece of exposition, as has been emphasized already, is withheld until the conclusion. An essay on this story's structure might consider what effects this delay produces in the story, and therefore the benefit (or detriment) of this kind of mystery or suspense structure.

It is also possible to devote the body of the essay not to the entire structure of the story, but to a major part, character, or action. Thus, the climax of a story might be the principal subject. Questions to be explored would be these. Where does the climax begin? What events are included in it? Is any new piece of information, or any new interpretation of existing details, introduced in the climax? Why then and not earlier? What is the expected or logical way in which the climax may be resolved? Is this resolution indeed the one created by the author? How and how soon does the reader learn what the resolution is going to be? Similar questions might be posed and answered if the topic of the essay is, say, the complication or the crisis. With such a concentration on only one aspect of structure, you would need to explain in your introduction why you are analyzing a part of the work rather than the whole.

If you should decide to write about the author's structuring of particular characters, it would be important to establish how the characters are introduced, how information is brought out about them, how they figure in the plot, and how they are treated in the resolution. With an action, it might be that one minor event is introduced to demonstrate the importance of fate, chance, or casual happenings in life. Or it might be that the action is not the one intended by the character or by a group. Thus, the event could be seen as it influences the structuring and arrangement of the story's outcome.

Conclusion

Here you may wish to highlight the main parts of the theme. Also, you may wish to deal briefly with the relationship of structure to the plot. If the work you have analyzed departs in any way from strict chronology, you might wish to emphasize the effects of the variations. Your aim should be to focus on the success of the work as it has been brought about by the author's choices in development.

Sample Theme

*The Structure of Eudora Welty's "A Worn Path"**

[1]   On the surface, Eudora Welty's "A Worn Path" is structured simply. The narrative is not difficult to follow, and things go forward in straight chronology. The main character is Phoenix Jackson, an old, poor black woman. She walks from her rural home in Mississippi through the woods to Natchez to get a free bottle of medicine for her grandson, who is a hopeless invalid. Everything takes place in just a few hours. This action is only the frame, however, for a skillfully and powerfully structured plot.° The masterly control of structure is shown in the story's locations, and in the way in which the delayed revelation produces both mystery and complexity.▫

[2]   The locations in the story are arranged to coincide with the increasing difficulties set out against Phoenix. The first and most obvious "worn path" is the rural woods, with all its physical difficulties. For most people the obstacles would not be especially challenging, but for an old woman they are formidable. In Natchez, the location of the next part of the story, Phoenix's inability to bend over to tie her shoe demonstrates the lack of flexibility of old age. In the medical office, where the final scene takes place, two major difficulties of the plot are brought out. One is Phoenix's increasing senility, and the other is the disclosure that her grandson is an incurable invalid. This set of oppositions, the major conflicts in the plot, thus coincide with locations or scenes to demonstrate the cumulative power of the conditions against Phoenix.

[3]   The most powerful of these conditions, the revelation about the grandson, makes the story something like a mystery. Because this detail is not known until the end, the reader is left in the dark to wonder what might happen next to Phoenix. In fact, some parts of the story are really false leads. For example, the episode with the dog is threatening, but it leads nowhere; Phoenix, with the aid of the hunter, is unharmed by the animal. Her theft of the nickel might seem at first to be cause for punishment, but the young hunter is ignorant of the missing coin, and he makes no accusations against her. Right up to the

---

* For the text of this story, please see Appendix C, pp. 331–37.
° Central idea
▫ Thesis sentence

[3] moment of her entering the medical building, therefore, there is no apparent pending resolution. The reader is still wondering what might happen.

Hence the details about the grandson, carefully concealed as they are until the end, make the story much more complex than it seems at first. Because of this concluding revelation, the reader must do a double take, a reconsideration of what has gone on before. Phoenix's difficult walk into town must be seen not as an ordinary errand but as a hopeless mission of mercy. Phoenix's

[4] character also bears reevaluation: She is not just a funny old woman who speaks to the objects and animals around her, but she is an amazingly brave although pathetic woman trying to carry on normally against crushing odds. These conclusions are not apparent for most of the story, and the bringing out of the carefully concealed details makes "A Worn Path" both forceful and powerful.

Thus the parts of "A Worn Path," while seemingly simple, are skillfully arranged. The key to the double take and reevaluation is Welty's withholding of the crucial detail of exposition right until the very end. As it were, parts of the exposition and complication merge with the climax at just about the same

[5] point near the end of the story in the speeches of the attendant and the nurse. In some respects, the detail makes it seem as though Phoenix's entire existence is a crisis, although she is not aware of this condition as she leaves the office to buy the paper windmill. It is this complex buildup and emotional peak that make the structure of "A Worn Path" the creation of a master writer.

COMMENTARY ON THE THEME

To highlight the differences between themes on plot and structure, the topic of this sample theme is Welty's "A Worn Path," the same story analyzed in the sample theme on plot. While both themes are concerned with the conflicts of the story, the theme on plot concentrates on the forces involved, while the theme on structure focuses on the placement and arrangement of the plot elements. Please note that neither the theme on plot nor that on structure is concerned with retelling the actual story, point by point, like a précis. Instead, these are analytical themes that explain the conflict (for plot) and the purposes of arrangement and layout (for structure). In both of these, the assumption is made that the reader has read the story being analyzed and already knows the details, whereas in the précis theme, the assumption is that the reader has not read the story.

The introduction of the essay on structure points out that the masterly structure accounts for the story's power. The second paragraph develops the topic that the geographical locations are arranged climatically to demonstrate the forces against the major character. Paragraph 3 deals with the delayed revelation about the invalid grandson, pointing out that the suspended detail leaves the reader concerned but baffled about the ultimate climax and resolution of the plot. The fourth paragraph deals with the complexity brought about by the delayed information: The necessary reevaluation of Phoenix's character and her mission to town. The concluding paragraph also deals with this complexity, accounting for the story's power by pointing out the merging of a number of plot elements near the very end to bring things out swiftly and powerfully.

chapter 4

Writing About Likes and Dislikes
Responding to Literature

As you read a work of literature—any work—you will respond to it emotionally, and you will be able to describe your response in few or many words.
There are numerous possible expressions of approval and disapproval.
The ones you should be developing as a disciplined reader are those that
are *informed* rather than uninformed. Sometimes the first response students
may express about a work is that it is "boring." Regrettably, this response
is usually only a mask to cover an incomplete, ineffective reading. It is
no more informative than it is informed.

As you study most works, however, you will discover that you get
drawn into them emotionally. One word that describes this process is
interest; that is, to identify yourself with the plans and actions of the major
characters (*interest* implies that you almost literally get taken right inside
the work). A comparable word is *involvement*; that is, to have your emotions
become almost rolled into the work, to get taken up by the characters,
problems, and outcomes. Sometimes both of these words are used defen-
sively, just like the word *boring*. It is easy, in other words, to say that
something you read is "interesting," or that you get "involved" in it,
and you might say just these things with a hope that no one will ask
you further about what you mean. But both interest and involvement do
indeed describe genuine responses to reading. Once you become interested,
you will recognize that fact. Your reading becomes less of a task than a
pleasure, and, although you may do some of the detailed assignments

grudgingly because of the needed time and effort, your deepening appreciation will be its own reward.

All of this leads to the topic of likes and dislikes of literary works. For most practical purposes, you may equate your interest in a work with liking it. You can carry the specifics of liking further, however, by considering some of the following as reasons for your favorable responses:

> You like and admire the characters and approve of what they do and stand for.
>
> You learn more about topics very important to you.
>
> You learn something you had never known or thought before.
>
> You gain new or fresh insights into things you had already known.
>
> You learn about characters from different ways of life.
>
> You are involved and interested in the outcome of the action or ideas, and do not want to put the work down until you have finished it.
>
> You feel happy because of reading the work.
>
> You are amused and laugh often as you read.
>
> You like the author's presentation.
>
> You find that some of the ideas and expressions are beautiful and worth remembering.

Obviously, if you find none of these things in the work, or find something that is distasteful, you will not like the work.

KEEP A NOTEBOOK FOR YOUR FIRST RESPONSES

No one can tell you what you should or should not like; liking is your own concern. In any consideration of your reactions, therefore, you should begin by keeping a notebook record of your responses and observations about a work. You might keep this record as your read, or immediately after you have finished, while your experience of reading is still fresh. What is important here is absolute frankness, for your responses should be based on a combination of what happens in the work together with your judgments and conclusions. Always try to explain the reasons for your responses, even if these reasons are brief and not completely thought through. If, with later thought and fuller understanding, you change or modify your first impressions, record these changes too. Here is such a notebook entry, about Guy de Maupassant's "The Necklace" (this story is the subject of the sample theme on pp. 314–19):

> I like "The Necklace" because of the surprise ending. It isn't that I like Mathilde's bad luck, but I like the way De Maupassant hides

the most important fact in the story until the end. Mathilde thus does all that work and sacrifice for no reason at all, and the surprise ending makes this point strongly.

This paragraph could easily be expanded as a part of a developing essay. The virtue of it is that it is a clear statement of the student's liking, followed by the major reasons for this response. The pattern, which might best be phrased as "I like [dislike] this work because . . . ," is necessary in your notebook entries.

The challenge in considering your responses of liking or disliking is that in a theme you will need to explain yourself in detail. For this reason, it is essential to try to pinpoint some of the specific things to which you have responded. If at first you cannot put into your notebook any full sentences detailing the causes of your responses, at least make a brief list of those things that you like or dislike. If you write nothing, you will probably forget your reactions, and recovering them at a later time, either for discussion or writing, will be difficult.

WHAT DO YOU DO WITH DISLIKES?

Although so far we have dismissed *boring* and stressed *interest, involvement,* and *liking,* it is important to know that disliking an entire work, or some thing in it, is acceptable. You do not need to hide this response. Here, for example, are two short notebook responses expressing dislike for "The Necklace":

1. I do not like "The Necklace" because Mathilde seems spoiled, and I don't think she is worth reading about.

2. "The Necklace" is not an adventure story, and I like reading only adventure stories.

These are both legitimate responses because they are based on a clear standard of judgment. The first stems from a distaste for an unlikable trait shown by the main character, the second from a preference for mystery or adventure stories, which contain rapid action to evoke interest in the dangers faced and overcome by main characters.

Here is a notebook-type entry that might be developed from the first response. What is important is that the reasons for dislike are explained. They would need only slightly more development to be expressed later in classroom discussion or in an essay form:

I do not like "The Necklace" because Mathilde seems spoiled and I do not think she is worth reading about. She is a phony. She nags her husband because he is not rich. She never tells the truth. I especially dislike her hurrying away from the party because she is afraid of being seen in her shabby coat. It is foolish and dishonest of her not to tell

Jeanne Forrestier about losing the necklace. It is true that she works hard to pay the debt, but she also puts her husband through ten years of unnecessary hardship and misery. If Mathilde had faced facts, she might have had a better life. I do not like her and cannot like the story because of her.

As long as you explain why you dislike something, as is done in this notebook paragraph, you can use your reasons for further study and consideration. Even though you yourself might modify or even change your mind later, it is better to record your honest responses of dislike than to force yourself to say you like something when you don't like it.

PUTTING DISLIKES INTO A LARGER CONTEXT

If it is important to be truthful about a response of dislike, however, it is equally important to broaden perspective and to expand taste. For example, the dislike based on a preference for only mystery or adventure stories, if it is applied generally, would cause a person to dislike most great works of literature. This seems unnecessarily self-limiting.

If a person can put negative responses into a larger context, it is possible to expand his or her likes in line with very personal responses. A young woman might be deeply involved in personal concerns and therefore be uninterested in seemingly remote literary figures. However, if by reading about literary characters she can gain insight into general problems of life, and therefore her own concerns, she can like just about any work of literature. A young man might like sports events and therefore not care for reading anything but sports magazines. But what likely interests him in sports is the competition. If he can find competition, or conflict, in a work of literature, he can like that work. The principle here is that already established reasons for liking something may be stimulated by works that at first did not seem to bring them out.

As an example, let us consider again the dislike based on a preference for adventure stories, and see if this preference can be analyzed. Here are some reasons for liking adventures:

1. Adventure has fast action.
2. Adventure has danger and tension, and therefore interest.
3. Adventure has daring, active characters.
4. Adventure has obstacles that the characters work hard to overcome.

No one could claim that "The Necklace" is described by the first three points, but the fourth point is promising. In looking at Mathilde Loisel, we can see that she works hard to overcome an obstacle—paying off the large debt. If our student likes adventures because the characters try to achieve worthy goals, then he or she can also like "The Necklace" for the same reason. The principle here is clear: If a reason for liking a favorite work can be found in another work, then there is also reason to like that new work. The problem is that the student must first be able to articulate responses to the favorite work; thought and analogy will then do the rest. Such a comparative method can become the basis for analyzing and developing responses to newly encountered works of literature.

The following paragraph shows how the thought processes of the comparison might work to form the basis for an entire essay on liking. (The sample essay is also developed along these lines.)

> I usually like only adventure stories, and therefore I disliked "The Necklace" because it is not adventure. But one of my reasons for liking adventure is that the characters work hard to overcome difficult obstacles like finding buried treasure or exploring new places. Mathilde, De Maupassant's main character in "The Necklace," also works hard to overcome an obstacle—helping to pay back the money and interest for the borrowed 18,000 francs used as part of the payment for the replacement necklace. I like adventure characters because they stick to things and win out. I see the same toughness in Mathilde. Her problems therefore get more interesting as the story moves on after a slow beginning. I came to like the story.

This example shows the ability to apply an accepted principle of liking to another work where it also applies. A person who adapts principles in this open-minded way can, no matter how slowly, redefine dislikes and expand the ability to like and appreciate many kinds of literature.

An equally open-minded way to develop understanding and to widen taste is to put dislikes in the following light: An author's creation of an unlikable character, situation, attitude, or expression may be deliberate. Your dislike might then result from the author's *intentions*. A first task of study therefore becomes the attempt to understand and explain the intention or plan. As you put the plan into your own words, you may find that you can like a work with unlikable things in it. Here is a paragraph that traces this pattern of thinking, based again on "The Necklace":

> De Maupassant apparently wants the reader to dislike Mathilde, and I do. He shows her as unrealistic and spoiled. She lies to everyone and nags her husband. Her rushing away from the party so that no one can see her shabby coat is a form of lying. But I can like the story itself because De Maupassant makes another kind of point. He does not hide her bad qualities, but makes me see that she herself is the cause of her trouble. If people like Mathilde never face the truth, they will get into bad situations. This is a good point, and I like the way De Maupassant makes it. The entire story is therefore worth liking even though I still do not like Mathilde.

Neither of the two ways shown here of broadening the contexts of response is dishonest to the original expressions of dislike. In the first paragraph, the thinker applies one of his principles of liking to include

"The Necklace." In the second, the writer considers her initial dislike in the context of the work, and discovers a basis of liking the story as a whole while still disliking the main character. The main concern in both responses is to keep an open mind despite initial dislike, and then to see if the unfavorable response can be more fully and broadly considered.

However, if, after consideration, you decide that your dislike over-balances any reasons you can find for liking, then you should be prepared to describe and defend your dislike of the work. As long as you relate your response accurately to the work, and measure it by a clear standard of judgment, your dislike of even a commonly liked work will be acceptable.

WRITING ABOUT RESPONSES: LIKES AND DISLIKES

In writing about your responses, you should rely on your initial informed reactions to the work you have been assigned. It is not easy to reconstruct your first responses after a lapse of time, so you will need your notebook observations as a guide. Try to be true to them. Develop your essay in terms of what interests you (or does not interest you) in the work.

A major difficulty in such a theme is to relate the details of the work to the point you are making about your ongoing responses. It might be easy to begin by indicating that you liked the work; then, in describing what it is that you liked, you might forget your response as you enumerate details. It is therefore necessary to keep stressing your involvement in the work as you bring out evidence from it. You can show your attitudes by indicating approval (or disapproval), by commenting favorably (or unfavorably) on the details, by indicating things that seemed new (or shopworn) and particularly instructive (or wrong), and by giving assent to (or dissent from) ideas or expressions of feeling.

Introduction

Begin by describing briefly the conditions that influence your response. Your central idea should be whether you like or dislike the work. The thesis sentence should list the major causes of your response, to be developed in the body of your essay.

Body

1. The most common approach is to consider the thing or things about the work that you like or dislike (for a list of possible reasons for liking a work, see above, p. 56). You may like a particular character, or maybe you got so interested in the story that you could not put it down. It may be that a major idea, a new or fresh insight, or a particular

outcome is the major point you wish to develop. The sample notebook paragraph earlier in this chapter (pp. 56–57) shows a "surprise ending" as the cause of a favorable response.

2. Another approach is to give details about how your responses occurred or changed in your reading of the work. This development requires that you pinpoint, in order, the various good (or bad) parts of the work and your responses to them. Because of the orderly introduction of details, you should avoid the pitfall of simply retelling a story or summarizing an argument. If you emphasize how the details bring out your responses, however, your essay will contain more thought and consideration than a précis.

3. Two additional types of response about which you may write are described in some detail above (pp. 58–60). Both approaches bring out a shift or development of response, either from negative to positive (most common) or vice versa. The first approach allows the writer to show that a principle for liking one kind of literature may be applied to the assigned work. (This approach is illustrated in the sample theme, below. The second suggests that a writer may first respond unfavorably to something about the work, but that on further consideration she or he has been able to establish a larger context, which permits a favorable response.

Conclusion

Here you might briefly summarize the reasons for your major response. You might also try to face any issues brought up by a change in your responses, if there was one. That is, if you have always held certain assumptions about your taste but liked the work despite these assumptions, you may wish to talk about your own change or development. This topic is personal, but in an essay about likes or dislikes, discovery about yourself is something you should aim for.

Sample Theme

Some Reasons for Liking Guy de Maupassant's "The Necklace"[*]

To me, the most likable kind of reading is adventure. Although there are many reasons for my preference, an important one is that adventure characters work hard to overcome obstacles. Because "The Necklace" is not adventure, I did not like it at first. But in one respect the story is like adventure:

[*] For the text of this story, please see Appendix C, pp. 314–19.

[1] Mathilde, with her husband Loisel, works hard for ten years to overcome a difficult obstacle. Thus, because Mathilde does what adventure characters also do, the story is likable.° Mathilde's appeal results from her hard work, strong character, and sad fate.□

[2] Mathilde's hard work makes her seem good. Once she and her husband are faced with the huge debt of 18,000 francs with interest, she works like a slave to pay it back. She gives up her servant and moves to a cheaper place. She does the household drudgery, wears cheap clothes, and bargains with shopkeepers for the lowest prices and greatest savings. Just like the characters in adventure stories, who sometimes must do hard and unpleasant things, she does what she has to, and this makes her admirable.

[3] Her strong character makes her endure, a likable trait. To do the bad jobs, she needs toughness. At first she is a nagging, spoiled person, always dreaming about wealth and telling lies, but she changes and gets better. She recognizes her blame in losing the necklace, and she has strength to help her husband redeem the debt. She sacrifices "heroically" (De Maupassant's word) not only her middle-class way of life, but also her youth and beauty. Her jobs are not the exotic and glamorous ones of adventure stories, but her force of character makes her as likable as an adventure heroine.

[4] Her sad fate also makes her likable. In adventure stories the characters often suffer as they do their jobs. Mathilde also suffers, but in a different way, because her suffering is permanent, while the hardships of adventure characters are temporary. This fact makes her pitiable, and even more so because all her sacrifices are not necessary. Thus, there is a sense of injustice about her plight which makes the reader take her side.

[5] Obviously "The Necklace" is not an adventure story, but some of the good qualities of adventure characters can also be seen in Mathilde. Also, the surprise revelation that the lost necklace was false is an unforgettable twist that makes her more deserving than she seems at first. De Maupassant has arranged the story so that the reader finally admires Mathilde. "The Necklace" is a skillful and likable story.

COMMENTARY ON THE THEME

The argument in this theme is that "The Necklace," which the writer claims at first not to have liked, can be liked because Mathilde, the major character, has many of the qualities that make adventure-story characters likable. Each of the reasons brought out for liking Mathilde is also a reason for liking adventure characters. Although the liking for adventure is thus a bridge that the writer crosses on the way to liking "The Necklace," some other reasons are brought out in the conclusion of the essay.

In the introduction, the writer uses as a central idea the common bonds that make Mathilde as likable as characters in adventure stories.

° Central idea
□ Thesis sentence

The thesis sentence lists three topics—hard work, strong character, and sad fate—which are to be developed in the body of the essay.

Paragraph 2 gives instances of Mathilde's hard work as a cause for liking, and concludes by comparing Mathilde and adventure characters as workers. The third paragraph gives examples of Mathilde's toughness of character and also compares her strength with the strength of adventure characters. In paragraph 4 a comparison is made between Mathilde's sacrifices and the hardship experienced by adventure characters; the pity and sympathy evoked by Mathilde are claimed as causes for liking her. The conclusion restates the comparison, and also lists the surprise ending and the development of the story as reasons for liking "The Necklace."

Throughout the theme, the central idea that the story is liked is brought out in words and expressions like "likable," "Mathilde's appeal," "strong character," "she does what she has to," "pitiable," and "take her side." These expressions, mixed as they are with references to many details from the story, create thematic continuity that shapes and develops the essay. It is the thematic development, together with the use of the details from the story as supporting evidence, that distinguishes the sample theme from a précis (Chapter 2).

chapter 5

Writing About Character

Character in literature is an extended verbal representation of a human being, the inner self that determines thought, speech, and behavior. Through dialogue, action, and commentary, authors capture some of the interactions of character and circumstance. Narratives and plays make these interactions interesting by portraying characters who are worth caring about, rooting for, and even loving, although there are also characters at whom you may laugh or whom you may dislike or even hate.

CHOICE AND CHARACTER

The choices that people make indicate their characters, if we assume they have freedom of choice. We always make silent comparisons with the choices made or rejected. Thus, if you know that John works twelve hours a day, while Tom puts in five, and Jim sleeps under a tree, you have a number of separate facts, but you do not conclude anything about their characters unless you have a basis for comparison. This basis is easy: The usual, average number of working hours is eight per day. With no more than this knowledge for comparison, you might conclude that John is a workaholic, Tom is lazy, and Jim is either unwell or a dropout. To be fair, you would need to know much more about the lives and financial circumstances of each person before you could make your conclusions definite.

In narrative and drama you may expect such completeness of context. You may think of each action or speech, no matter how small or seemingly unusual, as an accumulating part of a total portrait. Whereas in life things may "just happen," in literature all the actions, interactions, speeches, and observations are arranged to give you the details you need for conclusions about character. Thus, you read about important events like a first confession (O'Connor's "First Confession"), a long period of work and sacrifice (De Maupassant's "The Necklace"), the taking of a regular journey of mercy (Welty's "A Worn Path"), the murder of a husband by a wife (Glaspell's *Trifles*), or a sudden change from anger to love (Chekhov's *The Bear*). From these events in context you draw conclusions about the characters involved.

MAJOR CHARACTER TRAITS

In studying a literary character, you should determine the character's major **trait** or traits. A trait is a typical mode of behavior or response, such as acting first and thinking afterward, crowding another person closely while talking, looking directly into a person's eyes or avoiding eye contact completely, or habitually borrowing money and not repaying it. If we can learn enough about a person's separate traits, we can go a long way toward understanding that person. Often, of course, traits may be minor and therefore negligible. But sometimes a particular trait may be important enough to be considered the primary characteristic of a person, not only in literature but also in life. Thus, characters may be lazy or ambitious, anxious or serene, aggressive or fearful, assertive or bashful, open or secretive, confident or self-doubting, adventurous or timid, noisy or quiet, visionary or practical, reasonable or hotheaded, careful or careless, evenhanded or biased, straightforward or underhanded, a "winner" or a "loser," and so on.

With this sort of list, to which you may add at will, you can analyze and develop conclusions about character. For example, in preparing to write about Mathilde Loisel, the main character in De Maupassant's "The Necklace," you would note that she daydreams about wealth she cannot have. Such thoughts are not unusual, but she is so swept up in her longing for ease that she scorns the comparatively good life that she has in reality. It is fair to conclude that this trait is also a weakness, because her dream life in effect destroys her real life. By contrast, the narrator of Amy Lowell's poem "Patterns" (Appendix C) demonstrates the capacity to cover up her real feelings, even though all her plans for future happiness have just been destroyed by the news of her fiancé's death. This ability gives her the power to analyze her situation, and presumably to face it; as a result, she exhibits strength of character. From a combination of traits and actions such as these, you can get a "handle" on the characters you study in literature.

APPEARANCE, ACTION, AND CHARACTER

When you assemble materials for your essay on character, be sure to consider physical descriptions, but also be sure to relate the physical to the mental or psychological. Suppose your author stresses the neatness of one character and the sloppiness of another. Most likely, these descriptions can be related to your character study. The same also applies to your examination of what a character does. Go beyond the actions themselves and try to determine what they show about the character. Always try to get from the outside to the inside, for it is on the inside that character resides.

TYPES OF CHARACTERS: ROUND AND FLAT

In literature you will encounter two types of characters, which E. M. Forster (in *Aspects of the Novel*) calls "round" and "flat." The basic requirement for a **round character** is that he or she profit from experience and undergo a change or development. Round characters have many realistic traits and are relatively fully developed by the author. For this reason they are often given the names **hero** or **heroine.** Because many major characters are anything but heroic, however, it is probably best to use the more neutral word **protagonist,** which implies only that a character is a center of attention, not a moral or physical giant. The protagonist is central to the action, moves against an **antagonist,** and usually exhibits the human attributes we expect of rounded characters.

   To the degree that round characters have individual and unpredictable human traits, and because they undergo change or growth because of their experiences, they may be considered **dynamic.** In Glaspell's *Trifles*, for example, Mrs. Wright is a dynamic, round character (she is the subject of the sample theme, pp. 368–78). We learn that she was, when younger, a colorfully dressed and music-loving person, but we also learn that she has suppressed the assertiveness of her youth. Finally, however, after accepting her husband's insensitivity and contempt for thirty years, she has reasserted herself in an act of anger and violence. At the play's end, even though we may not approve of her murder of her husband, we do understand her change from subservience to violence. She is a dynamically conceived character.

In considering a round character, you may decide for yourself whether alterations are *change* or *growth*. Do human beings develop new traits as circumstances bring them out, or do circumstances merely draw out traits that are already present? Mrs. Wright has acted the role of victim for many years during her drab life, but she commits a violent act of anger and hatred. Does this act show a change from victim to victimizer, or does it show that she was potentially a victimizer all along, no matter how she suppressed this quality? With round or full characters, a question of this type is appropriate, for round characters are just as complex and as difficult to understand as living people. A round character therefore stands out, totally identifiable within the class, occupation, or circumstances of which she or he is a part. Obviously, in a brief story or play we cannot learn everything there is to know about a major character, but if the author is skillful, there will be enough significant detail in the work to add up to a dynamic character. Indeed, you may judge an author by how fully he or she brings round characters to life.

As contrasted with the round character, the **flat character** is undistinguishable from other persons in a particular group or class. Therefore, the flat character is not individual, but **representative.** Flat characters are usually minor, although not all minor characters are flat. They are mostly useful, adding background, local color, or service to the works in which they appear. They may be the parent or the brother or sister of a major character, may walk along a street and greet a major character, may be contrasted in some way with a major character, and may provide a service for a major character; they may poke around in rooms in a house, explain a procedure or custom that would otherwise not be explained, and perform the other important tasks in the development of a narrative or play. We learn little if anything about their traits and their lives. They are, in truth, peripheral to the main plot. Because they do not change or grow, they are **static,** not dynamic like round characters.

Sometimes flat characters are prominent in certain types of literature, such as cowboy, police, and detective stories, where the main characters need to be strong, tough, steadfast, and clever enough to overcome the obstacles before them or solve the crime. These and other types of works feature recurring situations and require characters to perform similar roles. The term **stock character** refers to characters in these repeating situations. Obviously, names, ages, and sexes are often changed, and places and offices may vary slightly, but stock characters have many common traits. Some of the many stock characters are the clown, the revenger, the foolish boss, the bewildered parent, the overbearing or henpecked husband, the servile or henpecking wife, the angry police captain, the lovable drunk, the younger or older sister or brother, and the town do-gooder.

Although these characters are not necessarily flat, they stay flat as long as they perform only their functions, exhibit conventional and unindividual traits, and then disappear from the story and from your memory. When stock characters possess no attitudes except those to be expected from their class, they are often given the label **stereotype,** because they all seem to be cast in the same mold. Often, in highly conventionalized works like cowboy and police stories and romances, even the major characters are flat and stereotypical even though they occupy center stage throughout as protagonists.

Complications occur when round characters are in stock roles and exceed their expected stereotypical behavior. Thus John Wright, the murdered husband in Glaspell's *Trifles*, is described as having been in life a typically insensitive and bluntly overbearing and even cruel person—a flat, stock character. The plot of the play develops, however, because Minnie Wright, having accepted her servility and unimportance as his wife for thirty years—in other words, having been a flat, stock servile wife—has been provoked to move out of this role and destroy her oppressor, her husband. Because of this complication, we know that she is a round character, even though we never see her firsthand, but only hear about her actions and draw our conclusions about her from the discoveries of the two women in the kitchen. Had she continued to acquiesce in her dreary lot with her husband, even to the point of accepting his deliberate cruelty, she would have continued to be flat, representative, and stereotypical, and there would have been no play. Mrs. Popov of *The Bear* is another character who emerges from a stock role as a grieving widow to become a round character. She gives up her supposedly lifelong devotion to her dead husband to accept and return the love of the outrageous creditor and then suitor, Smirnov.

HOW IS CHARACTER DISCLOSED IN LITERATURE?

In preparing your theme, you should consider that authors use four distinct ways to present information about characters. Remember that you must use your own knowledge of and experience with human beings to make judgments about the qualities—the flatness or roundness—of the characters being revealed.

1. *What the characters themselves say (and think, if the author expresses their thoughts).* On the whole, speeches may be accepted at face value to indicate the character of a speaker. Sometimes, however, a speech may be made offhandedly, or it may reflect a momentary emotional or intellectual state. Thus, if characters in deep despair say that life is worthless, you must balance this speech with what the same characters say when they

are happy. You must also consider the situation or total context of a statement. Macbeth's despair at the end of Shakespeare's play *Macbeth* is voiced after he has shown himself to be guilty of ruthless political suppression and assassination. In fact, his brooding self-condemnation indicates that he is at heart a good person, but that he has taken the wrong path; otherwise, he would not feel guilt. You should also consider whether speeches show change or development. A despairing character might say depressing things at the start but happy things at the end of a play or story. Your analysis of such speeches should indicate how they reflect change or development.

2. *What the characters do.* You have heard that "actions speak louder than words," and you should interpret actions as signs of character. Thus, you might consider Phoenix's trip through the woods (Welty's "A Worn Path") as a sign of a loving, responsible character, even though Phoenix herself nowhere claims to be loving and responsible. The difficulty and hardship she goes through on the walk, however, justify such a conclusion about her.

Often you will find that action is inconsistent with logic or expectation. Such behaviors may signal naiveté, weakness, deceit, a scheming personality, a change or realization of some sort, or strong inner conflicts. Here is a change: Smirnov, in Chekhov's play *The Bear*, would be crazy to teach Mrs. Popov how to use the dueling pistol properly, because she has threatened to kill him with it. But his change is his realization that he loves her, and his cooperative if potentially self-destructive act shows that his loving nature has overwhelmed his sense of self-preservation. The old man in Collier's "The Chaser" is a schemer. He is planning eventually to make the big sale of the death potion, the "chaser," and hence he speaks to Alan Austen indirectly and manipulatively; he is ostensibly selling love, but he really is selling death. A strong inner conflict is seen in the two women in Glaspell's play *Trifles*. They have an obligation to the law, but they feel a stronger obligation to the accused killer, Mrs. Wright; hence they remain silent even though they discover incriminating evidence against her.

3. *What other characters say about them.* In stories and in plays, as in life, people often talk about other people. If the speakers are shown as honest, you may usually accept their opinions as accurate descriptions of character. However, sometimes a person's prejudices and interests distort what he or she says. You know, for example, that the word of a person's enemy is likely to be prejudicial and untrue. Therefore, an author may give you a good impression of characters by having a bad or negative character say negative things about them (see, for example, Nora's comments about her brother, Jackie, in "First Confession"). Similarly, the word of a close friend may be biased in favor of a particular character, and thus may exaggerate that character's good qualities. You must always

consider the context and source of all remarks before you draw conclusions about a character.

4. *What the author says about them, speaking as storyteller or observer.* What the author, speaking with the authorial voice, says about a character is usually to be accepted as accurate. Naturally, the authorial voice must be accepted factually. However, when the authorial voice *interprets* actions and characteristics, the author assumes the role of a reader or critic, and any opinions may be either right or wrong. For this reason, authors frequently avoid interpretations and devote their skill instead to arranging events and speeches so that only readers themselves draw conclusions.

REALITY AND PROBABILITY: VERISIMILITUDE

You are entitled to expect characters in literature to be true to life. That is, their actions, statements, and thoughts must all be what human beings are likely to do, say, and think under the conditions presented in the work. This expectation is often called the standard of **verisimilitude** ("similar to truth"), **probability,** or **plausibility.** That is, there are persons in life who do seemingly impossible tasks (such as single-handedly capturing 200 enemy soldiers, or giving away a fortune). Such characters in literature would not be true to life, however, because they are not within our judgment of *normal* or *usual* human behavior. They are not probable or believable (unless they appear in a fantasy or fairy tale).

One should therefore distinguish between what can *possibly* happen and what would frequently or *most usually* happen. Some reactions do not belong in a work featuring full, round characters. Thus, for example, in De Maupassant's "The Necklace," it is possible that Mathilde could be truthful and tell her friend Jeanne Forrestier that she has lost the necklace. In light of the sense of pride, honor, shame, and respectability of Mathilde and her husband, however, it is more normal, more believable, for her to hide the fact, borrow money to buy a replacement necklace, and endure the ten-year penance to pay back the loans. The probable here has overshadowed the possible.

Nevertheless, probability does not rule out surprise or even exaggeration. Thus, in *The Bear*, the main characters, who are strangers when the short play opens, fall in love. This change is not as improbable as it seems at first, for Chekhov shows that both Mrs. Popov and Smirnov have deeply loving and emotional natures, and that they are given to suddenness or whim. Under the emotional crisis of their threatened duel, it is therefore not improbable that they would turn directly to loving each other. The action, though surprising and exaggerated, meets the standard of verisimilitude, or probability.

There are many ways of rendering the probable in literature. Fiction that attempts to mirror life—the realistic, naturalistic, or "slice of life" types of fiction like Welty's "A Worn Path"—sets up conditions and raises expectations about the characters that are different from those of works that attempt to portray a romantic, fanciful world. A character's behavior and speech in the "realistic" setting would be out of place in the romantic setting.

But the situation is more complex than this, for within the romantic setting a character might reasonably be *expected* to behave and speak in a fanciful, dreamlike way. Speech and action under both conditions are therefore probable, as we understand the word, although different aspects of human character are presented in these two different types of works.

It is possible that within the same work you might find some characters who are realistic and others who are not. In such works you have contrasting systems of reality. Mathilde in "The Necklace" exhibits such a contrast. Her dream world at the beginning is so powerful that she makes unrealistic demands on her husband. When the borrowed necklace is lost, her character as a dreamer has effectively destroyed her life in the real world.

You might also encounter works where there are *mythical* or *supernatural* figures, like the woodland guide in Hawthorne's "Young Goodman Brown." You may wonder how you should interpret the character of such figures. Usually, gods and goddesses embody qualities of the best and most moral human beings, and devils like Hawthorne's guide take on attributes of the worst. However, you might remember that the devil is often imagined as a character with many dashing and engaging traits, the easier to deceive poor sinners and lead them into hell. In judging characters of this or any type, your best guide is probability, consistency, and believability.

WRITING ABOUT CHARACTER

Usually you will have been assigned a major character, although it is possible that you might study a minor character or characters. Either way, the procedures you follow will be much the same. After your customary overview, begin taking notes. Determine as many traits as you can; also determine how the author has presented information about the character. When comments are made by other characters or by the authorial voice, determine whether these are true. When characters go into action, consider what these actions tell about their natures. If there are unusual traits, determine what they show.

Try to answer questions like these: Does the character come to life? Is he or she round or flat, lifelike or wooden? Are there admirable qualities or many shortcomings? What are they? Is the character central to the action, and therefore the hero or protagonist of the story? What traits make the character genuinely major? Do you like him or her? Why? Who or what is the antagonist? How does reaction to the antagonist bring out qualities in your character? What are they? Does the character exhibit any stock or stereotypical qualities? If so, does he or she rise above them, and how? What is the relationship of the character to the other characters? What do the others say or think about him? How accurate are their observations?

Once you have gathered materials in response to these and other questions, it will be possible to go ahead to do the classifying and sorting necessary for the composition of the essay.

Introduction

The introduction may begin with a brief identification of the character to be analyzed, which may be followed by reference to noteworthy problems in defining the character's qualities. The central idea is a statement about the major trait or quality of the character. The thesis sentence links the central idea to the main sections to be covered in the body.

Body

The organization is designed to illustrate the central idea and make it convincing. There is much freedom in the approach to take, such as the following:

1. *Organization around central traits or major characteristics.* Examples might be "kindness, gentleness, generosity, firmnness," or "resoluteness of will frustrated by inopportune moments for action, resulting in despondency, doubt, and melancholy." A body containing this sort of structure would demonstrate how these qualities are embodied in the work. For example, a particularly strong quality might be shown in one part of the work in speeches that a character makes about the major character, and in other parts of the work in speeches and actions of the character. Emphasizing the quality thus enables you to study three different ways in which the author presents the character; it also enables you to focus on separate parts of the work irrespective of the narrative or chronological development of the plot.

2. *Organization around the growth or change of a character.* The beginning of such a body would establish the traits the character possesses at the start of the story, and then describe the changes or developments that occur. It is important here to avoid retelling a narrative or dramatic action, and to stress the actual alterations as they emerge from the circumstances of the work. It is also important to determine whether the growth or change is genuine; do the traits belong clearly to the character, and are

they logically produced, or are they manufactured as needed by the events?

3. *Organization around central incidents, objects, or quotations that reveal primary characteristics, bring them out, or even cause them.* Certain key incidents may stand out in a work, as will objects closely associated with the character being analyzed and several key quotations spoken by the character or by someone else in the work. The body of a theme on character study might effectively be structured with these as signposts for the discussion. As with the second method of organization just described, it is important to stress in the topic sentences that the purpose is to illuminate the character, to show how the topics are keys or wedges to opening up an understanding of the character, not just to expand on the incidents, things, or quotations as separate topics themselves.

4. *Organization around qualities of a flat character or characters.* If the essay is about a character who is not round but flat, the body might treat topics like the function and relative significance of the character, the group of which the character is representative, the relationship of the flat character to the round ones and the importance of this relationship, and any additional qualities or traits discoverable in the work.

Conclusion

The conclusion is the location for statements about how the discussed characteristics are related to the story or play as a whole. If the person was good but came to a bad end, does this discrepancy elevate him or her to tragic stature? If the person was a nobody and came to a bad end, does this fact suggest any authorial attitudes about the class or type of which he or she is a part? Or does it seem to illustrate the author's general view of human life? Or both? Do the characteristics explain why the person helps or hinders other characters? Does the essay help in the clearing up of any misunderstandings that might have been present on a first reading? Questions like these may be raised and answered in the conclusion.

Sample Theme

The Character of Minnie Wright of Glaspell's Trifles[*]

---

[1]   Minnie Wright is the major character of Glaspell's *Trifles*. We learn about her, however, not from seeing and hearing her, for she does not appear or

[*] For the text of this play, please see Appendix C, pp 368–78.

[1] speak in the play, but only from secondhand evidence and observation. The major speaking characters tell much about her, and their evidence is augmented by the condition of her kitchen, which she had left when she was arrested the day before the action of the play. Lewis Hale, the neighboring farmer, tells about her behavior on the morning after she used a rope to strangle her husband, John, in his sleep. Martha Hale, Hale's wife, tells about Minnie's young womanhood and about how she became alienated from her nearest neighbors because of John's stinginess and unfriendliness. The many objects in the kitchen indicate the emotional upset she was in before the murder. From this information we get a full portrait of how Minnie has changed from passivity to destructive assertiveness.° Her change in character is brought out by a consideration of her clothing, her dead canary, and her unfinished patchwork quilt.□

[2] The clothes that Minnie has worn in the past and in the present indicate her character as a person of charm who has withered under neglect and contempt. Martha Hale mentions Minnie's attractive and colorful dresses as a young woman, even recalling a white dress with blue ribbon. This recollection prompts Mrs. Hale to observe that Minnie, when young, had been personable and attractive, though also somewhat shy ("sweet and pretty, but kind of timid and—fluttery"). Mrs. Hale also remarks that Minnie had changed, and changed for the worse, during her thirty years of marriage with John Wright, whom Mrs. Hale describes as having been like a "raw wind that gets to the bone." As more evidence for Minnie's acceptance of her drab life on the farm, Mrs. Peters, the sheriff's wife, says that Minnie asked for no more than an apron and a shawl as extra clothing for her period of arrest in the sheriff's home. These modest and uncolorful garments, as contrasted with the colorful garb of her youth, suggest her habitual suppression of spirit.

[3] The dead canary in Minnie's sewing box, however, indicates not only her love of music, but also the change brought about by inner rage against her husband. For twenty-nine years of marriage Minnie had endured her cheerless farm home, the contempt of her husband, her life of solitude, a general lack of pretty things, and the recognition that she could not share the social life of the local farm women as an equal. But her purchase of the canary the year before indicates both the continuance and the reemergence of her love of song, just as it also suggests at least a degree of self-assertion. That her husband wrung the bird's neck may thus be seen as the cause of her change or development, from the acquiescing, self-effacing wife to a person angry enough to kill.

[4] Like her love of song, her unfinished quilt indicates her capacity for creativity. In thirty years on the farm, never having had children, she had no better chance to be creative than to do needlework, such as the quilt that she had recently been piecing together in her kitchen. Both Mrs. Hale and Mrs. Peters remark about the beauty of her log-cabin design, and a stage direction draws attention to the "bright pieces" in the sewing basket. The inference is that even though Millie's life had been bleak, she had been able on at least a minor level to indulge her characteristic love of color and form— and also of warmth, granted the purpose of a quilt.

[5] Ironically, the quilt may also be taken to show the creativity in the murder of her husband. Both Mrs. Hale and Mrs. Peters interpret the breakdown of

° Central idea
□ Thesis sentence

her stitching on the quilt as signs of distress about the dead canary and also of her nervousness in planning revenge. Further, even though nowhere in the play is it said that John is strangled with a quilting knot, there is no other conclusion that one can draw. Both Mrs. Hale and Mrs. Peters agree that Minnie probably intended to knot the quilt rather than sew it in a quilt stitch, and Glaspell pointedly causes the men to learn about this probability also. In other words, Minnie's habitual outlet for creativity in needlework enables her to perform the murder in the only way she can—by quietly slipping a quilting knot around John's neck without waking him up, and then by quickly drawing this slip-proof knot tight. Even though her plan for the murder is deliberate, however (Mrs. Peters reports that the arrangement of the rope was "crafty"), she is by no means cold or remorseless. Her apparent fear and helplessness after the crime demonstrates that planning an elaborate scheme of evasion of guilt, beyond simple denial, is not in her character. In addition, she is probably not so diabolically creative that she plans or even perceives the irony of the method she uses to kill her husband—by tightening the rope around his neck and thus killing him just as he killed the bird by wringing its neck. The irony, however, is certainly intended by Glaspell.

[5]

It is important to emphasize again that Minnie does not appear in the play, and that the few short speeches she makes in response to Hale are only quoted. Readers, and viewers, can learn about her only from the words of others and from things seen or described. Nevertheless, the picture that Glaspell draws is fully realized, round, and poignant. For the greater part of her adult life, Minnie has been representative of women whose capacities for growth and expression have been stunted and virtually killed by both the grind of life and the cruelty and insensitivity of others. For her part, she has been patient and accepting of the dreary home with her husband that is so different from the high expectations of her youth. Amid such depressing surroundings, Minnie has suppressed whatever grudges she might have developed, just as she has suppressed her prettiness, colorfulness, and creativity. But the killing of the canary is clearly a last straw. It causes Minnie to change and to destroy her husband in an assertive and also systematic rejection of her subservient role. She is a woman who is slow to anger and who continues her concern about household matters even when in jail, but whose patience finally reaches the breaking point.

[6]

COMMENTARY ON THE THEME

For illustration, the opening paragraph of this theme begins by stressing the means by which readers learn about Minnie, the character being analyzed. The purpose is to establish the unusual fact that Minnie never appears in the play, and that therefore all conclusions about her are inferential, based on the words of others and the conclusions they reach from evidence of her actions. The central idea stresses Minnie's change from passivity to assertiveness; thus, she may be considered as round, not flat. The thesis sentence describes an organization for the theme stemming from particular objects closely associated with Minnie. This organization illustrates one of the types in the third approach described above. Other organizations could also have been chosen, such as the qualities of acquiescence, fortitude, and potential for anger (#1), or the change in Minnie from subservience to vengefulness (#2), or the reported actions of Minnie's singing, knotting quilts, and sitting in the kitchen on the morning after the murder (another type of #3).

In the body of the theme, paragraph 2 considers what Minnie's clothing, both past and present, shows about the suppression of her youthful potential for colorfulness. Paragraph 3 deals with the effect of the dead canary as a breaking point of Minnie's long acceptance of her acquiescent role. Paragraphs 4 and 5 consider the relationship of her unfinished quilt to her capacity for creativity, and also to the actual creativity she shows in the means by which she murders her husband. The last paragraph, 6, summarizes much of the theme, and it also considers how Minnie, though a round character, has a number of flat qualities because she is typical and representative of many other women in her position.

chapter 6

Writing About Point of View

Point of view is the position from which details in a narrative or poem are perceived and related to the reader. It is a method of rendering, a means by which authors create a speaking **voice, persona,** or **narrator,** a centralizing intelligence, a narrative personality, an intellectual filter through which you receive the narration or argument. Other terms describing point of view are *viewpoint, perspective, angle of vision, mask, center of attention,* and *focus.* Another helpful term is *coign of vantage,* which implies a high spot or corner—a vantage point—from which things below may be seen.

In practice, you can think of point of view as the character or **speaker** who does the talking. To write about point of view is to describe the effect of the speaker—his or her traits, motives, circumstances, and limitations—on the literary work.

You might respond that this definition means that authors do not use their own "voices" when they write, but somehow change themselves into another character who may be a totally separate creation. Actually, this response hits the nail right on the head. It is true that authors, as writers of their own works, always write and therefore control what gets written, but it does not follow that they always use their own voices as they write. It is not easy to determine exactly what one's "own voice" is. Test yourself: When you speak to your instructor, to your friend, to a child, to a person you love, or to a distant relative, your voice always sounds the same, but the personality—or persona—that you employ changes according to the person to whom you are talking.

In short, authors create not only stories and ideas, but also the speakers or voices of their works. The situation is very much like that of actors on stage. The actors are always themselves, but the roles they play are not those of their own identities or personal lives. Rather, they imitate characters like Hamlet or Othello, Desdemona or Lady Macbeth. Authors, too, may create separate roles for the speakers you hear in their works.

POINT OF VIEW AND "THROWING THE VOICE"

A helpful way to consider point of view is to think of the speaker as a ventriloquist's dummy and the author not as the speaker but the ventriloquist. The author "throws" the voice into the dummy, whose written words you actually read. Although the dummy or speaker is the one who is talking, the author is the one who makes the speaker believable and consistent. Consider the relationship as illustrated here:

Often this speaker, or voice, is separate and totally independent, a character who is completely imagined and consistently maintained by the author. A problem of identifying the voice occurs when the speaker seems to be the author in person. To claim that authors are also speakers, however, assumes that we have absolute biographical and psychological knowledge about them. Authors, like all people, change. They may have been changing even as they were writing the works you are reading. In addition, they may have been creating a separate personality, or aspect of themselves, as the voice they used when they wrote. Beyond all that, there is the general problem that human personality is elusive. For all these reasons, in works where the author seems to be talking directly, it is more proper to refer to the author's **authorial voice** as the speaker rather than referring to the author himself or herself.

It is most important to understand the potential complexity of these details. As an exercise, suppose for a moment that you are an author and are planning a set of stories. Try to imagine the speakers you would create to make stories out of the following situations:

> A happy niece who has just inherited $25 million from an uncle recalls a childhood experience with the uncle years ago.
>
> A disappointed nephew who was cut off without a cent describes a child-hood experience with the same uncle.
>
> A ship's captain who is filled with ideas of personal honor, integrity, and responsibility describes the life of a sailor who has committed a cowardly act.
>
> A person who has survived a youth of poverty and degradation describes a brother who has succumbed to drugs and crime.
>
> An economist looks at problems of unemployment.
>
> A person who has just lost a job looks at problems of unemployment.

In creating voices and stories for the various situations, you will recognize the importance of your imagination in the selection of point of view. You are always yourself, but your imagination enables you to speak like someone else totally distinct from yourself. Point of view is hence an imaginative creation, just as much a part of the author's work as the events narrated or the ideas discussed.

POINT OF VIEW AS A PHYSICAL POSITION

Thus far we have considered point of view as an interaction of personality and circumstance. There are also purely physical aspects, specifically (1) the speaker as one who sees and reports actions and statements, and (2) the speaker as one who receives and passes on information from others. If narrators have been at the scene of an action, this position gives them credibility because they are reporting events they actually saw or heard. Some speakers may have been direct participants in the action; others may have been bystanders. It is possible that a speaker may have overheard a conversation, or may have witnessed a scene through a keyhole. If the speakers were not on the spot, they must have gained their facts in a believable way. They could get them from someone else who was a witness or participant. They could receive letters, read newspaper articles, go through old papers in an attic or library, or hear things on a radio or television program. Sometimes the unidentified voice of the author comes from a person who seems to be hovering right above the characters as they move and speak. Such a speaker, being present everywhere without being noticed, is a reliable source of all information presented in the narrative.

DISTINGUISH POINT OF VIEW
FROM OPINION

It should be clear that point of view is not the same as opinion or idea. It is true that a person's opinions (most obviously about politics or religion) influence what that person says about a social issue or personal behavior. As a result, many students conclude that point of view is just another way of defining opinions. But this is not true. In examining point of view, therefore, you should try to draw as many conclusions as possible about the voice you are hearing, about the speaker who remains invisible but who nevertheless is doing the talking. Opinions are no more important in this discussion than closeness or distance from the events, capacities of understanding, personal or ideological involvement in the situation, and general personality. A discussion of point of view requires you to analyze the character and circumstances of the speaker who is relating the events of the story or poem.

KINDS OF POINTS OF VIEW

The kinds of points of view may be classified fairly easily. You may detect the point of view in any work by determining the dominant grammatical voice. Then, of course, you should go on to all the other considerations thus far discussed.

First Person

If the story is told by an "I," the author is using the **first-person** point of view—the voice of a fictional narrator and not the author's own voice. First-person speakers report significant things that they see, hear, and think; as they do, they convey not only the action of the work, but also some of their own background, thinking, attitudes, and prejudices.

Jackie, in O'Connor's "First Confession," is a first-person narrator who tells about events that occurred to him as a child. As he speaks he not only tells the story, but also tells a good deal about his feelings both as a child and as an adult.

In a first-person narration, the speaker's background and educational level have a great effect on the language of the work itself. Thus Jackie, who as an adult narrator is clearly well educated, includes some of the authentic rhythms and diction of his own childhood and also of the people he quotes. Langston Hughes, in the poem "Theme for English B" (yes, poetry also has speakers and can therefore be analyzed for point of view), creates another first-person narrator whose language reflects his status as a young black attending an urban university.

Depending upon the degree of involvement imagined for the situation or for the events being narrated, first-person speakers disclose information either firsthand or secondhand. One kind of speaker has acquired information because he or she was a direct participant in the action as a major character (or "major mover"). The unnamed speaker of Christina Rossetti's poem "Echo" speaks from firsthand recollections about having loved a person now dead, a situation also reflected by the speaker of Amy Lowell's "Patterns." Jackie of "First Confession" is another narrator who relates firsthand experiences. One type of major participant deserves special mention. This is a speaker like Dr. Watson in the well-known Sherlock Holmes stories. Watson is an involved or major participant, but is not a major mover, for that role is assigned to the brilliant master detective, Sherlock Holmes. Watson's first-person narration, however, is essential to the authenticity of the Holmes stories.

Both the age and the understanding of the narrators are significant in what they say and therefore in our perception of the events they describe or to which they respond. You may reasonably expect a speaker who is a mature adult to present intelligent and well-considered thoughts about a situation or action, as Emily Dickinson's speaker does in "After Great Pain a Formal Feeling Comes." A less aware, more naive narrator may have reached adulthood, but may not indicate an adult's understanding. Such a speaker is Jackie in "First Confession." If you have a writing assignment about works containing speakers like these, you not only need to understand and sort out details, but also need to judge the observations included by the narrator as commentary or response.

One thing is clear about stories and poems containing the first-person point of view. Whenever the speaker uses the "I" and comments on the action, that speaker is also an important part of the work. Everything we read is reported by the speaker. Therefore, his or her abilities, position as an observer, character, attitudes, and possible prejudices or self-interests are to be considered along with everything that is said. The first-person speaker of Amy Lowell's "Patterns" is considering her feelings upon receiving notice that her fiancé has been killed in battle. As she carries on her train of thought, we follow not only her own sorrow but also her developing anger against the irony and injustice of her solitude and her coming life of unfulfilled desires. Her position as a character and observer, like that of virtually all first-person speakers, is as much a focus of interest as the narrative or situation.

Second Person

Although a **second-person** narration (in which the narrator tells a listener what he or she has done and said, using the "you" personal pronoun) is possible, it is rare because in effect the second person requires a first-person speaker who tells the listener—the "you" of the narration— what he or she did at a past time. Thus, a parent might be telling a child what the child did during infancy, about which the child has no memory. Or a doctor might tell a patient with amnesia about the patient's earlier life before the injury that caused the loss of memory, or a lawyer might present a story of a crime directly to the accused criminal by way of accusation. In practice, the second-person point of view is of only passing use in most literature, and you will encounter it so rarely that you may consider it to be almost negligible. A. A. Milne uses it for a time at the beginning of the children's story *Winnie the Pooh*, but drops it as soon as the events of Pooh Bear and the rest of the animals get under way. Jay MacInerny, in *Bright Lights, Big City* uses it, but it is clear that the "you" being addressed really means "I" and "me." Hence MacInerny's second person is really first person.

Third Person

If the narrator is not introduced as a character, and if everything in the work is described in the third person (that is, *he, she, it, they*), the author is using the **third-person** point of view. There are three variants: dramatic or objective, omniscient, and limited omniscient.

DRAMATIC OR OBJECTIVE.   The basic mode of describing action and recording conversation or dialogue is the dramatic or objective point of view (also called **third-person objective**). The objective point of view is characteristic of plays, for which dramatists present speeches, descriptions of scenes, and stage directions or actions. Similarly, writers of fiction using the dramatic point of view try simply to "report the facts" scrupulously and objectively, without comment. They avoid telling that certain characters thought this or felt that, but instead allow the characters themselves to state what is on their minds. Shirley Jackson's "The Lottery" (the subject of the sample theme) is a prime example of the dramatic point of view in a story, as is John Collier's "The Chaser" (after the first two paragraphs). The narrator of the dramatic point of view perceives things and reports them in a way that is roughly analogous to a hovering or tracking motion-picture camera. Thus, characters in the out-of-doors may be seen and heard at a distance or up close, and when they move indoors or into a conveyance of some sort, the speaker continues to observe and report their activities and record their dialogue.

Though actions and dialogue are the main substance of the dramatic point of view, authors may allow certain characters to express their own attitudes and feelings, which then also become a part of the story. Old Man Warner in "The Lottery" is an example of the commentator who represents a conservative voice in favor of the institution of the lottery, even as he notes that persons in nearby communities want to give it up.

The key to the dramatic point of view is that the writer presents actions and dialogue, leaving conclusions and interpretations to the readers. Naturally, however, the author does not relinquish his or her shaping spirit with the choice of the dramatic viewpoint. Hence, the reader's conclusions are shaped by the author's ordering of the materials of the story.

OMNISCIENT. The third-person point of view is called **omniscient** (all-knowing) when the speaker not only presents the action and dialogue of the work, but also knows and reports how the characters are responding and thinking. In the third person omniscient point of view, authors take great responsibility: By delving into the minds of their characters, they assume a stance that exceeds our ordinary experience with other persons. The result is that an omniscient story is not realistic according to our present way of seeing things. On occasions, however, authors present the thoughts and goals of characters as a convenient way of adding explanations to actions.

LIMITED, OR LIMITED OMNISCIENT. More common than the omniscient point of view, therefore, is the limited or limited omniscient point of view, in which the author describes actions and records dialogue objectively while confining or limiting your attention to what a major character does, says, hears, sees, and thinks. Because this character is the center about whom events in the work turn, he or she may be called the **point of view character,** as in "Miss Brill" by Katherine Mansfield and "The Necklace" by Guy de Maupassant. Everything in these two stories is there because Miss Brill and Mathilde see it, hear it, respond to it, think about it, do it or share in it, try to control it, or are controlled by it. Often the limited omniscient mode of presentation is so focused on the major character that it brings out particular words and expressions that the point-of-view character might use, as in "Miss Brill." Obviously, there are variations in how deeply the limited omniscience may extend. Thus, we learn more about Miss Brill than about Mathilde, because Mansfield presents more responses and thoughts than does De Maupassant.

MINGLING POINTS OF VIEW

In most stories and narratives you will find a mingling of viewpoints. Hence, a point of view may be limited omniscient when focused on the thoughts of a major character, but dramatic when focused on the actions and dialogue. The writer may tell most of the story in one type of point of view but then shift at an important moment in order to sustain interest, create suspense, or put the burden of response entirely upon readers. For example, in "Miss Brill," Mansfield ends the focus on Miss Brill's thoughts and responses immediately after Miss Brill is insulted by the boy and girl on the park bench. After this action, the last paragraphs of the story are narrated from an objective point of view until the very last sentence. The result is that Miss Brill is made to seem totally alone in her grief, cut apart; readers can no longer share her sorrow as they earlier can share her observations about the many characters appearing in the park.

As you analyze point of view in various narratives and poems, you may find the following table helpful.

Points of View

1. First Person ("I"). First-person narrators may have (1) complete understanding, (2) partial or incorrect understanding, or (3) no understanding at all.
    a. Major participant
        i.   telling his or her own story as a major mover
        ii. telling a story about others and also about herself or himself as one of the major interactors
        iii. telling a story mainly about others; this narrator is on the spot and completely involved but is not a major mover.
    b. Minor participant, telling a story about events experienced and/or witnessed.
    c. Uninvolved character, telling a story not witnessed but reported to the narrator by other means.
2. Second person ("you"). Occurs only when speaker has more authority on a character's actions than the character himself or herself; for example, parent, psychologist, lawyer. This point of view cannot be sustained easily, and therefore it is used only in brief passages when necessary.

3. Third person ("she," "he," "it," "they").
   a. Dramatic or third-person objective. Speaker reports only actions and speeches. Thoughts of characters can be expressed only as dialogue.
   b. Omniscient. Omniscient speaker sees all, reports all, knows and explains the inner workings of the minds of any or all characters.
   c. Limited or limited omniscient. Action is focused on a major character, and thoughts and responses of this character may be reported.

POINT OF VIEW AND "EVIDENCE"

In considering point of view, you should analyze all aspects that bear on the presentation of the material. You may imagine yourself somewhat like a member of a jury. Jury members cannot accept testimony uncritically, for some witnesses may have much to gain by misstatements, distortions, or outright lies. Before rendering a verdict, jury members must consider all these possibilities. Speakers in literary works are usually to be accepted as reliable witnesses, but it is true that their characters, interests, capacities, personal involvements, and positions to view action may have a bearing on the material they present. A classic example is the Japanese film *Rashomon* (1950), directed by Akira Kurosawa, in which four different people tell a story as evidence in court. They all tell stories that make them seem more honest and honorable than they actually are, because each of them has something to hide. While most stories are not as complex as *Rashomon*, you should always consider the circumstances, interests, and character of the speaker of a story or poem before you make your judgment about the meaning of that work.

WRITING ABOUT POINT OF VIEW

In prewriting activity for a theme on point of view, you need to consider things like language, authority and opportunity for observation, selection of detail, characterization, interpretive commentaries, and narrative development. You might plan an analysis of one, a few, or all of these elements. Generally, your essay should explain how point of view has contributed to making the work unique. One of the major purposes in your study and preparation is to determine ways in which the narration is made to seem real and probable: Are the actions and speeches reported authentically, as they might be seen and reported in life? As you sketch out materials for your theme, try to apply this question to various parts of the work you are studying, so that you can determine whether the actual narration is just as "true" as the work itself.

Introduction

In your introduction you should get at the matters you plan to develop. Which point of view is used in the work? What is the major influence of this point of view on the work? (For example, "The omniscient point of view causes full, leisurely insights into many shades of character," or "The first-person point of view enables the work to resemble an exposé of back-room political deals.") To what extent does the selection of point of view make the work particularly interesting and effective, or uninteresting and ineffective? What particular aspects of the work (action, dialogue, characters, description, narration, analysis) do you wish to analyze in support of your central idea?

Body

The questions you raise here depend on the work you have studied. It is impossible to answer all the following questions in your analysis, but going through them should help you determine what to include in the body.

If you have read a work with a first-person point of view, your analysis concerns the speaker. Who is she (supposing, for the moment, a woman)? Is she a major or minor character? How reliable is she as an observer? What is her background? What is her relationship to the person listening to her (if there is a listener)? Does this situation make you, the reader, an eavesdropper on something private? Does she speak directly to you, the reader; if so, do you feel cast in the role of a listener? How does the speaker describe the various situations? Is her method uniquely a function of her character? How did she acquire the information she is presenting? How much does she disclose, or seem to hide? Why? Does she ever rely on the information of others for her material? How reliable are these other witnesses? Or (supposing a man), does the speaker undergo any changes that affect his presentation of material? Do his recollections and descriptions show strengths or limitations? Does he notice one kind of thing (for example, discussion) but miss others (for example, natural scenery)? What might have escaped him, if anything? Does the author put the speaker into situations that he describes but does not understand? Why? Is the speaker ever confused? Is he close to the action, or distant from it? Does he show emotional involvement in any situations? Are you sympathetic to his concerns or are you put off by them? If the speaker makes comments, are his thoughts valid? To what extent, if any, is the speaker of as much interest as the material he presents?

If you encounter any of the third-person points of view, try to determine the characteristics of the voice employed by the author. Does it seem that the author is speaking in an authorial voice, or that the narrator has a special voice? You can approach this problem by answering many of the questions relevant to the first-person point of view. Also try to determine the distance from the narrator to the action. How is the action described? How is the dialogue recorded? Is there any background information given? Do the descriptions reveal any bias toward any of the characters? Are the descriptions full or bare? Does the author include descriptions or analyses of a character's thoughts? What are these like? Do you see evidence of what you take to be the author's own philosophy? Does the choice of words direct you toward any particular interpretations? What limitations or freedoms devolve upon the story as a result of the point of view?

Conclusion

In your conclusion you should evaluate the success of the point of view: Was it consistent, effective, truthful? What did the writer gain (if anything) by the selection of point of view? What was lost (if anything)? How might a less skillful writer have handled similar material? After answering questions like these, you may end your theme.

PROBLEMS

1. In considering point of view, you will encounter the problem of whether to discuss the author or the speaker as the originator of attitudes and ideas. If the author is employing the first-person point of view, there is no problem. Use the speaker's name, if he or she is given one (for example, Jackie from "First Confession"), or else talk about the "speaker" or "persona" if there is no name (for example, the speaker of Jackson's "The Lottery"). You face a greater problem with the third-person points of view, but even here it is safe for you to discuss the "speaker" rather than the "author," remembering always that the author is manipulating the narrative voice. Sometimes authors emphasize a certain phase of their own personalities in their authorial voices. Many ideas are therefore common to both the author and the speaker, but your statements about these must be inferential, not absolute.

2. You may wander away from analysis of point of view into retelling the story or discussing the ideas. To keep on the topic, emphasize the presentation of the events and ideas, and the causes for this presentation. Do not emphasize the subject material itself, but use it only as it bears on your consideration of point of view. Your object is not just to interpret

the work, but also to show how the point of view *enables* you to interpret the work.

3. Remember that you are dealing with point of view in the entire work and not simply in single narrations and conversations. For example, an individual character has her own way of seeing things when she states something, but in relation to the entire work her speech is a function of the dramatic point of view. Thus, you should not talk about Character A's and Character B's point of view, but instead should state that "Using the dramatic point of view, Author Z allows the various characters to argue their cases, in their own words and with their own limitations."

4. Once again, be particularly careful to distinguish between point of view and opinions or beliefs. Point of view refers to the total position from which things are seen, heard, and reported, whereas an opinion is a thought about something. In this essay, you are to describe not the ideas, but the method of narration of an author.

Sample Theme

Shirley Jackson's Dramatic Point of View in "The Lottery"*

[1]   The dramatic point of view in Shirley Jackson's "The Lottery" is essential to the success with which the story renders horror in the midst of the ordinary.° But the story does not deal just with horror: It could also be called a surprise story, an allegory, or a portrayal of human obtuseness, passivity, and cruelty. But the validity of all other claims for "The Lottery" hinges on the author's control over point of view to make the events develop out of a seemingly everyday, matter-of-fact situation—a situation that could not be easily maintained if another point of view were used. The success of Jackson's point of view is achieved through her characterization, selection of details, and diction.□

[2]   Because of the dramatic point of view, the story presents the villagers as ordinary folks attending a normal, festive event—in contrast to the horror of their real purpose. This characterization depends upon a speaker who is remote and emotionally uninvolved. The speaker thus records only enough details about the villagers to permit the understanding that they are ordinary people, but not enough to give them life as round human beings. Similarly, Mr. Summers is presented as not much more than a middle-aged, pillar-of-society type. Tessie Hutchinson is the principal character in the story, but the speaker presents little more about her than that she is chatty, illiterate, and relatively inarticulate—all facts that are essential to her behavior at the end

---

*For the text of this story, please see Appendix C, pp. 337–53.
° Central idea
□ Thesis sentence

of the story when she objects not to the lottery itself but to the "unfairness" of the drawing. So it is also with the other characters. Their brief conversations are recorded, but no more. Because of the objective, remote point of view,

[2] we see them from a distance, as we would likely see any typical people at a public gathering. This distant, reportorial method of illustrating character is fundamental to the dramatic point of view, and the twist of cruelty at the end depends on the method.

While there could be much description, Jackson's speaker concentrates on only those details that in retrospect bring out the horror of the lottery drawing. At the beginning of the story, the speaker presents enough information about the lottery to make sense of it, but does not disclose that the prize for winning is instant death. Thus, the speaker establishes that the villagers are gathering

[3] rocks, but includes no mention of why. The short saying "Lottery in June, corn be heavy soon" is mentioned as a remnant of a more ritualistic kind of scapegoatism, but the speaker either does not know the meaning or chooses not to go into it (p. 297). All such references seem innocent as first presented by the speaker, and it is only after the ending is known that they are made to seem sinister.

Without exaggeration, another point of view would have required more detail, and therefore would have spoiled Jackson's doubletake of horror. A first-person speaker, for example, could not have been credible without explaining the situation in advance, or at least without revealing feelings that would have given away the brutal conclusion. (As an example, an "I" would need

[4] to say something like "The little boys gathered rocks without thinking about their forthcoming use in an execution.") An omniscient narrator would necessarily have expressed some commentary on the reactions of the townsfolk (otherwise, how could he or she be omniscient?) By contrast, the dramatic point of view can point out that characters hesitated, or looked worried, but can prevent us from learning why. Thus we get information, but not enough to give away the ending.

Appropriate both to the ending, and to the simple and unquestioning nature of the villagers, is the speaker's language. The speaker uses uncolored and unemotional words which are accurate and descriptive but not elaborate. When Tessie Hutchinson appears, she dries "her hands on her apron" (p.

[5] 339)—words that are functional and no more. Most of these simple, bare words may be seen as a means by which Jackson uses point of view to delay the reader's understanding of what is happening. The piles of stones, for example, are to be used in the ritual stoning of Tessie Hutchinson, yet one does not draw this conclusion when they are first described:

> Bobby Martin had already stuffed his pockets full of stones, and the other boys soon followed his example, selecting the smoothest and roundest stones; Bobby and Harry Jones and Dickie Delacroix—the villagers pronounced this name "Dellacroy"—eventually made a great pile of stones in one corner of the square and guarded it against the raids of the other boys (p. 338).

The speaker's references to the nicknames, and to the association of the stones with apparently normal boyhood games, both divert the reader's attention and obscure the horror that in just a short time the stones will be used in a ritual death. Even at the end, the speaker uses the word "pebbles" to describe the stones given to Tessie Hutchinson's son Davy. The implication is that the boy is going to a game, not to the killing of his own mother!

[6]   Such masterly control over point of view is a major cause of Jackson's success in "The Lottery." Her objective is to establish a superficial appearance of everyday, harmless reality, which she maintains up to the last few paragraphs. Indeed, she is so successful that a possible response to the stoning is that "such a killing could not take place among the common, earthy folks in this story." Yet it is because of this reality that a reader sees the validity of Jackson's vision. Horror is not to be found on moors and in haunted castles, but among everyday people like the villagers in Tessie Hutchinson's home town. Without Jackson's skill in controlling point of view, there could be little of this power of suggestion, and it would not be possible to claim such success for the story.

COMMENTARY ON THE THEME

For illustrative purposes, this theme analyzes Jackson's choice of the dramatic or objective point of view as it affects characterization, description, and diction. In your theme you might wish to consider all these aspects or only one, depending on the length of your assignment.

The introductory paragraph develops the relationship of the dramatic point of view to the success of the work as a story of both horror and suspense. The thesis sentence points out the areas to be developed in the body of the essay.

In the second paragraph, the aim is not to present a full character study (since the theme is about point of view, not about character), but rather to discuss the ways in which the dramatic point of view enables the characters to be rendered. The only idea about the characters that is needed for the paragraph is that they are to be judged not as complete human beings but as "ordinary folks." Once this idea is established, then the thrust of the paragraph is to show how the point of view is used to keep the reader at a distance sufficient to permit this conclusion.

In the same way, the paragraphs about detail (3 and 4) emphasize the sparseness of detail in keeping with the conception that the speaker is distant and relatively uninvolved. Note that in paragraph 4 the dramatic point of view is contrasted with other points of view that might have been used. This way of developing a discussion might be helpful for you to adapt in your own themes, for by imagining how the events might be described in another way you may derive a better understanding of the method used in the work you are studying.

The third section of the body (paragraph 5) emphasizes the idea that the flat, colorless diction defers the reader's awareness of what is happening in the story. Therefore, the point of view is vital in the development of horror and surprise. The concluding paragraph emphasizes the way in which general response to the story, and also its success, are conditioned by the detached, dramatic point of view.

chapter 7

Writing About Setting:
Place and Objects in Literature

Setting refers to the natural and artificial scenery or environment in which characters in literature live and move, together with the things they use. Times of day, conditions of sun and clouds, weather, hills and valleys, trees and animals, sounds both outside and inside, and smells—all these may go into the setting of a work. Setting may also include artifacts like walking sticks, paper windmills, dueling pistols, birdcages, bread knives, necklaces, large boxes, park benches, hair ribbons, and many other items. The setting of a work may also extend to references to clothing, descriptions of physical appearance, and spatial relationships. In short, the setting of a work is the sum total of references to physical and temporal objects and artifacts.

The setting of a story, novel, or poem is much like the sets and properties of the stage or the location for a motion picture. The dramatist writing for the stage is physically limited by what can be constructed and moved or carried onto the stage. Writers of nondramatic works, however, are limited only by probability and their imaginations. It is possible for them to include details of many places without the slightest external restraint.

The action of a story, play, or poem, while often taking place in one city, countryside, or house, may shift within an area or location as characters move about to perform their tasks. In a novel, the author may shift the characters to many different locations. Whether there is one location or many, however, the term *setting* refers to all the places and objects that are important in the work, whether natural or manufactured.

TYPES OF SETTINGS

Natural

The setting for a great number of works is the out-of-doors, and, as one might expect, Nature herself is seen as a force that shapes action and therefore directs and redirects lives. A deep woods may make walking difficult or dangerous, or may be a place for a sinister meeting of devil worshippers. The open road may be a place where one person seeks flight, others face a showdown, and still others may meet their fate. A park bench on a sunny afternoon may be the place where a person feels the deepest joy and also begins a descent into misery. A garden walk may occasion great anguish and sorrow. The ocean may be the location of a test of youth but also may provide the environment for the memory of vanished dreams. A distant star may be a guide to a young speaker's conduct and ideals. Nature, in short, is one of the major forces governing the circumstances of characters who experience life and try to resolve their conflicts in literary works.

Manufactured

Manufactured things always reflect the people who made them. A building or a room tells about the people who built it and live in it, and ultimately about the social and political orders that maintain its condition. A richly decorated house shows the expensive tastes and resources of the characters who own it. A few cracks in the plaster and some chips in the paint show the same persons declining in fortune and power. Ugly and impoverished surroundings may contribute to the weariness, insensitivity, negligence, or even hostility of the characters living in them.

Possessions may enter into character motivation and development. A bottle of medicine may cause a woman to take a journey of mercy, while a bottle of beer may embarrass a sensitive young boy. The loss of a borrowed but cheap necklace may plunge a young married couple into indebtedness and a life of drudgery. The destruction of a prized canary may produce uncontrollable rage in the bird's owner. The drawing of a lottery "prize" may unleash a collective community horror. As in life, literature includes all the forces that may be generated among people by objects of value and convenience.

STUDYING THE USES OF SETTING

In preparing to write about the setting of any work, your first concern should be to discover all the details that form a part of setting, and then to determine how the author has used these details. For example, as writers stress character, plot, or action, they may emphasize or minimize setting. At times a setting may be no more than a roughly sketched place where events occur, as in Collier's "The Chaser." In other works, the setting may be so prominent that it may almost be considered a participant in the action. An instance of such "participation" is Welty's "A Worn Path," where the woods and roadway are almost active antagonists against Phoenix as she walks on her worn path toward Natchez.

Setting and Credibility

One of the major purposes of setting is to lend realism or verisimilitude. As the description of setting is made more particular and detailed, the events of the work become more believable. Langston Hughes locates the speaker of "Theme for English B" in the area immediately near Columbia University in New York City, thereby giving the poem a geographically real location. In "First Confession," Frank O'Connor's use of the realistic details of the bread knife, the boy under the table defending himself against his sister, and Mrs. Ryan's candle flame lend credibility to the delightful story of young Jackie's first confession. Even futuristic, unrealistic, symbolic, and fantastic stories, as well as ghost stories, take on authenticity if the setting is presented as though the world of these stories is the one we normally see and experience. Nathaniel Hawthorne presents the realistic town of colonial Salem, and the woods surrounding it, as a background for the hero's nightmarish forest walk and confrontation with the evil that destroys all his trust, love, and happiness. Without a basis in detailed settings, such works would lose credibility, even though they make no pretenses at everyday realism.

Setting and Statement

Setting may be a kind of pictorial language, a means by which the author makes statements much as a painter uses certain images as ideas in a painting. Thus the paths in both "Young Goodman Brown" and "A Worn Path" may be understood as visual equivalents of the solitude, obstacles, and uncertainties of life, in which all persons must ultimately go their own ways, for better or for worse. Chekhov's inclusion of references to the horse, Toby, in *The Bear* suggests that people must leave past obligations as they make new commitments.

Setting and Character

In the same vein, setting may intersect with character as one of the means by which authors underscore the importance of place, circumstances, and time upon human growth and change. In the short play *Trifles*, Susan Glaspell sets the scene in the kitchen of the lonely, dreary Wright farm. The setting is a place where nothing but hard work, joylessness, oppression, and even cruelty existed, so readers and audience realize that Mrs. Wright, however bright and promising she had been as a young woman, was also vulnerable, so much so that her outburst of anger in murdering her husband is made to seem understandable. Here the setting is dominant in helping us shape our ideas of her character. A similar blending of the setting and the major character of Guy de Maupassant's "The Necklace" (pp. 314–19) is explored in the sample essay. In virtually every work where place and objects are important, a comparable relationship may be found and studied.

Setting and Organization

Authors might also use setting as a means of organizing their works. The various actions in Jackson's "The Lottery" are all related to the place of the lottery drawing in the village square, "between the post office and the bank," and the story begins at ten o'clock in the morning and ends almost exactly at noon—in other words, according to a pattern of before, during, and immediately after the drawing. In De Maupassant's "The Necklace," the action removes Mathilde and her husband from an acceptable though not lavish apartment on the Rue des Martyrs in Paris to an attic flat in a cheap neighborhood. The final scene of the story is believable only because Mathilde leaves her poor neighborhood to take a nostalgic walk on one of the most fashionable streets in Paris, the Champs Élysées. Without this shift of scene, she could not have met Jeanne again, for their ways of life would otherwise never intersect.

Another organizational application of place, time, and object may be thought of as a **framing** or **enclosing setting.** An author frames a story by opening with a description of a setting, and then returning to the same setting at the end. Like a picture frame, the setting constantly affects the reader's thoughts about the story. An example of this method is seen in Mansfield's "Miss Brill," which opens and closes with references to the heroine's shabby little fur piece. Welty's "A Worn Path" begins by describing the major character's difficult walk to Natchez, and ends with the beginning of her hopeless and pathetic walk away from it. In the same way, Collier's "The Chaser" is framed by Alan Austen's entering and leaving the establishment of the sinister old man. Another example is Hawthorne's "Young Goodman Brown," which is framed by Brown's leaving the town of Salem: When alive, at the beginning, he leaves to take his walk in the woods; when dead, at the end, he is carried in a funeral procession to his grave. In such ways, the framing or enclosing setting emphasizes that many things about life remain the same even though people may undergo constant growth and change.

Setting and Atmosphere

Setting also affects the **atmosphere** or **mood** of stories. You might note that the description of an action requires no more than a functional description of setting. Thus, an action in a forest needs just the statement that the forest is there. However, if you read descriptions of the trees, the shapes, the light and shadows, the animals, the wind, and the sounds, you may be sure that the author is working to create an atmosphere or mood for the action (as in Hawthorne's "Young Goodman Brown"). There are many ways of creating moods. Descriptions of "warm" colors (red, orange, yellow) may contribute to a mood of happiness. "Cooler" colors may suggest gloom. References to smells and sounds bring the setting even more to life by asking additional sensory responses from the reader. The setting of a story on a farm or in a city apartment may evoke a response to these habitats that may contribute to a story's atmosphere.

Setting and Irony

Just as setting is present as an element of agreement, reinforcement, and strengthening of character and theme, so may it work ironically—as an environment that is the opposite of what actually occurs in the work. For example, in "The Lottery" Jackson uses descriptions of the local towns-folk, their conversations, and their interests to set up the expectation that the winner of the small-town lottery drawing will receive a valuable prize. This location in normal, rural America makes the conclusion grimly ironic, for it is just real, everyday folks who cast the stones of ritual execution. Mansfield uses setting ironically in "Miss Brill," where the location, the circumstances, the musical background, and the sunlight are all appropriate to activities of happiness. However, amid this pleasant setting, the young man and woman appear to inflict the most crushing of insults upon the heroine, and her momentary happiness is totally shattered. A happier contrast is used in O'Connor's "First Confession," where the confessional, which young Jackie fears, is the source of great satisfaction and reward.

WRITING ABOUT SETTING

In preparing to write about setting, you should take notes directed toward the locations and artifacts that figure prominently in the work. Generally, you should determine if there is one location of action or more. Raise questions about how much detail is included: Are things described visually so that you can make a sketch or draw a plan (such a sketch might help you to organize your essay), or are the locations left vague? Why? What influence do the locations have upon the characters in the story, if any? Do the locations bring characters together, push them apart, make it easy for them to be private, make intimacy and conversation difficult? What artifacts are important in the action, and how important are they? Are they well described? Are they vital to the action? Are shapes, colors, times of day, locations of the sun, conditions of light, seasons of the year, and conditions of vegetation described? Do characters respect or mistreat their environment?

With answers to questions like these, you can formulate ideas for your essay. Remember to develop a central idea to enable you to avoid writing no more than a description of scenes and objects (such an essay is analogous to simply retelling a narrative). Emphasize the connection between setting and whatever aspect or aspects you choose about the story. A possible central idea might thus be, "The normal, everyday setting (of "The Lottery") not only is plainly described, but it also demonstrates that human evil is also common and ordinary," or "The dreary kitchen underscores the long-suffering ordeal of Mrs. Wright (of *Trifles*) and helps readers to understand her violent act of self-assertion." Emphasizing such ideas would encourage you to use description only as illustration and evidence, and not as an end in itself.

Introduction

The introduction should give a brief description of the setting or scenes of the story, with a characterization of the degree of detail presented by the author (that is, a little, a lot; visual, auditory; colorful, monochromatic; and so on). The central idea explains the relationship to be explored in the essay, and the thesis sentence determines the major topics in which the central idea will be traced.

Body

Following are five possible approaches to essays about setting. Which one you choose is your decision, but some works almost invite you to pick one approach over the others. Although each approach outlines a major emphasis in your essay, you may wish to bring in details from one of the others if and as they seem important.

1. SETTING AND ACTION.   Here you explore the use of setting in the various actions of the work. Among the questions to be answered are these: How detailed and extensive are the descriptions of the setting?

Are the scenes related to the action? (Are they essential or incidental?) Does the setting serve as part of the action (places of flight or concealment; public places where people meet openly or out-of-the-way places where they meet privately; natural or environmental obstacles; sociological obstacles; seasonal conditions such as searing heat or numbing cold, and so on)? Are details of setting used regularly, or are they mentioned only when they become necessary to an action? Do any physical objects figure into the story as causes of inspiration or conflict (for example, a walking stick, a pretty necklace, a coin, a dog, a horse, a toy windmill, a piece of candy, a pistol, a dead bird)?

2. SETTING AND ORGANIZATION. A closely related way of writing about setting is to connect it to the organization of the work. Some questions to help you get started with this approach are these: Is the setting a frame, an enclosure? Is it mentioned at various points, or at shifts in the action? Does the setting undergo any expected or unexpected changes as the action changes? Do any parts of the setting have greater direct importance in shaping the action than other parts? Do any objects, such as money or property, figure into the developing or changing motivation of the characters? Do descriptions made at the start become important in the action later on? If so, in what order?

3. SETTING AND CHARACTER. Your aim here is to pick those details important to your understanding of character, and write about their effects. The major question is the degree to which the setting seems to interact with or influence character. You might get at this topic through additional questions: Are the characters happy or unhappy where they live? Do they express their feelings, or get into discussions or arguments about them? Do they seem adjusted? Do they want to stay or leave? Does the economic, cultural, or ethnic level of the setting make the characters think in any unique ways? What jobs do the characters perform because of their ways of life? What freedoms or restraints do these jobs cause? How does the setting influence their decisions, transportation, speech habits, eating habits, attitudes about love and honor, and general folkways?

4. SETTING AND ATMOSPHERE. Here you should write about those aspects of setting that evoke a mood. Some questions are: Does the detail of setting go beyond the minimum needed for action or character? Do clear details help clarify the conflicts in the story, or do vague and amorphous details help to make these conflicts problematic? Are descriptive words used mainly to paint verbal pictures? To evoke a mood through references to colors, shapes, sounds, smells, or tastes? Does the setting establish a mood, say, of joy or hopelessness, lushness or spareness? Do things happen in daylight or at night? Do motions and actions suggest constantly recurring, typical human patterns (such as missions of mercy,

actions of futility, and conversations leading to love)? Does anything about the setting suggest impermanence (like footsteps in the sand, movement through water, or the procession for a funeral)? If temperatures are mentioned, are things warm and pleasant or cold and harsh? For any details of setting suggesting mood, what are the implications for life generally?

5. OTHER ASPECTS. In an earlier section of this chapter, "Setting and Statement" and "Setting and Irony" were listed as important uses of setting. Not all stories lend themselves to either treatment, but for stories that do, you could create an interesting theme. If the author has used setting as a means of underscoring the circumstances and ideas in the work, you might use the section on statement as a guide for the body of your paper. If you perceive a contrast between setting and content, that too could be the basis of an essay such as those described in the paragraph on "Setting and Irony."

Conclusion

You always have the option of summarizing your major points as your conclusion, but you might also want to write about anything you neglected in the body of your essay. Thus, you might have been treating the relationship of the setting to the action, and may wish to mention something about any noticeable connections that the setting has with character or atmosphere. You might also point out whether your central idea about the setting also applies to other major aspects of the work.

Sample Theme

De Maupassant's Use of Setting in "The Necklace" to Show
the Character of Mathilde

---

[1]   In "The Necklace" De Maupassant does not present vivid or detailed descriptions of setting. He does not even provide a description of the ill-fated necklace—the central object in the story—but states only that it is "superb." Rather than create extensive descriptions, he uses the setting of the story to reflect the character and changes in the major figure, Mathilde Loisel.° Her character and growth may be related to the first apartment, the dream-life mansion rooms, and the attic flat.□

*For the text of this story, please see Appendix C, pp. 314–19.
° Central idea
□ Thesis sentence

[2]   Details about the modest apartment of the Loisels on the Street of Martyrs (Rue des Martyrs) indicate Mathilde's peevish lack of adjustment to life. Though everything is serviceable, she is dissatisfied with the "drab" walls, "threadbare" furniture, and "ugly" curtains. She has domestic help but wants more than the simple country girl who does the household chores. Her dissatisfaction is also shown by details of her irregularly cleaned tablecloth and the plain and inelegant beef stew that is her husband's favorite food. Even her best dress, which she wears for the theater, provokes her unhappiness. All these details of setting clearly establish that Mathilde's dominant character trait at the start of the story is maladjustment, and therefore she seems unpleasant and unsympathetic.

[3]   Like the real-life apartment, the impossibly expensive setting of her reveries provokes her dissatisfaction and inhibits her capacity to face reality. In her daydreams, all her rooms are large, draped in silk, and filled with expensive furniture and bric-a-brac. Within this setting of her fantasies, she imagines private rooms for intimate talks, and big dinners with delicacies like trout and quail. With dreams of such a rich home, she feels even more despair about her apartment. Ironically, this despair, together with her inability to live with actuality, is the cause of her economic and social undoing. It is the root cause of her borrowing the necklace (which is just as unreal as her daydreams of wealth), and it is the loss of the necklace that forces reality upon her with the loss of her first apartment and the move to a life of want in the cheap attic flat.

[4]   Also ironically, the attic flat brings out coarseness in her character while at the same time it brings out her best qualities of cooperativeness, pride, and honesty. There is little detail about this flat except that it is cheap and that Mathilde must walk up many stairs to reach it. De Maupassant emphasizes the drudgery of the work she must do to maintain the flat, such as washing floors with large pails of water and haggling about prices with local tradespeople. Although she speaks loudly, gives up hair and hand care, and wears the cheapest dresses, all her efforts in keeping up the flat make her heroic, in the judgment of the narrator. As she cooperates to help her husband save money to pay back the loans, her dreams of a mansion fade, and all she has left is the memory of that one happy evening at the Minister of Education's reception. Thus, the attic flat brings out her physical change for the worse at the same time that it brings out her psychological and moral change for the better.

[5]   Other details of setting in the story also have a similar bearing on the character of Mathilde. Thus, the story mentions little about the big party scene, but emphasizes only that Mathilde was a great "success"—certainly a detail that shows her ability to shine if given the chance. When she and Loisel return to their first apartment and discover the loss of the necklace, De Maupassant includes details about the Parisian streets, the visits to loan sharks, and the jewelry and jewelry-case shops, to bring out Mathilde's sense of honesty and pride as she and her husband prepare for the long years to be lived in poor surroundings. Anything that is not focused on Mathilde is not needed in the story, nor is it included. Thus, in "The Necklace," De Maupassant uses setting as a means to highlight Mathilde's maladjustment, her needless misfortune, her loss of youth and beauty, and finally, her growth as a responsible human being.

COMMENTARY ON THE THEME

This theme illustrates the approach of how a writer may relate the setting of a work to a major character (type 3, above). While this approach necessarily requires emphasis on character traits, it is important to note that these traits are brought out only as they are related to details about place and objects. The topic is setting and its relationship to character, not character itself.

The introduction of the essay makes the point that De Maupassant uses just as much detail as he needs, and no more. The central idea is that the details of setting may be directly related to Mathilde's character and growth. The thesis sentence does not indicate a plan to deal with all the aspects of setting in the story, but only two real places and one imaginary place.

Paragraphs 2 and 3 show how Mathilde's real-life apartment and dream-life mansion bring out her maladjustment and inability to face reality. The fourth paragraph connects her attic flat in a cheaper neighborhood with both the dulling and coarsening of her character and also the emergence of her admirable qualities. The idea here is that while better surroundings at the start reinforce her inabilities and lack of adjustment, the poorer surroundings of the ugly attic flat are associated not only with the expected and predictable loss of her youth and beauty, but also with her unexpected development of honesty, cooperation, hard work, and endurance.

The conclusion cites additional examples of De Maupassant's use of setting, and makes the assertion that all details of setting are focused directly on Mathilde and her growth because she is the center of interest in "The Necklace."

chapter 8

Writing About a Major Idea, or Theme

The word **idea** is connected to actions of seeing and knowing; indeed, the words *view* and *wit* (in the sense of knowledge) are close relatives of *idea*. Originally, the word was applied to mental images that, once seen, could be remembered and therefore known. Because of this mental activity, an idea was considered a conceptual form as opposed to external reality. The word is now commonly understood to refer to a concept, thought, opinion, or belief. Some examples of ideas as recognized by philosophers and historians of ideas are these: *infinity, justice, right and good, necessity, the problem of evil, causation,* and, not unsurprisingly, *idea* itself. A full consideration of ideas like these requires much knowledge, understanding, and thought. In this respect, ideas involve the interrelation of thinking and knowing.

In literature, ideas are not so much about abstract and speculative definitions as about the human side of things. The ancient Greek philosopher Plato, in *The Republic,* attempts at great length to define the idea of *justice* in the abstract. By contrast, in "Theme for English B," the black American writer Langston Hughes creates a poem about one of the personal sides of justice—equality—by showing how his young speaker shares many traits in common with the teacher for whom he is writing his assignment. In "The Lottery," Shirley Jackson causes the unfortunate winner of the lottery to raise questions of fairness and justice as they have affected her in the drawing. When an idea is brought out in literary works like these, it is often given the name **theme.** This word refers to something laid down, a postulate, a central or unifying idea. Loosely, the *theme* of a work and its *major idea* or *central idea* may be considered synonymous.

IDEAS, ASSERTIONS, AND MEANING

As a writer creates a literary work, he or she usually has a major idea or theme in mind or a point to illustrate (although not always consciously or deliberately), and this idea may be discovered and traced by readers. Thus, a play about a man and woman like Smirnov and Mrs. Popov in Chekhov's *The Bear* involves an idea about *love,* while the story about a woman like Phoenix Jackson in Welty's "A Worn Path" illustrates something about the idea of *sacrifice. Growth* is a major idea of O'Connor's "First Confession," while *dedication* is an idea in Keats's poem "Bright Star." Other ideas that you may readily discover in literary works, in addition to these, are *power, honor, maturity, persecution, happiness, pain,* and many more.

Although an idea may be expressed in a phrase or single word, developing an essay about ideas in a work is difficult unless you formulate the idea in a complete sentence to make a clear **assertion.** Thus, we might find stories with assertions that love is necessary but also irrational; hatred is built on misunderstanding; slavery is worse than death; power destroys youthful dreams; or growth is difficult but exciting.

In other words, assertions that you can formulate in studying ideas in effect embody your understanding of a work's **meaning.** In answering the question, "What does this, or that, *mean?*" the response usually takes the form of an assertion about human nature, conduct, or motivation— that is, the form of an idea. For Eudora Welty's "A Worn Path," we might formulate an idea about the character of Phoenix Jackson as follows: "Phoenix illustrates the idea that human beings who are committed to caring for others may suffer for this commitment." Similarly, it might be argued that Mrs. Popov in Chekhov's *The Bear* embodies the idea that "Even if a commitment to the dead is strong, the commitment to life is stronger."

DISTINGUISHING IDEAS FROM SUMMARIES

As you try to phrase assertions about the ideas in a work, it is important for you to avoid the trap of simply describing plots or main actions. After reading O'Connor's "First Confession," for example, a reader might want to express the central idea in the story as follows: " 'First Confession' is a story about a young boy's family troubles before going to his first confession." This sentence does not state an idea, even though it accounts for the story's major action. In fact, the sentence gets in the way of understanding, since it directs further thought only toward what happens, and does not provide guidance for seeing the characters and events as they relate to an idea. A better way of preparing to discuss O'Connor's theme might be to assert that " 'First Confession' embodies the idea that fear and punishment are self-defeating means of reinforcing religious education." The result of this clearer formulation is that details from the story may be focused upon the main idea and away from a summary of events.

IDEAS AND VALUES

The idea or ideas that an author expresses in literature are closely tied to his or her values, or value system. Unless an idea is completely abstract, as in the idea of a geometric form, it usually implies a value judgment. In "Theme for English B," for example, Hughes's dominant idea is that all human beings are equal regardless of race. His values are made clear as he wittily demonstrates the similarities between his speaker and his teacher, and by extension, among all human beings of all races. It is not possible to discuss Hughes's ideas in the poem without considering his value system. As a general rule, then, we should assume that the ideas of authors grow out of their values, and that values are embodied in their works along with the ideas.

HOW DO YOU FIND IDEAS?

This question is important, because ideas do not just leap out at you from the page; you must look for them. Read the work carefully. Consider the main characters, situations, statements, and actions; evaluate such variables as tone, setting and symbolism. Always, several readings of the work are helpful. At some point in the process, you should formulate an assertion about an idea in the work. There is no hard and fast rule that all statements about ideas in a work should be the same; people notice different things, and individual formulations vary. In Hughes's "Theme for English B," for example, an initial expression about ideas may take any of the following forms: (1) Young people are ambitious, regardless of color. (2) Showing that human beings have similar tastes is a way of showing that persons of all races are also similar. (3) Despite many breakdowns of color barriers, whites are still more free than blacks. (4) Human beings become human through experiences that are faced by everyone. Although any one of these choices, as well as others, could be an idea around which to build a story of ideas in "Theme for English B," they all have in common the assertion that human interests and capacities transcend race, and that therefore color barriers are inhuman. If, in studying for ideas, you follow a similar process—making a number of formulations for an idea, and then revising them to arrive at a single idea to develop further—you will deal skillfully with ideas in whatever stories, poems, and plays you encounter.

With this in mind, you may study your work. As you look and think, you should be alert for the common methods by which authors convey ideas. You should remember, however, that the following classifications are neither exhaustive nor restrictive; rather, they are for convenience and reference. In actual practice, authors may be employing all the following methods (and more) at the same time.

Direct Statements by the Author's Unnamed Speaker

Often the unnamed speaker, who may or may not represent the author's exact views, states ideas directly, by way of commentary, to guide us or to deepen understanding. These ideas may be successful in helping our reading, but they might also disrupt our understanding of the story. In the second paragraph of "The Necklace," for example, De Maupassant's authorial voice states the idea that women without strong family connections must rely on their charm and beauty to get on in the world. This idea might seem sexist or patronizing today, but it is nevertheless an accurate restatement of what De Maupassant's speaker says. In considering it as an idea, just as you might consider other ideas expressed directly by any other author's unnamed speaker, you might want to adapt it somewhat in line with your own understanding of the story. Thus, an adequate restatement of the De Maupassant idea might be this: " 'The Necklace' shows the idea that women, with no power except their charm and beauty, are helpless against chance or bad luck."

Direct Statements by the Persona

(Please see Chapter 6, Writing About Point of View, pp. 77–90.) Often the first-person narrators or speakers state their own ideas. It is possible that these may be identical with ideas held by the author or the authorial speaker, for the author may use the speaker as a direct mouthpiece for ideas. But there is a danger in making a direct equation, for any ideas expressed by a persona speaking within a story represent only himself or herself; the author may not be underwriting the ideas, but only examining them. Careful consideration is therefore necessary to determine the extent to which the narrator's ideas correspond with or diverge from the author's ideas. Sometimes the narrators speak views that are directly opposed to what the author might stand for. Usually these instances are clear. Jonathan

Swift, for example, makes his speaker Gulliver, of *Gulliver's Travels* (1726), say many things that Swift himself clearly rejects. In addition, the author may cause the persona to make statements indicating a limited understanding of the situation he or she is telling about. Thus the adult Jackie, in O'Connor's "First Confession," says things that show some of his ideas to be immature.

Dramatic Statements Made by Characters

In many works, different characters state ideas that are in conflict. The English story writer and novelist Aldous Huxley, for example, frequently introduces "mouthpiece" characters specifically to state ideas related to the fictional story being developed. Authors may thus present thirteen ways of looking at a blackbird and leave the choice up to you; or they may provide you with guides for your interpretations. For instance, they may create an admirable character whose ideas may be the ones they respect. The reverse is true for a bad character.

Figurative Language

Authors often use figurative language to express or reinforce their ideas. In "Dover Beach," for example, Matthew Arnold introduces references to the retreating surf and to a distant and indistinct light to suggest that certainties about life are being lost. Keats, in the poem "Bright Star," uses the star to symbolize the constancy upon which the speaker wishes to model himself. Writers of fiction and drama also introduce such language. At the very opening of Mansfield's story "Miss Brill," the narrator introduces similes stressing images of gold and wine, which are ironically to be contrasted with the deep pain that the major character will soon experience. The idea is that individual misfortunes make human life less happy than the beauty of the earth would demand. In the play *Trifles*, Susan Glaspell compares the dead husband to "a raw wind that gets to the bone." With this language, she conveys the idea of bluntness, cruelty, and indifference that so adequately fits this character.

Characters Who Stand for Ideas

Although characters are busy in the action of their respective works, they may also symbolize ideas or values. Mathilde Loisel in "The Necklace" may be thought of as an embodiment of the idea that women of the nineteenth-century middle class, without the possibility of a career, are hurt by unrealizable dreams of wealth. Two diverse or opposed characters may represent ideas that can be compared or contrasted. Mrs. Ryan and the priest in O'Connor's "First Confession," for instance, represent opposing ideas about the way in which religion is to be instilled in the young.

In effect, characters who stand for ideas may assume symbolic status, as in Hawthorne's "Young Goodman Brown," where the character Brown symbolizes persons who, in becoming zealous about any cause, go too far and exclude themselves from both love and normal human company. The speaker of Frost's "Desert Places" invites identification as a symbol of those frightening qualities of emptiness and unconcern within individual human beings. Seen in this way, the statements and actions of characters like Brown, and like Frost's speaker, can be construed independently not only as narrative event and dramatic dialogue, but also as idea.

The Work Itself as it Represents Ideas

One of the most important ways in which authors express ideas is to render them as an inseparable part of the total impression of the work. All the events and characters may add up to an idea that is made forceful by the impact of the work itself. Thus, although an idea may not be directly stated in so many words, it will be clear after you have finished reading. For example, in "Theme for English B," Hughes makes objective the idea that the human reasons for bringing down racial barriers override the prejudice and socially convenient reasons for which they have been established. Although he never states this concept directly, the idea is clearly embodied in the poem. Similarly, Shakespeare's tragedy *Hamlet* dramatizes the idea that a person doing evil sets strong forces in motion that cannot be stopped until everything in their path is destroyed. Even "escape literature," which is ostensibly designed to enable readers to forget about problems, embodies conflicts between good and evil, love and hate, good spies and bad, earthlings and aliens, and so on. Such stories in fact *do* embody ideas and themes, even though they admittedly do not set out to strike readers with their boldness or originality.

WRITING ABOUT AN IDEA OR THEME

In preparing to write a theme about ideas, keep in mind that an idea pervades a work just as a key signature governs the notes in a musical composition. In a well-written story, poem, or play, most things are introduced only as they have a bearing on the idea. Thus, actions, characters, statements, symbols, and dialogue may be judged by how closely they relate to the idea or theme. In this sense, a major idea runs throughout a work and ties things together much like a continuous thread. As readers, we can trace such threads, with all the variations that writers work upon them. In Amy Lowell's "Patterns," for example, the details are related to the idea that all abstract ideals about personal or national honor are nothing when compared to the needs and rights of individual human beings.

As you take notes and sketch your plan of attack, you should explore all the methods of expressing ideas described above (pp. 103–6), and use as many as you think will give you the most useful information. It may be that you rely most heavily on the direct statements of the authorial voice, or on a combination of these and your interpretation of characters and actions. Or you might focus exclusively on a persona or speaker and use his or her ideas as a means of determining those of the author, as nearly as they can be established.

As you sketch out parts for your essay, you should make clear the various sources of your details, and also distinguish the source from your own commentary. The patterns to establish are like these:

> In "Young Goodman Brown," Hawthorne's anonymous narrator describes Brown's increasing hurry toward the forest meeting as the way in which human beings rush to do evil. This description illustrates his idea that evil is irresistible and even desirable as people increasingly lose their sense of perspective. [Here the first sentence refers to a statement by the author's unnamed persona. The second sentence interprets this statement.]

> In one of the last speeches in "The Chaser," the old man implies that his clients will someday return for his expensive poison so that they may eliminate the wives for whom they feel such youthful infatuation. It is clear that Collier introduces this speech to demonstrate the idea that life sometimes leads to unconquerable cyncism and evil. [Here the source of the detail in the first sentence is a dramatic statement by a character in the story. The second sentence is interpretive.]

> In "First Confession," the priest's thoughtful, good-humored treatment of Jackie, as contrasted with the harsh, punishing treatment he receives from others, shows the idea that religious incentive is best implanted by kindness and understanding, not by fear. [Here the idea, expressed as a single sentence, is derived from a consideration of the work as a whole.]

By locating the source of information in this way, and distinguishing it from your own conclusions, you focus on the topic of your essay—the ideas in a work rather than the narrative or dramatic details. You also help the reader of your essay in verifying and following your arguments.

In developing and writing you essay, you might answer questions like these: What is the best wording of the idea that you can make? What has the author done with the idea? How can the actions be related to the idea as you have stated it? Might any characters be measured according to whether they do or do not live up to the idea? What values does the idea suggest? Is the author proposing a particular cause (personal, social, economic, political, scientific, ethical, esthetic, or religious)? Does the idea affect the organization of the work? How? Does imagery or symbolism develop or illustrate the idea?

Introduction

In your introduction you might state any special circumstances in the work that affect ideas generally or your idea specifically. Your statement of the idea will serve as the central idea for your essay. Your thesis sentence should indicate the particular parts or aspects of the story that you will examine.

Body

The exact form of your essay is controlled by your goals, which are (1) to define the idea, and (2) to show its importance in the work. Each separate story, poem, or play invites its own approach, but here are a number of helpful strategies for developing the body:

1. THE FORM OF THE WORK AS A PLAN, SCHEME, OR LOGICAL FORMAT.   Example: "The idea makes for a two-part work, the first showing religion as punishment and the second showing religion as kindness and reward."

2. A SPEECH OR SPEECHES.   Example: "The priest's conversation and responses to Jackie show in operation the idea that kindness and understanding are the best means to encourage religious commitment."

3. A CHARACTER OR CHARACTERS.   Example: "Minnie Wright embodies the idea that a life lived amid alienation and insensitivity can lead to unhappiness and even to violence."

4. AN ACTION OR ACTIONS.   Example: "That Mrs. Popov and Smirnov fall in love rather than fight a duel indicates Chekhov's idea that love is so strong that it may almost literally rescue human lives."

5. SHADES OR VARIATIONS OF THE IDEA.   Example: "The idea of punishment as a corrective is brought out through the simplicity of the father's 'flaking' of Jackie, the spitefulness of Nora, and the sadistic threats of pain and cosmic intimidation by Mrs. Ryan."

6. A COMBINATION OF THESE TOGETHER WITH ANY OTHER ASPECT RELEVANT TO THE WORK.   Example: "The idea in *The Bear* that love is complex and contradictory is shown in Smirnov's initial scorn of Mrs. Popov because of his personal bitterness against women, his self-reproach when he realizes he is falling in love with her, and his actually embracing her at the end of the play." [Here the idea is to be traced as speech, character, and action in the play would reflect upon it.]

Conclusion

In your conclusion you might briefly summarize the idea. You might also add statements such as your evaluation of the idea's validity or force. If you have been convinced by the author's ideas, you might say that the author has expressed the idea forcefully and convincingly, or else you might show the relevance of the idea to current conditions. If you are not convinced, it is never enough just to say that you disagree; you should state reasons for your disagreement, or demonstrate the shortcomings or limitations of the idea. If you wish to mention an idea related to the one you have discussed, you might introduce this new idea here, being sure to stress the connections.

Sample Theme

The Idea of the Strength of Love in Chekhov's The Bear[*]

---

[1] In the one-act farce The Bear, Anton Chekhov shows a man and woman who have never met before falling suddenly in love. With such an unlikely main action, ideas may seem unimportant, but one can nevertheless find a number of ideas in the play. Some of these are that responsibility to life is stronger than that to death, that people may find justification for even the most contradictory actions, that love makes people do and say unusual and foolish things, and that lifelong commitments may be made with no more than minimal deliberation. One of the play's major ideas is that love and desire are powerful enough to overcome even the strongest obstacles.[°] This idea is shown as the force of love conquers commitment to the dead, renunciation of womankind, unfamiliarity, and anger.[□]

[2] Commitment to her dead husband is the obstacle to love shown in Mrs. Popov. She states that she has made a vow never to see daylight because of her mourning, and she spends her time staring at her husband's picture and comforting herself with her faithfulness. Her devotion to the dead is so intense that she claims at the start that she is already in her grave. In her, Chekhov has created a strong obstacle to love so that he might illustrate his idea that love conquers all. By the play's end, Mrs. Popov's embracing Smirnov is a visual example of the idea.

[3] Renunciation of women is the obstacle for Smirnov. He tells Mrs. Popov that his experience with women has made him bitter and that he no longer gives "a good goddamn" about them. His disillusioned words make him an impossible candidate for love. But, in keeping with Chekhov's idea, Smirnov

---

[*] For the text of this play, please see Appendix C, pp. 359–68.
[°] Central idea
[□] Thesis sentence

[3] is the one who is soon confessing to the audience that he has fallen in love suddenly and uncontrollably. For him, the idea about the force of love operates so strongly that he would even claim happiness at being shot by "those little velvet hands."

[4] As if these personal causes were not enough to prevent love permanently, a major obstacle is that the two people are strangers. Not only have they never met, they have never even heard of each other. According to the main idea, however, this unfamiliarity is not insurmountable. Chekhov is dramatizing the power of love, and shows that it is strong enough to overcome lack of familiarity or friendship. Indeed, that Smirnov and Mrs. Popov are total strangers may be almost irrelevant to the idea about love's strength as shown in the play.

[5] Anger and the threat of violence, however, make the greatest obstacle. The two characters become so irritated about Smirnov's demand for payment that, as a climax of their heated words, Smirnov challenges Mrs. Popov to a duel! Along with their own personal barriers against loving, it would seem that the threat of their shooting at each other, even if poor Luka could forestall it, would cause the beginning of lifelong hatred between the two. And yet love knocks down all these obstacles, in line with Chekhov's idea that love's power is irresistible.

[6] The idea, of course, is not new or surprising. It is the subject and substance of many popular songs, stories, and other plays and movies. What is surprising about Chekhov's use of the idea is that love in The Bear wins out suddenly against such unlikely conditions. These conditions bring up an interesting and closely related idea: Chekhov is suggesting that intense feelings, even irritation, anger, and professed hatred, may lead to love. In the speeches of Smirnov and Mrs. Popov, one can see hurt, disappointment, regret, frustration, annoyance, anger, and rage. Yet at the high point of these negative feelings, the characters fall in love. Could Chekhov be saying that it is a mixture of such feelings that brings out love, not unlike the way in which the universe was created out of chaos? Though The Bear is a farce, and a good one, Chekhov's use of the idea of love's power is based on an accurate judgment about human beings.

COMMENTARY ON THE THEME

This essay is derived from the dialogue, situations, soliloquies, and actions of the two major characters in Chekhov's play. Throughout, these sources are mentioned as the authority for the various conclusions.

The introduction notes that the play is a farce but that it nevertheless contains a number of ideas. The major idea to be developed is stated as the capacity of love to reach fulfillment in unlikely or even impossible conditions. In the thesis sentence, these conditions are identified as obstacles to be found in (1) Mrs. Popov, (2) Smirnov, (3) their being strangers with each other, and (4) their anger.

As the operative aspects of Chekhov's idea, paragraphs 2 through

5 detail the nature of the obstacles to be overcome by love. The obstacle discussed in paragraph 2, Mrs. Popov's commitment to her husband's memory, is "strong." The one in paragraph 3, Smirnov's dislike of women as a result of his previous experiences, seems to become "impossible." The one in paragraph 4, their being total strangers, is claimed as a "major" obstacle to be overcome. In paragraph 5, the obstacle of anger is detailed as seeming likely to produce not love but "lifelong hatred."

The concluding paragraph indicates that the distinguishing mark of Chekhov's use of this comparatively common idea is surprise. The related idea developed in paragraph 6 is that love, being a strong emotion, may stem easily out of the other strong emotions exhibited by the two characters. Once this last thought is established, the theme is concluded with a tribute to Chekhov's serious use of the major idea.

chapter 9

Writing About Imagery

In literature, **imagery** refers to language that triggers your mind to recall and recombine images—to fuse together old and new memories or mental pictures of sights, sounds, tastes, smells, and sensations of touch. A specific impression that you bring to mind is an image. When particular words or descriptions cause you to form mental images, you are using your imagination. That is, you put together selected memories and apply them to your understanding of what you are reading or hearing. (When you go just a step beyond, to write a story or develop a new way to do a particular task, you are also using your imagination.) Through the deliberate use of imagery, therefore, authors tap your selected experiences in order to make their works lively and stimulating.

For example, the word "lake" may cause you to imagine or visualize either a particular lake that you remember vividly, or it may present to your mind's eye a composite picture of a number of lakes. You may think of a distant view of calm waters reflecting blue sky, a nearby view of rippling waves stirred up by a wind, a close-up view from a boat looking at the lake bottom, or an overhead view of a sandy and sunlit shoreline. Similarly, the words "rose," "apple," "hot dog," "malted milk," and "pizza" all cause you to visualize these things at least to some degree, and in addition may bring to your memory their smells and tastes. Active and pictorial words such as "row," "swim," and "dive" cause you to imagine someone performing these actions. Words like these, which writers use to make your imagination work, are images.

THE VOCABULARY OF IMAGES
AND IMAGERY

We may use the word "image" when referring either to a single word or to the impression invoked by the word. The word "images" refers to a number of separate words or impressions. When we speak more generally about a writer's characteristic use of images within a work, or about changes from work to work or from time to time, the word "imagery" is appropriate. Thus, we speak of the image in line 5 of a poem, or the images in part 6 of a story. We might also speak of Frost's use of imagery in the poem "Desert Places." More extensive topics would be "Shakespeare's use of imagery in the sonnets," and even more broadly, "the development of Shakespeare's imagery."

IMAGERY AND ATTITUDES

Writers rely upon images to evoke commonly held attitudes and feelings. Thus, the phrase "beside a lake, beneath the trees," from Wordsworth's poem "Daffodils," prompts both the visualization of a wooded lakeshore and the related pleasantness of outdoor relaxation and happiness. In contrast, Masefield in "Cargoes" introduces unpleasant responses through images of things such as "pig lead" and "cheap tin trays." By thus relying upon imagery that is accompanied by certain associations, writers not only make their works vivid, but they also control reader responses.

OUR RESPONSES AND THE WRITER'S USE
OF DETAIL

In studying imagery, we need to determine how the writer brings the world alive so that we may reconstruct in our imaginations something like the set of pictures and impressions presented in the work. We must read the writer's words, but then let them simmer and percolate in our minds to develop what he or she intended. To get our imaginations stirring, we might follow Coleridge in this description from "Kubla Khan":

> A damsel with a dulcimer
> In a vision once I saw:
> It was an Abyssinian maid,
> And on her dulcimer she played,
> Singing of Mount Abora.

We do not read about the color of the damsel's clothing, or anything else about her appearance except that she is playing a stringed instrument, a dulcimer, and that she is singing a song about a mountain in a foreign, remote land. But Coleridge's reference is enough. From it we can imagine a magically distant, exotic, vivid picture of a woman singing and the loveliness of song. The image lives.

IMAGERY OF THE SENSES:

(1) SIGHT. Literary imagery consists of specific and concrete language evoking sense impressions and actions. Sight is the most significant of our senses, for sight is the key to our remembrance or recollection of other impressions. As might be expected, therefore, the most frequent imagery in literature is to things we can visualize either exactly or approximately—**visual images**. John Masefield, in his poem "Cargoes" (the subject of the sample theme, pp. 118–19), asks us to recreate mental pictures or images of ocean-going merchant vessels from three periods of human history. He speaks about a quinquereme (a ship with five tiers of oars) from the ancient Near East, associated with the biblical King Solomon; then he turns to a "stately Spanish galleon" at the time of the Renaissance; finally, he refers to a modern British ship caked with salt, carrying grubby, cheap items. His images are vivid as they stand, without the need for more detailed amplification. In order to reconstruct them imaginatively, we do not need ever to have seen the ancient biblical lands or waters, or ever to have seen or handled the cheap commodities on a modern merchant ship. We have seen enough in our lives, both in reality and in pictures, to *imagine* places and objects like these; hence Masefield is successful in implanting his visual images into our minds.

(2) SOUND. Obviously, writers create images derived from the other senses. **Auditory images,** or references to sound, are frequent. In Wilfred Owen's poem "Anthem for Doomed Youth," which is about needless death in warfare, the speaker asks what "passing bells" may be tolled for "those who die as cattle." He is referring to the traditional tolling of a parish church bell to announce the death ("passing") of a parishioner to the nearby community. Such a ceremonial ringing suggests a period of peace and order, a time when respect for the dead may be properly observed. But the poem then points out that the only sound for those who have fallen in battle is the "rapid rattle" of "stuttering" rifles—in other words, not the solemn, dignified sounds of peace, but the horrifying noises of war. Owen's auditory images evoke corresponding sounds in our imaginations, and help us experience the poem and hate the uncivilized depravity of war.

IMAGES OF (3) SMELL, (4), TASTE, AND (5) TOUCH. You will find images derived from the other senses as well. An **olfactory image** refers to smell, a **gustatory image** to taste, and a **tactile image** to touch. A great deal of love poetry, for example, includes observations about the fragrances of flowers. As a twist on this common olfactory imagery, Shakespeare in Sonnet 130, "My Mistress' Eyes," creates a speaker who amusingly contrasts a woman's breath with the beauty of the scent of roses.

Images derived from and referring to taste—gustatory images—are also common, though less frequent than those to sight and sound. In line 5 of Masefield's "Cargoes," for example, there is a reference to "sweet white wine," and in line 10 to "cinnamon." Although these gustatory images refer to these things as cargoes, the words themselves inevitably register in our minds because of their appeal to our sense of taste.

Tactile images of touch and texture are perhaps the least common in poetry because these are often more personal and subjective than sights and sounds. It is obvious that references to touching in love poetry, for example, would be sensual as well as sensuous.

OTHER TYPES OF IMAGES

The frames of reference of imagery may also take in virtually every sort of activity in which human beings may engage. Descriptions of motion and action come immediately to mind. Imagery referring to activities is termed *kinetic* if general motion is described, or *kinesthetic* if the imagery applies to human or animal activity. Masefield's reference to the British coaster butting through the channel is a kinetic image. Amy Lowell's reference to the speaker's walking in the garden after hearing about her fiancé's death is kinesthetic.

The areas from which kinetic and kinesthetic imagery may be derived are almost too varied to describe. Occupations, trades, professions, businesses, recreational activities—all these might furnish images in poetry and fiction. One poet introduces references from gardening, another from money and banking, another from modern real-estate developments, another from life within jungles. The freshness, newness, and surprise of literature result from the many and varied areas from which poets draw their images.

IMAGERY DERIVED PURELY FROM LORE AND IMAGINATION

Because there are few restrictions upon the human imagination, the references of imagery may not only be real, but also imagined. Hawthorne in "Young Goodman Brown" describes the protagonist's walk into the woods, an area that seems realistic but which turns into imagined regions of fantasy and nightmare. Coleridge in "Kubla Khan" gives us both reality and unreality in a single line about a "woman [real] wailing for her demon lover [unreal]."

IMAGERY, COMPLETENESS, AND TRUTH

Writers—poets, dramatists, and writers of fiction alike—do not create imagery just to present a series of pictures or other sensory impressions. Their aim is to help you see the world in a new way, to widen your understanding, to transfer their own ideas by the *authenticating* effects of the vision and perceptions underlying them. Strong, vivid images are thus a means by which literature renders truth. It would be difficult to give assent to Masefield's views about modern commercial life if his image of the "Dirty British coaster with a salt-caked smoke-stack" did not ring true. It does.

Comparable imagery used for a different purpose may be seen in Shakespeare's Sonnet 130, "My Mistress' Eyes." Here Shakespeare's speaker expressly denies the overly romanticized compliments that men give women, stressing instead that his woman friend lives in the everyday world. By this emphasis, Shakespeare gains assent to the view that everyday life is superior to dream life, if for no other reason than that it provides a basis for a relationship between people. As you read stories and poems, and find images in them, try in this way to determine their aptness, consistency, and reliability, for the life of literature is only as durable as the authenticity of its imagery.

WRITING ABOUT IMAGERY

In preparing to write, you should work with a thoughtfully developed set of notes. With imagery, it is particularly important to classify references to the various senses to which they belong (e.g., sight, sound). In determining other classifications, you may be able to find a consistent pattern of references to a particular activity or related set of activities. If accurate classification is not possible, you may be able to make much of your poet's diversity of images.

Introduction

Here you set out the main things that you plan for the body of your essay, such as that the writer refers predominantly to images of sight, sound, action, and so on. You central idea should clearly delineate your objective, and your thesis sentence should outline the aspects you will examine in the following paragraphs or groups of paragraphs, depending on the length of your essay.

Body

A number of aspects of imagery may be developed in the body of your essay. You might choose one of these exclusively, but quite likely you may bring in two or more of the following approaches:

1. THE TYPE OF IMAGES.   Is there a predominance of a particular type of imagery, such as references to sight, or is there a blending? Is there a bunching of types at particular points in the poem or story? What might be a reason for this bunching? Is there any shifting from type to type as the work develops? How do the images relate to the content, to the ideas, of the work? Are they appropriate? Do they assist in making the ideas seem convincing? If there seems to be any inappropriateness, what is its effect?

2. THE USE OF IMAGES TO SUGGEST IDEAS AND/OR MOODS.   Are the images directed to the establishment of any particular ideas or moods in the work? What might these ideas be? How can the images be construed to make these ideas plain? Do the images promote a sense of approval or disapproval? Do they seem cheerful? Melancholy? Exciting? Vivid? Do they seem to be conducive to humor or surprise? How does the writer manipulate the images to achieve these effects? Are the images consistent in their application, or might they be taken in a different way as the work progresses? (For example, the images in Masefield's "Cargoes" straightforwardly indicate first approval and then disapproval, with no ambiguity. By contrast, Shakespeare's references in "My Mistress' Eyes" might initially be construed as insults. However, in a total consideration of the sonnet, they may be seen not as insults but as compliments.)

3. THE DEVELOPMENT OF ANY SYSTEMS OF IMAGES.   In effect, this is another way of considering the appropriateness of the imagery, whether in a poem, story, or play. Is there a pattern of similar or consistent images, such as darkness (Hawthorne's "Young Goodman Brown") or brightness to darkness (Mansfield's "Miss Brill")? Do all the images adhere consistently to a particular frame of reference, such as a sunlit garden (Lowell's "Patterns"), an extensive recreational forest and garden (Coleridge's "Kubla Khan"), a kitchen (Glaspell's *Trifles*), or a group of seagoing vessels (Masefield's "Cargoes")? Is there anything unusual or unique about the set of images? Do they provide any unexpected or new responses to the situation and ideas of the work?

4. THE CREATION OF A CHARACTERISTIC MODE OF IMAGES.   Here you develop an idea about any noticeable reliance upon characteristic images. If you find such a characteristic or typical line of images, this line may be considered a mode for that poem or story, if not for the writer generally. It may be hard to determine a modal type on the basis of only one work,

but there are questions you may pursue to determine if there is a mode in the work you have studied. Does the imagery seem to rely upon shapes and colors (visual), sounds (auditory), actions (kinetic or kinesthetic)? Is it especially vivid, and if so, how does the poet achieve this vividness? Does the writer present the images completely or sketchily? Is one type of image used rather than another—for example, natural scenes and not interiors, loud as opposed to low sounds, facial expressions rather than grosser actions, bright colors rather than dull ones, shapes and locations rather than colors? What conclusions can you draw about the work and the author as a result of your answers?

Conclusion

While in the body of the essay you will have been developing a fairly detailed analysis of the types and appropriateness of the writer's images, in your conclusion you might stress any insights you have gained from your study. It would not be proper to introduce entirely new directions here, but you might briefly take up one or more of the conclusions you had reached but did not develop in the body. In short, what have you learned from your study of imagery in the work about which you have written?

Sample Theme

The Images of John Masefield's Poem "Cargoes"[*]

---

[1]
In the three-stanza poem "Cargoes," John Masefield develops imagery to create a negative impression of modern commercial life.[°] There is a contrast between the first two stanzas and the third, with the first two demonstrating the romantic, distant past and the third demonstrating the modern, gritty, grimy present. Masefield's images are thus both positive and lush, on the one hand, and negative and stark, on the other.[□]

[2]
The most evocative and pleasant images in the poem are included in the first stanza. The speaker asks that we imagine a "Quinquereme of Nineveh from distant Ophir," an ocean-going, many-oared vessel loaded with treasure for the biblical King Solomon. The visual impression is colorful, rich, and romantic. The imagery of richness is established with ivory (line 3), and is continued with the exoticism of "apes and peacocks" in all their strangeness and colorfulness. The speaker adds to the fullness of this scene by referring to sandalwood,

[*] See Appendix C for the text of this poem, p. 356.
[°] Central idea
[□] Thesis sentence

[2] cedarwood, and sweet white wine, thus adding images of smell and taste. The "sunny" light of ancient Palestine not only illuminates Masefield's scene, but invites readers to imagine the sun's warming touch. The references to animals and birds also suggest images of the sound these exotic creatures would make. Thus, in this lush first stanza, images derived from all the senses are introduced to create the life and impressions of a glorious past.

[3] Almost equally lush are the images of the second stanza, which completes the first part of the poem. Here the visual imagery evokes the royal splendor of a tall-masted, full-sailed galleon at the height of Spain's commercial power in the sixteenth century. The cargo of the galleon suggests great wealth, with diamonds and amethysts sparkling to the eye, and "gold moidores" of Portugal gleaming in colorful chests. With cinnamon in the second stanza's bill of lading, Masefield includes a reference to a pleasant-tasting spice.

[4] The negative imagery of the third stanza is in stark contrast to the first two stanzas. Here the poem draws the visual image of a modern "Dirty British coaster" to focus on the griminess and suffocation of modern civilization. This spray-swept ship is loaded with materials designed to pollute the earth with noise and smoke. The smokestack of the coaster (line 11) and the firewood it is carrying suggest the creation of choking smog. The "Tyne coal" (line 13) and "road-rails" (line 14) suggest the noise and smoke of puffing railroad engines. As if this were not enough, the "pig-lead" (line 14) to be used in various industrial processes indicates not just more unpleasantness, but also something more poisonous and deadly. In contrast to the lush and stately imagery of the first two stanzas, the images in the third stanza invite the conclusion that people now, when the "Dirty British coaster" butts through the English Channel, are surrounded and threatened by visual, olfactory, and auditory pollution.

[5] The poem thus establishes a romantic past and ugly present through images of sight, smell, and sound. The images of motion are also directed to agree with this view: In stanzas 1 and 2 the quinquereme is "rowing" and the galleon is "dipping." These kinetic images conveyed by participles of motion suggest dignity and lightness. The British coaster, however, is "butting," an image indicating bull-like hostility and blind force. These, together with all the other images, focus the poem's negative views of today's consumer-oriented society. The facts that life for both the ancient Palestinians and the Renaissance Spaniards included slavery (of those men rowing the quinquereme) and piracy (by those Spanish "explorers' who exploited the natives of the isthmus) should probably not be emphasized as a protest against Masefield's otherwise valid contrasts in images. His final commentary may hence be thought of as the banging of his "cheap tin trays," which makes a percussive climax of the oppressive images filling too large a portion of modern lives.

COMMENTARY ON THE THEME

The method illustrated in this sample theme is the second one described on p. 117, the use of images to develop ideas and moods. This method permits the introduction of imagery drawn from all the senses in order to demonstrate Masefield's ideas about the past and present. Other approaches might have concentrated exclusively on Masefield's visual images, or upon his images drawn from trade and commerce. It is unlikely that an essay could be devoted only to the images of sound or taste in "Cargoes." Such topics might be more properly developed in a single paragraph.

The introductory paragraph of the theme presents the central idea that Masefield uses his images climactically to lead to his negative view of modern commercialism. The thesis sentence indicates that the topics to be developed are those of (1) lushness, and (2) starkness.

Paragraphs 2 and 3 form a unit in which the lushness and exoticism of the images in stanzas 1 and 2 of the poem are stressed. All the examples—derived directly from the poem—emphasize the qualities of Masefield's images. The discussion in paragraphs 2 and 3 illustrates no more than the minimal use of imagination needed to make adequate sense of the images. Thus, in the real world, the peacocks of stanza 1 would have had feathers containing a number of bright, arresting colors, but these colors are not stressed in the sample theme beyond a reference to the general colorfulness of these birds. Ivory would unquestionably have been sculpted into various statues and ornaments, but because no mention is made by Masefield to any such shapes, the sample theme does not try to go beyond Masefield's general reference to "ivory." His images, in short, are considered only as they evoke an impression of lushness and richness, not as they might be further imaginatively amplified. The illustrative value of this discussion is that in interpretation, readers should not go beyond where writers invite them to go, no matter how great the temptation.

The fourth paragraph stresses the contrast of Masefield's images in stanza 3 with those of stanzas 1 and 2. To this end, the paragraph illustrates the need for a high enough degree of imaginative reconstruction to develop an understanding of this contrast. The unpleasantness, annoyance, and even the danger of the cargoes mentioned in stanza 3 are therefore emphasized as the qualities evoked by the images.

The last paragraph demonstrates that the imagery of motion—not much stressed in the poem—is in agreement with the rest of Masefield's imagery. As a demonstration of the need for fair, impartial judgment, the conclusion introduces the possible objection that Masefield's imagistic portraits may be slanted because they include not a full but more of a partial view of their respective historical periods. This demurrer, however, is not emphasized. Thus, the concluding paragraph adds balance to the analysis illustrated in paragraphs 2, 3, and 4.

chapter 10

Writing About Metaphor and Simile

Figurative language refers to expressions that conform to particular patterns and arrangements of thought. These patterns, or **rhetorical figures**, with special names, are used by writers to make their works effective, persuasive, and forceful. Although figures may be used in any kind of work, they are most commonly found in poetry.

There are many rhetorical figures, also called **devices**, but the two most important are **metaphor** and **simile**. These both refer to ways of making comparisons. Quite often the words *metaphor* and *metaphorical language* are used in general reference to both metaphors and similes. A metaphor ("a carrying out of a change") is the direct verbal equation of two things that at first seem unlike each other. The sentence "All the arts are sisters," for example, is a metaphor that emphasizes the close family relationship between poetry, music, sculpture, painting, architecture, and acting, to name the major arts. Notice that the metaphor does not claim that the arts are *like* sisters, but rather that the arts *are* sisters.

While a metaphor thus verbally merges identities, a simile ("the showing of similarity or oneness") is a figure of comparison, using "like" with nouns and "as" (also "as if" and "as though") with clauses, that draws attention to similarities about two things. Thus, the sentence "Come with . . . eyes as bright / As sunlight on a stream" (from Christina Rossetti's poem "Echo") makes a connection between the listener's eyes and a most attractive natural scene. This pleasant reference suggests the speaker's fond memory of the listener. Because the simile is introduced by "like," the speaker's emphasis is on the *similarity* of the listener's eyes to sunlight on a stream, not on the *identification* or *equation* of the two.

IMAGERY, METAPHOR, AND SIMILE

To see the relationship of metaphor and simile to imagery, you should remember that imagery requires readers to use their imaginations to remember experiences similar to sensory experiences described in a literary work. The images in the work arise more or less functionally and expectedly from the topic material of the work. By duplicating the images intellectually and emotionally, through the use of imagination, readers may understand and verify the work itself. Through the use of imagery, therefore, writers make their works accurate, vivid, stimulating, and memorable.

Metaphors and similes go a step beyond by introducing images that may not normally be expected in a given work, but which may be unusual, unpredictable, and even surprising. In effect, writers use metaphorical language to connect something to be communicated—an observation, attitude, idea, feeling, or action—with a new insight that is made objective through the comparison of a simile or the equation of a metaphor. These devices are therefore a mode of expression, but more fundamentally, they are an inseparable part of the way of seeing the world anew that is the special contribution of great literature.

For example, to communicate a character's joy and excitement, the sentence "She was happy" is accurate, but not interesting or effective. A more vivid way of saying the same thing is to use an image of an action, such as, "She jumped for joy." This image gives us a concrete picture of an action that a person might perform as a demonstration of happiness. But an even better way of communicating a happy state is the following simile: "She felt as if she had just inherited five million tax-free dollars." Because readers can easily understand and reconstruct for themselves the combination of excitement, disbelief, exhilaration, and joy that such an event would bring, they also readily understand the true range of the character's happiness. It is the simile that evokes this perception. No simple description can help a reader comprehend the same degree of emotion.

As a poetic example, let us refer to John Keats's poem "On First Looking into Chapman's Homer." Keats (1795–1821) wrote the poem after he first read the Elizabethan writer John Chapman's translation of *The Iliad* and *The Odyssey*, epic poems attributed to the ancient Greek epic poet Homer. Keats's main idea is that Chapman not only translated Homer's words but also transmitted his greatness. A brief paraphrase of the poem is this:

> I have enjoyed much art and read much European literature, and
> have been told that Homer is the best writer of all, but not knowing
> Greek, I could not appreciate his works until I discovered them in Chap-
> man's translation. To me, this experience was exciting and awe-inspiring.

This paraphrase also destroys the poem's sense of exhilaration and discovery. Contrast the second sentence of the paraphrase with the last six lines
of the sonnet as Keats writes them:

> Then felt I like some watcher of the skies
> When a new planet swims into his ken;
> Or like stout Cortez when with eagle eyes
> He star'd at the Pacific—and all his men
> Look'd at each other with a wild surmise—
> Silent, upon a peak in Darien.

If all we had of the poem were our paraphrase, we would probably
pay little attention to it. But in Keats's lines there are two powerful similes
("like some watcher" and "like stout Cortez"). These deserve special care.
In reading, we should not just read them and pass them by, but should
use our imaginations to experience them. We should read them, hear
them, mull them over, feel them, and dream about them. We should
suppose that we actually *are* an astronomer just discovering a new planet,
and that we actually *are* the first people to see the Pacific Ocean. As we
imagine ourselves in these roles, we should think of our accompanying
amazement, wonder, excitement, anticipation, joy, and sense of accom-
plishment. If we imagine these feelings, then Keats has unlocked experiences that the relatively unpromising title does not suggest. He has given
us something new. He has enlarged us.

CHARACTERISTICS OF METAPHORICAL
LANGUAGE

It would be difficult to find any good piece of writing that does not employ
metaphorical language at least to some extent. Such language is most
vital, however, in imaginative writing, particularly poetry, where it com-
presses thought, promotes understanding, and shapes response.

As we have seen in the section on imagery (above, pp. 112–20),
images are embodied in words or descriptions denoting sense experience
that leads to many associations. A single word naming a flower—say,
rose—evokes a positive response. A person might think of the color of a
rose, recall its smell, associate it with the summer sun and pleasant days,
and remember the love and respect that a bouquet of roses means as a
gift. But the word *rose* is not a metaphor or simile until its associations
are used in a comparative or analogical way, as in the opening lines of
"A Red, Red Rose" by Robert Burns:

> O my Luve's like a red, red rose,
>> That's newly sprung in June:

The first thing about these lines is that they are short. The speaker could probably go on forever about his sweetheart, but we all know that readers would quickly tire of such a disquisition. Instead, the speaker has recourse to a simile. To help us understand and even reduplicate his feelings, however, the speaker asks us to bring to our minds all the possible associations that we might have with roses, in addition to those already mentioned. After winter's drabness and leaflessness, springtime's lush growth marks a new beginning, an entirely new and colorful earth that contrasts with the monochrome dullness of winter. Thus, the rose suggests loveliness, colorfulness, the end of dreariness, love, and the seasonal fertility of the earth. Once we have expanded upon the simile in this way, we have come close to comprehending the speaker's enthusiasm about his lady. That a rose may have unpleasant associations, perhaps because of its thorns, should not be considered. Such an extension of meaning, although truthful, would likely be a misreading of the simile.

It would, that is, unless the writer deliberately calls some of these less happy ideas to mind. In one of the most famous poems about a rose, by Edmund Waller ("Go Lovely Rose," in which the speaker addresses a rose that he is about to send to his sweetheart), the speaker observes that roses, when cut, die:

> Then die—that she
> The common fate of all things rare
>> May read in thee:
> How small a part of time they share
> That are so wondrous sweet and fair.

Here the speaker is directing the reader's responses to the original comparison of the rose with the lady love. The structure of the poem is the full development of the simile (the speaker uses the phrase "resemble her to thee" in reference to this figure).

To see how metaphors, like similes, compress the thought of writers, let us briefly consider Shakespeare's Sonnet 30 (this poem, which is the subject of the sample essay at the end of this chapter, is printed on p. 129). Shakespeare's opening metaphor equates the business of a law court with personal reverie and self-evaluation:

> When to the sessions of sweet silent thought
> I summon up remembrance of things past, . . .

The word *sessions* is the legal name for that period of time during which judges, juries, lawyers, and witnesses carry out the court's business (i.e., "the court is now in *session*"; think also of "school is now in *session*").

The word *summon* is the legal word that describes an official commandment for a person to appear before a court, usually to stand as a defendant for an alleged wrongdoing. Through these metaphors, the speaker says that in moments of reflection he (assuming a male speaker) thinks about his past and passes judgment on it, thinking about past sorrows and regrets and wondering whether he always did the right things. In a way, the speaker asks us to visualize his "sweet silent thought" as though he is sitting as a combination lawyer-judge over his memories, which he has commanded to reappear. The implication of this metaphor is that the total experience of a person is constantly alive and present; that the memory is like an entire society with wrongs, shortcomings, and transgressions; that judgment and reassessment are constant, living processes; and that the consciousness of individuals is not an unchanging, solid state, but is instead a series of conflicting or contrasting impulses.

This development of Shakespeare's metaphor may seem at first like a great deal more than Shakespeare intended; indeed, we have used more words in prose than he uses in verse. Once we have understood his language, however, our minds are unlocked, and we may then allow ourselves this kind of expansion as we consider the full ramifications of the comparison or equation.

DEGREES OF DEVELOPMENT

As you prepare to write about metaphor and simile, you will find that these devices appear with varying degrees of development. Often a single word creates a metaphorical context. Shakespeare's use of the word "tell" in line 10 of Sonnet 30, for example, indicates a way of counting out past sorrows in the same way a bank teller counts ("tells") money. In Burn's "A Red, Red Rose," the speaker invites readers to consider that the rose has "newly sprung in June." In this way Burns focuses on the associations of fertility and growth. Sometimes the single word stretches out and covers nearby words to incorporate them into a metaphorical system, as in line 4 of Keats's "On First Looking Into Chapman's Homer," where Keats uses the word *fealty*. Here the reference is to the medieval feudal system of holding and developing land by the permission and authority of a more powerful lord or baron. The landholder, who was a person of considerable power, shared some of the benefits reaped from the land, and also owed military service and support. This arrangement was called holding the land in *fealty* to the lord. Because Keats equates writers with landholders, the poem states that writers exercise their craft with the consent and aid of God (called "Apollo" in the poem).

USING EXPLANATORY NOTES
AND A DICTIONARY

As you read, you will likely discover that an exhaustive expansion of metaphors and similes may not be easy the first time around. You can understand them, however, if you use your time and ingenuity, and also if you use explanatory notes (if they are available) or a dictionary to uncover meanings that may not be apparent at first. Thus, in Shakespeare's line "And heavily from woe to woe tell o're," the word "tell" is in common use and you may therefore miss its metaphorical meaning entirely unless you consult an explanatory note or a dictionary. Similarly, you will need an explanation of "fealty," such as the one above, or "demesne," from Keats's "On First Looking into Chapman's Homer," if you are to catch the meaning Keats intends. So be alert; do not ignore explanatory notes; and use your dictionary often. Allow the similes and metaphors to resonate in your mind. Try some solutions and some possibilities, and, if these do not seem probable, be willing to reject them. But keep working on applying new potential meanings that occur to you.

WRITING ABOUT METAPHOR
AND SIMILE

When you plan to write about metaphor and simile, you will not know what direction your theme will take. Thus, you will need to record your discoveries as you study the work. Determine the existence, line by line, of metaphors or similes. Obviously, similes are much easier to recognize than metaphors, because of the "like" or "as" with which they begin. Metaphors may be recognizable because of the transference of the subject to the actual meaning or tenor. If the subject is memory, for example, but the poem speaks of law courts, you are looking at a metaphor.

Once you have listed all the figures you can identify, try to formulate answers to questions like these: What metaphors or similes does the work contain? How extensive are they? Are they signaled by a single word, or are they more extensively detailed? Next, attempt to describe the thoughts embodied in the figures: What ideas can you locate and delineate there? What impressions of experience, what attitudes? How extensively do the figures bear the burden of thought and development in the work? Are the figures the major means of development, or are they no more than an embellishment of a more discursive or conversational development? If you have discovered a number of metaphors and similes, what relationships can you find among them (such as the judicial and financial relationships in Shakespeare's Sonnet 30)? How are the similes or metaphors related to the structure of the work? Do you find that one type of figure is used in a particular section while a second type predominates in another?

Once you have these guidelines sketched out in a set of notes, you are ready to begin developing the initial stages of your theme.

Introduction

In determining your central idea, you should relate the quality of the figures to the general nature of the work you are studying. Thus, metaphors and similes about suffering might be appropriate to a religious, redemptive work, while those of sunshine and cheer might be right for a romantic one. If there is any discrepancy between the metaphorical language and the topic material, you would find it necessary to consider that contrast as a possible central idea, for if such a discrepancy exists, your writer would clearly be developing an ironic perspective. Suppose that the topic of the poem is love, but the metaphors are those of darkness and cold: What would the writer be saying about the quality of love? You should also try to justify any claims you make about similes or metaphors. For example, one of the similes in Coleridge's "Kubla Khan" compares the sounds of a "mighty fountain" to the breathing of the earth in "fast thick pants." How is this simile to be taken? As a reference to the animality of the earth? As a suggestion that the fountain, and the earth, are dangerous? Or simply as a comparison suggesting immense, forceful noise? How do you explain the answer or answers you select? Your introduction is the place to establish ideas and justifications of this sort. Once you have determined your central idea, you should develop your thesis sentence to guide your reader for the remainder of your essay.

Body

There are a number of approaches for discussing simile and metaphor. They are not mutually exclusive, and you may combine them as you wish. Most likely, in fact, the essay you write will invariably bring in most of the following classifications.

1. THE MEANING AND EFFECT OF THE FIGURES. Here you explain your interpretation of the various similes and/or metaphors. In stanza 2 of "A Valediction: Forbidding Mourning," for example, Donne introduces a metaphor equating the condition of love with the structure of the church:

> 'Twere profanation of our joys
> To tell the laity our love.

Here Donne emphasizes the private, mystical relationship of two lovers, drawing the metaphor from the religious tradition whereby any explanation of religious mysteries is considered a desecration. The idea that Donne is expressing is that love is rare, heaven-sent, private, privileged, and so fragile that it would be hurt if it were generally known. In effect, this approach is direct, requiring that metaphors and similes be explained and expanded, with the introduction of necessary references and allusions to make your expansion fully meaningful.

2. **THE FRAMES OF REFERENCE OF THE FIGURES, AND THEIR APPROPRIATENESS TO THE SUBJECT MATTER.** Here you classify and locate the sources and types of the images, determining, as you do so, the appropriateness of this range of references to the subject matter of the poem. Questions to answer are similar to those you might bring out in a study of straightforward imagery: Does the writer favor figures from nature, science, warfare, politics, business, reading? Thus, Shakespeare in Sonnet 30, as we have seen, expands a metaphor equating personal reverie with courtroom proceedings. Because such proceedings are public and methodical, while personal self-evaluation is private and relatively unplanned, how appropriate is the metaphor? Does Shakespeare make it seem right as he develops it in the poem? How? In considering any metaphors and similes in the work you analyze, you would need similarly to classify according to sources, and try to determine the appropriateness of this body of figures to the poet's ideas.

3. **THE INTERESTS/SENSIBILITIES OF THE WRITER.** In a way, this approach is like the second one, but the emphasis here is on what the selectivity of the writer might show about his or her vision and interests. You might begin by listing the figures in the poem and then determining the sources, just as you would do in discussing the sources of images generally. But then you should raise questions like the following: Does the writer use figures derived from one sense rather than another (i.e., sight, hearing, taste, smell, touch)? Does he or she record color, brightness, shadow, shape, depth, height, number, size, slowness, speed, emptiness, fullness, richness, drabness? Has the writer relied on the associations of figures of sense? Do metaphors and similes referring to green plants and trees, to red roses, or to rich fabrics, for example, suggest that life is full and beautiful, or do references to touch suggest amorous warmth? This approach is designed to help you draw whatever conclusions you can about the author's—or the speaker's—taste or sensibility as a result of your study.

4. **THE EFFECT OF ONE FIGURE ON THE OTHER FIGURES AND IDEAS OF THE POEM.** The assumption of this approach is that each literary work is unified and organically whole, so that each part is closely related and inseparable from everything else. Usually it is best to pick a simile or metaphor that occurs at the beginning of the work and then determine how this figure influences your perception of the rest of the work. In an analysis of this sort, your aim is to consider the relationship of part to parts, and part to

whole. The beginning of Donne's "A Valedication: Forbidding Mourning," for example, contains a simile comparing the parting of the speaker and his woman friend to the quiet dying of "virtuous men." What is the effect of this comparison upon the rest of the poem? To help you in approaching such a question, you might always suppose something quite different— say, in this instance, the violent death of a condemned criminal, or the slaughter of a domestic animal. Such suppositions, out of place and inappropriate as they would obviously be in Donne's poem, may help you to see and then explain what is actually there in the work you are analyzing.

Conclusion

In your conclusion, you might summarize your main points, describe your general impressions, try to describe the impact of the figures, indicate your personal responses, or show what might further be done along the lines you have been developing in the body of your theme. If you know other works by the same writer, or other works by other writers with comparable or contrasting figures, you might briefly consider this other work and the light it might shed on your present analysis.

Sample Theme

A Study of Shakespeare's Metaphors in Sonnet 30

> When to the sessions of sweet silent thought,
> I summon up remembrance of things past,
> I sigh the lack of many a thing I sought,
> And with old woes new wail my dear time's waste:
> Then can I drown an eye (un-used to flow)   5
> For precious friends hid in death's dateless night,
> And weep afresh love's long since cancelled woe,
> And moan th'expense of many a vanished sight.
> And can I grieve at grievances foregone,
> And heavily from woe to woe tell o'er   10
> The sad account of fore-bemoaned moan,
> Which I new pay, as if not paid before.
> > But if the while I think on thee (dear friend)
> > All losses are restored, and sorrows end.

[1]   In this sonnet Shakespeare's speaker stresses the sadness and regret of remembered experience, but he states that a person with these feelings may be cheered by the thought of a friend. His metaphors, cleverly used,

[1]
create new and fresh ways of seeing personal life in this perspective.° He presents metaphors drawn from the public and business world of law courts, money, and banking or money handling.□

[2]
The courtroom metaphor of the first four lines shows that memories of past experience are constantly present and influential. Like a judge commanding defendants to appear in court, the speaker "summon[s]" his memory of "things past" to appear on trial before him. This metaphor suggests that people are their own judges and that their ideals and morals are like laws by which they measure themselves. The speaker finds himself guilty of wasting his time in the past. Removing himself, however, from the strict punishment that a real judge might require, he does not condemn himself for his "dear time's waste," but instead laments it (line 4). The metaphor is thus used to indicate that a person's consciousness is made up just as much of self-doubt and reproach as by more positive influences.

[3]
With the closely related reference of money in the next group of four lines, Shakespeare shows that living is a lifelong investment and is valuable for this reason. According to the money metaphor, living requires the spending of emotions and commitment to others. When friends move away and loved ones die, it is as though this expenditure has been lost. Thus, the speaker's dead friends are "precious" because he invested time and love in them, and the "sights" that have "vanished" from his eyes make him "moan" because he went to great "expense" for them (line 8).

[4]
Like the money metaphor, the metaphor of banking or money handling in the next four lines emphasizes that life's experiences are on deposit in the mind. They are recorded there, and may be withdrawn in moments of "sweet silent thought" just as a depositor may withdraw money. Thus, the speaker states that he counts out his woes just as a merchant or banker counts money ("And heavily from woe to woe *tell* o'er"). Because strong emotions still accompany his memories of mistakes made long ago, he pays again with "new" woe the accounts he had already paid with old woe in the past. The metaphor suggests that the past is so much a part of the present that a person never finishes paying both the principal and interest of past emotional investments. Because of this combination of banking and legal figures, the speaker indicates that his memory puts him in double jeopardy, for the thoughts of his losses overwhelm him in the present just as much as they did in the past.

[5]
The legal, financial, and money-handling metaphors combine in the last two lines to show how a healthy present life may overcome past regrets. The "dear friend" being addressed in these lines has the resources (financial) to settle all the emotional judgments that the speaker as a self-judge has made against himself (legal). It is as though the friend is a rich patron who rescues him from emotional bankruptcy (legal and financial) and the possible doom resulting from the potential sentence of emotional misery and depression (legal).

[6]
In these metaphors, therefore, Shakespeare's references are drawn from everyday public and business actions, but his use of them is creative, unusual, and excellent. In particular, the idea of line 8 ("And moan th'expense of many a vanished sight") stresses that people spend much emotional energy on others. Without such personal commitment, one cannot have precious friends and loved ones. In keeping with this metaphor of money and investment, one could measure life not in months or years, but in the spending of emotion

° Central idea
□ Thesis sentence

and involvement in personal relationships. Shakespeare, by inviting readers
[6]   to explore the values brought out by his metaphors, gives new insights into
the nature and value of life.

COMMENTARY ON THE THEME

This essay treats the three classes of metaphors that Shakespeare introduces
in Sonnet 30. It thus illustrates the second approach (p. 128). But the
aim of the discussion is not to explore the extent and nature of the comparison between the metaphors and the personal situations spoken about in
the sonnet. Instead, the goal is to explain how the metaphors develop
Shakespeare's meaning. This method therefore also illustrates the first
approach (pp. 127–28).

   In addition to providing a brief description of the sonnet, the introduction brings out the central idea and the thesis sentence. Paragraph 2 deals
with the meaning of Shakespeare's courtroom metaphor. His money metaphor is explained in paragraph 3. Paragraph 4 considers the banking or
money-handling figure. The fifth paragraph shows how Shakespeare's
last two lines bring together the three separate strands, or classes, of
metaphor. The conclusion comments generally on the creativity of Shakespeare's metaphors and also amplifies the way in which the money metaphor leads toward an increased understanding and valuation of life.

   Throughout the essay, transitions from one topic to the next are
brought about by linking words in the topic sentences. In paragraph 3,
for example, the words "closely related" and "next group" move the reader
from paragraph 2 to the new content. In paragraph 4, the words effecting
the transition are "like the money metaphor" and "the next four lines."
The opening sentence of paragraph 5 refers collectively to the subjects
of paragraphs 2, 3, and 4, thereby focusing them on the new topic of paragraph 5.

chapter 11

Writing About Symbolism and Allegory

Symbolism and **allegory** are like metaphor and simile because they are modes of literary expression that convey meaning through analogy and extension. They are unlike metaphors and similes, however, because their meaning is usually constant and continuous throughout a work. Symbolism (something "thrown together") implies a static meaning, while allegory ("something other than what is said") requires a moving, narrative structure. The idea underlying both modes is that writers use symbolism and allegory to express ideas and judgments that go beyond the surface texture.

SYMBOLISM

A symbol pulls or draws together (1) a specific thing with (2) ideas, values, persons, or ways of life, in direct relationship that normally would not be apparent. Another way to think of a symbol is to regard it as a stand-in or substitute for the elements being signified, much as the flag stands for the ideals of the nation.

In a literary work, whether story, drama, or poem, a symbol is a single person, thing, place, action, situation, or (sometimes) thought. It possesses its own reality and meaning, and may function at a level of reality compatible with the work. There is often a topical or integral relationship between the symbol and the things it stands for, but a symbol may also have no apparent connection and therefore may be arbitrary. What is important, however, is that a symbol points beyond itself to greater and more complex meaning. It is a conventionalized, shorthand form of conveying meaning. When a symbol is introduced, like a key opening a lock, it signifies a specific combination of attitudes, a sustained constancy of meaning, and the potential for wide-ranging application. A symbol might appear over and over again in the same work, and it always maintains the same meaning. Thus you might think of a symbol as a constant among variables, a theme with variations.

To test whether something is a symbol, you need to judge if it consistently refers beyond itself to a significant idea, emotion, or quality. For example, the ancient mythological character Sisyphus is a symbol because he has been connected with a specific set of ideas. According to legend, he is doomed for eternity to roll a large boulder up a high hill in the underworld. Just as he gets it to the top, it rolls down, and then he is fated to roll it up again, and again, and again. His plight is symbolic because it is a typical human condition: A person rarely if ever completes anything. If one day goes well, there is always the next day. Work needs doing again and again, and the same problems occur with only slight variations in all societies and governments at all times. In the light of such infinitely fruitless effort, life seems to have little meaning. Nevertheless, there is hope. Even people who are frustrated like Sisyphus do not give up, but stay involved. For this reason, work itself—the constant engagement in effort—gives life meaning; keeping busy makes sense even if things never seem to be finished. Any writer referring to Sisyphus would clearly intend symbolism of this kind.

Other symbols, like the myth of Sisyphus, are generally or universally recognized, and authors referring to them rely on this common understanding. Such symbols are *universal* or *cultural*. They embody ideas and emotions that writers and readers share as heirs of the same historical and cultural history. In using universal symbols, writers assume that readers already know their meaning. Thus water, the substance used in the sacrament of baptism, is recognized as a symbol of life. When clear water spouts up in a fountain, it symbolizes optimism (as upwelling, bubbling life). A stagnant pool, however, symbolizes the pollution and diminution of life. In terms of psychology, water is understood as a reference to sexuality. Thus, lovers may meet by a quiet lake, a cascading waterfall, a murmuring stream, a wide river, or a stormy sea. The condition of the water in each instance may be interpreted as a symbol of their romantic relationship. Another generally recognized symbol is the serpent, which represents the Devil, or Satan, or evil straight and simple. (It was in the form of a serpent, you may remember from Genesis 3:1–7, that Satan tempted Eve

in the Garden of Eden.) In "Young Goodman Brown," Nathaniel Hawthorne describes a walking stick that resembles a serpent, in this way
instantly evoking the idea of satanic evil.

Many objects and descriptions do not have this generally established
rank as symbols, and therefore they can be developed as symbols only
within an individual work. These types of symbols are *private, authorial,*
or *contextual.* Unlike universal symobls, these are not derived from our
common cultural or religious heritage, but rather gain their symbolic meaning within the context of a specific work. For example, the jug of beer
(porter) carried by Jackie's grandmother in "First Confession" (pp. 325–
31) symbolizes for Jackie the grandmother's peasantlike and boorish habits.
Similarly, Amy Lowell invests symbolic significance in the word "patterns"
in the poem "Patterns." There it is made clear that patterns symbolize
not only confining and stultifying cultural expectations, but the destructive
implementation of warfare. Symbolism of this sort, however, applies only
within the context of an individual work. If you encounter references to
porter or patterns in a context other than "First Confession" and "Patterns,"
they would not necessarily be symbolic unless they were designed to be
so by the author of that other work.

In determining whether a particular object, action, or character is a
symbol, you need to judge the context of the work. If the item in question
appears to be particularly important and also maintains a constancy of
meaning, you can justify claiming symbolic value for it. Miss Brill's fur
piece in Mansfield's "Miss Brill," for example, appears at the beginning
and ending of the story, and it contextually symbolizes her poverty and
isolation. At the end of Welty's "A Worn Path," Phoenix, the major character, plans to spend all her money for a toy windmill for her sick grandson.
Readers may conclude that the windmill is small and will break soon,
like her life and that of her grandson, but she wants to give the boy a
little pleasure despite her poverty and the hopelessness of both their lives.
For all these reasons, it is correct to interpret the windmill as a contextual
or authorial symbol of her strong character, generous nature, and pathetic
existence.

ALLEGORY

Like symbolism, an allegory describes one thing in terms of another. However, allegory is more complex and sustained than symbolism. An allegory
is to a symbol as a motion picture is to a still picture; allegory puts symbols
into sustained and consistent action. In form, an allegory is a complete
and self-sufficient narrative, but it also signifies another series of events
or conditions as expressed in a philosophy or religion. While some works

are allegories from beginning to end, many works that are not allegories contain sections or episodes that may be considered allegorically.

Allegories and the allegorical method do not exist simply to enable authors to engage in literary exercises. Rather, thinkers and writers have concluded that readers learn and memorize stories more easily than moral lessons. Thus, the allegorical method evolved so that listeners could be entertained and instructed at the same time. In addition, thought and expression have not always been free: The threat of censorship and reprisal has sometimes caused authors to express their views indirectly in the form of allegory rather than to write directly and risk being accused of libel or political attack.

As you study a work for allegory, you should try to determine how an entire story, or a self-contained episode, may be construed as having an extended, allegorical meaning. The recent popularity of the film *Star Wars* and its sequels, for example, is attributal at least partly to the fact that it is an allegory about the conflict between good and evil. Obi-Wan Kenobi (intelligence) enlists the aid of Luke Skywalker (heroism, boldness), and instructs him in "the Force" (moral or religious faith). Thus armed and guided, Skywalker opposes Darth Vader (evil, even though he dies a hero) to rescue the Princess Leia (purity and goodness) with the aid of the latest spaceships and weaponry (technology). The story is accompanied by ingenious visual effects and almost tactile sound effects and music; hence, as an adventure film, it stands by itself. With the obvious allegorical overtones, however, it stands for any person's quest for self-fulfillment.

To see how the allegory works, let us consider that Vader is so strong that he imprisons Skywalker for a time, and Skywalker must exert all his skill and strength to get free and overcome Vader. In the allegorical application of the episode to people generally, this temporary imprisonment signifies those moments of doubt, discouragement, and depression that people experience while trying to better themselves through education, work, self-improvement, friendship, marriage, or whatever. The idea is that as long as they persist, they will be able to overcome difficulty and win out.

In one form or another, this interpretation of life has been represented again and again in allegorical form. In ancient Greece, two such allegories were the story of Jason, who sails the *Argonaut* to distant lands to gain the golden fleece, and Bellerephon, who rides Pegasus to destroy the monster Chimera. In Old English times another story was about Beowulf, who rescues many people by destroying the bloodthirsty Grendel and his equally monstrous mother. In Bunyan's *The Pilgrim's Progress*, the hero, Christian, overcomes difficulties and temptations to reach the Heavenly City. Allegory, in short, is as old as the capacity of human beings to embody their views of life in literary form. As long as the parallels between a story and its allegorical counterpart are consistent, like those mentioned here, an extended allegorical interpretation has validity.

FABLE, PARABLE, AND MYTH

Three additional forms that are close to allegory, but which are special types, are **fable, parable,** and **myth.**

FABLE.   A fable is a short story, often featuring animals with human traits, to which writers and editors attach morals or explanations. Such stories are often called *beast fables*. The ancient writer Aesop's fable of "The Fox and the Grapes," for example, signifies the human tendency to demean things we cannot have. More recent contributions to the fable tradition are Walt Disney's stories about Mickey Mouse and Walt Kelly's comic strips about Pogo.

PARABLE.   A parable is a short, simple allegory. Parables are associated with Chirst, who used them in his teaching to embody religious insights and truth. Parables like those of the Good Samaritan and the Prodigal Son are interpreted to show God's active love, concern, understanding, and forgiveness for human beings.

MYTH.   A myth, like the myth of Sisyphus, is a story associated with the religion, philosophy, and collective psychology of various societies or cultures. Myths embody truths for prescientific socieities, and codify the social and cultural values of the civilization in which they were written. Unfortunately, the word *mythical* is sometimes used to mean "fanciful" or "untrue." This minimizing of the word reflects a limited appreciation of the psychological, philosophical, and scientific value of myths. In fact, the truths embodied in mythology are not to be found literally in the stories themselves, but rather in their symbolic or allegorical interpretations.

ALLUSIVENESS IN SYMBOLISM AND ALLEGORY

Universal or cultural symbols and allegories often allude to other works from our cultural heritage, such as politics, current events, the Bible, ancient history and literature, and works of the British and American traditions. For example, a major character in Hawthorne's "Young Goodman Brown" is Brown's wife, Faith, who stays at home when he leaves to go on his journey. Later, in the forest, when Brown is seeing his vision of sinful human beings, he exclaims, "My Faith is gone" (p. 310). On the primary level of reading, this statement makes perfect sense, because Brown has concluded that his wife is lost. However, the symbol of his being married to Faith takes on additional meaning when one notes that it is also an allusion to the biblical book of Ephesians (2:8), and to the Protestant-Calvinist tradition that faith is a key to salvation:

> For by grace you have been saved through faith; and this is not your own doing, it is the gift of God—

This biblical passage might easily take a volume of explication, but in brief the allusion makes clear that Brown's loss of faith also indicates his belief that he has been abandoned by God. Here is an instance where a symbol gains its resonance and impact through allusion.

This example brings up the issue of how much background you need for detecting allusions in symbolism and allegory. You can often rely on your own knowledge. Sometimes, however, an allusion may escape you if you do not pursue the point in a dictionary or other reference work. The scope of your college dictionary will surprise you. If you cannot find an entry in your dictionary, however, try one of the major encyclopedias, or ask your reference librarian about standard guides like *The Oxford Companion to English Literature*, *The Oxford Companion to Classical Literature*, and William Rose Benet's *The Reader's Encyclopedia*. A useful aid in finding biblical references is *Cruden's Complete Concordance*, which has been used by scholars and readers in various editions for more than two centuries (since 1737). This work lists all the major words used in the King James Version of the Bible, so that you may easily locate the chapter and verse of any biblical quotation. If you still have trouble after using sources like these, see your instructor for more help.

WRITING ABOUT SYMBOLISM
OR ALLEGORY

Take careful notes on your story, and, in the light of the introductory discussion in this chapter, test the material to determine parallels that establish the presence of symbolism or allegory. A helpful aid in studying symbolism is to make a list, the purpose of which is to show how qualities of the symbol may be lined up with qualities of a character or action. Such a list can give you the substance for much in your essay, and it can also help you in thinking more deeply about the effectiveness of the symbol. Here is such a list for the symbol of the toy windmill in Welty's "A Worn Path":

Qualities in the Windmill	Comparable Qualities in Phoenix and Her Life
1. Cheap 2. Breakable 3. A gift 4. Not practical 5. Colorful	1. Poor, but she gives all she has for the windmill 2. Old, and not far from death 3. Generous 4. Needs some relief from reality and practicality 5. Same as 4

An aid for figuring out an allegory or allegorical passage can work well with a diagram of parallel lines or boxes. You can place corresponding characters, actions, things, or ideas along these lines as follows (using the film *Star Wars* as the specimen work):

STAR WARS

Luke Skywalker	Obi Wan Kenobi	Darth Vader	Princess Leia	Capture	Escape, and defeat of Vader

ALLEGORICAL APPLICATION TO MORALITY AND FAITH

Forces of good	Education and faith	Forces of evil	Object to be saved, ideals to be rescued and restored	Doubt, spiritual negligence	Restoration of faith

ALLEGORICAL APPLICATION TO PERSONAL AND GENERAL CONCERNS

Individual in pursuit of goals	The means by which goals may be reached	Obstacles to be overcome	Occupation, happiness, goals	Temporary failure, depression, discouragement, disappointment	Success

Introduction

When you discuss symbolism and allegory, try to relate your topic to the general nature of the work. Thus, symbols of one type might appear at the beginning of a work; symbols of another type might be appropriate at the end. At the beginning of "Young Goodman Brown," for example, the symbols are colorful and domestic, while at the end they are infernal and dark. The opening of "First Confession" introduces symbols of the home and kitchen, but the ending includes the symbols of both confessional and candy; these refer to the rightness and, by extension, the sweetness of the boy hero's religious initiation. In Mansfield's "Miss Brill," the opening and closing of the box containing Miss Brill's fur piece may be construed as symbols of her solitude. You should also briefly explain and justify whatever claims you make about symbolism and allegory. In Glaspell's *Trifles*, for example, two women discover a dead canary in Mrs. Wright's sewing box. Why does this bird symbolize her life with her murdered husband, and how does it explain her actions? Your introduction is the right place to present an overview of fuller answers and explanations to follow. Your central idea and thesis sentence should be here, to prepare your reader for the body of your essay.

Body

You have a number of choices in your approach to symbolism and allegory. You might wish to use one exclusively, or a combination.

If you write about symbolism, you can proceed in one of the following ways:

1. THE MEANING OF A MAJOR SYMBOL.   Here you interpret the symbol and show what it stands for both inside and outside the work. A few of the questions you might pursue are these: How do you determine that the symbol is a symbol? How do you derive from the work a reasonable interpretation of the symbolic meaning? What is the extent of the meaning? Does the symbol undergo any modification if it reappears in the work? By the same token, does the symbol affect your understanding of other parts of the work? How? Does the author create any ironies by using the symbol? Does the symbol give any special strength to the work?

2. THE MEANING AND RELATIONSHIP OF A NUMBER OF SYMBOLS.   What are the symbols? Do they have any specific connection or common bond? Do they suggest a unified reading or a contradictory one? Are the symbols contextual or universal? How can you justify your answer to this question? Do the symbols control the form of the work? How? For example, Mrs. Popov's attitude toward the horse, Toby, in *The Bear* symbolizes the shifting of her love and loyalty, which constitutes one of the major structures in the play. The symbol of the barren waste in Frost's "Desert Places" develops a dual meaning as the poem unfolds, referring clearly both to bleakness of soul and the natural landscape. The star that the speaker addresses in Keats's "Bright Star" is a symbol that governs the movement of ideas from personal integrity to love. Other questions you may consider are whether the symbols fit naturally or artificially into the context of the

work, or whether and how the writer's symbols make for unique qualities or excellences.

If you write about allegory, you might use one of the following approaches:

1. THE APPLICATION OF THE ALLEGORY. Does the allegory (fable, parable, myth) refer to anything or anyone specific? Does it refer to an action important in a particular period of history? Or does the allegory refer more broadly to general ideas or certain aspects of human character? Does it illustrate, either closely or loosely, particular philosophies or religious views? If so, what are these? If the original meaning of the allegory seems apparently dated or obsolete, how much meaning can be applied to life at the present time?

2. THE CONSISTENCY OF THE ALLEGORY. Is the allegory maintained consistently throughout the work, or is it intermittently used and dropped? Explain and detail this use. If the work does not seem to be an allegory from beginning to end, can you say that parts of it are allegorical? That is, can you determine that particular actions or scenes of the work lend themselves to allegorical interpretation? For example, the details about the natural obstacles in the woods in Welty's "A Worn Path" may be taken as allegorical equivalents of various difficulties in life. The walk that Nora and Jackie take from home to the confession may be read allegorically to refer to the religious idea that God's ways are not human ways. Positively, does such an allegorical interpretation seem functional and consistent with the scope and ideas of the work, or, negatively, does it in any way seem digressive or inconsistent?

Conclusion

You might summarize your main points, describe your general impressions, try to describe the impact of the symbolic or allegorical methods, indicate your personal responses, or show what further might be done along the lines you have been developing in the body. You might also assess the quality of the symbolism or allegory and make a statement about the appropriateness of the specific details to the applied ideas.

Sample Theme

Allegory and Symbolism in Hawthorne's "Young Goodman Brown"[*]

[1] It is hard to read beyond the third paragraph of "Young Goodman Brown" without finding allegory and symbolism. The opening seems realistic—Goodman Brown, a young Puritan, leaves his home in colonial Salem to take an overnight trip—but his wife's name, "Faith," immediately suggests a symbolic reading. As soon as Brown goes into the forest, however, it becomes clear that his journey is an allegorical trip into the acquisition of evil. The idea that Hawthorne shows by the walk is that rigid and rigorous belief destroys the best human qualities, such as understanding and love.[°] He develops this thought in the allegory and in many symbols, particularly the sunset, the walking stick, and the path.[□]

[2] The allegory portrays how individuals may develop destructively rigid views on life. Most of the events that occur on the walk are dreamlike and unreal, and the ideas that Brown acquires are similarly unreal and unfounded. After the weird night, he thinks of his wife and neighbors not with love, but with hatred for their supposed depravity, which he learns about during the "witch meeting" deep in the dream forest. Because he finds certainty despite the unreality of his dream vision, he rigidly and rigorously sees evil in everyone around him, and he lives out his remaining life in unforgiving harshness. The story thus allegorizes the loss of perspective that makes it acceptable and even orthodox for people to value wrongful ideals more than understanding, forgiveness, and love.

[3] Hawthorne's attack on such dehumanizing belief is found not just in the allegory, but also in his many symbols. For example, the seventh word in the story, "sunset," is a symbol. In reality, sunset merely indicates the end of day. Coming at the beginning of the story, however, it suggests that Goodman Brown is beginning the long night of his hatred, his spiritual death. For him the night will never end because his final days are shrouded in "gloom" (p. 332). The symbol suggests that Brown, like anyone else who gives up on human beings, is cut off from humanity, and is locked within an inner prison of bitterness.

[4] The next symbol, the walking stick, suggests the ambiguous and arbitrary standard by which Brown judges his neighbors. The stick is carried by the guide who looks like Brown's father. It "might almost be seen to twist and wriggle itself like a living serpent" (pp. 305–6). The serpent symbolically suggests Satan, who tempted Adam and Eve (Genesis 3:1–7). However, the staff is also still a walking stick, and in this respect it is just a normal and innocent part of life. This double meaning squares with the speaker's attribution to Brown of "the instinct that guides mortal man to evil" (p. 310). Such evil is

---

[*]See Appendix C for the text of this story, pp. 304–13.
[°]Central idea
[□]Thesis sentence

[4]   the passionate suspicion and condemnation of wrong in others, even without
        the support of facts.
               In the same vein, the path through the forest is a major symbol of the
        destructive mental confusion that overcomes Brown. As he walks, the path
        before him grows "wilder and drearier, and more faintly traced," and "at length"
        it vanishes (p. 310). This is like the biblical description of the "broad" way
        that leads "to Destruction" (Matthew 7:13). As a symbol, the path shows that
        most human acts are bad, while a small number, like the "narrow" way to
[5]   life (Matthew 7:14), are good. Goodman Brown's path is at first clear, as though
        sin is at first unique and unusual. Soon, however, it is so indistinct that he
        can see only sin wherever he turns. The symbol suggests that as people
        follow evil, their moral vision becomes blurred and they cannot choose the
        right way even if it is in front of them. With such vision, their best instincts
        are buried, and they become agents of evil rather than of the good they profess
        and claim to represent.
               Through Hawthorne's allegory and symbols, then, "Young Goodman
        Brown" presents the paradoxes of how a seemingly good system can lead to
        bad results and also of how noble beliefs can backfire destructively. Goodman
        Brown's life is dreary and unproductive, and he dies in gloom because he
        cannot see anything beyond his own misguided beliefs. He himself symbolizes
        the form of evil that is the hardest to overcome, because wrongdoers who
[6]   are convinced of their own goodness are beyond reach. Such a blend of evil
        and self-righteousness, whether cloaked in the apparent virtues of Puritanism
        or of some other blindly rigorous doctrine (political as well as religious), causes
        Hawthorne to write that "the fiend in his own shape is less hideous than
        when he rages in the breast of man" (p. 310). Young Goodman Brown thus
        is the central symbol of the story. He is one of those who walk in darkness
        while thinking that he is bathed in the light of true faith.

COMMENTARY ON THE THEME

The introduction justifies the treatment of allegory and symbolism because
of the way in which Hawthorne early in the story invites such a reading.
The central idea relates Hawthorne's method to the idea that rigid belief
destroys the best human qualities. The thesis sentence outlines two major
areas of discussion: (1) allegory and (2) symbolism.

Paragraph 2 considers the allegory as a criticism of rigid Puritan
morality. Paragraphs 3, 4, and 5 deal with three major symbols: sunset,
walking stick, and path. The aim of this discussion is to show the meaning
and applicability of these symbols to Hawthorne's attack on rigidity of
belief. Throughout these three paragraphs the central idea—the relationship of rigidity to destructiveness—is stressed. Hawthorne's allusions to
both the Old and New Testaments are pointed out in paragraphs 4 and
5. The last paragraph raises questions leading to the conclusion that Brown
himself symbolizes Hawthorne's idea that the primary cause of evil is
the inability to separate reality from unreality, which results in instant condemnation and morose alienation rather than a search for understanding.

chapter 12

Writing About Comparison-Contrast and Extended Comparison-Contrast

In a theme of this type you may compare and contrast different authors, two or more works by the same author, different drafts of the same work, or characters, incidents, and ideas in the same work or different works. Not only is comparison-contrast popular in literature courses, but it is one of the more useful approaches for other disciplines. The ideas of philosophers may be compared, or views of human behavior, or economic or political theories, or approaches to painting or sculpture. The possibilities for comparison-contrast are extensive.

COMPARISON-CONTRAST AS A WAY TO KNOWLEDGE

Comparison and contrast are important ways to gain understanding because individual characteristics of a thing stand out when it is placed side by side with something else. For example, a comparison may enhance our understanding of both Shakespeare's Sonnet 30, "When to the Sessions of Sweet Silent Thought," and Christina Rossetti's lyric poem "Echo" (see pp. 129 and 217–18). We immediately see that both poems treat personal recollections of past experiences. In each poem, a speaker is imagined to be addressing a presumed listener, and we as readers are cast in the role of looking on and overhearing the speech. We may notice that each poem refers to persons now dead, with whom the speaker was closely involved.

There are important differences, however. In Shakespeare's poem, the dead persons are "precious friends" who are mentioned incidentally as a part of the focus on the speaker's regret and sorrow, while Rossetti refers specifically to a dead person with whom the speaker had been in love. In fact, the speaker is addressing this dead person. Rossetti's topic is the sorrow of lost love, the irrevocability of past events, and the present loneliness of the speaker. Shakespeare includes the references to dead friends as a way of accounting for current sadness, but then his speaker turns to the present and asserts that thinking about the "dear friend" being addressed (who is alive) enables him to overcome past "losses" and "sorrows." There is no such reconciliation of past and present in Rossetti's poem; instead, the speaker focuses entirely upon the sadness of the present moment. Thus, though both poems are retrospective, Shakespeare's poem moves toward the present while Rossetti's remains in the past.

There is much more to the poems, but you may see that such comparison enables the viewing of each work in perspective and thereby facilitates understanding of the works separately. No matter what works you use for comparison-contrast, the method will be similarly effective in helping you isolate and highlight individual characteristics, because the quickest way to get at the essence of an artistic work is to compare it with something else. Similarities are brought out by comparison, and differences are shown by contrast. In other words, you can find out what a thing *is* by using comparison-contrast to discover what it *is not*.

CLARIFY YOUR INTENTION

Your first problem in planning a theme of comparison-contrast is to decide on a goal, for you may use the method in a number of ways. One objective may be the equal and mutual illumination of both (or more) works. Thus, an essay comparing O'Connor's "First Confession" with Hawthorne's "Young Goodman Brown" (see pp. 325–31 and 304–13) might be designed (1) to compare ideas, characters, or methods in these stories equally, without stressing or favoring either. But you might also wish (2) to emphasize "Young Goodman Brown," and therefore you would use "First Confession" as material for highlighting Hawthorne's work. In addition, you might also use the comparison-contrast method (3) to show your liking of one work at the expense of another, or (4) to emphasize a method or idea that you think is especially noteworthy or appropriate.

A first task is therefore to decide what to emphasize. The first sample essay (pp. 151–53) reflects a decision to give equal time to both works being considered, without any claims for the superiority of either. Unless you want to pursue a different rhetorical goal, you may find this essay a suitable model for most comparisons.

FIND COMMON GROUNDS
FOR COMPARISON

The second stage in planning and sketching out the theme is to select the proper material—the grounds of your discussion. It is pointless to compare dissimilar things, for then your conclusions will be of limited value. You need to put the works or writers onto common ground. Compare like with like: idea with idea, characterization with characterization, imagery with imagery, point of view with point of view, problem with problem. Nothing much can be learned from a comparison of "Welty's view of courage and Chekhov's view of love," but a comparison of "The relationship of love to stability and courage in Chekhov and Welty" suggests common ground, with the promise of important things to be learned through the examination of similarities and differences.

In seeking common ground, you may need to be ingenious. You know, for example, that you cannot easily add dissimilar mathematical fractions unless you first develop a common denominator. The same thing applies if you compare works of literature—say, De Maupassant's "The Necklace" and Chekhov's *The Bear*—for this story and play seem just as unlike as three fourths and two thirds. Yet a common denominator can be found, such as "The Treatment of Self-Deceit," "The Effects of Chance on Human Affairs," and "The View of Women," among others. Although at first appearance many other works may seem more dissimilar than these, it is usually possible to find a suitable frame of reference that permits analytical comparison and contrast. Much of your success in writing this theme depends on your ingenuity in finding a workable basis—a common denominator—for comparison.

METHODS OF COMPARISON

Let us assume that you have decided on your rhetorical purpose and on the basis or bases of your comparison. You have done your reading, taken your notes, and have an idea of what you want to say. The remaining problem is the treatment of your material.

A common treatment is to make your points first about one work, and then to do the same for the other. This method serves the purpose, but it has the drawback of making your paper seem like two big lumps (i.e., "work 1" takes up one half of your paper, and "work 2" takes up the other half). Also, the method causes repetition, because the treatment of the second work requires restatement of the points of comparison established with the first. While this method is satisfactory, it has obvious defects.

A superior method, therefore, is to treat the major aspects of your main idea, and to refer to the two (or more) writers as their works support your arguments. Thus, you refer constantly to both writers, sometimes within the same sentence, and remind your reader of the point of your discussion. There are reasons for the superiority of this method: (1) You do not repeat your points needlessly, for you document them as you raise them. (2) By constantly referring to the two works in relation to your common ground of comparison, you make your points without requiring a reader with a poor memory to reread previous sections. Frequently such readers do not bother to reread (alas), and as a result they are never clear about what you have said.

As a model, here is a paragraph from a student essay on "Natural References as a Basis of Comparison in Frost's 'Desert Places' and Shakespeare's Sonnet 73, 'That Time of Year Thou Mayest in Me Behold' " (for texts, see pp. 344 and 355–56). The virtue of the paragraph is that it uses material from both poems simultaneously (as nearly as the time sequence of sentences allows) as the substance for the development of the ideas:

> [1] Both writers link their ideas to events occurring in the natural world. [2] Night as a parallel with death is common to both poems, with Frost speaking about it in his first line, and Shakespeare introducing it in his seventh. [3] Along with night, Frost emphasizes the onset of winter and snow as a time of death and desolation. [4] With this natural description, Frost also symbolically refers to empty, secret, dead places in the inner spirit—crannies of the soul where bleak winter snowfalls correspond to selfishness and indifference to others. [5] By contrast, Shakespeare uses the fall season, with the yellowing and dropping of leaves and also the flying away of birds, to stress the closeness of real death and therefore also the need to love fully during the time remaining. [6] Both poems thus share a sense of gloom, because both present death as inevitable and final, just like the oncoming season of barrenness and waste. [7] Because Shakespeare's sonnet is addressed to a listener who is also a loved one, however, it is more outgoing than the more introspective poem of Frost. [8] Frost turns the snow, the night, and the emptiness of the universe inwardly in order to show the speaker's inner bleakness, and by extension, the bleakness of many human spirits. [9] Shakespeare instead uses the bleakness of seasons, night, and dying fires to state the need for loving "well." [10] The poems thus use common and similar references for different purposes and effects.

Letting *S* and *F* stand for ideas about Shakespeare and Frost respectively, the paragraph may be schematized as follows (numbers refer to the bracketed sentence numbers):

1 = F,S; 2 = F,S; 3 = F; 4 = F; 5 = S; 6 = F,S; 7 = F,S; 8 = F; 9 = S; 10 = F,S.

The scheme shows that this model paragraph links Shakespeare's references to nature with those of Frost. Half the sentences speak of both authors together; three speak of Frost alone, and two of Shakespeare alone, but all the sentences are unified topically. This interweaving of references indicates that the writer has learned both poems well enough to think of them at the same moment. Mental "digestion" has taken place.

You can learn from this example: If you develop your essay by putting your two subjects together constantly, you will write more economically and pointedly than by the first method (not only for themes, but also for tests). Beyond that, if you actually digest the material as successfully as this method indicates, you demonstrate that you have fulfilled one of the major goals of education—the assimilation and *use* of material. Too often, because you learn things separately (in separate courses, in separate works, at separate times), you may keep them distinct and compartmentalized in your mind. But instead, you should always try to relate them, to put them together, to *synthesize* them. Comparison and contrast help in this process of putting together, of seeing things not as separate fragments but as parts of wholes.

AVOID THE "TENNIS-BALL" METHOD

As you make your comparison, do not confuse an interlocking method with a "tennis-ball" method, in which you bounce your subject back and forth constantly and repetitively, almost as though you were hitting observations back and forth over a net. The tennis-ball method is shown in the following example from a comparison of the characters Mathilde (De Maupassant's "The Necklace") and Miss Brill (Mansfield's "Miss Brill"):

> Mathilde is young and married, while Miss Brill is an aging spinster. Mathilde has a social life, while Miss Brill is alone and lonely. Mathilde's daydreams about wealth bring about her fussiness and her resulting misfortune, but Miss Brill's daydreams about her self-importance do not hurt her until they are shattered by the rude boy and girl. Therefore, Mathilde is made unhappy because of her own shortcomings, while Miss Brill is a helpless victim. The focus in Mathilde's case is on adversity causing not only trouble but also the strengthening of character, and in Miss Brill's case the focus is on the weak getting hurt and therefore being made weaker.

This 1,2—1,2—1,2 order might be acceptable for a few sentences, or even for a paragraph, but try to imagine an entire theme written in this way (don't scream). Aside from the repeated and unvaried patterning of subjects, the tennis-ball method does not permit much illustrative development. You should not feel so cramped that you cannot take a number of sentences to develop a point about one writer or subject before you include comparative references to another. If you remember to interlock the two subjects of comparison, however, as in the paragraph about Frost and Shakespeare, your method will give you the freedom to develop your topics fully.

THE EXTENDED COMPARISON-CONTRAST THEME

For a longer essay, such as a limited research paper or the sort of extended theme required at the end of a semester, the technique of comparison-contrast may be used for three, four, or many works. The extended theme may also be adapted for tests, including general, comprehensive questions. Such questions require that you treat ideas, influences, or methods in a number of works (see also pp. 292–94).

For themes of this larger scope, you will still need to develop common grounds for comparison, although with more than two works you will need to modify the method.

Let us assume that you have been assigned not just two works but five or six. You need first to find a common ground to use as your central, unifying idea, just as you do for a comparison of only two works. When you take your notes, sketch out your ideas, make your early drafts, and rearrange and shape your developing materials, try to think about the works as they relate to your points of comparison. As an illustration, please note that the second sample theme (pp. 154–57) compares all the works on the common basis that they speak about the nature of love and devoted service. While each work is unique, they are all alike in dealing with this single topic, this "common denominator."

Once you establish a topic for comparison, you should classify or group your works on the basis of whether they are alike or different with regard to the topic. Let us assume that three or four works treat a topic in one way, while two or three do it in another. In writing about these works, you might treat the topic itself in a straightforward comparison-contrast method, but use details from the works within the groupings as the material that you use for illustration and argument. To make your theme as specific as possible, it is wise to stress only two major works with each of your subpoints. Once you have established these points in detail, there is no need to go into similar detail with all the other works being discussed. Instead, you may refer to the other works briefly, with your purpose being to strengthen your points but not to create more and more examples. Once you go to another subpoint, you may stress different works, so that by the end of your theme you will have given due attention to each work in your assignment. In this way—by treating many works as groups of twos—you can keep your essay within limits, for there is no need for unproductive detail.

As an example of how works may be grouped in this way, please refer to the second sample essay (pp. 154–57). There, four works are included in a general category of how love and service offer guidance and stability. This group is contrasted with another group of three works (including two characters from one of the works in the first group), in which love is shown as an escape or retreat.

DOCUMENTATION AND THE EXTENDED COMPARISON-CONTRAST THEME

For the longer comparison-contrast paper you may find a problem in documentation. Generally, you do not need to locate page numbers for references to major traits, ideas, and actions. For example, if you refer to the end of O'Connor's "First Confession," where the priest gives Jackie some candy, you may assume that your reader is also familiar with this action. You do not need to do any more than make the reference.

But if you quote lines or passages, or if you cite actions or characters in special ways, you may need to use parenthetical page references, as described in Joseph Gibaldi and Walter S. Achtert, *MLA Handbook for Writers of Research Papers*, 2nd ed. (discussed in Appendix B, pp. 299–302). If you are using lines or parts of lines of poetry, use line numbers parenthetically, as in the second sample essay. Be guided by the following principle: If you make a specific reference that you think your reader might want to examine in more detail, supply the line or page number. If you refer to minor details that might easily have been unnoticed or forgotten, also supply the line or page number. Otherwise, if you refer to major ideas, actions, or characterizations, be sure to make your internal reference clear enough so that your reader can easily recall it from his or her memory of the work. Then you will not need to provide line or page numbers.

WRITING A COMPARISON-CONTRAST ESSAY

First, narrow and simplify your subject so that you can handle it conveniently. For example, if you compare Amy Lowell and Wilfred Owen (as in the first sample theme), pick out one or two poems of each poet (on identical or approximately equal topics), and write your theme about these. You must be wary, however, of the limitations of your selection, because generalizations made from one or two works may not apply to all works of the same writers.

Introduction

State what works, authors, characters, or ideas are under consideration. Then show how you have narrowed the topic of your comparison. Your central idea should be a brief statement highlighting the principal grounds of comparison and contrast, such as that both works treat a common topic, exhibit a similar idea, use a similar form, develop an identical attitude, and so on, and also that major or minor differences between the works are important in making each of them unique. You may assert that one work is superior to the other if you wish to make this judgment and defend it. Your thesis sentence should contain the topics you plan to develop in the body of the theme.

Body

The body of your theme depends on the points you have chosen for comparison. You might be comparing two works on the basis of point of view or the use of metaphorical language, two authors on ideas, or two characters on their character traits. In your discussion, you would necessarily use the same methods as for writing about a single work, except that here (1) you exemplify your points with more than one subject, and (2) your main purpose is to shed light on both topics of comparison.

In this sense, your discussions of point of view, metaphorical language, or whatever are not so much designed to explain these topics as topics, but rather to explore similarities and differences between the two works. Let us say that you are comparing ideas. Of course you will need to explain the idea or ideas, but only enough to make your point clear that the two works are either similar or different. As you develop this theme about comparative ideas, you might illustrate your arguments by referring to the authors' uses of elements like setting, point of view, or metaphor. When you introduce these new subjects, you will be right on target as long as you use them comparatively.

No matter what evidence you introduce, you should use your explanations to help achieve your overall goal of comparison and contrast. Thus, in stories, different points of view might show authorial certainty or uncertainty about an idea, about human nature, or about life in general. In plays, similar characters may reflect similar religious or philosophical outlooks. In poems, dissimilar uses of similar topics might indicate dissimilar sensitivities or perceptions by the poets. What you decide to say about such topics will depend on the points you have chosen for comparison.

Conclusion

Here you may reflect on other ideas or techniques in the works you have compared, make observations about similar qualities, or summarize briefly the grounds of your comparison. The conclusion of an extended comparison-contrast theme should represent a final bringing together of your materials. In the body of your theme, you may not have referred to all the works in each paragraph; however, in your conclusion you should try to include them all.

If your writers belong to any "period" or "school," you also might wish to show in your conclusion how they relate to these larger movements. References of this sort provide an obvious common ground for comparison and contrast.

First Sample Theme (Two Works)

*The Treatment of Human Responses to War in Amy Lowell's "Patterns" and Wilfred Owen's "Anthem for Doomed Youth"**

---

[1]
    "Patterns" and "Anthem for Doomed Youth" are both powerful and unique condemnations of war.° Owen's short poem speaks broadly and generally about the ugliness of war and also about large groups of bereaved people, while Lowell's longer poem focuses upon the personal grief of just one person. In a real sense, Lowell's poem begins where Owen's ends, a fact that accounts for both the similarities and differences between the two works. The anti-war themes may be compared on the basis of their subjects, their lengths, their concreteness, and their use of a common major metaphor.□

[2]
    "Anthem for Doomed Youth" attacks war more directly than "Patterns." Owen's opening line, "What passing bells for those who die as cattle," suggests that in war human beings are depersonalized before they are slaughtered, like so much meat, while his observations about the "monstrous" guns and the "shrill, demented" shells unambiguously condemn the horrors of war. By contrast, in "Patterns" warfare is far away, on another continent, intruding only when the messenger delivers the letter stating that the speaker's fiancé has been killed (lines 63–64). Similar news governs the last six lines of Owen's poem, quietly describing the responses of those at home to the news that their loved ones have died in war. Thus, the anti-war focus in "Patterns" is the contrast between the calm, peaceful life of the speaker's garden and the anguish of her responses, while in Owen's poem the stress is more the external horrors of war which bring about the need for ceremonies honoring the dead. Both poems attack war, but in different ways.

[3]
    Another difference, which is perhaps something of a surprise, is that Owen's poem is less than one seventh as long as Lowell's. "Patterns" is an interior monologue or meditation of 107 lines, but it could not realistically be shorter. In the poem the speaker thinks about the present and past, and contemplates the future loneliness to which her intended husband's death has doomed

---

*For the texts of these poems, see Appendix C, pp. 353 and 357.
° Central idea
□ Thesis sentence

her. Her final outburst, "Christ, what are patterns for?" could make no sense if she does not explain her situation as extensively as she does. On the other hand, "Anthem for Doomed Youth" is brief—a fourteen-line sonnet—because it is more general and less personal than "Patterns." Although Owen's speaker shows sympathy for individuals, he or she views the sorrows of others distantly, unlike Lowell, who goes right into the mind and spirit of the grieving woman. [3] Owen's use, in his last six lines, of phrases like "tenderness of patient minds" and "drawing down of blinds" is a short but powerful represention of deep grief. He presents no further detail even though thousands of individual stories might be told. In contrast, Lowell tells one of these stories as she focuses on her solitary speaker's lost hopes and dreams. Thus, the contrasting lengths of the poems are governed by each poet's treatment of the topic.

Despite these differences of approach and length, both poems are similarly concrete and vivid. Owen moves from the real scenes and sounds of battlefields to the homes of the many doomed soldiers who are now dead, while Lowell's scene is a single place—the garden of the estate where the speaker has just received news of her lover's death. Her speaker walks on gravel along garden paths that contain daffodils, squills, a fountain, and a [4] lime tree. She thinks of her clothing and her ribboned shoes, and also of her fiancé's boots, sword hilts, and buttons. The images in Owen's poem are equally real, but are not associated with any individuals: cattle, bells, rifle shots, shells, bugles, candles, and window blinds. While the poems thus reflect the reality of life, Owen's details are more general, public, and comprehensive, whereas Lowell's are more centralized, personal, and intimate.

Along with this concreteness, the poems share a major metaphor: that cultural patterns both control and frustrate human wishes, plans, and hopes. In "Patterns" this metaphor is shown in warfare itself (line 106), which is the supremely destructive political structure, or pattern. Further examples of the metaphor are found in details about clothing (particularly the speaker's stiff, confining gown in lines 5, 18, 21, 73, and 100, but also the lover's military boots in lines 46 and 49); the orderly, formal garden paths in which the speaker is walking (lines 1, 93); her restraint at hearing of her lover's death; and her courtesy, despite her grief, in ordering that the messenger take refreshment (line 69). Within such rigid patterns, her hopes for happiness have vanished, [5] along with the sensuous spontaneity represented by her lover's plans to make love with her on a "shady seat" in the garden (lines 85–89). The metaphor of the constricting pattern may also be seen in "Anthem for Doomed Youth," except that in this poem the pattern is the funeral, not love or marriage. Owen's speaker contrasts the calm, peaceful tolling of "passing bells" (line 1) with the frightening sounds of war represented by the "monstrous anger of the guns," "the rifles' rapid rattle," and "the demented choirs of wailing shells" (lines 2–8). Thus, while Lowell uses the metaphor to reveal the irony of hope and desire being destroyed by war, Owen uses it to reveal the irony of war's nullification and perversion of peaceful ceremonies.

Though the poems in these ways share topics and some aspects of treatment, they are distinct and individual. "Patterns" is mainly visual and kinesthetic, whereas "Anthem for Doomed Youth" is strongly auditory. Both [6] poems conclude on powerfully emotional although different notes. Owen's poem dwells on the pathos and sadness that war brings to many unnamed people, while Lowell's expresses the most intimate thoughts of a particular woman in the first agony of sorrow. Although neither poem directly attacks the usual platitudes and justifications for war (the needs to mobilize, to sacrifice, to

achieve peace through fighting, and so on), the attack is there by implication, for both poems make their appeal by stressing how war destroys those relation-
[6]   ships that make life worth living. For this reason, despite their differences and their uniqueness, both "Patterns" and "Anthem for Doomed Youth," are parallel anti-war poems, and both are strong portrayals of human feeling.

COMMENTARY ON THE THEME

This example illustrates how approximately equal time can be given to each work being compared, with the goal of explaining similarities and differences on a common ground of comparison. Because the theme shifts continually from one work to the other, particular phrases may be noticed. When the works are similar or even identical, terms are "common," "share," "and," "both," "similar," and "also." For comparative situations, words like "longer" and "more" are useful. Differences are marked by "by contrast," "while," "whereas," "different," "dissimilar," and "on the other hand." Transitions from paragraph to paragraph are not different in this type of theme from those in other themes. Thus, "despite," "along with this concreteness," and "in these ways" are used here, but they could be used anywhere for the same purpose.

The central idea of the theme is that the poems mutually condemn war. This idea is brought out in the introductory paragraph, together with the supporting idea that the poems blend into each other because both show responses to news of battle casualties. The thesis sentence concluding the first paragraph indicates four topics to be explored in the body of the theme.

Paragraph 2, the first in the body, discusses how each poem brings out its attack on warfare. Paragraph 3 explains the differing lengths of the poems as a function of differences in perspective. Because Owen's sonnet views war and its effects at a distance, it may be short, while Lowell's interior monologue views death intimately, needing consequent detail and length. The point of paragraph 4 is that both poems are commonly concrete and real, but that the specificity (about personal things and public ceremonies) points the poems in different directions. Paragraph 5, the last in the body, considers the similar and dissimilar ways in which the poems treat a common metaphor.

The final paragraph summarizes the central idea; it also stresses the ways in which both poems, while similar, are distinct and unique.

Second Sample Theme
(Extended Comparison-Contrast)

*The Complexity of Love and Devoted Service as Shown
in Six Works*[*]

[1] On the surface, at least, love and devotion are simple, and their results should be good. A person loves someone, or serves someone or something. This love may be romantic or familial, and the service may be religious or national. But love is not simple. It is complex, and its results are not uniformly good.° Love and devotion should be ways of saying "yes," but ironically, they sometimes become ways of saying "no," too. This idea can be traced in a comparison of six works: Shakespeare's Sonnet 116, Arnold's "Dover Beach," Hardy's "Channel Firing," Chekhov's *The Bear*, O'Connor's "First Confession," and Welty's "A Worn Path." The complexity in these works is that love and devotion do not operate in a vacuum but rather in the context of personal, philosophical, economic, and national difficulties. The works show that love and devotion may be forces for stability and refuge, but also for harm.□

[2] Ideal and stabilizing love, along with service performed out of love, is shown by Shakespeare in Sonnet 116 and by O'Connor in "First Confession." Shakespeare states that love gives lovers strength and stability in a complex world of opposition and difficulty. Such love is like a "star" that guides wandering ships (line 7), and like a "fixed mark" that stands against the shaking of life's tempests (lines 5 and 6). A character who is similarly aware of human tempests and conflicts is the "young priest" who hears Jackie's confession in "First Confession." He is clearly committed to service, and is "intelligent above the ordinary" (p. 329). With service to God as his "star," to use Shakespeare's image, he is able to talk sympathetically with Jackie and to send the boy home with a clear and happy mind.

[3] For both Shakespeare and O'Connor, love and service grow out of a great human need for stability and guidance. To this degree, love is a simplifying force, but it simplifies primarily because the "tempests" complicating life are so strong. Such love is one of the best things that happen to human beings, because it fulfills them and prepares them to face life.

[4] The desire for love of this kind is so strong that it can also be the cause for people to do strange and funny things. The two major characters in Chekhov's short comedy-farce *The Bear* are examples. At the play's start, Chekhov shows that Mrs. Popov and Smirnov are following some of the crackbrained and negative guides that people often confuse for truth. She is devoted to the memory of her dead husband, while he is disillusioned and cynical about women. But Chekhov makes them go through hoops for love. As the two argue, insult each other, and reach the point of dueling with real pistols,

---

[*]For the texts of these works, please see Appendix C, pp. 325, 331, 344, 350, 352, 359.
° Central idea
□ Thesis sentence

[4]   their need for love overcomes all their other impulses. It is as though love happens despite everything going against it, because the need for the stabilizing base is so strong. Certainly love here is not without at least some complexity.

[5]   Either seriously or comically, then, love is shown as a rudder, guiding people in powerful and conflicting currents. The three works studied so far show that love shapes lives and makes for sudden and unexpected changes.

[6]   This thought is somewhat like the view presented by Eudora Welty in "A Worn Path." Unlike Chekhov and Shakespeare, and more like O'Connor, Welty tells a story of service performed out of love. A poor grandmother, Phoenix Jackson, has a hard life in caring for her incurably ill grandson. The walk she takes along the "worn path" to Natchez symbolizes the hardships she endures because of her single-minded love. Her service is the closest thing to pure simplicity that may be found in all the works examined, with the possible exception of the love in Chekhov's play.

[7]   But even her love is not without its complexity. Hardy in "Channel Firing" and Arnold in "Dover Beach" describe a joyless, loveless, insecure world overrun by war. Phoenix's life is just as grim. She is poor and ignorant, and her grandson has nowhere to go but down. If she would only stop to think deeply about her condition, she might be as despairing as Arnold and Hardy. But her strength may be her ability either to accept her difficult life or to ignore the grimness of it. With her service as her "star" and "ever-fixed mark," she is able to keep cheerful and to live in friendship with the animals and the woods. Her life has meaning and dignity.

Arnold's view of love and devotion under such bad conditions is different from the views of Shakespeare, Chekhov, O'Connor, and Welty. For Arnold, the public world seems to be so far gone that there is nothing left but personal relationships. Thus love is not so much a guide as a refuge, a place of sanity and safety. After describing what he considers the worldwide shrinking of the "Sea of Faith," he states:

[8]
> Ah, love, let us be true
> To one another! for the world, which seems
> To lie before us like a land of dreams,
> So various, so beautiful, so new,
> Hath really neither joy, nor love, nor light,
> Nor certitude, nor peace, nor help for pain;
> And we are here as on a darkling plain
> Swept with confused alarms of struggle and flight
> Where ignorant armies clash by night.
>
> —lines 29–37

Here the word *true* should be underlined, as Shakespeare emphasizes "true minds" and as O'Connor's priest is a *true* servant of God. "True" to Arnold seems to involve a pledge to create a small area of certainty in the mad world like that of "Channel Firing," where there is no certainty. Love is not so much a guide as a last place of hope, a retreat where truth can still have meaning.

[9]   In practice, perhaps, Arnold's idea of love as a refuge is not very different from the view that love is a guide. Once the truthful pledge is made, it is a force for goodness, at least for the lovers making the pledge, just as love works for goodness in Shakespeare, O'Connor, Chekhov, and Welty. Yet Arnold's view is weaker. It does not result from an inner need or conviction, but

[9] rather from a conscious decision to let everything else go and to look out only for the small relationship. In an extreme form, this could lead to total withdrawal. Such a passive relationship to other affairs could be harmful by omission.

The idea that love and devotion as a refuge could be actively harmful is explored by O'Connor in other characters in "First Confession." Nora and Mrs. Ryan seem to think only of sinfulness and punishment. They seek the love of God out of a desire for protection. Their devotion is therefore a means to an end, not the pure goal that operates in Shakespeare, Welty, and O'Connor's own priest. As Jackie says of Mrs. Ryan:

[10]
> She . . . wore a black cloak and bonnet, and came every day to school at three o'clock when we should have been going home, and talked to us of hell. She may have mentioned the other place as well, but that could only have been by accident, for hell had the first place in her heart (p. 326).

[11] Love and devotion for her and for Nora take the form of observing ritual and following rules, such as being sure that all confessions are "good" (that is, complete, with no sins held back). If this obedience were only personal, it would be a force for security, as it is on the personal level for Arnold. But from the safety of their refuge, Mrs. Ryan confuses children like Jackie by describing devilish, sadistic tortures, while Nora tells her father about the bread knife and thus brings down punishment (the "flaking") and a "scalded" heart on Jackie. Even though Mrs. Ryan is not a bad soul, and Nora is no more than a young girl, their use of religion is negative. Fortunately, their influence is counterbalanced by the priest.

[12] Mrs. Ryan and Nora are minor compared with those unseen, unnamed, and distant persons firing the big guns during the "gunnery practice out at sea" in Hardy's "Channel Firing" (line 10). Hardy does not treat the gunners as individuals but as an evil collective force made up of persons who, under the sheltering claim of devotion to country and obedience to orders, are "striving strong to make/Red war yet redder" (lines 13, 14). For them, love of country is a refuge, just like the love of God for Mrs. Ryan and Nora and the true pledge to love for Arnold's speaker. As memebers of the military they obey orders and, as Hardy's God says, they are not much better than the dead because they do nothing "for Christés sake" (line 15). They operate the ships and fill the columns of Arnold's "ignorant armies," for Hardy makes clear that their target practice takes place at night (line 1).

[13] In summary, love and devotion as seen in these various works may be compared with a continuous line formed out of the human need for love and for the stability and guidance that love offers. At one end love is totally good and ideal; at the other it is totally bad. Shakespeare, Welty, Chekhov, and O'Connor (in the priest) show the end that is good. Still at the good end, but moving toward the center, is Arnold's use of love as a refuge. On the other side of the line are Mrs. Ryan and Nora of "First Confession," while all the way at the bad end are the insensible and invisible gunners in "Channel Firing."

[14] The difficulty noted in all the works, and a major problem in life, is to devote oneself to the right, stabilizing, constructive part of the line. Although in his farce Chekhov makes love win against almost impossible odds, he shows the problem most vividly of all the authors studied. Under normal conditions, people like Mrs. Popov and Smirnov would not find love. Instead, they would continue following their destructive and false guides. They would be unhappy and disillusioned, or else they might become more like Mrs. Ryan and spread

[14] talk about their own confused ideas (as Smirnov actually does almost right up to his conversion to love). Like the military and naval forces of Arnold and Hardy, they would then wind up at the destructive end of the line.

[15] Change, opposition, confusion, anger, resignation, economic difficulty—these are only some of the forces that attack people as they try to find the benefits of love. If they are lucky they find meaning and stability in love and service as in Sonnet 116, "First Confession," *The Bear*, "A Worn Path," and, to a small degree, "Dover Beach." If confusion wins, they are locked into harmful positions, like the gunners in "Channel Firing" and Mrs. Ryan and Nora in "First Confession." Thus love is complicated by circumstances, and it is not the simple force for good that it should ideally be. The six works compared and contrasted here have shown these difficulties and complexities.

COMMENTARY ON THE THEME

This theme compares and contrasts six works—three poems, two stories, and a play—on the common ground or central idea of the complexity of love and service. The complexity is caused by life's difficulties ("tempests," as Shakespeare calls them) and by bad results. The theme develops the central idea in terms of love as an ideal and guide (paragraphs 2 to 7) and love as a refuge or escape (8 to 12), with a subcategory of love as a cause of harm (10 to 12).

The various works are introduced as they are grouped according to these sections. For example, Sonnet 116, "First Confession" (because of the priest), *The Bear*, and "A Worn Path" are together in the first group—love as an ideal and guide. Because "Dover Beach" and "Channel Firing" are in the second group, these works are brought in earlier, during the discussion of the first group. For this reason, both poems are used regularly for comparison and contrast throughout the theme.

The use of the various works within groups may be seen in paragraph 8. There, the principal topic is the use of love as a refuge or retreat, and the central work of the paragraph is "Dover Beach." However, the first sentence contrasts Arnold's view with the four works in the first group; the fifth sentence shows how Arnold is similar in one respect to Shakespeare and O'Connor; and the sixth sentence shows a similarity of Arnold and Hardy. The paragraph thus brings together all the works being studied in the theme.

The technique of comparison-contrast used in this way shows how the various works may be defined and distinguished in relation to the common idea. Paragraph 13, the first in the conclusion, attempts to summarize these distinctions by suggesting a continuous line along which each of the works may be placed. Paragraphs 14 and 15 continue the summary by showing the prominence of complicating difficulties, and, by implication, the importance of love. Thus, the effect of the comparison of all the works collectively is the enhanced understanding of each of the works separately.

chapter 13

Writing About a Problem

A **problem** is any question you cannot answer easily and correctly about a body of material that you know. The question, "Who is the major character in *Hamlet*?" is not a problem, because the obvious answer is Hamlet.

Let us, however, ask another question: "Why is it correct to say that Hamlet is the major character?" This question is not as easy as the first, and for this reason it is a problem. It requires that we think about our answer, even though we do not need to search very far. Hamlet is the title character. He is involved in most of the actions of the play. He is so much the center of our liking and concern that his death causes sadness and regret. To solve this problem has required a set of responses, all of which provide answers to the question *why*. With variation, most readers of Shakespeare's play would likely be satisfied with the answers.

More complex, however, and more typical of most problems, are questions like these: "Why does Hamlet talk of suicide in his first soliloquy?" "Why does he treat Ophelia so coarsely in the 'nunnery' scene?" "Why does he delay in avenging his father's death?" Essays on a problem are normally concerned with questions like these. Simple factual responses do not answer such questions. A good deal of thought, together with a number of interpretations knitted together into a whole essay, is required.

THE USEFULNESS OF PROBLEM SOLVING

The techniques of problem solving should be useful to you in most of your classes. In an art course, for example, you might need to write on the problem of representationalism as opposed to impressionism. In philosophy you may encounter the problem of whether reality is to be found in particulars or universals. You should know what to do with problems of this sort.

Without question, you have already had a good deal of experience in problem solving. The classroom method of questions and answers has required that you put facts and conclusions together just as you do for an essay on a problem.

The process of solving problems is one of the most important experiences in the development of people's abilities as good readers and thinkers. Uncritical readers do not think about what they read. When they are questioned, they are embarrassed by what they do not remember or understand. However, if they create and answer their own questions as they read, they will need to search the material deeply and try to command it. In dealing with their questions, they must test a number of provisional solutions and develop their responses. As they do these tasks, they develop their ability to be good critical readers.

STRATEGIES FOR AN ESSAY ABOUT A PROBLEM

The first purpose in an essay about a problem is to convince your reader that your solution is a good one. You do this by making sound conclusions from supporting evidence. In nonscientific subjects like literature you rarely find absolute proofs, so your conclusions will not be proved in the way you prove triangles congruent. But your organization, your use of facts from the text, your interpretations, and your application of general or specific knowledge should all be designed to make your conclusions convincing. Your basic strategy is thus persuasion.

Because problems and solutions change with the work being studied, each essay on a problem is different from any other. Despite these differences, however, a number of common strategies might be adapted to whatever problem you face. You might wish to use one or more of these strategies throughout your theme. Always, you should be trying to solve the problem—to answer the question—and you should achieve this goal in the most direct, convenient way.

STRATEGY 1: THE DEMONSTRATION THAT CONDITIONS FOR A SOLUTION ARE FULFILLED.   In effect, this development is the most basic in writing— namely, illustration. In your theme, you first explain that certain conditions need to exist for your solution to be plausible. Your central idea—really a brief answer to the question—is that the conditions do indeed exist. Your development is to show how the conditions may be found in the work.

Let us suppose that you are writing on the problem of why Hamlet delays revenge against his uncle, Claudius (who before the play opens has murdered Hamlet's father, King Hamlet, and has become the new king of Denmark). Suppose that in your introduction, you make the point that Hamlet delays because he is not completely sure Claudius is guilty. This is your "solution" to the problem. In the body of your essay you would support your answer by showing the flimsiness of the information Hamlet receives about the crime (i.e., the two visits from the Ghost and Claudius's distress at the play within the play). Once you have attacked these sources of data on the grounds that they are unreliable, you have succeeded. You have proposed a fair solution to the problem and have shown that your solution is consistent with the facts of the play.

STRATEGY 2: THE ANALYSIS OF WORDS IN THE PHRASING OF THE PROBLEM. Another good approach is to explore the meaning and limits of important words or phrases in the question as it has been put to you. Your object is to clarify the words and show how applicable they are. You may wish to define the words and show whether they have any special meaning.

You will find that attention to words might give you enough material for all or part of your essay. The sample theme in this chapter, for example, briefly considers the meaning of the word "effective" when applied to Robert Frost's poem "Desert Places." Similarly, a theme on the problem of Hamlet's delay would benefit from a treatment of the word *delay*: What, really, does *delay* mean? For Hamlet, is there a difference between delay that is reasonable and delay that is unreasonable? Does Hamlet in fact delay unreasonably? Is his delay the result of a psychological fault? Would speedy revenge be more or less reasonable than the delay? By the time you have asked such pointed questions about so important a word, and answered them, you will also have written a goodly amount of material to use in a full essay on the problem. Of course, you could use just a part of this material as you go in new directions in fashioning your solution.

STRATEGY 3: THE REFERENCE TO LITERARY CONVENTIONS OR EXPECTATIONS. What might appear to be a problem can often be treated as a normal characteristic, given the particular work you are studying. In this light, your best argument may be to establish that the problem can be solved by reference to the literary mode or conventions of a work, or to the work's own self-limitations. For example, a question might be raised about why Mathilde in "The Necklace" does not tell her friend Jeanne right away about the loss of the necklace. A plausible answer might be that, all motivation aside, the story builds up to a surprise at the end, and that an early disclosure would spoil the surprise. To solve the problem, in other words, one has recourse to the actual structure of the story—to the literary convention that De Maupassant was observing when he wrote "The Necklace."

Similarly, a problem about Dickinson's "After Great Pain a Formal Feeling Comes" may be whether the poem is sufficiently detailed to substantiate what it says about the nature of sorrow. Because the poem is only a short lyric, however, it cannot, by its very nature, be filled with extensive details. Instead, an understanding of the poem presupposes that readers will supply their own details about pain and grief, thus enabling the speaker to concentrate exclusively on the topic—the ritualized pattern of sorrow following a personal tragedy. In other words, the solution to problems like these depends upon the assumptions and limitations of the works themselves; one cannot expect what was never intended.

Other problems that may be dealt with in this way concern levels of reality. Hawthorne's "Young Goodman Brown," for example, is fanciful and dreamlike (or nightmarish). In everyday life, things could not happen as they do in the forest near Hawthorne's Salem. Similarly, although Jackson's "The Lottery" is presented as an apparently realistic gathering of village folk at a public event, the stoning at the end indicates that the story is not to be taken as a representation of everyday reality. Thus, problems about whether such a lottery could actually occur, or whether Young Goodman Brown could take such a fantastic walk, can be answered by reference to the nature of both works as being dreamlike or symbolic. In the same way, a question about whether Mrs. Popov and Smirnov could in reality fall in love as rapidly as they do in Chekhov's *The Bear* can be answered with reference to the play's being a farce: Because in farces unlikely things occur rapidly and sometimes illogically, such a quick infatuation is not unusual at all. The principal strategy in dealing with questions like these is to resolve apparent difficulties by establishing a context in which the difficulties vanish. Problems, in other words, may be seen as resulting from no more than normal occurrences within the particular works being discussed. With variations, this method can work for many similar problems.

STRATEGY 4: THE ARGUMENT AGAINST POSSIBLE OBJECTIONS: PROCATALEPSIS. With this strategy, you raise an objection to your solution and then argue against the objection. This strategy, called **procatalepsis** or **anticipation,** is useful because it helps you to sharpen your own arguments. That is, the need to answer objections forces you to make analyses and use facts that you might ordinarily overlook. Although procatalepsis may be used point by point throughout your theme, you may find it most useful at the end. (Please see the last paragraph of the sample theme.) The situation you visualize is that someone might object to your arguments even after you have made your major points. If you can raise the objections first, before they are made by someone else, and then answer them, your essay will be that much more powerful and convincing.

Your aim with the strategy of procatalepsis should be to show that, compared with your solution, the objection (1) is not accurate or valid, (2) is not strong or convincing, or (3) is based on an exception, not a rule. Here are some examples of these approaches. The objections raised are underlined, so that you can easily distinguish them from the answers.

a. The objection is not accurate or valid. Here you reject the objection by showing that either the interpretation or the conclusions are wrong and also by emphasizing that the evidence supports your solution.

> Although Hamlet's delay is reasonable, the claim might be made that his greater duty is to kill Claudius in revenge as soon as the Ghost accuses Claudius of his murder. This claim is not persuasive because it assumes that Hamlet knows everything the audience knows. The audience accepts the Ghost's word, right from the start, that Claudius is guilty, but from Hamlet's position there is every reason to doubt the Ghost and not to act. Would it not seem foolish and insane for Hamlet to kill Claudius, who is king legally, and then to claim that he did it because the Ghost told him to do so? The argument for speedy revenge is not good, because it is based on an incorrect view of the situation Hamlet faces.

b. The objection is not strong or convincing. Here you concede that the objection has some truth or validity, but you then try to show that it is weak and that your own solution is stronger.

> One might claim that Claudius's distress at the play within the play is evidence for his guilt and that therefore Hamlet should carry out his revenge right away. This argument has merit, and Hamlet's speech after Claudius has fled the scene ("I'll take the Ghost's word for a thousand pound") shows that the King's conscience has been caught. But this behavior is not a strong enough cause for killing him. Hamlet could justify a claim for an investigation of his father's death on these grounds, but he could not justify a revenge killing. Claudius could not be convicted in any court on the strength of testimony that he was disturbed at seeing the murder of Gonzago on stage. Even after the play within the play, the reasons for delay are stronger than those for action.

c. The objection is an exception, not a rule. Here you reject the objection on the grounds that it could be valid only if normal conditions were suspended. The objection depends on an exception, not a rule.

> The case for quick action is simple: Hamlet should kill Claudius right after seeing the Ghost (I.3), or else after seeing the King's reaction to the stage murder of Gonzago (III.2) or else after seeing the Ghost

again (III.4). This argument wrongly assumes that due process does not exist in the Denmark of Hamlet and Claudius. Redress under these circumstances, goes the argument, must be both personal and extra-legal. However, the fact is that Hamlet's Denmark is a civilized place where legality and the rules of evidence are precious. Thus Hamlet cannot rush out to kill Claudius, because he knows that the King has not had anything close to due process. The argument for quick action is poor because it rests on an exception being made from civilized law.

WRITING ABOUT A PROBLEM

Writing a theme on a problem requires you to argue a position: Either there is a solution or there is not. To develop this position requires that you show the steps that have led you to your conclusion. The general form of your theme is thus (1) a description of the conditions that need to be met for the solution you propose, and then (2) a demonstration that these conditions exist. If your position is that there is no solution, then your form would be the same for the first part, but your second part—the development—would show that these conditions have *not* been met.

As with most themes, you may assume that your reader is familiar with the work you have read. Your job is to arrange your materials convincingly around your main point. You should not use anything from the work that is not relevant to your central idea. You do not need to discuss things in their order of appearance in the work. You are in control and must make your decisions about order so that your solution to the problem can be brought out most effectively.

Introduction

Begin right away with a statement of the problem, and refer to the conditions that must be established for the problem to be solved. It is unnecessary to say anything about the author or the general nature of the work unless you plan to use this material as a part of your development. Your central idea is your answer to the question, and your thesis sentence indicates the main heads of your development.

Body

The body should contain the main points of argument, arranged to convince your reader that your solution to the problem is sound. In each paragraph, the topic sentence is an assertion that you believe is a major aspect of your answer, and should be followed with enough detail to support the topic. Your goal should be to bring about your reader's agreement with your answers.

You might wish to use one or more of the strategies described in this chapter. These are, again, (1) the demonstration that conditions for a solution are fulfilled, (2) the analysis of words in the phrasing of the problem, (3) the reference to literary expectations or limitations, and (4) the argument against possible objections. You might combine these if a combination helps your argument. Thus, if we assume that you are writing to explain that Hamlet's delay is reasonable and not the result of a character flaw, you might begin by considering the word *delay* (strategy 2). Then you might use strategy 1 to explain the reasons for which Hamlet does delay. Finally, in order to answer objections to your argument, you might show that he is capable of action when he feels justified in acting (strategy 4). Whatever your topic, the important thing is to use the method or methods that best help you to make a good case for your solution to the problem.

Conclusion

In your conclusion you should affirm your belief in the validity of your solution in view of the supporting evidence. You might do this by reemphasizing those points that you believe are strongest. You might also summarize each of your main points. Or you might think of your argument as continuing and thus might use the strategy of procatalepsis to raise and answer objections that could be made against your solution, as in the last paragraph of the sample theme.

Sample Theme

The Problem of Frost's Use of the Term "desert places" in the Poem "Desert Places"[*]

---

[1] In the last line of "Desert Places," the meaning suggested by the title undergoes a sudden shift. At the beginning it clearly refers to the snowy setting described in the first stanza, but in the last line it refers to a negative state of soul. The problem is this: Does the change happen too late to be effective? That is, does the new meaning come out of nowhere, or does it really work as a good closing thought? To answer these questions, one must grant that the change cannot be effective if there is no preparation for it before the last

[*] For the text of this poem, please see Appendix C, p. 355.

line of the poem. But if there is preparation—that is, if Frost does provide hints that the speaker feels an emptiness like that of the bleak, snowy natural world—then the shift is both understandable and effective even though it comes at the very end. It is clear that Frost makes the preparation and therefore that the change is effective.° The preparation may be traced in Frost's references, word choices, and concluding sentences.□

[2] In the first two stanzas Frost includes the speaker in his reference to living things being overcome. The scene described in line 4 is "weeds and stubble showing last." Then come the hibernating animals "smothered in their lairs" in line 6. Finally, the speaker focuses on his own mental state. He says that he is "too absent-spirited to count," and that the "loneliness" of the scene "includes" him "unawares" (7, 8). This movement—from vegetable, to animal, to human—shows that everything alive is changed by the snow. Obviously, the speaker will not die like the grass or hibernate like the animals, but he indicates that the "loneliness" overcomes him. These first eight lines thus connect the natural bleakness with the speaker.

[3] In addition, a number of the words in the third stanza are preparatory because they may be applied to human beings. The words "lonely" and "loneliness" (line 9), "more lonely" (10), "blanker" and "benighted" (11), and "no expression, nothing to express" (12) may all refer equally to human or to natural conditions. The word "benighted" is most important, because it suggests not only the darkness of night, but also, on the human level, to intellectual or moral ignorance. Because these words invite the reader to think of negative mental and emotional states, they provide a context in which the final shift of meaning is both logical and natural.

[4] The climax of Frost's preparation for the last two words is in the sentences of the fourth stanza. All along, the speaker claims to feel an inner void that is similar to the bleakness he finds in the cold, snowy field. This idea emerges as the major focus in the last stanza, where in two sentences the speaker talks about his own feelings and his sense of emptiness or insensitivity:

> They cannot scare me with their empty spaces
> Between stars—on stars where no human race is
> I have it in me so much nearer home
> To scare myself with my own desert places.

[5] In the context of the poem, therefore, the shift in these last two words does not seem sudden or illogical. They rather pull together the two parts of the comparison that Frost has been building from the very first line. Just as "desert places" refers to the snowy field, it also suggests human coldness, blankness, unconcern, insensitivity, and maybe even cruelty. The phrase does not spring out of nowhere, but is a strong climax of the major directions of the poem.

[6] Although Frost's conclusion is effective, a critic might still claim that it is weak because Frost does not develop the thought about the negative soul. He simply mentions "desert places" and stops. But the poem is not a long psychological study. To ask for more than Frost gives would be to expect more than sixteen lines can provide. A better claim against the effectiveness of the concluding shift of meaning is that the phrase "desert places" is both vague and perhaps overly humble. If the phrase were taken away from the

---

° Central idea
□ Thesis sentence

poem, this criticism might be acceptable. But the fact is that the phrase is in the poem, and that it must be judged only in the poem. There, it takes on the connotations of the previous fifteen lines, and does so with freshness and surprise. Thus, the shift of meaning is a major reason for Frost's success in "Desert Places."

COMMENTARY ON THE THEME

The introductory prargraph states the problem of whether or not the shift of meaning at the end of Frost's poem is effective. It is emphasized that the poem must prepare the reader for this shift if effectiveness is to be claimed for it. The central idea indicates that the poem satisfies this requirement and that the shift is effective. The thesis sentence indicates three subjects for development.

The first half of paragraph 2 draws attention to three references to the snow's bleakness. These are considered in the second half, and thus the paragraph shows that there is preparation early in the poem for the shift. Paragraph 3 continues this line of development, illustrating the relationship of certain words in the third stanza to the human state, and thus to the shift in the poem from the vegetable to the human world. The fourth paragraph asserts that the concluding sentences build toward a climax of Frost's pattern or development.

Paragraphs 5 and 6 form a two-part conclusion to the theme. The fifth paragraph summarizes the arguments and offers an interpretation of the phrase. The last paragraph deals with two objections against the effectiveness of the phrase. The theme thus shows that a careful reading of the poem eliminates the grounds for claiming that there is any problem about the last line.

The general development of this essay illustrates strategy 1 described in this chapter (p. 159). The attention to the word *effective* in paragraph 1 briefly illustrates the second strategy (p. 160). The concluding paragraph shows two approaches to the fourth strategy (p. 161), using the arguments that the objections are not good because they (4a) are not accurate or valid (here the inaccuracy is related to strategy 3), and (4c) are based on the need for an exception, namely that the phrase in question be removed from the context in the poem.

chapter 14

Writing About Tone:
The Writer's Control
over Attitudes and Feelings

Tone refers to the methods by which writers reveal attitudes or feelings, although the discussion of tone sometimes becomes focused on attitudes themselves. You should remember, however, that tone refers not to attitudes, but to those techniques and modes of presentation that *reveal* or *create* these attitudes.

LITERARY TONE AND SPEAKING TONE OF VOICE

For literary study, the word *tone* is borrowed from the phrase *tone of voice* in speech. Tone of voice reflects your attitudes toward a particular thing or situation and also toward your listeners. Let us suppose that Mary has a difficult school assignment, on which she expects to work all day. Things go well, and she finishes quickly. She happily tells her friend Anne about the work, saying, "I'm so pleased. I needed only two hours for that." Then Mary goes to a theater to buy tickets for a popular play, and the line is long and slow. After she finally gets the tickets and is walking away, she tells a group of people waiting in the back of the line, "I'm so pleased. I needed only two hours for that." The sentences are exactly the same, but by changing her emphasis and vocal inflection, Mary conveys the idea that she is disgusted with the difficulty and slowness of the line, and also that she understands the annoyance of those behind her, who will have a similarly long wait. By controlling the *tone* of her statements, in other words, Mary conveys pleasure at one time, and indignation and anger (and also sympathy) at another.

TONE AS SHOWN BY CHARACTERS WITHIN A WORK

The assumption of a study of tone is that all authors, like our real-life speaker Mary, have a choice about what to say and how to say it, and that they make their choices in full consideration of their readers. One obvious authorial judgment is that readers are intelligent and can perceive the intricacies of both real and fictional human interchanges. As a specific literary example, John Collier, at the beginning of the grim story "The Chaser" (the topic of the first sample theme, pp. 175–177, creates a difficult situation: A young man, Allan Austen, comes to a chemist's shop seeking a love potion. The chemist, an old man, wants to tell Austen about a deadly and untraceable poison. Here, the proper tone is absolutely essential. Collier must heed the integrity of his two characters, for the situation requires that not all things can be stated directly if the aims and goals of each are to be fulfilled. Therefore, he has the old man speak indirectly about the poison, as follows:

> "I look at it like this," said the old man. "Please a customer with one article, and he will come back when he needs another. Even if it *is* more costly. He will save up for it, if necessary."

The indirect, veiled style of this speech shows the old chemist's assessment of Austen. If he were to say outright that Austen will eventually come back for the poison to kill the woman whom he now wants so desperately, Austen would flee in horror. So the old man uses the phrase "come back when he needs another" to suggest that in the future Austen may indeed remember these words and fit himself into the category of men wanting the other product, the poison. The speech, therefore, is right for the circumstances. The example shows how an author may judge and control tone by the careful crafting of characters and their speeches within a work.

TONE AND THE AUTHOR'S ATTITUDE TOWARD READERS

In addition, also by controlling the style of the speech of the old man, Collier demonstrates confidence in the perceptiveness of his readers, who are able to judge whether the dialogue in the story is truly realistic. Suppose that Collier had written an interchange in which the old man does indeed tell Austen that someday he will return for the poison. Could one then expect sophisticated and intelligent readers to believe that Austen would continue his mission to buy the love potion? Obviously Collier's answer is no. The point is that Austen, *at the moment of the story*, is young, romantic, and idealistic; but *at a future time* he will become cynical, and will grow so weary of his sweetheart that he will want to kill her. He will then remember that the old man will sell him the poison. The story therefore goes forward as it does, with the old man speaking ambiguously and ominously, and Austen hearing but not understanding. Collier thus shows not only a due regard for the probability of the characters and situation, but also a clear acknowledgment of the intelligence and perceptiveness of readers.

This example illustrates that aspect of tone involving the author's attitude toward his or her audience. As it were, the author recognizes that readers are participants in the creative act, and that all elements of a work must take audience response into account. Readers would know instantly that any departures from normally expected behavior—from verisimilitude—would strain credibility, as would any inappropriate language, settings, motivation, chronology, and so on.

LAUGHTER, COMEDY, AND FARCE

A major aspect of tone is laughter and the methods of comedy and farce. Everyone likes to laugh, but not everyone can explain the reasons for laughing. It seems clear that smiles, shared laughter, and good human relationships go together, so that laughter is essential to a person's mental health. Laughter is unplanned, often unpredictable, and sometimes personal and idiosyncratic. It resists close analysis. Despite the difficulty of explaining the causes for people's laughter, however, it is nevertheless possible to note common elements. These are:

1. AN OBJECT TO LAUGH AT. There must be something to laugh at, whether a person, thing, situation, custom, or a habit of speech or dialect or an arrangement of words.

2. INCONGRUITY. Human beings know what to expect under given conditions, and anything that violates these expectations may cause laughter. When the temperature is 100 degrees Farenheit, for example, you would reasonably expect people to dress lightly. If you saw a person dressed in a heavy overcoat, a warm hat, a muffler, and large gloves, who was shivering, waving his arms, and stamping his feet as though to keep them warm, this person would have violated your expectations. His garments for the day would be inappropriate or *incongruous*, and you

would likely laugh at him and his clothing. If you hear a stand-up comedian say, "Yesterday afternoon I was walking down the street and turned into a drugstore," this remark is funny because "turned into" can have two incompatible meanings. Here the language itself furnishes its own incongruity. A student once wrote that in high school he had sung in the "archipelago choir." This inadvertent verbal mistake is called a *malapropism*, after Mrs. Malaprop, a character in Richard Sheridan's eighteenth-century play *The Rivals*. If you know about unaccompanied choirs, you expect to see *a capella*, or at least a recognizable misspelling of the phrase. When you see *archipelago*, however, a word that makes sense (if you are speaking about islands) and that looks something like *a capella*, you laugh, or at least smile. Incongruity is the quality common to all these instances of laughter. In the literary creation of such verbal slips, the tone is directed against the speaker, and both readers and author alike share the enjoyment.

3. **SAFETY AND/OR GOOD WILL.** Seeing a person slip on a banana peel and hurtle through the air may cause laughter as long as we ourselves are not that person, for our laughter depends on our being insulated from danger and pain. In farce, where much physical abuse takes place (such as falling through trap doors or being hit in the face by cream pies), the abuse never harms the participants. The incongruity of such situations causes laughter, and one's safety from personal consequences, together with the insulation from pain of the participants, prevents grave or even horrified responses. Good will enters into laughter in romantic comedy or in works where you are drawn into general sympathy with the major figures, such as Smirnov and Mrs. Popov in Chekhov's *The Bear*. Here the infectiousness of laughter and happiness governs your responses. As the author leads the characters toward the admission of their love, your involvement with them produces happiness, smiles, and even sympathetic laughter.

4. **UNFAMILIARITY, NEWNESS, UNIQUENESS, SPONTANEITY.** Laughter depends on seeing something new or unique, or on experiencing a known thing freshly. Because laughter is prompted by a flash of insight or a sudden revelation, the circumstances promoting laughter are always spontaneous. Perhaps you have had someone explain a joke or funny situation, only to find that the explanation dampened the spontaneity needed for laughter. Although spontaneity is most often a quality of the unfamiliar, it is not lost just because a thing is well known. Indeed, the task of the comic writer is to develop ordinary materials to a point where spontaneity frees the reader to laugh. Thus, it is possible to read and reread *The Bear* and laugh each time because, even though you know what is going to happen, the work leads you to expect one outcome, but then gives you a surprisingly different one. The love between Smirnov and Mrs. Popov

is and always will be comic because it is so illogical, unexpected, incongruous, and spontaneous.

IRONY

One of the most human traits is the capacity to have two or more attitudes toward someone or something. We know that people are not perfect, but we love a number of them anyway. Therefore, we speak to them not only with love and praise, but also with banter and criticism. (And they may choose to inform us, in their turn, about our own imperfections.) On occasions, you may have bought greeting cards which are amusing or even mildly insulting rather than directly sentimental. If you give such cards, you do so in the expectation that your loved ones will not be affronted, but instead will be amused. As you share smiles and laughs, you also remind your loved ones of your affection for them.

The word **irony** describes such situations and expressions, by which a writer conveys a specific idea or attitude by stating something apparently opposite or contradictory. Irony is natural to human beings who are aware of the ambiguities and complexities of life. It is a function of the realization that life does not always measure up to promise, that friends and loved ones may sometimes be angry and bitter toward each other, that the universe contains incomprehensible mysteries, that doubt exists even in the certainty of knowledge and faith, and that human character is built through chagrin, regret, and pain as much as through emulation and praise. In expressing an idea ironically, writers pay the greatest compliment to their readers, for they assume that readers have sufficient skill and understanding to see through the quizzical or ambiguous surface statement to the clarity beneath.

The major types of irony are *verbal*, *situational*, and *dramatic*. **Verbal irony** is a statement in which one thing is said and another is meant. For example, one of the American astronauts was once asked how he would feel if all his reentry safety equipment failed as he was coming back to earth. He answered, "A thing like that could ruin your whole day." His words would have been appropriate for day-to-day minor mishaps, but since failed safety equipment would cause his death, his answer was ironic (doubly so since the 1986 loss of the space shuttle *Challenger*). This form of verbal irony is **understatement.** By contrast, **overstatement** or **hyperbole** is deliberate exaggeration for effect, as in "And I will love thee still, my Dear, / Till all the seas go dry" (lines by Robert Burns).

Often verbal irony is ambiguous, having double meaning or **double entendre.** At the end of Collier's "The Chaser," for example, the old man responds to Austen's "Good-bye" with the French farewell salutation "Au revoir." This phrase, meaning "Until I see you again," is not especially unusual, and on the surface it seems fairly innocent, but the context makes clear that these final words are a dire prediction that Austen will return one day for the untraceable poison. In other words, the old man's statement has two meanings, one innocent and the other sinister. Ambiguity of course may be used in relation to any topic. Quite often double entendre is used in statements about sexuality and love, usually for the amusement of listeners or readers.

The terms **situational irony** or **irony of situation** refer to conditions measured against forces that transcend and overpower human capacities. These forces may be psychological, social, political, or environmental. Collier's "The Chaser," for example, is based on the irony of the situation in which an unrealistic desire for romantic possession leads people inevitably toward destructiveness rather than everlasting love. A happier example of situational irony is in Chekhov's *The Bear*, for the two characters shift from anger to love because they are in the grips of emotions that are "bigger than both of them."

A special kind of situational irony that develops out of a pessimistic or fatalistic view of life is **cosmic irony,** or **irony of fate.** By the standard of cosmic irony, the universe is indifferent to individuals, who are subject to blind chance, accident, perpetual misfortune, and misery. Even if things temporarily seem to be going well, people's lives will inevitably end badly, and their best efforts will not rescue them or make them happy. A work illustrating cosmic irony is Glaspell's *Trifles*, which develops out of the stultifying conditions of farm life experienced by Minnie Wright. She has no other profession, no other home to which to return, no other life open to her except life on the lonely, dreary farm—nothing. After twenty-nine years of wretchedness, she buys a canary who sings for her and makes life at least a little pleasant. But after a year, her crude husband wrings the bird's neck; she, in turn, with her only meager pleasure destroyed, strangles him at night in his bed. The cosmic irony of her situation virtually requires that this violent murder be the only action open to her. She thus illustrates the irony of fate, for she is caught in a hopeless web of circumstance from which there is no constructive escape.

Like cosmic irony, **dramatic irony** is a special kind of situational irony; it applies when a character perceives a situation in a limited way while the audience, including other characters, may see it in greater perspective. The character therefore is able to understand things in only one way, while the audience can perceive two ways. Allan Austen in "The Chaser" is locked into such irony; he believes that the only potion he will ever need is the one to win him love, while the old man and the readers know that one day he will return for the poison. The classic example of dramatic irony is found in the play *Oedipus Rex* by the ancient Greek dramatist Sophocles. All his life Oedipus has been driven by fate, which he can never escape. As the play draws to its climax and Oedipus believes that he is about to discover the murderer of his father, the audience knows—as he does not—that he is approaching his own self-destruction: As he condemns the murderer, he also condemns himself.

WRITING ABOUT TONE

In preparing to write about tone, you will, as always, need to begin with a careful reading. As you study, note those elements of the work that touch particularly on attitudes or authorial consideration. Thus, for example, you may be studying Collier's "The Chaser," where it would be necessary to consider whether the story asks too much of the reader: Is the old man's prediction really the horror at the end of the road for all romantic loves? In this respect, the story may cause a certain mental squirming. But is this right? Does Collier want the squirming to occur? Perhaps if the question is phrased another way, the tone might be more adequately understood. If Allan Austen is seen to want "overly possessive love" rather than simply "romantic love," the story may seem less disturbing. In seeking answers like this, you will find that the author has been directing you and guiding your responses; that is, the author's control over tone is firmly established.

Similar questions apply when you study internal qualities such as style and characterization. Do all the speeches seem right for speaker and situation? Are all descriptions appropriate, all actions believable? If the work is comic, does the writer seem to be involved with the things, characters, situations, language, or objects at which she or he directs laughter? In serious situations, does the work give evidence of pity? Does the writer ask you to lament the human condition? What kind of character is evidenced by the speaker? Is he or she intelligent? Friendly? Idealistic? Realistic? Do any words seem unusual or especially noteworthy, such as dialect, polysyllabic words, foreign words or phrases that the author assumes you know, or especially connotative or emotive words?

Introduction

The introduction describes the general situation of the work and the mood or impression that it may leave with you. The central idea should be about the aspect or aspects that you plan to develop in the body, such as that the work leads to cynicism, as in "The Chaser," or to laughter and delight, as in *The Bear*. Or your central idea might be that the diction of the work is designed to portray the life of ordinary people, or to show the pretentiousness of various speakers or characters, or to call upon the reader's ability to visualize experience. Problems connected with interpreting the tone of the work should also be mentioned here. The thesis sentence contains the major aspects to be explored in the body.

Body

In the body, you should examine all aspects bearing on the tone of the work. Some of the things to cover might be these:

1. THE AUDIENCE, SITUATION, AND CHARACTERS. Is any person or group directly addressed by the author's voice? What attitude seems to be expressed (love, respect, condescension, confidentiality, confidence, etc.)? What is the basic situation in the work? Do you find irony? If so, what kind is it? What does the irony show about the author's apparent attitudes (optimism or pessimism, for example)? How is the situation controlled to shape your responses? That is, can actions, situations, or characters be seen as expressions of attitude or as embodiments of certain favorable or unfavorable ideas or positions? What is the nature of the speaker or persona? Why does the speaker seem to speak exactly as he or she does? How is the speaker's character manipulated to show apparent authorial attitude and to elicit reader response? Does the work promote respect, admiration, dislike, or other feelings about character or situation? How? Through what ways are these feelings made clear?

2. DESCRIPTIONS, DICTION. Analysis of these is stylistic, but your concern here is to relate style to attitude. Are there any systematic references, such as to colors, sounds, noises, natural scenes, and so on, that collectively reflect an attitude? Do connotative meanings of words control response in any way? Does it seem that special knowledge of any sort is expected of the reader to understand references and words? What is the extent of this knowledge? Do speech or dialect patterns indicate attitudes about speakers or their condition of life? Are speech patterns normal and standard, or slang or substandard? What is the effect of these patterns? Are there unusual or particularly noteworthy expressions? If so, what attitudes do these show? Does the author use verbal irony? To what effect?

3. HUMOR. Is the work funny? How funny, how intense? How is the humor achieved? Does the humor develop out of incongruous situations or language, or both? Is there an underlying basis of attack in the humor, or are the objects of laughter still respected or even loved despite having humor directed against them?

4. IDEAS. Ideas may be advocated, defended mildly, or attacked. Which tack is taken in the work you have been studying? How does the author make his or her attitude clear—directly, by statement, or indirectly, through understatement, overstatement, or the language of a character? In what ways does the work assume a common ground of assent between author and reader? That is, are there apparently common assumptions about religious views, political ideas, moral and behavioral standards, and so on? Are these commonly assumed ideas readily acceptable, or is any concession needed by the reader to approach the work? (For example, a major subject of "First Confession" is the proper preparation for a child about to take first confession in the Catholic faith. Not everyone can grant the importance of this action of faith, but even an irreligious reader might find common ground in the psychological situation of the story, or in the desire to learn as much as possible about human beings.)

5. UNIQUE CHARACTERISTICS OF THE WORK. Each work has unique properties that may contribute to the tone. Dickinson's "After Great Pain a Formal Feeling Comes," for example, considers deep personal hurt, but does not disclose the specific causes, so that the reader must energetically recall personal instances of sorrow to develop assent to the ideas. Glaspell's *Trifles* develops out of the inquisitiveness and also the feminine understanding of the two women on stage throughout the play. Without them, we would not learn about Minnie, for their husbands understand nothing about her plight. Be alert for such special circumstances in any work, whether story, poem, or play, and as you plan and develop your theme, try to take these things into account.

Conclusion

The conclusion may summarize the main points of the essay and from there go on to any concluding thoughts about the tone of the work. Redefinitions, explanations, or afterthoughts might belong here, together with reinforcing ideas in support of earlier points. If there are any personal thoughts, any changes of mind, or any awakening awarenesses, a brief account of these would also be appropriate here, as long as you demonstrate that they rise out of your study and writing for the assignment. Finally, you might mention some other major aspect of the work's tone that you did not develop in the body of the essay. Any or all of these details would fit here, so long as you emphasize the writer's technique.

First Sample Theme (The tone of a story)

The Situational and Verbal Irony of Collier's "The Chaser"*

---

[1]   John Collier's "The Chaser" is based on the situational irony of the unreal hope of youth as opposed to the extreme disillusion of age and experience. Collier builds the brief story almost entirely in dialogue between a young

* For the text of this story, please see Appendix C, pp. 323–25.

man, Alan Austen, who is deeply in love and wants to possess his sweetheart entirely, and an unnamed old man who believes in a life free of romantic involvement. The situation reflects disillusionment so completely that the story may in fact be called cynical.° This attitude is made plain by the situation, the old man, and the use of double meaning.▫

[2] The situation between the two men establishes the story's dominant tone of cynicism. Austen, the young man full of illusions and unreal expectations about love, has come to the old man to buy a love potion so that his sweetheart, Diana, will love him with slavelike adoration. Collier makes it clear that the old man has seen many young men like Austen in the grips of romantic desire before, and he therefore knows that their possessive love will eventually bore and anger them. He knows, because he has already seen these disillusioned customers return to buy the "chaser," which is a deadly, untraceable poison, so that they could kill the women for whom they previously bought the love potion. Thus, Collier creates the ironic situation of the story—the beginning of an inevitable process in which Austen, like other young men before him, are made to appear so unrealistic and self-defeating that their enthusiastic passion will someday change into hate and murderousness.

[3] The sales method used by the old man reveals his cynical understanding of men like Austen. Collier makes clear that the old man knows why Austen has come: Before showing his love potion, the old man describes the untraceable poison, which he calls a "glove cleaner" or "life cleaner." His aim is actually to sell the expensive poison by using the love potion as inexpensive bait. Thus, we see the old man's art of manipulation, for even though Austen is at the moment horrified by the poison, the seed has been planted in his mind. He will always know, when his love for Diana changes, that he will have the choice of "cleaning" his life. This unscrupulous sales method effectively corrupts Austen in advance. Such a calculation on the old man's part is grimly cynical.

[4] Supporting the tone of cynicism in the old man's sales technique is his use of double meaning. For example, his concluding words, "Au revoir" ("Until I see you again"), carry an ironic double meaning. On the one hand, the words conventionally mean "good-bye," but on the other, they suggest that the old man expects a future meeting when Austen will return to buy the poison to kill Diana. The old man's acknowledgment of Austen's gratitude shows the same ironic double edge. He says,

> I like to oblige. . . . Then customers come back, later in life, when they are better off, and want more expensive things.

Clearly the "expensive" thing is the "chaser," the undetectable poison. Through such ironic speeches, the old man is politely but cynically telling Austen that his love will not last and that it will eventually bore, irritate, and then torment him to the point where he will want to murder Diana rather than to continue living with her potion-induced possessiveness.

[5] Before "The Chaser" is dismissed as cynical, however, we should note that Austen's ideas about love must inevitably produce just such cynicism. The old man's descriptions of the total enslavement that Austen has dreamed about would leave no breathing room for either Austen or Diana. This sort of love, because it excludes everything else in life, suffocates rather than pleases. It is normal to wish freedom from such psychological imprisonment, even if the prison is of one's own making. Under these conditions, the cynical tone

° Central idea
▫ Thesis sentence

of "The Chaser" suggests that the desire to be totally possessing and possessed—to "want nothing but solitude" and the loved one—can lead only to disaster for both man and woman. The old man's cynicism and the young man's desire suggest the need for an ideal of love that permits interchange, individuality, and understanding. Even though this better ideal is not described anywhere in the story, it is compatible with Collier's situational irony. Thus, cynical as the story unquestionably is, it does not exclude an idealism of tolerant and more human love.

COMMENTARY ON THE THEME

This theme presents a way in which you can write about a story of dominating pessimism and cynicism without giving in to the underlying negative situational irony. Therefore, the theme illustrates how a consideration of tone can aid the development of objective literary judgment.

The introductory paragraph indicates that the aspect of tone to be discussed will be an ironic situation—youthful but unrealistic hope in the context of aged cynicism. The thesis sentence indicates that the body of the theme will deal with (1) this situation and how it is related to (2) the sales method of a major character—the old man—and (3) his speeches containing double meaning.

The second paragraph establishes the situational irony by describing the desires of Austen and the cynical attitude of the old man. In the third paragraph, the topic is the sinister manipulation of Austen as a result of the old man's skillful and subtle salesmanship. By stressing that the old man plants the seeds of corruption in Austen, this paragraph continues the topic of the tone of cynicism which is the thematic basis of the essay. The subject of the fourth paragraph, the last in the body of the theme, is Collier's use of double meaning in the speeches of the old man to emphasize that Austen will someday want to kill his wife.

The concluding paragraph is reflective. In view of the cynical tone of the story, this paragraph suggests that a more realistic and optimistic attitude about love is possible—a view that is not stated in the story, but which nevertheless provides a basis for judging the characters.

Second Sample Theme (The tone of a poem)

The Tone of Confidence in "Theme for English B"* by Langston Hughes

[1] "Theme for English B" grows from the situational irony of racial differences. The situation is unequal opportunity, seen from the perspective of a college student from the oppressed race. This situation might easily produce bitterness, anger, outrage, or vengefulness. However, the poem contains none of these. It is not angry or indignant; it is not an appeal for revenge or revolution. It is rather a declaration of personal independence and individuality. The tone is one of objectivity, daring, occasional playfulness, but above all, confidence.° These attitudes are made plain in the speaker's situation, the ideas, the poetic form, the diction, and the expressions.□

[2] Hughes's treatment of the situation is objective, factual, and personal, not emotional or political. The poem contains a number of factual details presented clearly, like these: The speaker is black in an otherwise all-white college English class. He has come from North Carolina, and is now living alone at the Harlem YMCA, away from family and roots. He is also, at 22, an older student. The class is for freshman (English B), yet he is the age of many seniors. All this is evidence of disadvantage, yet the speaker does no more than present the facts objectively, without comment. He is in control, presenting the details straightforwardly, in a tone of total objectivity.

[3] Hughes's thoughts about equality—the idea underlying the poem—are presented in the same objective, cool manner. The speaker writes to his instructor as an equal, not as an inferior. In describing himself, he does not deal in abstractions, but rather in reality. Thus, he defines himself in language descriptive of everyday abilities, needs, activities, and likes. He is cool and direct here, for his presentation takes the form of a set of inclusive principles emphasizing the sameness and identity of everyone regardless of race or background. The idea is that everyone should put away prejudices and begin to treat people as people, not as representatives of any race. By causing the speaker to avoid emotionalism and controversy, Hughes makes counterarguments difficult, if not impossible. He is so much in control that the facts themselves carry his argument for equality.

[4] The selection of a poetic form demonstrates bravery and confidence. One would normally expect a short prose theme in response to an "assignment" in an English class, but a poem is unexpected and therefore daring and original. It is as though the speaker is showing his mettle and imagination, thereby personally justifying the idea that he is on an equal footing with the instructor. The wit behind the use of the form itself is a basis for equality.

---

* For the text of this poem, see Appendix C, p. 359–58.
° Central idea
□ Thesis sentence

Hughes's diction is in keeping with the tone of confidence and daring. The words are studiously simple, showing the confidence of the speaker in the directness and truth of his ideas. Almost all the words in the poem are short, of no more than one or two syllables. This high proportion of short words reflects a conscious attempt to keep the diction clear and direct. A result is that Hughes avoids any possible ambiguities, as the following section of the poem shows:

[5]

> Well, I like to eat, sleep, drink, and be in love.
> I like to work, read, learn, and understand life.
> I like a pipe for a Christmas present,
> or records—Bessie, bop, or Bach.

With the exception of what it means to "understand life," these words are straightforward, descriptive, and free of emotional overtones. They reflect the speaker's confidence that the time for recognizing human equality has replaced the time for allowing inequality and prejudice to continue.

A number of the speaker's phrases and expressions also show this same confidence. Although most of the material is expressed straightforwardly, one can perceive playfulness and irony, too. Thus, in lines 18–20 there seems to be a deliberate use of confusing language to bring about a verbal merging of the identities of the speaker, the instructor, Harlem, and the greater New York area:

> Harlem, I hear you:
> hear you, hear me—we two—you, me talk on this page.
> (I hear New York, too.) Me—who?

The speaker's confidence is strong enough to allow him to write and keep in the poem and expression that seems almost childish. This expression is in
[6] the second line of the following excerpt:

> I guess being colored doesn't make me not like
> the same things other folks like who are other races,

There is also whimsicality in the way in which the speaker treats the irony of the black-white situation:

> So will my page be colored that I write?

Underlying this last expression is an awareness that, despite the claim that people are equal and are tied to each other by common humanity, there are also strong differences among individuals. The speaker is confidently asserting grounds for independence as well as equality.

Thus, an examination of "Theme for English B" reveals vitality and confidence. The poem is a statement of trust and an almost open challenge on the personal level to the unachieved ideal of equality. Hughes is saying that since it is American to have such ideals, there is nothing to do but to live up
[7] to them. He makes this point through the almost conscious naiveté of the speaker's simple words and descriptions. Yet the poem is not without irony, particularly at the end, where the speaker mentions that the instructor is "somewhat more free" than he is. "Theme for English B" is complex and engaging. It shows the speaker's confidence through objectivity, daring, and playfulness.

COMMENTARY ON THE THEME

The central idea is that the dominant attitude in "Theme for English B" is the speaker's confidence, and that this confidence is shown in the similar but separable attitudes of objectivity, daring, and playfulness. The purpose of the theme is to discuss how Hughes makes plain these and other related attitudes. The tone is studied as it is shown in five separate aspects of the poem.

Paragraph 2 deals with the situational irony of the speaker in relation to a larger set of social and political circumstances, in this case racial discrimination (see approach 1, above). Paragraph 3 considers the idea of equality as Hughes presents it through the speaker's eyes (approach 4). The aim of the paragraph, however, is not to consider equality *as an idea*, but to show how the speaker expresses his attitude toward it. Paragraph 4 contains a discussion of how the selection of the poetic form is a mark of the speaker's assurance (approach 5). Paragraphs 5 and 6 consider the stylistic matters of word choice and expression (approach 2). The attention given to monosyllabic words is justified by the high percentage of such words in the poem.

The concluding paragraph stresses again the attitude of confidence in the poem, and also notes additional attitudes of trust, challenge, ingenuousness, irony, daring, and playfulness.

Because this theme embodies a number of approaches by which tone may be studied in any work (situation, common ground, diction, special characteristics), it is typical of many essays that use a combined, eclectic approach to tone. The fourth paragraph is particularly instructive, for it shows how a topic that might ordinarily be taken for granted, such as the basic form of expression, can be seen as a unique feature of tone.

chapter 15

Writing Three Themes on Prosody:
Rhythm, Segments, and Rhyme

I. THE RHYTHM OF POETRY:
BEAT, METER, AND SCANSION

Rhythm in poetry—also called *beat, metrics, versification, mechanics of verse,* and *numbers*—refers to the comparative speed and loudness in the flow of words spoken in poetic lines. Poets, being especially attuned to sounds, build certain rhythms into their language. They select words not just for content but also for sound, and they arrange words so that important ideas and climaxes of sound coincide. Sensitive readers, when reading poetry aloud, interpret the lines to develop an appropriate speed and expressiveness of delivery—a proper *rhythm*. Indeed, some persons think of rhythm as the *music* of poetry, since it refers to measured sounds much like rhythms and tempos in music. Like music, poetry requires some regularity of beat, although the tempo and loudness of poetry may be freer and less regular. To achieve emphasis during the reading of many parts of a poem—often within individual lines—the speaking voice may be accelerated or retarded, intensified or softened.

It is important to emphasize that rhythm is never to be separated from the content of a poem. It is important only as it supports and underscores content. Alexander Pope wrote that "the sound [of poetry] must seem an echo to the sense." This idea is important, for in poetry each word must count. Everything—not just the meanings of the words but their sounds and their positions in lines and in the entire poem—should work to convey ideas and attitudes. Words must be placed in the most effective location so that they may furnish emphasis through the comparative speed and loudness of their pronunciation as well as through their meaning and position within a train of thought, description, or narrative. The poet uses every linguistic skill to strike your mind and spirit, to fix the poem in your memory. Thus, the study of rhythm and beat is an attempt to determine how poets have arranged the words of their poems to make sound complement content.

THINGS TO CONSIDER IN STUDYING RHYTHM

It is difficult to undertake a study of rhythm without a grasp of a few basic linguistic facts. Fortunately, you have the essential details readily at hand as a result of your own experience as a speaker and reader. Let us say once again that rhythm refers to the relative loudness and tempo of words as pronounced in groups. Large units of words, poetry aside, make up sentences and paragraphs. Smaller units make up phrases, or *cadence groups* and, in poetry, *metrical feet*. Principally, we will be concerned here with cadence groups and metrical feet, for these form the basic blocks of rhythmical analysis.

CADENCE GROUPS

Words do not function alone but are meaningful only when they are related to other words, as a part of sentences. This interdependence of words is a fact of any language, and one should never ignore it in studying the rhythm of a poem. Sentences do not stretch out forever, but rather they are composed of phrases and clauses that relate to each other through principles of coherence. The term used to describe the coinciding of speaking units with grammatical units, separated by slight pauses (or *junctures*), is **cadence group.** The words *on* and *to*, for example, are, grammatically, prepositions, but they are not very meaningful alone. In phrases like *on this continent* and *to the proposition*, however, they become part of a unit of meaning—prepositional phrases—that when spoken are also cadence groups. As another example, the word *nation* conveys a certain amount of meaning, but the phrase *a new nation* forms a syntactic and rhythmical unit, a cadence group. We do not utter words separately, but rather put them together into cadence groups that coincide both grammatically and rhythmically. Let us for the moment consider the beginning of Abraham Lincoln's Gettysburg Address. If we use separate lines and spaces to indicate both the noticeable and slight vocal pauses that separate the various cadence groups, we can see that it is made up of these units of both rhythm and meaning:

> Fourscore and seven years ago
> our fathers brought forth   on this continent
> a new nation
> conceived in liberty
> and dedicated to the proposition
> that all men   are created equal.

This sentence is famous prose, and you can see that a sympathetic reading of it would be difficult without a grouping of the words approximately as they are laid out here. The following lines by Walt Whitman are spaced according to such cadence groups:

> When lilacs last   in the dooryard bloom'd,
> And the great star   early droop'd
> in the western sky   in the night.

Such groups may or may not correspond to regular rhythmical configurations in poetry. Here is an example of poetry (from Alexander Pope's *Essay on Man*) in which the cadence groups are patterned upon a rhythmical norm:

> O happiness!   our being's end and aim!
> Good,   pleasure,   ease,   content!   whate'er thy name:
> That something still   which prompts th'eternal sigh,
> For which we bear to live,   or dare to die.

You may observe that *O happiness, that something still,* and *or dare to die* are rhythmically similar: the second and fourth syllables in each of these groups are pronounced more emphatically than the first and third. You may also perceive the same rhythmical similarity of the groups *our being's end and aim, which prompts th'eternal sigh,* and *for which we bear to live.* This kind of poetry, in which cadence groups create a recurring pattern, is called **traditional poetry,** or poetry having a **closed form.** Poetry like Whitman's, however, in which cadence groups are arranged according to meaning and the poet's apparent wishes rather than according to rhythmical regularity, is called **free verse,** or poetry having an **open form.** Whether they use the open or closed form, all poets desire to create effective, moving ideas through the manipulation of cadence groups. However, the open-form poet relies almost exclusively on the arrangements of cadence groups, whereas the poet of closed form merges cadence groups and regular rhythmical patterns. Thus, open verse takes no apparently regular shape; lines may be long or short as the poet wishes to expand or concentrate the ideas. Traditional, closed verse takes on a more formal appearance, and its rhythms can be systematically measured.

SYLLABLES

Words are made up of **syllables,** the individual units of meaning and rhythm. A syllable is a separately pronounced part of a word or, in some cases, a complete word. Thus, *nation* is a complete word of two syllables, while *word*, also complete, has only one syllable. A syllable may be made up of (1) a vowel alone, as in the indefinite article *a* ("*a* star"), or (2) a vowel with a consonant, as in *to* in the word *together*, or (3) two consonant sounds enclosing a vowel, as in *geth* in *together*. There are other combinations. For example, in the word *abide* the portion *bide* is a single syllable because the final *e* is not pronounced (sometimes this type of *e* is called a "silent *e*" or "diacritic *e*"). In the word *through* there are two consonant sounds (*th* and *r*) preceding the *oo* sound of *ough*, but they do not create a separate syllable. Because the *gh* combination is not pronounced at all, *through* is a word of only one syllable. In words ending in *tion*, consonants enclose two vowels. However, the *ti* combines to form the *sh* sound (one consonant), and the letters hence make up only one syllable (as in *nation*). A concluding *es* or *ed* may make up a new syllable in words such as *musses* and *suited*, but quite often there is no new syllable at all, as in *mussed* and *fashioned*. Thus, in Francis Thompson's line "fashioned so purely," the syllables may be determined as follows:

> Fash - ioned   so   pure - ly.

This line has five distinctly pronounced syllables. Sometimes people experience difficulty in distinguishing the syllables in words. Hence, as a first step in perceiving rhythm, it is important to make an effort to recognize syllables. The word *merrier*, for example, is a three-syllable, not a two-syllable, word (*mer-ri-er*), as is *solitude* (*sol-i-tude*). If you have difficulty in recognizing syllables, a good idea is to read each word aloud, pronouncing every syllable, before reading the words in poetic context. If you are still not sure about the locations of syllables, consult a dictionary. The practice of reading poetry aloud is good in any event. If you have been encouraged to read for speed, you will be better off slowing down when you read poetry.

STRESS, METER, FEET, BEAT, AND METRICAL SCANSION

When you speak, and especially when you read poetry, you naturally give more force, intensity, or loudness to some syllables than to others. Those syllables that receive more force are *heavily stressed* or *heavily accented*, and those receiving less force are *lightly stressed* or *lightly accented*. In Browning's line "All that I know," for example, *all* and *know* are more heavily accented than *that* and *I*. In Pope's line "For fools rush in where angels fear to tread," the syllables receiving major stress are *fools, rush, an-, fear,* and *tread.* The syllables with less emphasis are *for, in, where, -gels,* and *to.*

BEAT AND THE METRICAL FOOT.   The beat or accent of the lines just cited, and of all lines of poetry, is determined by the syllables receiving major stress, and the rhythm of a line is determined by the relationship of heavily and lightly stressed syllables. The building block of a line of poetry is a **metrical foot,** which usually consists of one heavily stressed syllable and one or more lightly stressed syllables. There are various types of feet, each with a characteristic pattern. Poets writing in traditional forms usually fill their lines with a specific number of the same feet, and that number determines the regular **meter,** or measure, of that line. Thus five feet in a line are **pentameter,** four are **tetrameter,** three are **trimeter,** and two are **dimeter.** (To these may be added the less common line lengths **hexameter,** a six foot line, **heptameter** or **septenary,** seven feet, and **octameter,** eight feet.) In terms of accent or beat, a trimeter line has three beats (or stressed syllables), a pentameter line five beats, and so on.

Frequently, rhetorical needs cause poets to substitute other feet for the regular foot established in the poem. Whether there is **substitution** or not, however, the number and kind of feet in each line constitute the metrical description of that line. In order to discover the prevailing metrical system in any poem, you **scan** the poem. The act of scanning is called **scansion.**

A NOTATIONAL SYSTEM TO INDICATE RHYTHMS.   In scansion, it is important to use an agreed-upon notational system to record **stress** or **accent.** A heavy or primary accent is commonly indicated by a prime mark or acute accent (´) and a light accent may be indicated by a short accent (˘). (A circle or degree symbol may also be used for a light accent.) To separate one foot from another, a virgule (/) or slash is used. Thus, the following line, from Coleridge's "The Rime of the Ancient Mariner," may be schematized formally in this way:

Wa - tĕr, / wá - tĕr, / ev́ - eŕy whére,

Here the virgules show that the line may be divided into 2 two-syllable feet and 1 three-syllable foot.

METRICAL FEET

Equipped with this knowledge, you are ready to scan a poem to determine the rhythmical pattern of feet. The most important ones, the specific names of which are derived from Greek poetry, may be classed as the two-syllable foot, the three-syllable foot, and the imperfect (or one-syllable) foot.

The Two-Syllable Foot

1. IAMB.   A light stress followed by a heavy stress:

thĕ winds

The iamb is the most common foot in English-language poetry because it most nearly reflects the natural rhythmic cadences of the language. It is among the most versatile of poetic feet, capable of great variation. Even within the same line, iambic feet may vary in intensity, so that they may support or undergird the shades of meaning designed by the poet. For example, in this line from Wordsworth, each foot is unique:

Thĕ winds / thăt will / bĕ howl - / ĭng at / all hours.

Even though *will* and *at* are stressed syllables, they are not as heavily stressed as *winds*, *howl-*, and *hours* (indeed, they are also less strong than *all*, which is in an unstressed position). Such variability, approximating the stresses and rhythms of actual speech, makes the iambic foot suitable for just about any purpose, serious or light. The iamb therefore assists poets in focusing attention on their ideas and emotions. If they use it with skill, and vary it, it never becomes monotonous, for it does not distract the reader by drawing attention to its own rhythm.

2. TROCHEE.   A heavy accent followed by a light:

flow - ĕr

The iamb and the trochee deserve special attention. Most English words of two syllables or more are trochaic; for example:

region, watĕr, snowfăll, author, willŏw, morning, early

assurăncĕ, consider, returning, dĕpéndĕd

Words of two syllables having an iambic pattern are usually words with prefixes, or else they have been borrowed from a foreign language, such as French:

Words with prefixes: control, bĕcause, dĕspair, sŭblime

French words: măchine, gărage, tĕchnique, chĕmise

Trochaic rhythm is often called *falling, dying, light,* or *anticlimactic,* and iambic rhythm is usually called *rising, elevating, serious,* and *climactic.* A major problem encountered by many English poets has been to fit trochaic words into iambic patterns. A common way to deal with the problem—

and a way consistent with the natural word order of English—is to place a definite or indefinite article, a possessive pronoun, or some other single-syllable word, before a trochaic word. For example:

the cúrfĕw;   ă présĕnce;   whăt máttĕr;   hăs ópenĕd;   whĕn yéllŏw

Such additions produce an iamb followed by the light stress needed for the next iamb. For example, Thomas Gray, when developing the third line of the "Elegy Written in a Country Churchyard," an iambic poem, introduced the definite article *the* before the trochaic word *ploughman*. Next he wrote a two-syllable adverb, *homeward*, which is also trochaic. After this he placed *plods*, a one-syllable verb, and completed the line with a three-word phrase, *his weary way*. Notice his use of a single-syllable pronoun before the trochaic word *weary* in order to fit this word into the iambic pattern. The complete line is a perfectly regular iambic line of five feet (*iambic pentameter*).

Thĕ plóugh - / măn hóme - / wărd plóds / hĭs wéar - / y̆ wáy. /

Shakespeare does virtually the same thing in this line from his sonnet "Let Me Not to the Marriage of True Minds":

Wĭth - ín / hĭs bénd - / ĭng síck - / lĕ's cóm - / păss cóme. /

Here Shakespeare begins the second foot with the possessive pronoun *his*, a one-syllable word that enables him to include three successive trochaic words within the iambic pattern. The inclusion of the single-syllable word *come* at the end of the line completes the pattern and makes the line an example of regular, and very skillfully composed, iambic pentameter.

Another obvious means of using trochaic words is to substitute them for iambs, a device often used at the beginning of a line, as Yeats does here:

Túrn - ĭng / ănd túrn - / ĭng ín / ă wíd - / ĕn - ĭng gýre.

Often poets avoid the problem entirely by reducing the number of polysyllabic words in their lines and relying heavily on one-syllable words, as Shakespeare does in this line:

Tŏ lóve / thăt wéll / whĭch thóu / mŭst leáve / ĕre lóng.

In scanning a poem, you might wish to consider the number of polysyllabic words and observe the methods by which the poet arranges them to fit or to conflict with the basic metrical pattern.

3. SPONDEE.   Two successive, equally heavy accents, as in *men's eyes* in Shakespeare's line:

When, ĭn / dĭs - gráce / wĭth fór - / tŭne ańd / men's eyes.

The spondee—sometimes called a **hovering accent**—is primarily a substitute foot in English because successive spondees develop the rhythms of iambs or trochees. For this reason it is virtually impossible within traditional metrical patterns for an entire poem to be written in spondees (but see the section on strong-stressed verse, pp. 190–91). As a substitute, however, as in the case of "men's eyes," the spondee emphasizes the image or idea being expressed by the poet. The usual way to indicate the spondee in metrical scansion is to link the two syllables together with chevronlike marks (⋀).

4. Pyrrhic. Two unstressed syllables (even though one of them may be in a position normally receiving stress), as in *on their* in Pope's line:

Nŏw sléep - / ĭng flócks / oń theĭr / soft fleece - / ĕs lĭe.

The pyrrhic foot consists of weakly accented words like prepositions and articles. Like the spondee, it is usually substituted for an iamb or trochee, and therefore a complete poem cannot be written in pyrrhics. As a substitute foot, however, the pyrrhic acts as a rhythmic catapult to the next strongly accented syllable; therefore, it undergirds the ideas connected to the words that are accented.

The Three-Syllable Foot

1. Anapest.   Two light stresses followed by a heavy:

Bў the dáwn's / ear - lў líght

2. Dactyl.   A heavy stress followed by two lights:

míght - ĭ - est

Both of these meters are relatively rare in English and American poetry, but both have been employed with some success. We can see an example of anapestic tetrameter in Clement Moore's well-known poem "A Visit from St. Nicholas" (1822):

Twăs the níght / befŏre Chríst - / măs ańd aíl / thrŏugh the hoúse

Dactyllic verse is used by Robert Browning in "The Lost Leader" (1845):

Júst fŏr ă / hándfŭl ŏf / sílvĕr hĕ / léft ŭs.

The Imperfect Foot

The imperfect foot consists of a single syllable: (˘) by itself, or (´) by itself. This foot is a variant or substitute occurring in a poem in which one of the major feet forms the metrical pattern. The second line of "The Star-Spangled Banner," for example, is anapestic, but it contains an imperfect foot at the end:

What so proud - / ly we hailed / at the twi - / light's last gleam - / ing.

Most scansion of English verse can be carried out with reference to the metrical feet described above. The following lines illustrate all the feet listed.

trochee   *iamb*   *iamb*   *anapest*   *spondee*

How in / my thoughts / those hap - / pi - est days / shine forth—

troche   *dactyl*   *iamb*   *pyrrhic*   *spondee*

Days of / mel - o - dy / and love / and a / great dream.

Uncommon Meters

In many poems you might encounter variants other than those described above. Poets like Browning, Tennyson, Poe, and Swinburne experimented with uncommon meters. Other poets manipulated pauses or *caesurae* (discussed below) to create the effects of uncommon meters. For these reasons, you might need to refer to other metrical feet, such as the following.

1. Amphibrach. A light, heavy, and light, as in the following line from Swinburne's "Dolores":

Ah, feed me / and fill me / with plea - sure.

The amphibrach is the major foot in Browning's "How They Brought the Good News from Ghent to Aix"; for instance:

And in - to / the mid - night / we gal - loped / a - breast.

2. Amphimacer or cretic. A heavy, light, and heavy, as in Browning's lines: "Love is best" and "praise and pray."

The amphimacer occurs mainly in short lines or refrains, and also may be seen as a substitute foot, as in the last foot of this line from Tennyson's "Locksley Hall":

In the / spring a / young man's / fan - cy / light - ly / turns to / thoughts of love.

3. Bacchius or bacchic. A light followed by two heavy stresses, as in "Some late lark" in this line from W. E. Henley's "A Late Lark Twitters":

Sŏme láte lárk / síng - ĭng.

The bacchius often occurs as a substitute for an anapest, as in the last foot of this line from Browning's "Saul":

Whĕre thĕ lóng / gră̄ss - ĕs stí - / flĕ thĕ wá - / tĕr wĭth - ín / thĕ

stréam's bĕd.

4. Dipody or sizygy. Dipodic measure (literally, "two feet" combining to make one) develops in longer lines when a poet submerges two normal feet, usually iambs or trochees, under a stronger beat, so that a "galloping" or "rollicking" rhythm results. The following line from Browning's "A Toccata of Galuppi's," for example, may be scanned as trochaic heptameter (seven feet), with the concluding foot being an amphimacer or cretic:

Dĭd yŏŭng / péople / táke thĕir / pléas - ŭre / whĕn thĕ / séa wă̄s /

wárm ĭn Máy?

In reading, however, a stronger beat is superimposed, which creates dipodic feet:

Dĭd yŏŭng péoplĕ / tăke thĕir pléasŭre / whĕn thĕ séa / wă̄s wărm ĭn

Máy?

The dipodic foot can be used for a homespun, naive effect, as in James Whitcomb Riley's "When the Frost Is on the Punkin," where the foot overpowers the trochees:

Ŏh ĭt séts / my hĕart ă̆ clícklĭn' / lĭke thĕ tíckĭn' / ŏf ă̆ clóck,

Whĕn thĕ fróst / ĭs ŏn thĕ púnkĭn / ănd thĕ fóddĕr's / ĭn thĕ shóck.

T. S. Eliot, in the burlesque poem "Macavity: The Mystery Cat," superimposes dipodic measure over iambs for comic effect:

Măcávĭty̆, / Mă̄cávĭty̆, / thĕre's nó onĕ lĭke / Mă̆cávĭty̆,

Hĕ's brókĕn / evĕry húmăn lăw, / hĕ bréaks thĕ lăw / ŏf grávĭty̆.

5. Accentual, strong-stress, and "sprung" rhythms. A number of modern poets do not use traditional meters in their poems, but instead build their lines out of major stresses, regardless of the number of lightly stressed words and syllables. These accentual, or strong-stress, lines are historically derived from the type of poetry composed a thousand years ago during the age of Anglo-Saxon English. At that time, each line was divided in two, with two major stresses occurring in each half. In the nineteenth century Gerard Manley Hopkins (1844–1889) developed "sprung" rhythm, or a rhythm in which the major stresses would be released or "sprung" from the poetic line. The method is complex, but one characteristic is the juxtaposing of one-syllable stressed words, as in this line from "Pied Beauty":

With swíft, slów; swéet, sóur; ădázzle, dím;

Here a number of elements combine to create six major stresses in the line, which contains only nine syllables. Many of Hopkins's lines combine alliteration and strong stresses in this way to create the same effect of heavy emphasis.

Note: In scanning a poem to determine its formal meter, always try to explain the lines simply, by reference to the more common feet, before turning to the less common ones. If a line can be analyzed as iambic, for example, do not attempt to fit the bacchius or the amphibrach to it unless these feet are unmistakably indicated. The following line is iambic pentameter with a substitute spondee as the third foot.

The fíle / ŏf mén / rode forth / ă - móng / thĕ hílls. /

It would be a mistake to scan it thus:

The / fíle ŏf mén / róde / forth ă - mong / thĕ hílls. /

This incorrect analysis correctly accents "file of men" and "forth among," but by describing these phrases as two amphimacers, it must resort to the explanation that "The" and "rode" are imperfect feet. Such an analysis creates unnecessary complications.

THE CAESURA, OR PAUSE

The pause separating cadence groups, however brief, is called a **caesura** (the plural is **caesurae**). For noting scansion, the caesura is indicated by two diagonal lines or virgules (/ /) to distinguish it from the single virgule separating feet. The following line by Ben Jonson contains two caesurae:

Thŏu árt / nŏt, / / Péns - / hurst, / / buílt / tŏ én - / viŏus shów. /

If a caesura follows an accented syllable, it may be called a *stressed* or *rising* caesura; if it follows an unaccented syllable, *unstressed* or *falling*. In

the following line from William Blake, a stressed caesura follows the word
divine:

Wíth hánds / dĭvíne / / hĕ móv'd / thĕ gén - / tlĕ Sód. /

The following line from the same poem ("To Mrs. Anna Flaxman") contains
a falling caesura after the word *lovely*:

Ĭts fórm / wăs lóve - /lў / / bút / ĭts cŏí - / ouŕs paíe. /

The word *caesura* is usually reserved for references to pauses within
lines, but when a pause ends a line—usually marked by a comma, semicolon, or period—such a line is **end-stopped.** If you are writing about a
poet's use of pauses, you should treat not only the caesurae but also the
end-stopping; you might use the double virgules to show the concluding
pause, as in the following line from Keats's "Endymion" (1818):

Ă thíng / ŏf béau - / tў / / ís / ă jóy / fŏrévĕr. / /

If a line has no punctuation at the end and runs over to the next line, it
is called **run-on.** A term also used to indicate run-on lines is **enjambement.**
The following passage, a continuation of the line from Keats, contains
three run-on lines:

Its loveliness increases; / / it will never
Pass into nothingness; / / but still will keep
A bower quiet for us, / / and a sleep
Full of sweet dreams, / / . . .

EMPHASIS BY FORMAL SUBSTITUTION

Most poems are written in a pattern that can readily be perceived. Thus
Shakespeare's plays usually follow the pattern of **blank verse** (unrhymed
iambic pentameter); Milton's *Paradise Lost* follows this same pattern. Such
a pattern is no more than a rhythmical norm, however. For interest and
emphasis (and because of the nature of the English language) the norm
is varied by *substituting* other feet for the normal feet.

The following line is from the "January" eclogue of Spenser's *Shep-
herd's Calendar*. Although the abstract pattern of the line is iambic pentameter, it is varied by the substitution of two other feet:

Áll ĭn / ă sún - / shine day, / / ăs díd / bĕ - fáll.

All in is a trochee, and *shine day* is a spondee. This line shows **formal
substitution;** that is, a separate, formally structured foot is substituted

for one of the original feet. The effect of these substitutions is to enable one's voice to emphasize *all* as a strong syllable, almost a separate imperfect foot. Then the phrase *in a sun* rolls off the tongue as an anapest, and the spondee on *shine day* enables the voice to emphasize the words. In the context, Spenser has just been stressing the miseries of winter, and this line with its substitutions encourages the reader to think of spring as the voice lingers on the words:

> A shepherd's boy (no better do him call)
> When winter's wasteful spite was almost spent,
> All in a sunshine day, as did befall,
> Led forth his flock, that had been long ypent [enclosed].

When you study rhythm, try in this way to relate the substitutions to the ideas and attitudes of the poet.

EMPHASIS BY RHETORICAL VARIATION

The effect of formal substitution is to create opposing or contrasting internal rhythms. The same effect is also achieved by the manipulation of the caesura. Placing the caesura in a regular line has the same effect, in a spoken line, as if formal substitution had occurred. This variation may be called **rhetorical substitution**. A noteworthy example in an iambic pentameter line is this one by Pope:

> Hĭs ác - /tiŏns', / / pás - /siŏns', / / bé - /inğ's, / / uśe / and énd;

Ordinarily there is one caesura in a line of this type, but in this one there are three, each producing a strong pause. The line is regularly iambic and should be scanned as regular. But in reading, the effect is different. Because of the pauses in the middle of the second, third, and fourth feet, the line is read as an amphibrach, a trochee, a trochee, and an amphimacer, thus:

> Hĭs ác - tiŏns', / / pás - siŏns', / / bé - inğ's, / / uśe and énd;

Although the line is regular, the practical effect—the rhetorical effect—is of variation and tension. In the following well-known line from Shakespeare's *Twelfth Night*, rhetorical substitution may also be seen:

> If music / / be the food of love, / / play on!

This line is regularly iambic except perhaps for a spondee in *play on*, but the reading of the line conflicts with the formal pattern. Thus, *If music* may be read as an amphibrach and *be the food* is in practice an anapest because of the short pause after *music* and the light stress on the word *be* following the caesura. The words stressed in the line are *music*, *food*, *love*, and the command *play on*. The line reads like normal speech even though it is in a formal rhythmical structure, and Shakespeare has provided us with the best of both worlds.

In whatever poetry you study, your main concern in noting substitutions is to determine the formal metrical pattern and then to analyze the formal and rhetorical variations on the pattern and the principal causes and effects of these variations. Always show how these variations have assisted the poet in achieving emphasis.

WRITING ABOUT RHYTHM IN POETRY

Because studying for poetic scansion requires a good deal of specific detail and, ultimately, much specific description, it is best to limit your choice of poem to a short passage or a complete short poem. A sonnet, a stanza of a lyric poem, or fragment from a long poem will usually be of sufficient length for your study. If you choose a fragment, it should be a self-contained one, such as an entire speech or short episode or scene (as in the example from Tennyson chosen for the sample essay in the second part of this chapter (pp. 206–9).

The analysis of even a short poem, however, can become long because of the need to describe the positions of words and stresses, and the need to determine various effects. For this reason, you do not have to exhaust all aspects of your topic. Try to make your reading selective and representative of the rhythms of the passage you have chosen.

Your first reading in preparation for your theme might be a reading for comprehension. On second and third readings, however, try to make yourself aware of sound and accent by reading the poem aloud. One student helped herself to a comprehension of rhythm by reading aloud in an exaggerated fashion in front of a mirror. If you have privacy, or are not especially self-conscious, you might do the same. Let yourself go a bit. As you dramatize your reading, you might find that certain heightened levels of reading also accompany important ideas. Mark these spots for later study, so that you can make points about the relationship of rhythm to content.

In planning a theme on scansion, it is important to prepare materials that will later be helpful, and make sure that you make your observations exactly and correctly, for your conclusions may go astray if some of your factual analysis is wrong. The job of writing can be facilitated by a careful preparation of materials. Therefore, the first task in developing your essay is to make a triple-spaced copy of the poem or passage. Leave spaces between syllables and words for the marking out of the various feet of the poem. Ultimately, this duplication of the passage, with your markings, should be included as a first page, as in the sample theme.

Carry out your study of the passage in the following way:

1. Number each line of the passage, regardless of length, beginning with 1, so that you may use these numbers as location references in your essay.

2. Determine the formal pattern of feet, using the short acute accent for heavily stressed syllables (´), and the short symbol for lightly stressed syllables (either ˘ or °). Use chevrons to mark spondees (⋀).

3. Indicate the separate feet by a diagonal line or virgule (/). Indicate caesurae and the pauses at end-stopped lines by double virgules (/ /).

4. Underline, or mark with various colored pencils, any formal and rhetorical substitutions, and provide a numbered key at the bottom of the page. Colored pencils have proved particularly useful in the distinguishing of the various effects, and often they prevent mistakes that result from confusion about monochromatic markings.

5. When sketching out and preparing drafts of your essay, use your worksheet as a reference. In the final writing of your essay, however, it will not be sufficient just to point out line numbers as your supporting data. Instead, you will need to make your examples specific and illustrative at the spot where they are relevant (using, for example, words, phrases, and entire lines, with proper marks and accents), just as they should be for essays on other topics.

Once you have fully analyzed the effects of meter in the poem under consideration and have recorded these on your worksheet and in your notes, you will be ready to formulate a tentative central idea and organization for the essay. The focus for the theme should reflect what you have found to be the most significant feature of metrics as it applies to some other element of the poem, such as speaker, tone, or ideas.

After forming a tentative idea for the theme, you can begin to gather examples of metrical evidence to support your central assertion. These examples can be grouped into units of related or similar effects that will eventually become paragraphs in the body of the theme. Make sure that all your examples are relevant to your central idea. If you find the metrical evidence leading you in new directions, rethink the theme and revise the central idea accordingly.

Introduction

The introduction should lead as quickly as possible to the central idea. After a brief description of the poem (such as that it is a sonnet, a two-stanza lyric, a short satirical piece in tetrameter couplets, an iambic pentameter description of a character, a dipodic burlesque poem, and so on), try to establish the scope of your essay. You might wish to discuss all aspects of rhythm, or perhaps just one, such as the poet's use of (1) regular meter, (2) a particular subsitution, such as the anapest or the trochee, and (3) the caesura and its effects. (For comprehensiveness, the sample essay treats all these topics, but an essay might deal with just one or two of them.) Your central idea will outline the thought you wish to carry out in your metrical analysis, such as that regularity of meter is consistent with the desire to be constant (as in the sample theme), or that the meter undergirds particular aspects of description, or that the poet builds up particular ideas so that they are rhythmically as well as logically stressed. Your thesis sentence should outline the aspects you plan to treat in the body of the theme.

Body

You should first establish the formal metrical pattern. What is the dominant metrical foot? Are the lines of consistent length, or do they vary? If there is variable length, what relationship do the variations have with the subject matter? If the poem is a lyric, or a sonnet, you should determine if the poet is successful in placing important words and syllables in stressed positions to achieve emphasis. Try to relate line lengths to whatever exposition and development of ideas and whatever rising and falling of emotion you find. It is also important to look for repeating or varying metrical patterns as the subject matter reaches peaks or climaxes. Generally, deal with the relationship between the formal rhythmical pattern and the poet's ideas and attitudes.

In writing about substitutions, you might analyze the formal variations and the principal effects of these, as nearly as you can determine what the effects are. The aim is to relate substitutions to ideas and emotions emphasized by the poet. If you decide to concentrate on one particular metrical substitution, try to describe any apparent pattern in its use; that is, its locations, recurrences, and effects on meaning.

In the analysis of caesurae, treat the effectiveness of the poet's control. Can you see any pattern of use? Are the pauses regular, or do they seem randomly placed? What conclusions can you draw as a result of your answer? Describe any noticeable principles of placement, such as (1) the creation of rhythmical similarities in various parts of the poem, (2) the development of particular rhetorical effects, or (3) the creation of interest through rhythmical variety. Do the caesurae lead to important ideas and attitudes? Are the lines all end-stopped, or do you discover enjambement? How do these rhythmical characteristics aid in the poet's expression of subject matter?

Conclusion

Beyond summarizing your main idea in the theme, you might develop a short evaluation of the poet's metrical performance. Without going into excessive detail (and in effect writing another body for the theme), can you say here any more than you have in the body? What has been the value of your study to your understanding and appreciating this particular poem? If you think your analysis has helped you to develop new awareness of the craft of poetry generally, it would be appropriate in your conclusion to describe what you have learned.

Sample Theme

The Rhythms of Keat's Sonnet "Bright Star"

1 Bright star! / / would I / were stead- / fast / / as /thou art/ — / /
                           — 2 —————

2 Not in / lone splen- / dor / / hung / a-loft / the night, / /

3 And watch- / ing, / / with / e- ter- / nal lids / a- part, / /

4 Like Na- / ture's pa- / tient / / sleep- / less E- / re- mite, / /

5 The mov- / ing wa-/ ters / / at / their priest- / like task

6 Of pure / ab-lu- / tion / / round / earth's hu- / man shores, / /
                           — 2 —

7 Or gaz- / ing / / on / the new / soft- fall- / en mask

8 Of snow / up- on / the moun- / tains / / and / the moors— / /

9 No— / / yet / still stead- / fast, / / still / un -change- / a-ble, / /

10   Pill-₇owed / up- ón / mў fáir / love's ₁ripe- / nĭng bréast, / /

11   Tŏ feél / forev ₅- / er / / its / soft ₁fall / ănd swéll, / /
                                — 2 ———

12   Ă-wáke / forév-₅ / er / / ín / ă sweet₆ / un- rést, / /

13   Still, / / still₁ / / tŏ héar / hĕr tén- / dĕr-tá- / kĕn bréath, / /

14   Ănd só / live ₁ev- / er— / / or / else ₁swoon / tŏ deáth. / /
                                  —2———

1 = spondee   5 = effect of amphibrach
2 = effect of bacchius   6 = effect of anapest
3 = effect of imperfect foot   7 = trochee
4 = effect of amphimacer   8 = effect of trochee

[1]   This personal poem, in which Keats's speaker describes the wish to be
a "steadfast" lover like the "bright star" that is a witness to the earth's waters
and snows, is a fourteen-line sonnet. Keats emphasizes steadiness and regularity, and his meter, too, is constant, even in its variations.° The regularity is
apparent in the formal iambic pattern, the substitutions, and the caesurae.□

[2]   Because the sonnet, being made up of only one long sentence, is difficult
to follow, Keats relies on metrical regularity to help the reader. Twelve of the
fourteen lines are end-stopped, ending on stressed syllables in iambic feet,
to climax particular ideas and descriptions. The two lines that are enjambed
are 5 and 7. Even these create an identical pattern, however, because they
are first and third in the second quatrain, and the carry-over words are alike
both grammatically and metrically (task / Of pure, and mask / Of snow). Keats
uses parallel patterns in 3 and 7 (And watch- / ing, and Or gaz- / ing). The
iambic-infinitives to feel and to hear appear in 11 and 13, and the accented
single-syllable verbs live and swoon are balanced together in the last line.
The iambic preposition upon is repeated in the second feet of 8 and 10, and
the adverb for-ev- / er recurs in 11 and 12.

[3]   The same regularity can be seen in Keats's substitutions, mainly spondees. He frames his first line with opening and closing spondees (Bright star
and thou art). For balance, he uses spondees again in the second and fourth
feet of the concluding line, an effective inner frame. He uses a total of fourteen
spondees. The spondee appears in the fourth foot of five separate lines (6,
7, 10, 11, and 14), enough to undergird his idea of steadfastness. Keats uses

° Central idea
□ Thesis sentence

two successive spondees in the first line (*Bright star, / would I/*) and uses this rhythm again at the start of line 9, as his thought shifts from the star to himself (*No—yet / still stead- /*). He also uses a spondee at the opening of the last couplet (*Still, still*), thus employing this substitution at the beginning of each major grouping of the sonnet (lines 1–8 as group one; 9–12 as two; and 13 and 14 as three). He uses one spondee in 11 (*soft fall*) to echo another one he uses in 7 (*soft fall- / en*). All these strategically placed spondees help unify Keats's thought. The trochees in lines 1, 2, and 10 are not by themselves enough to be seen as part of any trochaic pattern of substitution.

More to the effect of trochaic patterning is Keats's regularity in his use of caesurae. In eight lines, the caesura is in the middle, after the fifth syllable, thereby causing a trochaic or falling rhythm in the previous two syllables. This pattern is exemplified in line 4:

falling rhythm

Like Nát- / ure's(pa- / tient)/ /(sleep- / less)É- / re- mite,

[4] The caesura in such a position creates not just apparent trochees, as in *patient* and *wa-ters* in 4 and 5, but also the effects of amphibrachs, as in *ab-lu-tion* and *fore-ver* in 6 and 11. Keats also puts caesurae after uneven-numbered syllables in four of the other lines (1, 2, 5, and 14). Only two internal caesurae are rising ones after even-numbered syllables (1 and 13). Thus, the characteristic mode of caesurae for this poem is a falling one. In a real sense, the falling rhythm, balanced by the rising rhythm at the ends of the end-stopped lines, may be compared to the "fair love's" breathing described in lines 10 and 11.

[5] It would be possible to add still more descriptions of other recurring rhythmical effects by which Keats unites the poem (for example, the effect of the bacchius repeated twice in the opening and closing lines: *were stead-fast* and *as thou art*, and *and so live* and *or else swoon*). It is enough here, however, to restate that his metrics are used and varied with regularity. They reinforce his speaker's main theme—the wish to be as eternally steadfast as the bright star.

COMMENTARY ON THE THEME

Detailed as it is, this theme is a selective discussion of the rhythms of Keats's poem. It would be possible, for example, to extend the essay with a more searching study of the tension caused by the rhetorical variations which result from the placement of the caesurae.

The introductory paragraph relates the metrics to the constant, steadfast star. Paragraph 2 stresses the way in which the regularly placed accents help the reader to comprehend the poem, which consists of a single sentence. Note is made of the repeated words and grammatical forms which are also repeated rhythmical units.

The third paragraph treats the spondee as a regular substitution throughout the poem. Paragraph 4 deals with the caesurae and relates these to the central idea by submitting that the falling rhythms before the caesurae, balanced by the rising rhythms of the end-stopped lines, suggests the regular breathing of the speaker's "fair love."

The final paragraph suggests, as has been already mentioned, that there might be other aspects of the rhythm that could be examined. The essay, however, concludes here, on the principle that the writer has demonstrated a satisfactory understanding of rhythm.

II. SOUNDS AND SEGMENTS

Just as poetry stresses rhythm, it also emphasizes the sounds of individual words. These sounds have been classified by linguists as **segments.** Each segment is a sound essential to the meaningful understanding of words. Thus, in the word *top* there are three segments: *t, o,* and *p.* It takes three letters—*t, o,* and *p*—to spell **(graph)** the word, because each letter is identical with a segment. Sometimes it takes more than one letter to spell a segment. In *enough,* for example, there are four segments but *six* letters: *e, n, ou,* and *gh.* The last two segments (*ŭ* and *f*) require two letters each (two letters forming one segment are called a **digraph**). In the word *through* there are three segments but *seven* letters. To be correctly spelled in this word, the $\overline{oo}$ segment must have four letters, *ough.* Note, however, that in the word *flute* the $\overline{oo}$ segment requires only one letter, the *u.*

Segments may be treated as **vowel sounds** and **consonant sounds** (including **semivowels**). It is important to emphasize the word *sound* as distinguished from the letters of the alphabet, for the same letters often represent different sounds.

To study the effects of sounds and segments in poetry, we need an acceptable notational system for indicating sounds. The most readily available systems of pronunciation are those in the collegiate dictionaries; they take into account regional differences in pronunciation. If questions arise about syllabication and the position of stresses, you should use your dictionary as your authority.

VOWEL SOUNDS

Vowel sounds are vibrations resonating in the space between the tongue and the top of the mouth. Some are relatively straight and "short," such as *ĭ* (f*ĭ*t), *ŭ* (f*ŭ*n), and *ĕ* (s*ĕ*t). Some are long, such as *ō* (sn*o*w), *ā* (st*a*y), *ē* (fl*e*e), and $\overline{oo}$ (f*oo*d). There are three **diphthongs**—that is, sounds that begin with one vowel sound and move to another—namely *ī* (fl*y*), *ou* (h*ou*se), and *oi* (f*oi*l). A great number of vowel sounds in English are pronounced as a *schwa* (the *e* in "th*e* boy"), despite their spellings. Thus "*a*bout," "stag*e*s," "rap*i*d," "nati*o*n," and "circ*u*s" are spelled with the vowels *a*, *e*, *i*, *o*, and *u*, but all these different vowels make the same *schwa* sound.

CONSONANT SOUNDS

There are various classifications of consonant sounds, but basically they are of three types: (1) **Stop sounds** are made by the momentary stoppage and release of breath either when the lips touch each other or when the tongue touches the teeth or palate. The stop sounds are *p*, *b*, *t*, *d*, *k*, and *g* (as in "*g*ull"). (2) **Continuant sounds** are produced by the steady release of the breath in conjunction with various positions of the tongue in relation to the teeth and palate, as in *n*, *ng*, *l*, *r*, *th* (*th*orn), *th* (*th*e), *s*, *z*, *sh* (*sh*arp), and *zh* (plea*s*ure); or with the touching of the lower lip and upper teeth for the sounds *f* and *v*; or with the touching of both lips for the sound *m*. Two sounds, called **affricates,** begin with the stops *t* (*ch*ew) and *d* (*j*aw) and then become the continuants *sh* and *zh*. (3) **Semivowel sounds** or **glides** are midway between vowels and consonants. These are *w* (*w*agon), *y* (*y*es, *u*nion), and *h* (*h*ope).

Another way of classifying consonant sounds is according to whether they are **voiced,** that is, produced with vibration of the vocal chords (*b*, *d*, *v*, *z*), or **voiceless,** produced by the breath alone (*p*, *t*, *f*, *s*).

DISTINGUISHING SOUNDS
FROM SPELLING

When discussing segments, it is important to distinguish between spelling, or **graphics,** and pronunciation, or **phonetics.** Thus the letter *s* has three very different sounds in the words *sweet*, *sugar*, and *flows*: *s*, *sh*, and *z*. On the other hand, the words *shape*, *ocean*, *nation*, *sure*, and *machine* use different letters or combinations of letters to spell the same *sh* sound.

Vowel sounds may also be spelled in different ways. The *ē* sound, for example, can be spelled with *i* in *machine*, *ee* in *speed*, *ea* in *eat*, *e* in *even*, and *y* in *funny*, yet the vowel sounds in *eat*, *break*, and *bear* are not the same even though they are spelled the same. Remember: With both consonants and vowels, do not confuse spellings with actual sounds.

SEGMENTAL POETIC DEVICES

Poets use segments in various patterns to link sound with sense. A poet may use words containing the same segments and thereby impress your memory by merging sound and idea. In descriptive poetry, the segments may combine, with rhythm, to imitate some of the things being described. The segmental devices most common to poetry are *assonance, alliteration,* and *onomatopoeia.*

ASSONANCE. The repetition of identical *vowel* sounds in different words—for example, short *ĭ* in "swift Camĭlla skĭms," is called **assonance.** It is a strong means of emphasis, as in the following line by Spenser, where the *ŭ* sound connects the two words *lull* and *slumber,* and the short *ĭ* connects *him, in,* and *his*:

And more, to lŭll hĭm ĭn hĭs slŭmber soft

In some cases, poets use assonance quite elaborately, as in this line from Pope's "Essay on Criticism":

'Tĭs hard to say, ĭf greater want of skĭll

Here the line is framed and balanced with the short *ĭ* in *'Tis, if,* and *skill.* The *ä* in *hard* and *want* forms another, internal frame, and the *ā* in *say* and *greater* creates still another. Such a balanced use of vowels is unusual, however, for in most lines assonance is used more randomly for sound to connect sense.

In studying assonance, a reader must avoid selecting isolated instances of a particular sound. If, for example, a line in a poem includes three words that contain a long *ā* sound, these form a pattern of assonance. A word containing the same long *ā* sound that occurs six lines later, however, is not part of this pattern because it is too far removed from the original instances of the sound.

ALLITERATION. Like assonance, **alliteration** is a means of highlighting ideas by the selection of words containing the same *consonant* sound— for example, the repeated *m* in "*m*ixed with a *m*urmuring wind," or the *s* sound in Waller's "Your never-failing *s*word made war to *c*ease," which emphasizes the connection between the words *sword* and *cease.*

There are two kinds of alliteration. (1) Most commonly, alliteration is regarded as the repetition of identical consonant sounds that begin syllables in relatively close patterns—for example, Pope's "La*b*orious, heavy, *b*usy, *b*old, and *b*lind," and "While *p*ensive *p*oets *p*ainful vigils keep." Used sparingly, alliteration gives strength to a poem by emphasizing key words, but too much can cause comic consequences. (2) Another form of alliteration occurs when a poet repeats identical or similar consonant sounds that do not begin syllables but nevertheless create a pattern—for example, the *z* segment in the line "In these places freezing breezes easily cause sneezes," or the *b, m,* and *p* segments (all of which are made *bilabially,* that is, with both lips) in "The *m*u*mb*ling and *m*ur*m*uring *b*eggar throws *p*egs and *p*e*bb*les in the *bubb*ling *p*ool." Such deliberate patterns are hard to overlook.

ONOMATOPOEIA. **Onomatopoeia** is a blending of consonant and vowel sounds designed to imitate or suggest a sense or action. It is thus one of the most vivid and colorful aspects of poetry. Onomatopoeia depends on the fact that many words in English are *echoic*; that is, they are verbal echoes of the action they describe, such as *buzz, bump, slap,* and so on. In the following passage from John Donne's sonnet "Batter My Heart," we may see onomatopoeia in action:

> Batter my heart, three-personed God; for you
> As yet but knock, breathe, shine, and seek to mend,
> That I may rise, and stand, o'erthrow me, and bend
> Your force, to break, blow, burn, and make me new.

Notice here the words *batter, knock, seek, bend, break, blow,* and *burn.* These sounds, like the abrupt sounds of blows, provide a tactile illustration of the spiritual "violence" described in the lines.

Shakespeare created a memorable use of onomatopoeia in lines spoken by Cleopatra just before she commits suicide to avoid capture (*Antony and Cleopatra,* V.ii. 284–285):

> Now no more
> The juice of Egypt's grape shall moist this lip.

Here the bilabial *m* and *p* segments (like the sounds described in the previous section) in *more, Egypt's, grape, moist,* and *lip* all put spoken empha sis on the lips, to which people put glasses in the act of drinking. Shakespeare thus makes Cleopatra's reference to wine drinking a vivid verbal experience.

EUPHONY AND CACOPHONY

Words describing either positive or negative qualities of sound, particularly resulting from the placement of consonants, are *euphony* and *cacophony*. **Euphony** ("good sound") refers to words containing consonants that permit an easy and pleasant flow of spoken sound. Although there is no rule that some consonants are inherently more pleasant than others, students of poetry often cite continuant sounds like *m, n, ng, l, v,* and *z,* together with *w* and *y,* as offering especially easy pronunciation. The conclusion of Keats's line, "Thy hair soft-lifted by the winnowing wind," for example, is euphonious. The opposite of euphony is **cacophony** ("bad sound"), in which the words do not flow smoothly but rather bump against each other harshly and jarringly. As with euphony, there are no particularly "bad" sounds, for it is the combination that makes for harshness, as in tongue-twisters like "black bug's blood" and "selfish shellfish." Obviously, unintentional cacophony is a mark of imperfect control. When a poet deliberately creates cacophony for effect, however, as in Tennyson's "The bare black cliff clang'd round him," Pope's "The hoarse, rough verse should like the torrent roar," and Donne's lines from "Batter My Heart" quoted above, cacophony is a mark of poetic skill. Although poets generally aim to provide easily flowing, euphonious lines, cacophony does have a place, always depending on the poet's intention and subject matter.

WRITING ABOUT SOUNDS AND SEGMENTS IN POETRY

In writing a theme on segments in poetry, you should assume that all the words in a poem or passage are there because the poet chose them not only for meaning, but also for sound. There is thus nothing accidental; all the effects are intended. Readers sometimes claim that the relationship of sound to sense is subjective and murky. While there is an element of subjectivity, it is possible to show the objective basis for all conclusions. Thus, if a number of words with identical segments appear close together in a poem, this closeness justifies your study of them as a pattern.

The greatest subjectivity occurs when you make observations about onomatopoeia. Should a poet be describing a strong wind, however, and if the description contains many words with *h*, *th*, *f*, and *s* segments (all of which require a continuous, breathy release of air), you would be justified to claim that the sounds echo the description—an instance of onomatopoeia. If you are thus able to objectify your interpretation of sounds, your claims will stand most challenges.

As with themes on meter or rhythm, the aim in a theme on segments is to demonstrate the connection between a poem's sounds and its content. You cannot write about sound in isolation; segmental effects are normally linked to another aspect of the poem, such as speaker, tone, or meaning. Thus, the first step in planning your theme is to choose an appropriate poem or passage and discover as much as you can about its speaker, setting and situation, imagery, ideas, and so on.

When you are ready to move from these general considerations to a specific examination of sound, you should prepare a worksheet on which you can note segmental patterns. This worksheet should provide a triple-spaced copy of the poem or passage, with each line numbered. A carefully prepared worksheet will simplify the planning and writing of the theme and, if handed in with the theme, will help your readers significantly.

Scrutinize the poem or passage carefully for patterns of assonance and alliteration and for instances of onomatopoeia, and indicate these on your worksheet with different-colored pencils or markers. Use one color for each segment, and draw lines to indicate connections. If you use only one pencil or marker (as in the sample theme below), you might employ a system of dotted, dashed, and unbroken lines to signify connections. At the bottom of the worksheet, make an explanatory key to your circles and lines. Use a standard pronunciation guide from a dictionary to describe sounds, and indicate in a footnote which dictionary you are using.

After you have identified all the segmental patterns and your worksheet is covered with interconnected sounds, you can begin to isolate the most significant and effective instances. At this point in prewriting, selectivity and focus come into play. You will rarely use all your discoveries about sound in a single theme. Instead, look for those segmental patterns that have the most noticeable effect on the way you experience the poem.

The central idea for the theme will normally emerge from this connection between sound and content. If you are exploring Poe's poem "The Bells," for example, you might determine that onomatopoeia and repetition have the strongest impact on your reading, and a tentative central idea might assert that Poe employs onomatopoeia and repetition to bring the images of the poem alive and to make sound echo sense. The patterns of sound and segment that lead you to such conclusions about the poem under consideration will become the supporting evidence in the body of the theme.

Introduction

In a sentence or two, make a brief overview of your poem or passage. Is it descriptive, reflective? Does it contain much action? Is it down-to-earth and "real," or is it romanticized or idealized? Is it about love, friendship, loyalty, selfishness, betrayal, or what? Try to fashion your central idea as a link between the subject matter and the sound. Is there a strong relationship, or does it seem that any segmental effects are unsystematic or unintended? Your thesis sentence should outline the topics for the body.

Body

The body should report your linkage of sound and sense. Be sure to establish that the instances you choose have occurred systematically enough to be grouped as a pattern. Illustrate sounds by including the relevant words within parentheses. You might wish to make separate paragraphs on alliteration, assonance, onomatopoeia, and any seemingly important pattern of segments. Also, because space in an essay is at a premium, you might concentrate on one noteworthy effect, like a certain pattern of assonance, rather than on everything in the poem. Throughout your discussion, always keep foremost the relationship between the content and the sounds you are considering.

As a means of making illustrations clear, underline all sounds to which you are calling attention. If you use an entire word to illustrate a sound, underline only the sound and not the entire word, but put the word within quotation marks (for example, The poet uses a t ["tip," "top," and "terrific"]). When you refer to entire words containing particular segments, however, underline these words (for example, The poet uses a t in tip, top, and terrific.).

Conclusion

Here you might make a brief evaluation of the poet's use of segments. A poem is designed not only to inform, but also to transfer attitudes and to stimulate the reader. To what degree does sound contribute to these goals? Any personal reflections or discoveries that you have made as a result of your study are appropriate here. If it seems too difficult to write an evaluation, it would be possible here, as in any essay, to conclude with a short summary.

Sample Theme

A Study of Tennyson's Use of Segments in "The Passing of Arthur," lines 349–360

Note: The other sample themes in this chapter analyze a sonnet and a lyric. For illustrative purposes, this theme analyzes a passage from a long poem: Tennyson's "The Passing of Arthur," which is part of Idylls of the King. Containing 469 lines, "The Passing of Arthur" describes the last battle and death of Arthur, legendary king of early Britain. After the fight, in which Arthur has been mortally wounded by the traitor Modred, only Arthur and his follower Sir Bedivere remain alive. Arthur commands Bedivere to throw the royal sword, Excalibur, into the lake from which it had been originally given to Arthur. After much hesitation, Bedivere does throw the sword into the lake, and a hand rises out of the water to catch it. Bedivere then carries Arthur to the shore of the lake, where the dying king is taken aboard a magical funeral barge by three queens, who are "black-hooded" and "black-stoled" and who wear "crowns of gold." The barge carries Arthur away to die, leaving Bedivere alone to tell the story.

The passage analyzed here is the description of Bedivere carrying Arthur from the chapel at the battlefield down the hills to the shore of the lake.

WORKSHEET NO. 1: ALLITERATION

But the other (s) wiftly (s) trode from ridge to ridge,   1

Clothed with his breath, and looking, as (h) e walked,   2

Larger than (h) uman on the frozen (h) ills.   3

(H) e (h) eard the deep be (h) ind (h) im, and a cry   4

Before. (H) is own thought drove him like a goad.   5

Dry (c) lashed (h) is (h) arness in the icy (c) aves   6

And (b) arren (ch) asms, and all to left and right   7

The (b) are (b) (l) ack (c) (l) iff (c) (l) anged round him, as he (b) ased   8

His feet on juts of s (l) ippery (c) rag that rang   9

Sharp-smitten with the dint of armed heels—   10

And on a sudden, (l) o! the (l) evel (l) ake,   11

And the (l) ong g (l) ories of the winter moon.   12

⌇⌇⌇⌇⌇ = s   ——— = b

--------- = h   ～～～～ = l as second consonant
                                                                        sound in words

············· = k

——·——·——·— = l

WORKSHEET NO. 2: ASSONANCE ⃰

But the other sw (i) ftly str (o) de from r (i) dge to r (i) dge,   1

Cl (o) thed w (i) th h (i) s breath, and looking, as he walked,   2

Larger than human on the fr (o) zen hills.   3

He heard the deep beh (i) nd him, and a cr (y)   4

Before. His (ow) n thought dr (o) ve him l (i) ke a g (oa) d.   5

Dr (y) clashed his harness in the (i) cy caves   6

And barren ch (a) sms, and all to left and r (i) ght   7

The bare bl (a) ck cliff cl (a) nged round him, as he based   8

H (i) s feet on juts of sl (i) ppery cr (a) g that r (a) ng   9

Sh (ar) p-sm (i) tten w (i) th the d (i) nt of (ar) med heels—   10

And on a sudden, lo, the level lake,   11

And the long glories of the winter moon!   12

——————— = ō ⃰   •—•—•—•—• = ä

- - - - - - - - = ī   ⌇⌇⌇⌇⌇⌇ = ĭ

• • • • • • • • = a

⃰ Pronunciation symbols as in *Webster's New World Dictionary*, 2nd ed.

[1]
In this passage from "The Passing of Arthur," Tennyson describes Sir Bedivere's effort in carrying the dying King Arthur from the chapel near the battlefield to the shores of the nearby lake. Many of Tennyson's words contain sounds which support and echo his descriptions of setting and action.° This blending of sound and meaning is shown in Tennyson's use of alliteration, assonance, general segmental texture, and onomatopoeia.□

[2]
Tennyson's use of alliterative words ties together key ideas and assists in oral interpretation. In line 1, s's begin the words swiftly and strode. In 7 and 8, b's connect barren, bare, black, and based. Aspirated h's appear in 2–6 on human, hills, heard, behind, and harness. There are also h's in he, him, and his in these lines, but these words do not require the same breathy h pronunciation. Hard k sounds are repeated in nouns and active verbs in 6–9 (clashed, caves, chasms, cliff, clanged, crag). Two sets of l's appear. One is made up of the second segments in heavy, ringing words in 8 and 9 (black, cliff, clanged, and slippery). The other is the first segment in words describing the lake in 11 and 12 (lo, level, lake, long; note also glories). In their contexts, these l's assist in producing contrasting effects. They seem heavy and sharp in 8 and 9, but in 11 and 12 they help the voice to relax.

[3]
Through assonance, Tennyson gains the same kind of emphasis. To choose a notable example from many, the long o segment appears in six words in the first five lines. The first three words are descriptive and metaphoric (strode, clothed, and frozen), while the next three describe Bedivere's troubled spirit as he struggles on the barren crags (own, drove, and goad). By sound alone, therefore, the long o ties the physical to the psychological.

[4]
Combining assonance with a skillful use of segmental texture, Tennyson creates a remarkable contrast at the end of the passage. In lines 8 through 10 he introduces words containing vowels pronounced with the tongue forward and high in the mouth (he, based, feet, heels; and the short i assonance in cliff, him, his, slippery, smitten, with, and dint). These segments are penetrating and sharp, in keeping with Bedivere's exertion as he climbs down the dreary hills. By contrast, in the last two lines Tennyson uses words that invite a lowering of vocal pitch and a relaxed and lingering pronunciation. These are on, sudden, lo, long, glories, of, and moon (particularly long, glories, and moon). In reading, the contrast is both sudden and effective, a memorable and euphonious conclusion.

[5]
Also in these last two lines, and elsewhere in the passage, onomatopoeia may be noted. The l sounds in lo, level, lake, long, and glories suggest the gentle lapping of waves on a shore. At the start of the passage, in line 2, Tennyson indicates that the mountainous ridges are so chilly that Bedivere's condensing breath resembles clothing. In the next five lines there are a number of words, already noted, that contain the breathy h. In the context, these sounds remind one of Bedivere's labored breathing as he carries his royal burden. Similarly, the stop sounds in 6–10 (b and k, which have been noted, and also d [in dry, dint] and t [clashed, left, right, based, feet, juts, smitten, dint]) are cacophonous, like the sounds Bedivere would have made in struggling to keep his feet on the "juts of slippery crag."

[6]
Thus Tennyson's choice of words with identical or similar sounds is designed to undergird his descriptions of Bedivere's heroic efforts. These sounds, in context, have their own complementary meaning. They help Tennyson emphasize the grandeur of both Arthur and his faithful follower. As long as there are readers for the poem, this grandeur may be remembered.

° Central idea
□ Thesis sentence

COMMENTARY ON THE THEME

The sample theme demonstrates the clear and significant connection between patterns of sound and descriptions of setting and action in the passage from Tennyson's "The Passing of Arthur." The introductory paragraph briefly describes the topic material of the passage from Tennyson. The central idea connects many of the segments with his descriptions. The thesis sentence indicates that four topics will be developed.

Paragraph 2 examines all the instances of alliteration discovered in the analysis, with particular attention to the two groups of *l* sounds. Even within a comprehensive treatment, in other words, it is possible and desirable to go into detail on a single subtopic that is especially noteworthy.

The third paragraph considers assonance, not selecting all instances but instead providing detail about only a single pattern (the long *o*) and its effects. Such a treatment helps to keep the theme reasonably brief. The worksheets, which pinpoint all the noted instances of assonance, forestall a potential criticism that the discussion focuses on only one point because all the other points were not discovered.

Paragraph 4 deals with the specific effects of vowel quality in the last two lines. To make this treatment meaningful, the paragraph contrasts vowels in the preceding three lines with the vowels in the last two.

The fifth paragraph considers three separate instances of onomatopoeia, enough to justify the claim in the central idea that there is a close connection between sound and sense.

The concluding paragraph stresses the heroism and grandeur that Tennyson tried to evoke about his subject, and the paragraph also stresses the place of sound in this evocation.

Because confusion might result if both assonance and alliteration were marked together on only one worksheet, a single sheet is devoted to each aspect. The numbering, the circles, the connecting lines, and the key are all designed to assist readers in following the theme and in verifying the conclusions.

III. RHYME

Rhyme, the most easily recognized physical characteristic of poetry, means the repetition of identical concluding syllables in different words, most often at the ends of lines. Words with the same concluding vowel sounds rhyme; such rhymes are a special kind of assonance. Thus *day* rhymes with *weigh, gray, bouquet,* and *matinee,* even though all these words are spelled differently. Rhyme may also combine assonance and identical consonant sounds, as in *ache, bake, break,* and *opaque,* or *turn, yearn, fern,* and *adjourn.*

Rhyme is a means of emphasis, a way of reinforcing and pointing up ideas. It is a powerful way of "clinching" a thought by the physical link of identical sounds. In its simplest form it jingles in the mind, with rhymes like *bells* and *tells*. Everyone has learned common jingles and sayings like "Five, six, / Pick up sticks," and "An apple a day / Keeps the doctor away." To hear such rhymes once is to know them forever, so strongly do they impress themselves in our memories.

RHYME AND POETIC QUALITY

Wherever rhyme is used skillfully, it leads the mind into new and fresh turns of thought. Poets may thus be judged on their rhymes. Alexander Pope criticized "easy" rhymers who always pair obvious words like "trees" and "breeze." Such a rhymer is a follower of language, not a leader who sees rhyme in poetry as one means of reaching the goals of freshness and newness. The seventeenth-century poet John Dryden admitted that the need for rhymes led even him into turns of thought that he had not anticipated. In such a sense, rhyme had—and still has—a vital role in poetic creativity.

Rhyme not only has a serious role in poetry, but it may lead to surprising comic effects. The name *Julia* is rhymed with *peculiar* in a turn of-the-century popular song. Samuel Butler rhymed *ecclesiastic* with *a stick* in his long poem *Hudibras*. Sometimes rhymes may involve puns, as *futile* instead of *feudal* in a rhyme with *noodle*. A part of a word may be used as a rhyme, with the rest of the word carrying over to the next line, as in

> He would adorn
> Himself with orn-
> Aments.

Rhymes are often comic, as in this limerick:

> There once was a man from Tarentum
> Who gnashed his false teeth till he bent 'em.
> When asked the cost
> Of what he had lost,
> He said, "I can't say, for I rent 'em."

RULES AND VARIANTS IN RHYME

Unlike languages like Italian or French, English does not contain large numbers of rhyming words. Therefore there are not many "rules" for poets using rhymes. About the only restriction is that the same forms are not to be used, even if they appear in different words. *Turn* should not be matched with *taciturn*, *verse* with *universe*, or *stable* with *unstable*. Aside from this, the major guide is taste and propriety. A poet of serious verse would destroy a poem with rhymes like those in the limerick.

Also, because of the difficulty of finding rhyming words in English, a wide latitude in rhyming forms has been accepted. There is *eye rhyme* or *sight rhyme*, the pairing of words that look alike but that do not sound alike. Thus according to sight rhyme "I *wind* [a clock]" may be joined to "the North *wind*." In *slant rhyme* the rhyming vowel segments are different while the consonants are the same; for example *bleak* and *broke*; *could* and *solitude*.

RHYME AND RHYTHM

The effects of rhyme are closely connected with rhythm. In general, rhymes falling on accented syllables lend themselves to serious effects. These rhymes have traditionally been called *masculine*, although terms like *heavy-stress rhyme* or *accented rhyme* are now more appropriate. The accenting of heavy-stress rhyme may be seen in the opening lines of Robert Frost's "Stopping by Woods on a Snowy Evening":

Whose woods / these are / I think / I know.

His house / is in / the vil- / lage though.

Rhymes concluding with either one or two light stresses have been called *feminine*, but this term may now be distasteful. Preferable terms are the accurate *trochaic* or *double rhyme* for rhymes of two syllables, and *dactylic* or *triple rhyme* for rhymes of three syllables. Abstractly, such rhymes are called *falling* or *dying*. Falling rhymes, like those in lines 1, 2, and 5 of the limerick above, are most appropriate in comic and light subject matter. It is difficult for any poet to use falling rhymes and maintain seriousness at the same time. The accents in falling rhyme, in this example trochaic or double rhyme, may be seen in the second and fourth lines of the first stanza of "Miniver Cheevy," by Edwin Arlington Robinson:

Miniver Cheevy, child of scorn,

Grew lean while he assailed the *seasons*;

He wept that he was ever born

And he had *reasons*.

Dactylic or triple rhyme is unusual. It may be seen in these lines from Browning's "The Pied Piper of Hamelin," which also illustrate *internal rhyme*; that is, a rhyming word within a line:

Small feet were *páttĕriñg*, wooden shoes *cláttĕriñg*,

Little hands clapping and little tongues *cháttĕriñg*.

And, like fowls in a farm-yard when barley is *scáttĕriñg*, . . .

DESCRIBING RHYMES

In the description of rhymes, alphabetical letters are used. Each repeated letter indicates a rhyme (a, a). Each new letter indicates a new rhyme (b, b; c, c; d, d; etc.). An *x* indicates no rhyme. To formulate a rhyme pattern, you should include (1) the meter and number of feet of each line, and (2) the letters indicating rhymes. Here is such a formulation:

Iambic pentameter: a, b, b, a, c, c, a.

This scheme shows that all the lines are iambic, with five feet in each line. The rhyming lines are 1, 4, and 7; 2 and 3; and 5 and 6.

Should the number of feet in lines vary, show this fact with a number in front of each letter:

Iambic: 5a, 5b, 4a, 3a, 2b, 6a.

Always make a note of any deviations from the predominant pattern. If there is a variation in the meter of any of the rhymes, note that variation the first time you use the letter, as follows:

Iambic: 5a, 4b (trochee), 5a, 4b, 5a, 5b.

Here lines 2, 4, and 6 are rhyming trochees; there is no need to indicate this fact on any but the first use of the letter, because the following appearances of the letter automatically indicate the variation.

RHYME SCHEMES

Along with line length, rhyme is a determinant in the classification of poetic forms. Here are the major ones:

1. The Couplet.

a, a; b, b; c, c; d, d; etc.

Couplets of iambic pentameter are called *heroic* or *neoclassic*. Also common, especially for light and satiric purposes, are couplets in iambic tetrameter (four iambic feet).

2. The Italian or Petrarchan Sonnet.

Iambic pentameter: a, b, b, a, a, b, b, a, c, d, c, d, c, d.

The first eight lines form the *octave*, the last six the *sestet*. There is usually a shift in thought from the octave to the sestet.

3. The Shakespearean Sonnet.

Iambic pentameter: a, b, a, b, c, d, c, d, e, f, e, f, g, g.

Note that the Shakespearean sonnet has seven rhyming sounds, contrasted with the four in the Italian sonnet. The rhyming groups of four lines, like any four-line group, are called *quatrains*. Each quatrain usually contains a separate development of the thought, with the couplet providing a conclusion or climax.

4. Ballad Measure, or Common Measure.

Iambic: 4x, 3a, 4x, 3a; 4x, 3b, 4x, 3b; etc.

Each quatrain forms a separate unit, analogous to the paragraph, called a *stanza*. A typical ballad consists of many stanzas. Ballads are often narrative in development, like the anonymous "Sir Patrick Spens." Coleridge uses ballad measure for "The Rime of the Ancient Mariner" and added variations with extra lines for some of his stanzas.

5. The Song.

The song is a free stanzaic form designed to be sung to a repeated melody. The scheme for one stanza therefore describes all the stanzas. There is no limit to the number of stanzas, although there are usually no more than five or six. Here are some rhyme schemes of song stanzas:

Donne's "The Canonization":
    Iambic: 5a, 4b, 5b, 5a, 4c, 4c, 4a, 3a

Browning's "Two in the Campagna":
    Iambic tetrameter: a, b, a, b, (3)x.
Note that line 5 is not paired in rhyme with any of the other lines and that this line has three rather than four feet.

Burns's "To a Mouse":
    Iambic tetrameter: a, a, b, (2)c, b, (2)c.
In stanzas 1, 2, 4, and 6 the rhyming feet are in amphibrachs.
In stanzas 3, 5, 7, and 8 the rhyming feet are iambic.

A regular variant of the song is the *hymn*, a song used in religious services. Hymns usually contain from three to six stanzas. Common measure is most frequently used, but there are many schemes. To enable hymns to be sung to a number of separate tunes, most hymnals contain an analytical table of the hymns based on the number of syllables in each line of the stanza.

6. The Ode.

The ode is a stanzaic form more complex than the song, with varying line lengths and sometimes intricate rhyme schemes. Some odes have repeating stanzaic patterns, whereas others are totally free. Although some odes have been used as a setting for music, they usually do not fit repeating melodies. There is no set form for the ode; poets have developed their own types according to their needs. Keats's great odes were particularly congenial to his ideas, as in the "Ode to a Nightingale," which consists of ten stanzas in iambic pentameter, with the repeating form a, b, a, b, c, d, e, (3)c, d, e. By contrast, the pattern of none of Wordsworth's ten stanzas in the "Intimations of Immortality" ode is repeated.

7. Terza Rima.

Terza rima is a rhyming pattern of three lines in iambic pentameter: a, b, a; b, c, b; c, d, c; etc. Dante invented this form for *The Divine Comedy*. Shelley used it in the five stanzas of "Ode to the West Wind." Roethke used it in "The Waking."

WRITING ABOUT RHYME

For your analysis, select either a short, representative passage from a long poem, or an entire shorter poem such as a sonnet or three-stanza song. At the beginning of the theme, as for the other themes on prosody, include a worksheet. This should contain a double-spaced copy of the poem or passage, with each line numbered beginning with 1. List the numbers of feet in each line (you do not need to provide a complete scansion), and mark any variations in the predominant meter of the rhymes. Letter each rhyme (a, b, b, a, etc.). Underline or otherwise draw attention to particularly notable or outstanding aspects of the rhyme.

Introduction

Here you should make any general remarks you wish about the poem, but concentrate on the relationship of the rhyme to the content. That is, is the rhyme wholly integrated into the poem? Partially? Not at all? Try to define and describe this relationship. Your thesis sentence should cover the topics in the body of the theme.

Body

While stressing your central idea, you should include the following aspects of rhyme:

1. The physical description, including the rhyme scheme and variants, the lengths of the rhyming words, the rhythms of the rhymes, and noteworthy segmental characteristics.

2. The grammatical features of the rhymes. As a general principle, the forms of rhyming words should not be the same but should vary. In your poem, what kinds of words are used for rhymes? Are they all the same? Does one form predominate? Is there variety? Can you determine the grammatical positions of the rhyming words? Is it possible to relate your discoveries to the idea or theme of the poem?

3. The qualities of the rhyming words. Are the words specific? Concrete? Abstract? Are there any particularly striking rhymes? Any surprises? Are there any rhymes that are clever or witty? Do any rhymes give unique comparisons or contrasts? How?

4. Particularly striking or unique effects in the rhyme. Without becoming overly subtle or farfetched, you can make satisfying and sometimes even startling conclusions. Try to raise some of the following issues: Do any sounds in the rhymes appear (as assonance or alliteration) elsewhere in the poem to an appreciable degree? Do the rhymes assist in any onomatopoeic effects? Generally, can you detect any aspects of the rhyme that are uniquely effective because they are at one with the thought and mood of your poem?

Conclusion

Here you might include additional observations about the rhyme as well as comparisons between the rhyme in your poem and in other poems by the same poet or other poets. A short summary of your main headings is here, as always, appropriate.

Sample Theme

The Rhymes in Christina Rossetti's Poem "Echo"

1	Come to me in the silence of the night; *[n]*		5a
2	Come in the speaking silence of a dream; *[n]*		5b
3	Come with soft rounded cheeks and eyes as bright *[adj]*		5a
4	As sunlight on a stream; *[n]*		3b
5	Come back in tears, *[n]*		2c
6	O memory, hope, love of finished years. *[n]*		5c
7	O dream how sweet, too sweet, too bitter sweet, *[adj]*		5d
8	Whose wakening should have been in Paradise, *[n]*		5e
9	Where souls brimful of love abide and meet; *[v]*		5d
10	Where thirsty longing eyes *[n]*		3e
11	Watch the slow door *[n]*		2f
12	That opening, letting in, lets out no more. *[adv]*		5f
13	Yet come to me in dreams, that I may live *[v]*		5g
14	My very life again though cold in death: *[n]*		5h

Repeated words:

∼∼∼	dream, dreams	n = noun
———	sweet	v = verb
–.–.–.	breath	adj = adjective
......	low	adv = adverb
- - - -	long ago	
∼∼∼∼	come	

                                     v

15   Come back to me in dreams, that I may give   5g

                           n

16   Pulse for pulse, breath for breath: 3h

                     adj

17   Speak low, lean low,   2i

                            adj

18   As long ago, my love, how long ago!   5i

[1]   In the three-stanza lyric poem "Echo," Christina Rossetti uses rhyme as a virtually coequal way of saying that one might regain in dreams a love that is lost in reality.° As the dream of love is to the real love, so is an echo to an original sound. From this comparison comes the title of the poem and also Rossetti's unique use of rhyme. Aspects of her rhyme are the lyric pattern, the forms and qualities of the rhyming words, and the special use of repetition.□

          The rhyme pattern is simple, and, like rhyme generally, it may be thought of as a pattern of echoes. Each stanza contains four lines of alternating rhymes concluded by a couplet, as follows:

       Iambic: 5a, 5b, 5a, 3b, 2c, 5c.

[2]   There are nine separate rhymes throughout the poem, three in each stanza. Only two words are used for each rhyme; no rhyme is used twice. Of the eighteen rhyming words, sixteen—almost all—are of one syllable. The remaining two words consist of two and three syllables. With such a great number of single-syllable words, the rhymes are all rising ones, on the accented halves of iambic feet, and the end-of-line emphasis is on simple words.

          The grammatical forms and positions of the rhyming words lend support to the inward, introspective subject matter. Although there is variety, more than half the rhyming words are nouns. There are ten in all, and eight are placed within prepositional phrases as the objects of prepositions. Such enclosure is not unexpected in this lyric, personal poem, where the speaker states the yearning to relive her love within dreams. Also, the repeated verb "come" in stanzas one and three is in the form of commands to the absent lover. Thus, most of the verbal energy in the stanzas is in the first parts of the lines, leaving the rhymes to occur in elements modifying the verbs, as in

[3]   these lines:

       Come to me in the silence of the *night* (1)

       Yet come to me in dreams, that I may *live* (13)
       My very life again though cold in *death*; (14)

      Most of the other rhymes are also in such internalized positions. The three rhyming verbs occur in subordinate clauses, and the nouns that are not the objects of prepositions are the subject (10) and object (11) of the same subordinate clause.

[4]   The qualities of the rhyming words are also consistent with the poem's emphasis on the speaker's internal life. Most of the words are impressionistic.

° Central idea
□ Thesis sentence

[4] Even the concrete words—*stream*, *tears*, *eyes*, *door*, and *breath*—reflect the speaker's mental condition rather than describe reality. In this regard, the rhyming words of 1 and 3 are starkly effective. These are *night* and *bright*, which contrast the bleakness of the speaker's condition, on the one hand, with the vitality of her inner life, on the other. Another effective contrast is in 14 and 16, where *death* and *breath* are rhymed. This rhyme may be taken to illustrate the sad fact that even though the speaker's love is past, it can yet live in present memory just as an echo continues to sound.

[5] It is in emphasizing how memory echoes experience that Rossetti creates the special use of rhyming words. There is an ingenious but not obtrusive repetition of a number of words—echoes. The major echoing word is of course the verb *come*, which appears six times at the beginnings of lines in stanzas 1 and 3. But rhyming words, stressing as they do the ends of lines, are also repeated systematically. The most notable is *dream*, the rhyming word in 2. Rossetti repeats the word in 7 and uses the plural in 13 and 15. In 7 the rhyming word *sweet* is the third use of the word, a climax of "how *sweet*, too *sweet*, too bitter *sweet*." Concluding the poem, Rossetti repeats *breath* (16), *low* (17), and the phrase *long ago* (18). This special use of repetition justifies the title "Echo," and it also stresses the major idea that it is only in one's memory that past experience has reality, even if dreams are no more than echoes.

[6] Thus rhyme is not just ornamental in "Echo," but integral. The skill of Rossetti here is the same as in her half-serious, half-mocking poem "Eve," even though the two poems are totally different. In "Eve," she uses very plain rhyming words together with comically intended double rhymes. In "Echo," her subject might be called fanciful and maybe even morbid, but the easiness of the rhyming words, like the diction of the poem generally, keeps the focus on regret and yearning rather than self-indulgence. As in all rhyming poems, Rossetti's rhymes emphasize the conclusions of her lines. The rhymes go beyond this effect, however, because of the internal repetition—echoes—of the rhyming words. "Echo" is a poem in which rhyme is inseparable from meaning.

COMMENTARY ON THE THEME

Throughout the theme, illustrative words are italicized, and numbers are used to indicate the lines from which the illustrations are drawn.

The introductory paragraph asserts that rhyme is important in Rossetti's poem. It also attempts to explain the title, "Echo." The thesis sentence indicates the four topics to be developed in the body.

Paragraph 2 deals with the mechanical, mathematical aspects of the poem's rhyme. The high number of monosyllabic rhyming words is used to explain the rising, heavy-stress rhyme.

The third paragraph treats the grammar of the rhymes. For example, an analysis and count reveal that there are ten rhyming nouns and three rhyming verbs. The verb of command "come" is mentioned to show that most of the rhyming words exist within groups modifying this word, and three lines from the poem illustrate this fact. The grammatical analysis is related to the internalized nature of the subject of the poem.

Paragraph 4 emphasizes the impressionistic nature of the rhyming words and also points out two instances in which rhymes stress the contrast between real life and the speaker's introspective life.

The fifth paragraph deals with repetitions within the poem of five rhyming words. This repetition is seen as a pattern of echoes, in keeping with the title of the poem.

In the concluding paragraph, the rhymes in "Echo" are compared briefly with those in "Eve," another poem by Christina Rossetti. The conclusion is that Rossetti is a skilled rhymer because she uses rhyme appropriately in both poems. At the end of the theme, the central idea is reiterated.

chapter 16

Writing Two Themes Based on a Close Reading:
I. General content and
II. Style

A theme on a close reading is a detailed study of a passage of prose or poetry. The passage may be a fragment of a longer work, such as an entire speech from a play, story, or novel, or it may be a paragraph of descriptive or analytic prose. It may also be an entire short poem, such as a sonnet or short lyric.

The close-reading theme is at once specific and general. It is specific because it requires you to concentrate on the selected passage. It is general because you do not need to study a single topic (such as character, setting, or point of view), but need to deal with any or all of those things that may be found in the passage. Should your passage describe a specific person, of course, you would need to discuss character, but your emphasis would be on what the passage itself brings out about the character. You would also stress action, setting, and ideas, or even make comparisons, if you find that these matters are important. In other words, the content of a close-reading theme is variable; your passage dictates your content.

STUDYING YOUR PASSAGE

Whenever you are to write a close-reading theme, you should first read the *entire* work, so that you can understand the relationship of all the parts. Read carefully. Then study the passage you are to write about.

First, be sure to use a dictionary to help you understand all words that are even slightly obscure. Sometimes you may not get the sense of a passage on the first or second reading, perhaps because some of the words are not clear to you, even though they may appear so at first. Therefore, look up *all* the words, even the simple ones, in the obscure sentence or sentences. In Shakespeare's Sonnet 73, for example, this famous line occurs:

> Bare ruined choirs, where late the sweet birds sang.

If you think *choirs* means organized groups of singers (as you might at first), you will be puzzled by the line. The dictionary will tell you that *choirs* is also an architectural term for that part of a church in which singers are often placed. Thus Shakespeare's word takes in the range of both empty branches and destroyed churches, and the phrase *sweet birds* refers to vanished human singers as well as birds that have flown away because of winter's cold. Let us take another line, this time from John Donne's first *Holy Sonnet*:

> And thou like Adamant draw mine iron heart.

Unless you look up *Adamant* and realize that Donne uses it to mean a magnet, you will not understand the sense of *draw*. You will thus miss Donne's image and his idea of God's immense power over human beings.

Once you have mastered the words to the best of your ability, look at the sentence structures, particularly in poetry, where you will often find variations in the ordinary English subject-verb-object word order. If you read the line "Thy merit hath my duty strongly knit," be sure that you get the subject and object straight (i.e., "Thy merit hath strongly knit my duty"). Or, look at lines 15 and 16 from Pope's *Essay on Criticism*:

> Let such teach others who themselves excell,
> And censure freely who have written well.

On first reading these lines are difficult. A person might conclude that Pope is asking the critic to condemn those writers who have written well (but as an exercise, look up *censure* in the *Oxford English Dictionary*), until the lines are unraveled:

> Let such who themselves excell teach others,
> And [let such] who have written well censure freely.

There is a great difference here between the misreading and the correct reading. What you must keep in mind is that an initial failure to understand a sentence structure that is no longer common can prevent your full understanding of a passage. Therefore, you must be sure to untie all the syntactic knots.

TYPES OF CLOSE-READING THEMES

There are two types of close-reading themes. The first deals with the general content of the passage and its relationship to the entire work. The second type is also concerned with the general content but goes on to deal with the style of the passage.

I. THE GENERAL CONTENT OF A PASSAGE

This kind of close-reading theme emphasizes the content of the passage and the relationship of the passage to the rest of the work. The theme is designed as a first approach to close reading and does not require detailed knowledge about diction, grammar, and style. Thus, although you may wish to discuss special words and phrases, it should be your aim primarily to consider the content of your passage.

Once you have clarified the passage to your satisfaction, you should develop materials for your theme. Try to make some general statements about your passage: Does the passage (1) describe a natural or artificial scene, (2) develop a character or characters, (3) describe an action, (4) describe or analyze a character's thoughts, or (5) develop an argument? Is the passage a speech by one character or a dialogue or discussion by two or more? What is the content of the passage? That is, are there themes and ideas that are brought up elsewhere in the work? In this respect, how does the passage connect to what has gone on before and to what comes after? (To deal with this question, you may assume that your reader is familiar with the entire work.) Some obvious points to think about are these:

For an Early Passage

For an early passage, you may expect that the author is setting things in motion. Thus, you should try to determine how ideas, themes, characterizations, and arguments that you find in the passage are related to these matters as they appear later in the work. You may assume that everything in the passage is there for a purpose. Try to find that purpose.

For a Later, Midpoint Passage

For a later passage, which might be characterized as a "pivot" or "turning point," a character's fortunes take either an expected or unexpected turn. If the change is expected, you should explain how the passage focuses the various themes or ideas and then propels them toward the climax. If the change is unexpected, it is necessary to show how the contrast is made in the passage. It may be that the work is one that features surprises, and the passage thus is read one way at first, but on second reading may be seen to have a double meaning. Or it may be that the speaker has had one set of assumptions while the readers have had others, and that the passage marks a point of increasing self-awareness on the part of the speaker. Many parts of works are not what they seem at first reading, and it is your task here to determine how the passage is affected by events at or near the end of the work.

For a Concluding Passage

You may assume that a passage at or near the end of the work is designed to solve problems or to be a focal point or climax for all the situations and ideas that have been building up. You will need to show how the passage brings together all themes, ideas, and details. What is happening? Is any action described in the passage a major action, or a step leading to the major action? Has everything in the passage been prepared for earlier?

GENERAL PURPOSES OF THE CLOSE-READING THEME

In light of what we have seen, the general purposes of a close-reading theme should be clear. If you can read a paragraph, you can read the entire book; if you can read a speech, you can read the entire play or story; if you can read one poem by a poet, you can read other poems by the same poet. This is not to say that the writing of a close-reading theme automatically means that at first reading you will understand every work by the same author. Few people would insist that reading passages from Joyce's *Dubliners* makes it possible to understand *Finnegans Wake*. What a close-reading theme gives you is a skill upon which you can build, an approach to any other text you will encounter.

You will find use for the general technique of close reading in other courses also. In political science, for example, parts of political speeches can be, and should be, scrutinized carefully, not just for what is said but for what is half-said or left out entirely. A close study of a philosophical work or biblical passage will yield much that might not be found in a casual first reading. No matter what course you are taking or what your personal interests may be, you can use close-reading techniques to improve your understanding.

WRITING ABOUT GENERAL CONTENT
IN A PASSAGE

Introduction

Because the close-reading theme is concerned with details in the passage, you may find a problem in creating a thematic structure. This difficulty is surmountable if you work either with a generalization about the passage itself or else with a central idea based on the relationship of the passage to the work. Suppose, for example, that the passage is factually descriptive, or intensely emotional, or that it introduces a major character or idea, or that it sets in motion forces that will create a climax later in the work. Any one of these observations may serve as your central idea.

Body

You may develop the body according to what you find in the passage. Suppose you have a passage of character description; you might wish to analyze what is said about the character, together with a comparison of how these qualities are modified later. In addition, you might consider how these qualities are to affect other characters and/or later events in the work. Suppose your passage is particularly witty, and you decide to discuss the quality of the wit and then show how this wittiness bears upon earlier and later situations. The idea here is to focus on details in the passage and also on the relationship of these details to the entire work.

Conclusion

As you make your major points for the body of the theme, you may also notice subpoints that are worth mentioning but do not merit full consideration. You might bring these points into your conclusion. For example, there may be a particular word or type of word, or there may be an underlying assumption that you found in the passage, or there may be some quality that you find hard to describe. The conclusion is the place for you to mention these things. If you haven't discussed anything about the way some of the things are said, but want to say that the diction is plain and monosyllabic, or difficult and polysyllabic, and if you do not believe that you can go into great detail about these matters, then you can bring them up in your conclusion. You may also, of course, summarize your main points from the body of your theme.

NUMBERS FOR EASY REFERENCE

Include a copy of your passage at the beginning of your theme, as in the two samples in this chapter. For the convenience of your reader, number lines in poetry and sentences in prose.

Sample Theme (Study of a Prose Passage)

An Analysis of a Paragraph from Frank O'Connor's "First Confession"

---

[1] Nora's turn came, and I heard the sound of something slamming, and then her voice as if butter wouldn't melt in her mouth, and then another slam, and out she came. [2] God, the hypocrisy of women. [3] Her eyes were lowered, her head was bowed, and her hands were joined very low down on her stomach, and she walked up the aisle to the side altar looking like a saint. [4] You never saw such an exhibition of devotion; and I remembered the devilish malice with which she had tormented me all the way from our door, and wondered were all religious people like that, really. [5] It was my turn now. [6] With the fear of damnation in my soul I went in, and the confessional door closed of itself behind me.

This paragraph from Frank O'Connor's "First Confession" appears midway in the story. It is transitional, coming between Jackie's recollections of his childhood troubles at home and his happier memory of his first confession.

[1] Although the short episode might have been painful for the child, the passage itself reflects geniality and good nature.° This mood is apparent in the comments of the narrator, the comic situation, and the narrator's apparent lack of self-awareness.□

[2] More impressionistic than descriptive, the paragraph concentrates in a good-humored way on the direct but prejudiced responses of the narrator, Jackie. The two major events described are (a) that Nora enters the confessional, says her confession, and leaves, and (b) that Jackie then enters the confessional. But the narrator, now an adult, relates these details through his own disapproval and limited perceptions. Thus, he states that Nora, while confessing, sounds "as if butter wouldn't melt in her mouth." As he is about to describe her prayerful walk away from the confessional, he exclaims, "God, the hypocrisy of women" (sentence 2). When he himself enters the confessional, he does so with "the fear of damnation in . . . [his] soul" (sentence 6). These comments show prejudice and lack of understanding, but in the context of recollections of childhood they add to the charm and humor of the passage.

---

*For the text of this story, please see Appendix C, pp. 344–50.
° Central idea
□ Thesis sentence

[3] It is from these remarks that the comedy of the passage develops. Much of the humor rests on the inconsistency between Nora's sisterly badgering of Jackie and her pietism at the confession. Since Jackie is careful here to stress Nora's "devilish malice" against him (sentence 4), readers might smile when thinking about her saintly pose. But readers surely know that Nora is not unusual; she has been behaving like any typical older brother or sister. So there is also a comic contrast between her normal actions and Jackie's opinion that she is "devilish." The humor is thus directed by the author toward the narrator.

[4] In fact, it may be that the narrator's lack of self-awareness is the major cause of humor in the passage. Jackie is an adult telling a story about his experience as a seven-year-old. Readers might expect him to be mature and therefore to be compassionate about his childhood anger against his sister. But his child's-eye view seems still to be controlling his responses. Comments about Nora such as "looking like a saint" (sentence 3) and "You never saw such an exhibition of devotion" (sentence 4) are not consistent with a person who has put childhood in perspective. Hence, readers may smile not only at the obvious comedy of Nora's hypocrisy, but also at the narrator's lack of self-awareness. As he comments on his sister with his still-jaundiced attitude, he shows his own limitation and in this way directs much amusement against himself.

[5] Readers are more likely to smile at Jackie's remarks, however, than to object to his adult character. The thrust of the paragraph is thus on the good-natured comedy of the situation. For this reason the paragraph is successful. In its context it is a turning point between Jackie's disturbing experiences with his sister, grandmother, and father, on the one hand, and the pleasant confession with the kind, thoughtful, and genial priest on the other. The child goes into confession with the fear of damnation in his thoughts, but after the farce that is to follow, he finds the assurances that his fears are not justified and that his anger is normal and can be forgiven. Surely, the good nature of the passage extends far beyond the simple, common episode described there.

COMMENTARY ON THE THEME

A number of central ideas might have been made about the passage chosen for analysis: that it is dramatic, that it centers on the religious hypocrisy of Jackie's sister, that it brings together the major themes of the story, or that it creates a problem in the character of the narrator. The central idea of the sample theme as brought out in the first paragraph, however, is that the passage reflects geniality and good nature. The theme does deal with Nora's hypocrisy and also with the problem in the narrator's character, but these points are brought out in connection with the central idea.

In the body of the theme, the second paragraph shows that the narrator's comments about his sister and his own spiritual condition add to the good nature of the passage. The third paragraph explains the relationship between Jackie's remarks and the comedy in the passage. In paragraph

4, the adult narrator's unwitting revelation of his own shortcomings is related to the good humor and comedy. The concluding paragraph connects the passage to the latter half of the story, suggesting that the good nature of the passage is like the divine forgiveness that is believed to follow the act of confession.

Because this theme is based on a close reading of the passage chosen for analysis, its major feature is the use of many specific details. Thus, the second paragraph stresses the action of the passage and some of the narrator's comments about it. The third paragraph stresses the details about Nora's posture and Jackie's comments about her. Paragraph 4 emphasizes more of the narrator's comments and the limitations of character that they show. Finally, the concluding paragraph includes the detail about Jackie's entering the confessional.

II. THE STYLE OF A PASSAGE

The second type of close-reading theme is like the first because both deal with a passage in the context of the entire work. The second goes beyond the first, however, because it concentrates on the style of the passage rather than the content.

To carry out a discussion of style, you will need to apply many of the things you have previously learned or are learning about the mechanics of language. You might feel hesitant at first, but you will unquestionably find that you know much more than you think you know. In addition, many of the approaches you might try are not especially difficult. As an instance, the sample theme shows what might be done with the application of no more than a moderate knowledge of language.

The word *style* is not easy to define to everyone's satisfaction, but for the present theme you may deal with it as an analysis of word choice and sentence development resulting from an author's judgment about the following matters:

1. The speaker, or narrator, of the work
2. The character being analyzed or described
3. The circumstances of the passage
4. The type or purpose of the work
5. The audience

Any close reading for style should take these and related elements into account as they become relevant to the details of the passage.

And they do become relevant. Authors do not always write in their own persons, but take on the voice of a particular narrator, or they present the speech of a character just as they think that character would likely say it. (For further development of this fact, please see Chapter 6, Writing About Point of View.) Also, the writer's perception of his or her audience governs the amount of detail and kinds of diction that you will find in your passage. It is not possible to write a close-reading theme for style without also considering the entire context of the passage.

EXAMPLES OF STYLE AND ITS RELATION TO CHARACTER

To look at a specific example, let us consider the character of Portia from Shakespeare's *The Merchant of Venice*. Late in the play Portia masquerades brilliantly as a lawyer, and because of her ingenuity in argument she brings Antonio out of danger. It would seem natural that Shakespeare, in giving her speeches elsewhere in the play, would emphasize and demonstrate her intelligence. In I.ii, for example, Portia says the following:

> If to do were as easy as to know what were good to do, chapels had been churches and poor men's cottages princes' palaces. It is a good divine that follows his own instructions: I can easier teach twenty what were good to be done, than to be one of the twenty to follow mine own teaching.

From the style of this passage, one may conclude that Shakespeare is indeed showing that Portia has a rapid mind. Her first sentence uses simple diction but a complex structure. Of her first fourteen words, six are infinitives and two are verbs; that is, more than half of the words (about 57 percent) are verbs or verbals. One may conclude that such a proportion suggests great mental power. Also, the first fourteen words form an *if*-clause, dependent on the verb in the following main clause. The ability to control subordination in sentences is regarded as the mark of a good mind and a good style. Portia shows an ability to use rhetoric— in this sentence ellipsis in a parallel structure: the main clause of the first sentence equals two clauses, but the verb is used only once: "chapels had been churches and poor men's cottages [had been] princes' palaces." Portia's language is concrete and vivid, and she has control over her balanced sentence.

To be contrasted with Portia's speech is this one by Ophelia in *Hamlet*, IV. v:

> Well, God 'ild you. They say, the owl was a baker's daughter. Lord, we know what we are, but not what we may be. God be at your table.

Ophelia makes this speech after she has gone mad. Her words are simple, and her sentences are disconnected. Just when she seems to become coherent (in sentence 3) her thought is broken, and her last sentence seems as random as her first. Had Shakespeare introduced the mental toughness of Portia's speech here, he would not have shown a broken mind but an alert one in all its powers. Thus, he gives Ophelia these disconnected sentences, so unlike her coherent speeches earlier in the play.

The point about both passages is that the differences in style are appropriate to the two characterizations and also to the differing dramatic situations. Please note that our analyses of style are related to the contexts of the plays. It would not be fruitful to discuss style independently of the context, particularly in a dramatic passage, for the language is likely to be indicative of the immediate situation and is also likely to involve comparisons with other sections of the work.

TWO MAJOR APPROACHES TO STYLE

There are two major topics, or approaches, to close reading for style: (1) diction, and (2) rhetoric. Technically, rhetoric includes diction, but here they are separated for ease of analysis. Naturally, either approach can become complex and subtle, so much so that any aspect, such as connotation or parallelism, can furnish materials for an entire theme.

DICTION: CHOICE OF WORDS

The study of style begins with words, and **diction** refers to a writer's selection of specific words. The selection should be accurate and explicit, so that all actions and ideas are clear. It is perhaps difficult to judge accuracy and completeness, inasmuch as often we do not have any basis of comparison. Nevertheless, if a passage comes across as effective, if it conveys an idea well or gets at the essence of an action vividly and powerfully, we may confidently say that the words have been the right ones. In a passage describing action, for example, there should be active verbs, whereas in a description of a place there should be nouns and adjectives that provide locations, relationships, colors, and shapes. An explanatory or reflective passage should include a number of words that convey thoughts, states of mind and emotion, and various conditions of human relationships.

Formal, Neutral, and Informal Diction

Words fall naturally into three basic groups, or classes, that may be called **formal** or *high*, **neutral** or *middle*, and **informal** or *low*. Formal or high diction consists of standard and often elegant words (frequently polysyllabic), the retention of correct word order, and the absence of contractions. The sentence "It is I," for example, is formal. The following sentences from Poe's "The Masque of the Red Death" use formal language:

> They resolved to leave means neither of ingress nor egress to the sudden impulses of despair or of frenzy from within. The abbey was amply provisioned. With such precautions the courtiers might bid defiance to contagion.

Note here words like *ingress, egress, provisioned, bid defiance,* and *contagion.* These words are not in ordinary, everyday vocabulary; they have what we may call *elegance.* Though they are used accurately and aptly, and though the sentences are brief and simple, the diction is high.

Neutral or middle diction is ordinary, everyday, but still standard vocabulary, with a shunning of longer words but with the use of contractions when necessary. The sentence "It's me," for example, is neutral, the sort of thing many people say in preference to "It is I" when identifying themselves on the phone. The following passage from Langston Hughes's poem "Theme for English B" illustrates middle, neutral diction:

> I am twenty-two, colored, born in Winston-Salem.
> I went to school there, then Durham, then here
> to this college on the hill above Harlem.
> I am the only colored student in my class.

> —lines 7–10

In this passage the words are easy and ordinary, words that are in common use in everyday conversation. They do not draw attention to themselves, but are centered directly on the topic. In a sense, such words in the neutral style are chosen because they are like clear windows, while words of the high style are more like stained glass.

Informal or low diction may range from colloquial—the language used by people in relaxed, common activities—to the level of substandard or slang expressions. A person speaking to a very close friend is likely to use diction and idiom that would not be appropriate in public and formal situations, and even in some social situations. Low language is thus appropriate for dialogue in stories and plays, depending on the characters speaking, and for stories told in the first-person point of view as though the speaker is talking directly to a group of sympathetic and relaxed close friends. An amusing example of low diction may be seen in the first sentence of the following speech from Chekhov's *The Bear.* Smirnov, the speaker, talks angrily and insultingly to a servant, using low words. The humor develops when he shifts to a formal style speaking to the aristocratic lady, Mrs. Popov:

> SMIRNOV (*to* LUKA). You idiot, you talk too much. . . . Ass! (*Sees* MRS. POPOV *and changes to dignified speech.*) Madam, may I introduce myself: retired lieutenant of the artillery and landowner, Grigory Stepano-

vich Smirnov! I feel the necessity of troubling you about a highly important matter. . . .

By graphically juxtaposing low and high diction, the passage marks Chekhov's skill over comic dramatic style.

Specific-General and Concrete-Abstract Language

Specific refers to a real thing or things that may be readily perceived or imagined; "my pet dog" is specific. **General** statements refer to broad classes of persons or things. "Dogs make good pets" is a generalization. **Concrete** refers to words that describe qualities or conditions; in the phrase "a cold day," the word *cold* is concrete. You cannot see cold, but you know the exact difference between cold and hot, and therefore you understand the word in reference to the external temperature. **Abstract** refers to qualities that are more removed from the concrete, and abstract words can therefore refer to many classes of separate things. On a continuum of qualities, ice cream may be noted as being cold, sweet, and creamy. If we go on to say that it is *good*, however, this word is so widely applicable that it is abstract and therefore difficult to apply. Anything may be good, including other food, scenes, actions, words, and ideas. If we say only that something is *good*, we indicate approval but very little else about our topic.

Usually, good narrative and descriptive writing features specific and concrete words in preference to those that are general and abstract. If a narrative passage contains much general and abstract diction, it is difficult to understand because it is not easy to apply the words to any imaginable reality. Let us look at two examples of prose, the first from Hemingway's novel *A Farewell to Arms*, the second from Theodore Dreiser's *The Titan*:

In the late summer of that year we lived in a house in a village that looked across the river and the plain to the mountains. In the bed of the river there were pebbles and boulders, dry and white in the sun, and the water was clear and swiftly moving and blue in the channels. Troops went by the house and down the road and the dust they raised powdered the leaves of the trees. The trunks of the trees too were dusty and the leaves fell early that year and we saw the troops marching along the road and the dust rising and leaves, stirred by the breeze, falling and the soldiers marching and afterward the road bare and white except for the leaves.

From New York, Vermont, New Hampshire, Maine had come a strange company, earnest, patient, determined, unschooled in even the primer of refinement, hungry for something the significance of which, when

they had it, they could not even guess, anxious to be called great, determined so to be without ever knowing how.

Hemingway's diction is specific; that is, many of the words, such as *house,
river, plain, mountains, dust, leaves,* and *trees,* describe things that can be
seen or felt. In describing aspects of the scene, Hemingway uses concrete
words, like *dry, clear, swiftly moving, dusty, stirred, falling, marching,* and
bare. These words indicate clearly perceivable actions or states. Dreiser's
words are in marked contrast. The names of states are specific, but *company*
is a general word for a group of any sort, unlike Hemingway's *troops.*
Dreiser's key descriptive words are *strange, earnest, patient, determined, hungry,* and *anxious.* Because none of these words describes anything that
can be perceived, unlike *dry* and *dusty,* they are abstract. Obviously the
two passages are on different topics, and both are successful in their ways,
but Hemingway's diction indicates an attempt to present a specific, concrete
perception of things, while Dreiser's indicates an attempt at psychological
penetration.

Denotation and Connotation

Another way of getting at style is to be alert for the author's manage-
ment of *denotation* and *connotation.* **Denotation** refers to what a word means,
and **connotation** to what the word suggests. It is one thing to call a person
skinny, for example, another to use the word *thin,* and still something
else to say *svelte* or *shapely.* Similarly, both *cat* and *kitten* are accurate words
denotatively, but *kitten* connotes more playfulness and cuteness than one
might associate with a cat. If a person in a social situation behaves in
ways that are described as *friendly, warm, polite,* or *correct,* these words
all suggest slight differences in behavior, not because the words are not
approximately synonymous, but because the words have different connotations.

It is through the careful choice of words not only for denotation
but also for connotation that authors create unique effects even though
they might be describing similar or even identical situations. Let us look,
for example, at the concluding paragraph of Joseph Conrad's novel *Nostromo*
(1904). The hero of the novel, Nostromo, has just died, and the woman
who loves him has cried out in grief:

In that true cry of love and grief that seemed to ring aloud from Punta
Mala to Azuera and away to the bright line of the horizon, overhung by
a big white cloud shining like a mass of solid silver, the genius of the
magnificent *capataz de cargadores* dominated the dark gulf containing
his conquests of treasure and love.

This circumstance is not uncommon, for people die every day, and their
loved ones grieve for them. But through connotative words like *bright*

line, shining, solid silver, genius, magnificent, and *dominated,* Conrad suggests that Nostromo was more than ordinary, a person of great worth and power, a virtual demigod.

In contrast, here is the concluding paragraph of Hemingway's *A Farewell to Arms*:

> But after I had got them out and shut the door and turned off the light it wasn't any good. It was like saying good-by to a statue. After a while I went out and left the hospital and walked back to the hotel in the rain.

Hemingway's situation is similar to Conrad's. The heroine, Catherine Barclay, has died, and the hero, Frederick Henry, expresses his grief. He had loved her deeply, but their dreams for a happy future have been destroyed. Hemingway is interested in emphasizing the finality of the moment and he does so through phrases like *shut the door, turned off the light, went out,* and *walked back.* These expressions are all so common that you might at first be surprised to find them at so emotional a point in the book. But these flat, bare words serve a purpose; they suggest that death is as much a part of life as shutting a door and turning off a light. Both passages show how control over connotation creates different effects.

RHETORIC

Broadly, **rhetoric** refers to the art of persuasive writing and, even more broadly, to the general art of writing. Any passage can be studied for its rhetorical qualities. For this reason it is necessary to develop both the methods and the descriptive vocabulary with which to carry out an analysis. Some things that may easily be done involve counting various elements in a passage and analyzing the types of sentences the author uses.

Counting

Doing a count of the number of words in a sentence; or the number of verbs, adjectives, prepositions, and adverbs; or the number of syllables in relation to the total number of words, can often lead to valuable conclusions about style, especially if the count is related to other aspects of the passage. The virtue of counting is that it is easy to do and therefore it provides a "quick opening" into at least one aspect of style. Always remember that conclusions based on a count will provide *tendencies* of a particular author rather than absolutes. For illustration, let us say that Author *A* uses words mainly of 1 or 2 syllables, while Author *B* includes many words of 3, 4, and 5 syllables. Going further, let us say that *A* uses an average of 12 words per sentence while *B* uses 35. It would be fair to conclude that Author *A* is brief while Author *B* is more expansive. This is not to say that Author *A*'s passage would be superior, however, for a long string of short sentences with short words might become choppy and tiresome and might cause your mind to wander.

Sentence Types

You can often learn much about a passage by determining the sorts of sentences it contains. Though you have probably learned the basic sentence types at one time or another, let's review them here:

1. **Simple sentences** contain one subject and one verb, together with modifiers and complements. They are often short and are most appropriate for actions and declarations. Often they are idiomatic, particularly in dialogue.

2. **Compound sentences** contain two simple sentences joined by a conjunction (*and*, *but*, *for*, *or*, *nor*, and so on) and a comma, or by a semicolon without a conjunction. Frequently, compound sentences are strung together as a series of three or four or more simple sentences.

3. **Complex sentences** contain a main clause and a subordinate clause. Because of the subordinate clause, the complex sentence is often suitable for describing cause-and-effect relationships in narrative, and also for analysis and reflection.

4. **Compound-complex sentences** contain two main clauses and a dependent clause. In practice, many authors produce sentences that may contain a number of subordinate clauses together with many more than two main clauses. Usually, the more clauses, the more difficult the sentence.

Loose and Periodic Sentences

A major way to describe sentences in terms of the development of their content is to use the terms *loose* and *periodic*. A **loose sentence** unfolds easily, with no surprises. Because it is fairly predictable, it is the most commonly used sentence in stories. Here is an example:

In America, the idea of equality was first applied only to white males.

Periodic sentences are arranged as much as possible in an order of climax, with the concluding information or thought being withheld to make the sentence especially interesting or surprising. Usually the periodic sentence begins with a dependent clause so that the content may be built up to the final detail, as in this sentence:

Although in America the idea of equality was first applied only to males of European ancestry, in this century, despite the reluctance and even the opposition of many men who have regarded equality as a mark of their own status and not as a right for everyone, it has been extended to women and to persons of all races.

In narrative prose, sentences of this type are usually carefully placed in spots of crucial importance. Often the sentence alone might be said to contain the crisis and resolution at the same moment, as in this example from Edgar Allan Poe's "The Fall of the House of Usher":

For a moment she remained trembling and reeling to and fro upon the threshold, then, with a low moaning cry, fell heavily inward upon the person of her brother, and in her violent and now final death-agonies, bore him to the floor a corpse, and a victim to the terrors he had anticipated.

Parallelism

To create interest, authors often rely on the rhetorical device called **parallelism,** which is common and easily recognized. Parallelism is the repetition of the same grammatical form (nouns, verbs, phrases, clauses) to balance expressions, conserve words, and build up to climaxes. Here, for example, is another sentence from Poe, which occurs in the story "The Black Cat":

I grew, day by day, more moody, more irritable, more regardless of the feelings of others.

Arrangements like this are called *parallel* because they may actually be laid out graphically, according to parts of speech, in parallel lines, as in the following (with the phrase "day by day" left out):

              more moody
I grew   more irritable
              more regardless of the feelings of others

Poe's sentence achieves an order of increasing severity of psychological depression developing from the personal to the social.

The same parallel arrangements may be seen also in individual sentences within a paragraph or longer unit. In the story "The Necklace," for example, De Maupassant uses parallel sentences to describe Mathilde's ten years of household drudgery. The effect of the repeated patterns—"she" followed by active past-tense verbs—is to suggest the sameness and also the boredom of her life:

She learned to do heavy housework, dirty kitchen jobs. She washed the dishes, wearing away her manicured fingernails on greasy pots and encrusted baking dishes. She handwashed dirty linen, shirts, and dish towels that she hung out on the line to dry. Each morning, she took the garbage down to the street, and she carried up water, stopping at each floor to catch her breath. And, dressed in cheap house dresses, she went to the fruit dealer, the grocer, the butcher, with her basket under her arms, haggling, insulting, defending her measly cash penny by penny.

CUMULATIO OR ACCUMULATION.　The paragraph from "The Necklace" also illustrates another rhetorical device much used by writers, namely **cumulatio** or **accumulation.** While *parallelism* refers to grammatical constructions, *cumulatio* refers to the building up of details, such as the materials in the "she" sentences in De Maupassant's paragraph. The device is therefore a brief way of introducing much information, for once the parallel rhythm of the buildup begins, readers readily accept new material. The device thus acts as a series of quick glimpses or vignettes, and vividness is established through the parallel repetition.

CHIASMUS OR ANTIMETABOLE.　Also fitting into the pattern of parallelism is a favorite device called **chiasmus** or **antimetabole.** This pattern is designed to create vividness through memorable repetition. The pattern is *A B B A*, which can be arranged graphically at the ends of an *X* (which is the same as the Greek letter *chi*):

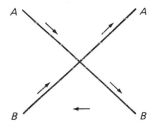

Mark Twain, in the story "Luck," creates a sentence that shows the pattern:

　A　　　　　　　*B*　　　　　　　*B*　　　　　　　*A*
I drilled him and crammed him, and crammed him and drilled him.

You may not always encounter such easily observed patterns, but you should always be alert to positions and arrangements that you think are particularly noticeable or effective. Even though you may not be able to use a technically correct name, your analysis should go well as long as you focus your attention on noticeable aspects of effective writing.

WRITING ABOUT THE STYLE
OF A PASSAGE

In prewriting, you should consider the selected passage in the context of the entire story. What sort of passage is it? Narrative? Descriptive? Does it contain any dialogue? Is there a speaker with clearly established characteristics? How does the passage reflect his or her personality? Try to determine the level of the diction: Did you need to use a dictionary to discover the meaning of any of the words? Are there any unusual words? Any especially difficult or uncommon words? Do any of the words distract you as you read? Is there any slang? Are any words used only in particular occupations or ways of life (such as words used about drink, or automobiles, or horses, words from other languages, and so on)? Are there any contractions? Do they indicate a conversational, intimate level of speech? Are the words the most common ones that might be used? Can you think of more difficult ones? Easier ones? More accurate ones? Are there many short words? Long words?

Can you easily imagine the situations described by the words? If you have difficulty, can you find any reasons that stem out of the level of diction?

Are the sentences long or short? Is there any variation in length? Can you observe any relationship between length and topic material? Are the sentences simple, compound, or complex? Does one type predominate? Why? Can you describe noteworthy rhetorical devices? Are there any sentences that are periodic rather than loose? What effect is gained by this sentence or sentences? Are there any other noticeable devices? What are they? How are they used? What is their effect?

Introduction

In your introduction you should establish the particulars about the passage you are studying and should present a central idea that relates the style to these particulars. You should mention the place of the passage in the work, the general subject matter, any special ideas, the speaker, the apparent audience (if any except the general reader), and the basic method of presentation (that is, monologue, dialogue, or narration, all of which might be interspersed with argument, description, or comparison).

Body

In the body of your theme you should describe and evaluate the style of the passage. Always remember to consider the style in relationship to the circumstances of the work. For example, suppose the speaker is in a plane crashing to the ground, or in a racing car just approaching the finish line, or hurrying to meet a sweetheart; or suppose the speaker is recalling the past or considering the future. Such conditions must be kept foremost throughout your analysis.

To focus your theme, you might wish to single out one aspect of style, or to discuss everything, depending on the length of the assignment. Be sure to treat things like levels of diction, categories like specific-general and concrete-abstract, the degree of simplicity or complexity, length, numbers of words (an approach that is relatively easy for a beginning), and denotation-connotation. In discussing rhetorical aspects, go as far as you can with the nomenclature at your command. Consider things like sentence types and any specific rhetorical devices you notice and are able to describe. If you can draw attention to the elements in a parallel structure by using grammatical terms, do so. If you are able to detect the ways in which the sentences are kept simple or made complex, describe these ways. Be sure to use examples from the passage to illustrate your point; indent them and leave spaces between them and your own material.

The sort of theme envisaged here is designed to sharpen your levels of awareness at your own stage of development as a reader. Later, to the degree that you will have gained sharper perceptions and a wider descriptive vocabulary, you will be able to enhance the sophistication of your analyses.

CONCLUSION.   Whereas the body is the place for detailed descriptions and examples, your conclusion is the place where you can make evaluations of the author's style. To what extent have your discoveries in your analysis increased or reinforced your appreciation of the author's technique? Does the passage take on any added importance as a result of your study? Is there anything elsewhere in the work comparable to the content, words, or ideas that you have discussed in the passage?

Numbers for Easy Reference

Include a copy of your passage at the beginning of your theme, as in the example. For your reader's convenience, number the sentences in the passage, and use these numbers as they become relevant in your theme.

Sample Theme (Style in a Passage from a Play)

Hamlet's Self-Revelation: A Reading of Hamlet, I. v. 92–109

Oh all you host of Heaven! Oh Earth; what else?	*92*
And shall I couple Hell? Oh fie: hold my heart;	*93*
And you my sinews, grow not instant old;	*94*
But bear me stiffly up: Remember thee?	*95*
Aye, thou poor Ghost, while memory holds a seat	*96*
In this distracted globe: Remember thee?	*97*
Yea, from the table of my memory,	*98*
I'll wipe away all trivial fond records,	*99*

100	All saws of books, all forms, all pressures past,
101	That youth and observation copied there;
102	And thy commandment all alone shall live
103	Within the book and volume of my brain,
104	Unmixed with baser matter; yes, yes, by Heaven:
105	Oh most pernicious woman!
106	Oh villain, villain, smiling damned villain!
107	My tables, my tables; meet it is I set it down,
108	That one may smile, and smile and be a villain;
109	At least I'm sure it may be so in Denmark;

In this passage from Act I of Hamlet, Hamlet is alone after the Ghost of his father has left the stage. His speech builds upon the Ghost's command to be remembered, and he begins by addressing that departed figure. After the first thirteen lines, however, he really is addressing himself, in soliloquy.

[1]   A close reading of the speech reveals Hamlet as an imaginative, reflective person undergoing great stress.° These qualities are apparent in the scholarly diction, the development of the "book and volume" comparison, the blending of grammatical structure and line, the poetic rhythms, and the contradiction within the speech.□

[2]   The diction indicates Hamlet's background as a student, for many of his words might be expected from someone who has been immersed in arguments and ideas. Table, records, saws (sayings) of books, copied, book and volume, set it down—all these smack of the classroom. They show that Hamlet, who before the play's opening has returned from the university for his father's funeral (and his mother's marriage), turns naturally to the language of a student even under stress, or perhaps especially under stress.

[3]   A turn of mind characteristic of a student is shown in lines 97–103. This is the knack of seizing a thought and developing it fully. Hamlet is promising to remember the Ghost, but he goes beyond that. He deals at great length with the thought that his memory is like a "book and volume" on which all his previous life's experiences have been written. He states that he will "wipe away" this entire record, which is "trivial" compared to the "commandment" for vengeance that the Ghost has just made. In short, Hamlet is the sort of person who pursues an idea to its logical extension, using the exactly right vocabulary.

The grammatical control in the passage seems also designed to suggest Hamlet's mental strength. Everything is correct. The adverbial clause while . . . globe modifies the opening verb Remember (95), which itself echoes the Ghost's departing words. The long sentence extending from 98 to 104 shows a perfect blending of grammar and poetic lines. Thus, 98 contains an adverb (prepositional) phrase modifying the main clause of 99. Line 100 contains three noun units which are in apposition to the noun in 99 (records). Lines 102 and 104 contain the second element in the compound sentence, and the major parts of this, too, are coextensive with their respective lines. In 103 the phrase Within . . . brain modifies the verb shall live in 102, and the phrase in 104 (Unmixed . . . matter) complements the same verb. The reader must here assume that Shakespeare is exerting this control over the lines to show that Hamlet's mind is powerful, and under the right circumstances capable of great control. Fortinbras says, after Hamlet's death, that the young Prince was potentially a great leader. Surely the control over language shown in

° Central idea
□ Thesis sentence

[4] this passage is evidence of the capacity for analysis and discernment that should characterize leadership.

Against this mental power, however, there are many rhythmic indications that Hamlet is going through stress. The large number of interjections throughout the speech creates heavy interruptions in the thought, most likely to suggest a mind that is being upset and overwhelmed. These are: *Aye* (96) *Yea* (98); *yes, yes, by heaven* (104); the exclamations against Gertrude and Claudius which take up lines 105 and 106; and the repetition of *smile* (108). In addition, the major rhythm of the speech from 104 to the end is complementary to the morbidity that characterizes Hamlet in the rest of the play. This section contains many trochaic rhythms, which would have been described in Shakespeare's day as having a "dying fall." There are falling rhythms on

[5]

yés, bў héavėn

and

Ȏ víllaȋn, víllȃin, smȋlȋng dámnĕd víllȃin.

The last two lines end with trochees (*villain*; *Denmark*). These rhythms anticipate the interjections in the "To be or not to be" soliloquy, where Hamlet is so depressed that he thinks of suicide.

Along with these rhythmic indications, a close reading of the content of the speech reveals great agitation. Hamlet is a person of normal sensibility, and a normal person would be upset by much less than he has just been through. A natural result, however brief, would be a loss of composure, with wrong words, hesitations, or even contradictions in thought. While Shake-[6] speare sees to it that Hamlet's diction is perfect, he leads Hamlet into an apparent contradiction. Thus, after he exclaims that his mother is "pernicious" and his uncle is a "villain," he frantically writes in his "tables" that one "may smile, and smile, and be a villain." Here the contradiction between his promise to forget trivialities and his writing this platitude indicates his confused state after seeing the Ghost.

Because this passage reveals the disturbance in Hamlet's character so fully, it is important to the rest of the play. From this point on, Hamlet is goaded by his promise to the Ghost that he will think of nothing but revenge. He will feel guilty and will be overwhelmed with self-doubt and self-destructive-[7] ness, because he delays acting on this promise. His attitude toward Claudius, which previously was scorn, will now be hatred and the obsession for vengeance. His love for Ophelia will be wrecked by this obsession, and as a result Ophelia, a tender plant, will die. Truly, this passage may be regarded as the climax of the first act, and it points the way to the grim but inevitable outcome of the play.

COMMENTARY ON THE THEME

This theme is based on the details of style that may be discussed after a careful but not exhaustive close reading. Thus, the discussion of diction in paragraph 2 deals only with those words that reflect Hamlet's concerns as a student. In paragraph 3 the "book and volume" analogy is related to this same studiousness. While the details of this analogy are mentioned, they are not examined extensively.

The most detailed paragraph is the fourth, where the connection is made between grammar and Hamlet's mental power. An operative use of grammatical terms is illustrated here to describe constituent parts of sentences. Although the paragraph may seem detailed and hard to follow, the nomenclature is neither obscure nor difficult. To write a comparable paragraph, you would need to lay out the sentences of a passage grammatically, relying on whatever methods you have learned about parsing or structural analysis.

The discussion of rhythm in paragraph 5 is focused on two prominent aspects of Hamlet's speech: the interjections to indicate mental turbulence, and the trochees to complement the growth of Hamlet's morbid frame of mind. The sixth paragraph is based on the interpretation (which the concentration in a close reading permits) that Hamlet's contradictory behavior is a normal response to his just having seen the Ghost. Throughout the theme there is an effort to fit the passage into the context of the play, and the concluding paragraph relates Hamlet's mental state, as revealed in the speech, to important aspects of the later acts.

chapter 17

Writing About Film

Film is the word used most often in discussing motion pictures, although often you may hear *picture*, or simply *movie*. It is a highly specialized kind of drama, which, like drama, utilizes the techniques of dialogue, monologue, and action. Also like drama, it employs movement and spectacle. Unlike drama, it embodies other techniques that result from the technology of photography and lighting, film chemistry, sound, and editing. In writing about film, many of your considerations may be purely literary, such as character, structure, tone, ideas, or symbolism. In addition, the techniques of film are so specialized—so much an extension of what you normally see on a printed page—that discussing film also requires considering film techniques, or at least taking them into account.

FILM AND STAGE PLAYS

Film may be compared with the stage production of a play. A written play may be produced many times, in many different places, with many different people. In bringing a play to life, the producer and director not only employ actors to speak the parts, but in planning and arranging for the production they also use artists, scene designers, carpenters, painters, lighting technicians, costume makers, choreographers, music directors, and musicians. Each production is therefore different from every other, because not only the actors, but also the actual appurtenances of the staging, are unique. A film, however, because of high production costs, and also because it reaches a mass audience through movie theaters and television and video cassette performances, exists in only one version (with the exception of remakes). Thus, Shakespeare's play *Hamlet* has been produced thousands of separate times since Shakespeare's Globe Theatre company first performed it at the beginning of the seventeenth century, while Orson Welles's *Citizen Kane* (1941) is in only one form, and will likely never change from that form.

As might be expected, stage and movie productions are quite different. Stage productions are limited by the physical conditions of a stage. Human beings enter, speak to each other, and remain in front of the audience until they exit. Although many directors and producers augment their performances with brief sections of film, slides, and tape recordings (such as for the witches in *Macbeth,* or the Ghost in *Hamlet*), and spectacular devices and machines such as wires, trapdoors, and revolving platforms, the stage itself limits the freedom of the production.

Aside from budget, the makers of film have few limitations. Film is therefore similar to a novel or a story, in which the absence of restrictions other than the writer's imagination permits the inclusion of any detail whatever, from the description of a chase to the reenactment of a scene in the Napoleonic wars. When you read a story, you use your imagination to bring things graphically to your mind. When you see a film, however, the filmmaker has replaced your imagination with his or hers: Is there a scene on a desert island? The filmmaker has gone on location to such an island, and presents it in the film, complete with beach, sand dunes, palm trees, native huts, and authentic natives-turned-actors. Nothing is left to your imagination. Is there a scene on a distant planet? Obviously the filmmaker cannot go on location there, but he or she creates a substitute working location in the studio, with lighting, props, costumes, and special effects. Film, in short, enables a dramatic production to approach the freedom of novels and stories.

THE PAINTER, THE PHOTOGRAPHER, AND THE FILMMAKER

To the degree that film is confined to a screen, it may be compared visually to the art of the painter. There is a whole language of visual art. One object in a painting may take on special relationships to others as the artist directs the eyes of the observer. A color used in one part may be balanced with the same color, or its complement, in another part. Painters may introduce certain details as symbols, and may suggest allegorical interpretations through the inclusion of mythical figures or universally recognized allegorical objects. Particular effects may be achieved with the use of the textures of paint. The techniques and effects are extensive.

Still photographers have many of the same resources as the painter, except that they cannot create the same textures with their cameras and chemicals as the painter can with paint. Basically, photographers transfer an image of reality to a finished print or slide. They do have freedom of focus with lenses, however, and can focus one object clearly while making others appear fuzzy. They also have the freedom to select shutter speeds, and can either stop an action at 1/1000 second or let it remain blurred at 1/30 second. With the exacting control of special lenses and development, they can create many monochromatic, textured, and impressionistic images. Techniques such as these give photographers much interpretive freedom in handling the external reality that is the basis of their art.

The filmmaker is able to utilize most of the resources of the still photographer and many of those of the painter, and may augment these with computer-created and -enhanced effects. Artistically, the most confining aspect of film is the rectangular screen, but aside from that, film is quite free. With a basis in a dramatic text called a *script* or *film script*, it uses words and their effects, but it also employs the language of visual art, especially the particular truth to life of moving pictures.

When discussing a film, then, you should realize that film communicates not just by words, but also by various other techniques. You can treat the ideas, the problems, and the symbolism in a film, but while treating them you should recognize that the visual presentation is inseparable from the medium of film itself.

TECHNIQUES

There are many techniques of film, and a full description and documentation of them can, and has, become extensive.[1] In preparing to write a theme about film, however, you need to familiarize yourself only with those aspects of technique that have an immediate bearing on your responses and interpretations.

---

[1] See, for example, Rudolph Arnheim, *Film as Art* (Berkeley: University of California Press, 1969); Daniel Talbot, ed., *Film: An Anthology* (Berkeley: University of California Press, 1969); Louis D. Giannetti, *Understanding Movies*, 4th ed. (Englewood Cliffs, N.J.: Prentice-Hall, Inc., 1987) and James Monaco, *How to Read a Film*, rev. ed. (New York: Oxford University Press, 1981).

EDITING OR MONTAGE: THE HEART
OF THE FILMMAKER'S CRAFT

A finished film is not a continuous work, filmed from start to end, but is instead a composite. The putting together of the film is the process of *editing*, or *montage* (assemblage, mounting, construction), which is a method of cutting and gluing. Depending on the flexibility or inflexibility of the film script, the various parts or scenes of the film are planned before actual shooting begins, but the major task of montage is done in a studio by special film editors.

If we may once again compare film with a stage play, the continuity of a typical film is not the same as in a theater, where the play moves continuously, with pauses only between scenes and acts. Your perception of the action is determined by your distance from the stage (perhaps aided by opera glasses or binoculars). Also, even as you move your eyes from one character to another, you still perceive the entire scene, or stage. In a film, however, the directors and editors create these perceptions for you by mounting together many different camera shots (hence "montage"). The editors may begin with many takes of scenes, along with many more scenes than will finally appear. What they select, or mount, will be the film—we never see the acting and pictures that they have rejected. Thus, it is editing, or montage, that puts everything together.

The Uses of Montage

NARRATIVE CONTINUITY.   A number of characteristics are achieved through montage. The first, already suggested, is narrative continuity. A journey, for example, may be illustrated by selected shots of a person buying a bus ticket, boarding the bus, viewing the passing countryside, and walking in a bus terminal. A climb up a steep cliff may be shown at the bottom, in the middle (with backward slips and falls to show the danger of the climb and to make viewers catch their breaths), and at the top as the character pauses to look back and down. All such narrative sequences result from the assembling of individual pieces, each representing phases of the activity. A noteworthy example of a large number of separate parts forming a narrative unit is the well-known shower murder in Alfred Hitchcock's *Psycho* (1959), where a forty-five-second sequence is made up of more than seventy different shots (e.g., the woman in the shower, the murderer behind the curtain, the attack, the slumping figure, the running water, the dead woman's eye, the bathtub drain, etc.).

EXPLANATION OF CHARACTER AND MOTIVATION.   Montage can be used in flashbacks to explain current, ongoing actions or characteristics; as illus-

tration of a particular character's thoughts and memories; or as brief examples from the unremembered past of a character suffering from amnesia
to explain the character's forgotten identity. It also supplies direct visual
explanation of human character. A famous example occurs in Welles's
Citizen Kane (the subject of the sample theme, pp. 252–55). The concluding
scene shows overhead views of Kane's vast collection of statues and me-
mentos. At the very end, the camera focuses on a raging incinerator,
into which workmen have thrown his boyhood sled, which bears the
brand name "Rosebud" (and which we have fleetingly seen him playing
with as a boy). Because "Rosebud" is Kane's dying word, which everyone
in the film is trying to learn about, this final scene is intended to show
that Kane, at the time of his death, is remembering his lost boyhood,
before he was taken away from his parents, and that his unhappy life
may have resulted from lifelong feelings of rejection and personal pain.

DIRECTORIAL COMMENTARY.   In addition, montage is used symbolically as commentary on particular situations, as in an early sequence in
Sir Charles Chaplin's *Modern Times* (1936) that shows a large group of
workingmen rushing to their factory jobs. Immediately following this scene
is a view of a large, milling herd of sheep. By this use of montage, Chaplin
suggests symbolically that the men are being herded and dehumanized
by modern industry. Thus, montage and editorial statement go hand in
hand.

OTHER USES.   Montage may also produce other characteristics through
the choice of camera work, development, and special effects. For example,
filmmakers may gain a comic effect by reversing an action to emphasize
its illogicality or ridiculousness. Editing may also speed up action (which
makes even the most serious things funny), or slow things down. It may
also blend one scene with another, or juxtapose two or more actions in
quick succession to show what different people may be doing while they
are separated. The possibilities for creativity and uniqueness are extensive.

VISUAL TECHNIQUES

The Camera

While editing or montage is a finishing technique, the work of film
begins with the motion picture camera, which permits great freedom in
the presentation of characters and actions. In a film, the visual viewpoint
may shift. Thus, a film may begin with a distant shot of the actors—a
long shot—much like the sight you might see when looking at actors on
stage in a theater. Then the camera may zoom in to give a close-up, or
zoom out to present a wide and complete panorama. Usually a speaking

actor will be the subject of a close-up, but the camera may also show close-ups of other actors reacting to the first actor's statements. You must decide on the effects of close-ups and long shots yourself, but it should be plain that the frequent use of either—or of middle-distance photographs—is a means by which film directors control perceptions of their characters and situations.

The camera may also move rapidly, or slowly, from character to character, or from character to a natural or manufactured object. In this way a film can show a series of reactions to an event. It can also concentrate your attention on the attitude of a particular character, or it can represent a visual commentary on his or her actions. If a man and woman are in love, as an example, the camera may shift, either directly or through montage, from the couple to flowers and trees, thus associating their love visually with objects of beauty and growth. Should the flowers be wilted and the trees leafless, however, the visual commentary might be that the love is doomed and hopeless.

The camera may also create effects that no other medium can convey. Slow motion, for example, can focus on a certain aspect of a person's character. The concentrated focus on a child running happily in a meadow (as in *The Color Purple* [1985] by Steven Spielberg) suggests the joy inherent in such movement. Surprisingly, speed is often indicated by slow motion, in order to demonstrate the muscular efforts of particular characters (as in the running scenes in Hugh Hudson's *Chariots of Fire* [1981]).

Many other camera techniques bear on action and character. The focus may be sharp at one point, indistinct at another. Moving a speaking character out of focus may suggest that listeners are bored. Sharp or blurred focus may also show that a character has seen things exactly or inexactly. In action sequences, the camera may follow a moving character, a technique called "tracking" because often the camera is mounted in a car on rails. It is possible to track from an automobile, truck, or boat, which may follow running human beings or horses, speeding bicycles and cars, or moving sailboats, canoes, speedboats, or rowboats. A camera operator on foot may also be the tracker, or the camera may shoot movement from a helicopter or airplane. Movement may also be captured by a rotating camera that follows a character from one point to another. Then, too, the camera may be held fixed and the moving character may simply walk, run, or ride across the scene.

Light, Shadow, and Color

As in the theater, the filmmaker utilizes light, shadow, and color as a means of communication. Because characters are seen in settings, both real and symbolic, you should recognize that the cinematic manipulation of setting is even more a part of the statement of the film than it might be in a story, where even an alert reader may miss such relationships. A scene in sunshine, which brings out colors, and the same scene in rain and clouds or in twilight, all of which mute colors, create different moods. Characters filmed in a bright light are presumably open, frank, and clear in their motivations, whereas characters in shadow or darkness may be hiding something, particularly in black-and-white films. The use of flashing or strobe lights might show a changeable, mercurial, and perhaps sinister character or situation.

Colors, of course, have much the same meaning as in any other artistic medium. Blue sky and clear light suggest happiness, while greenish-tinged light may indicate something ghoulish. A memorable use of color occurs midway through David O. Selznick's *Gone With the Wind* (1939), when Scarlet O'Hara reflects upon the devastation of her plantation home, Tara. She resolves never to be hungry again, and as she speaks she is silhouetted against a bright, flaming, orange sky—an angry background that suggests how totally the way of life she knew as a young woman has been destroyed. As in this example, you may always expect colors to be carefully arranged to underscore the story of the film. Thus, lovers may wear clothing with the same or complementary colors, while people who are not "right" for each other may wear clashing colors.

ACTION AND THE HUMAN BODY

Action

The strength of film is direct action. Actions of all sorts—running, swimming, driving a car, climbing a ladder, fighting, embracing and kissing, or even just sitting; chases, trick effects, ambushes—all these and more make an immediate appeal to the viewer's sense of reality, and all are tied (or should be) to the development of the film. Scenes of action may run on for several minutes, with little or no accompanying dialogue, to carry on the story of the film, or to convey ideas about the interests and abilities of the characters.

The Body

Closely related to the portrayal of action is the way in which film may show the human body, together with bodily motion and gesture (body language) to augment the dialogue. The view or perspective that the filmmaker presents is particularly important. A usual torso shot of a character may stress no more than the content of a character's speech. A close-up shot, however, with the character's head filling the screen, may focus not only on the content but also on the character's motives. The camera may also distort our ordinary expectations of reality. With wide-angle lenses and close-ups, for example, the filmmaker can make human subjects bizarre or grotesque, as with the numerous faces in the crowd in Woody Allen's *Stardust Memories* (1980). Sometimes the camera creates other bodily distortions, enlarging certain limbs, for example, as with the forest dweller in Ingmar Bergman's *The Virgin Spring* (1959), or throwing into unnatural prominence a scolding mouth or a suspicious eye. If distortion is used, it invites interpretation: Perhaps the filmmaker is showing that certain human beings, even supposedly normal ones, are especially menacing, or a little wacky or even psychotic.

SOUND

Dialogue and Music

The first business of the sound track in a film is the spoken dialogue, which is "mixed" as a part of the editing process to be synchronized with the action. There are many other elements in the sound track. Music, the most important, is introduced to create and augment particular moods. A major or minor theme, or a slow or fast tempo, may alter our perception of identical or similar actions. If a character is meditating or thinking deeply, muted strings may create a mellow sound to complement the mood. But if the character is going insane, the music may become discordant, percussive, and cacophonous. Sometimes music is designed to give a film a special identity. In Hudson's *Chariots of Fire*, for example, Vangelis Papathanassiou wrote music that has become separately popular, but which is always identified with the film. In addition, musical accompaniments can be so interwoven with the action that dramatic statement can be rendered effectively without the use of dialogue. An example occurs in Welles's *Citizen Kane*. Beginning that portion of the narrative derived from the autobiography of a character who is now dead (the scene first focuses on his statue), the musical sound track by Bernard Herrmann quotes the *Dies Irae* theme from the traditional Mass for the Dead. The instrumentation, however, creates a funny, not serious, effect, and as a result we do not grieve for the character, but smile instead. Herrmann, incidentally, varies this theme elsewhere in the film, usually to comic effect.

Special Sound Effects

Special sound effects may also augment a film's action. The sound of a blow, for example, may be enhanced electronically to cause an impact similar to the force of the blow itself (as in the boxing scenes from the many *Rocky* films). At times some sounds—such as the noises of wailing people, squeaking or slamming doors, marching feet, or moving vehicles under power—may be filtered through an electronic apparatus to create weird or ghostly effects. Often a character's words may echo rapidly and sickeningly to show dismay or anguish. In a word, sound is a vital part of film.

WRITING ABOUT FILM

Obviously the first requirement for writing a theme is to see the film. At one time, viewing films required going to a theater, but these days you can find many films in an audio-visual lab or in video cassette rental stores. The existence of video cassettes, in fact, has revolutionized the viewing of films. No matter how you see the film you are planning to write about, it is wise to see it at least twice, making notes as you go, because your discussion takes on value the more thoroughly you know the material. Write down the names of the director and the principal actresses and actors. If particular speeches are worth quoting from the movie, remember the general circumstances of the quotation and also, if possible, key words. Try to recall uses of costume and color, or (if the film is in black and white) uses of light and shade. You will need to rely on memory, but if you have the film on videotape, you can always go to particular spots to check details.

Introduction

State your central idea and thesis sentence here. You should also include the background necessary to support points to be made in the body. It is also appropriate to name directors, producers, and major actresses and actors.

Body

The most difficult choice is your topic. If you have no other instructions, you might decide on subjects like those described in other chapters of this book, such as characterization, ideas, setting, or problems. Remember, however, to widen your discussion by considering not only dialogue but also techniques of film.

In discussing the film's action, you might consider some of the following questions: What is the relationship of action to theme? Does the action have any bearing on the characters, or is it no more than action for its own sake? Is the action particularly realistic? Does the camera stay at a distance, showing the persons as relatively small in a vast natural or artificial world? Do close-ups show smiles, frowns, eagerness, or anxiety? Is any attempt made to render temperature by action—say, cold by a character's stamping of feet, or warmth by the character's removing a coat or shirt? Does the action show any changing of mood, from sadness to happiness, for example, or from indecision to decision? What particular aspects of the action point toward such conclusions?

Then, too, you may stress cinematographic techniques, showing their relationship to the theme of the film, their appropriateness, and their quality. If you discuss technique, be sure to have good notes, so that your supporting details are accurate and vivid. A good method is to concentrate on only a few special scenes and the techniques you find in them. If you wish to analyze the effects of montage, for example, you may use your stop-action control (for a video cassette recorder) to go over the adjoining scenes a number of times.

In judging a film, you might also emphasize the quality of the acting. You do not need to be a drama critic to supply answers to some of the following questions: How well do the actors adapt to the medium of film? How convincing are their performances? Do they control their facial expressions? Does their appearance lend anything to your understanding of their characters? How well do they control bodily motion? Are they graceful? Awkward? Does it seem that the actors are genuinely creating their roles, or just reading through the parts?

You may wish to write a general review, bringing in all these various aspects that go into the total package that is the film. If you write a review, consult Chapter 17 for ideas on how to proceed.

Conclusion

You might conclude by evaluating the effectiveness of the cinematographic form to story and idea. Are all the devices of film used in the best possible way? Is anything overdone? Is anything underplayed? Is the film good, bad, or indifferent up to a point, and then does it change? Why? How? The development of answers to questions like these are appropriate here.

Sample Theme

Orson Welles's Citizen Kane: *Whittling a Giant Down to Size*

Citizen Kane (1941) is a well-crafted film in black and white. The script is by Herman Mankiewicz and Orson Welles, with photography by Gregg Toland, music by Bernard Herrmann, direction by Welles, and the leading role played by Welles. It is the story of a wealthy and powerful man, Charles Foster Kane, who exemplifies the American Dream of economic self-sufficiency, self-determination, and self, period. The film does not explore the "greatness" of the hero, however, but rather exposes him as a misguided, unhappy person who tries to buy love and remake reality to suit himself.° All aspects of the picture—characterization, structure, and technique—are directed to this goal.□

[1]

At the film's heart is the characterization and deterioration of Kane, the newly deceased newspaper magnate and millionaire. He is not all bad, for he begins well and then goes downward, in a tragic sequence. For example, the view we see of him as a child, being taken away from home, invites sympathy. When we next see him as a spoiled young man, his idealism causes him to take control of a daily newspaper, the Inquirer. This idealism makes him admirable, and also makes his deterioration tragic. His attempt to use his newspaper for truth and social good shows his goodness. But the film is not about a good man's greatness, but rather about how he turns sour. As he says to Thatcher, in a moment of insight when he has to give up the paper, he could have been a great person if he had not been wealthy. His corruption begins when he tries to change facts to suit his own wishes. The major example of this unreality is his insane attempt to make an opera star out of his second wife, Susan, and his related attempt to shape critical praise for her despite her terrible singing. Even though he builds an opera house for her, and also sponsors many performances, he cannot change reality. It is this tampering with truth that indicates how completely he deserts his youthful dedication and integrity.

[2]

The structure is progressively arranged to bring out such weaknesses in Kane. The film flows out of the opening newsreel, which presents highlights in the life of Kane, who has just died. It is then that we learn that the word "Rosebud" (the sled that Kane used as a boy), spoken at the beginning by a person whose mouth is shown in close-up, is his dying word. The newsreel director, wanting to get the inside story, assigns a reporter named Thompson to learn about Rosebud. Thompson's search then unifies the rest of the film; he goes from place to place and person to person to read an autobiography and conduct interviews that disclose Kane's increasing strangeness and alienation. At the end, although the camera leaves Thompson to focus on the burning sled, Rosebud, he has been successful in uncovering the story of Kane's deterioration (even though he himself never learns what Rosebud means). Both the sled and the reporter therefore connect and tie together the many aspects of the film.

[3]

It is through Thompson's searches that the film presents the flashbacks rendering the story of Kane's deterioration. The separate persons being interviewed (including the handwritten account by Thatcher) each contribute something different to the narrative because their experiences with Kane have all been unique. Because of their individual points of view, the story takes on great intricacy. We learn in the Bernstein section, for example, that Jedediah proudly saves the copy of Kane's idealistic declaration about truth in reporting. We do not learn in Jedediah's interview, however, that he, Jedediah, sends the copy back to Kane as an indictment of Kane's betrayal of principle. Rather, it is in Susan's account that we learn about the returned declaration, even though she herself understands nothing about it. This subtlety, so typical of the film, marks the ways in which the biography of Kane is perceptively revealed.

° Central idea
□ Thesis sentence

[4]   Thus, the major importance of these narrating characters, although they are independently interesting, is to reveal and reflect the disintegration of Kane. Jedediah (Joseph Cotten) is a person of principle, who goes along with Kane for a long time, but after the lost election he rebels when he understands the falseness of Kane's personal life. He is totally alienated after his unfinished attack on Susan's performance is completed by Kane. Jedediah's change, or perhaps the reassertion of his own principles, thus reveals Kane's increasing

[5]   corruption. Susan, Kane's second wife (Dorothy Comingore), is naive, sincere, and warm, but her drinking, her attempted suicide, and her final separation show the harm of Kane's warped visions of life. Bernstein (Everett Sloane), the first person interviewed by Thompson, is a solitary figure who, as far as Kane is concerned, is uncritical, but it is he who first touches the theme about the mystery of Kane's motivations. Bernstein also takes on life when he speaks poignantly of his forty-five-year memory of the girl in white. Even though this revelation is brief, it suggests layers of feeling and longing.

       In addition to these perceptive characterizations that are used structurally, the film shows a mastery of film techniques. The camera focuses are sharp, with clear depths of field. In keeping with both the disintegration and mysteriousness of Kane, the screen is rarely bright. Instead, the film makes strong use of darkness and contrasts, almost to the point at times of blurring distinctions between people. Unique in the camera work are the many shots taken from

[6]   waist height or below, which distort the bodies of the characters by distancing their heads—suggesting that the characters are removed, out of focus, preoccupied with their own concerns, and oblivious to normal perspectives. Nowhere is this distortion better exemplified than in the scene between Kane and Jedediah in the empty rooms after the lost election. These rooms emphasize the solitude of the two men as Jedediah asks permission to leave for Chicago and thus to break their long association.

       As might be expected in a film so dominated by its central figure, the many symbols also create strong statements about character. The most obvious is the sled, Rosebud, the dominating symbol of the need for love and acceptance in childhood. Another notable symbol is glass and, in one scene, ice. In the party scene where the employees of the Inquirer are at the table, two ice statues are in the foreground. In another scene, a bottle is placed in front of Jedediah, who is drunk. In another, a pill bottle and drinking glass are in

[7]   front of Susan, who has just used them in her suicide attempt. The suggestion of these carefully photographed symbols is that life is brittle, fleeting, and breakable. Particularly symbolic is the bizarre entertainment in the party scene. Because Kane joins the dancing and singing, the action suggests that he is doing no more than taking a role in life, never being himself or knowing himself. Symbols that frame the film are the wire fence and the No Trespassing sign at both the beginning and ending. These symbols suggest that even if we understand a little about Kane, or anyone, there are boundaries we cannot pass, depths we can never reach.

       There are also amusing symbols that suggest not only the diminution of Kane, but also of the other characters. An example is Bernstein's high-backed chair, which makes him look like a small child. Equally amusing is the gigantic fireplace at Xanadu, which makes both Kane and Susan seem like pygmies—a symbol that great wealth does not improve life, but rather dwarfs and dehumanizes it. Kane's picnic at Xanadu is also comically grandiose. In going into the country, Kane and his friends do not walk, but ride in a long line of cars along the seashore—more like a funeral procession than a picnic—

and stay overnight in a massive tent. Quite funny is the increasing distance between Kane and Emily, his first wife, in the rapid-fire shots that portray their developing separation. Even more comic is the vast distance at Xanadu between Kane and Susan when they discuss their life together. They are so far apart that they must shout to be heard. Amusing as these symbols of diminution and alienation are, however, they are also pathetic, because at first Kane finds closeness with both his wives.

[8]

In all respects, *Citizen Kane* is a masterly film. This is not to say that the characters are likable, or that the amusing parts make it a comedy. Instead, the film pursues truth, suggesting that greatness and wealth cannot provide happiness. It is relentless in whittling away at its major figure. Kane is likable at times, and he is enormously generous (as shown when he sends Jedediah $25,000 in severance pay). But these high moments show the contrasting depths to which Kane falls, with the general point being that people who are powerful and great may deteriorate even at their height. The goal of the newsreel director at the beginning is to get at the "real story" behind the public man. There is more to any person than a two-hour film can reveal, but within its limits, *Citizen Kane* gets at the real story, and the real story is both sad and disturbing.

[9]

COMMENTARY ON THE THEME

The central idea is how the major figure, Kane, is reduced. In this respect the theme illustrates the analysis of character as described in Chapter 5 (see pp. 64–76), and it therefore emphasizes that film is first to be considered as a form of literature. Also shown in the theme are other methods of literary analysis: structure (see pp. 46–54) and symbols (pp. 132–42). Of these topics, only the use of symbols, because they are presented visually in the film, is unique to the medium of film as opposed to the medium of words.

Any one of the topics might be developed as a separate essay. There is more than enough about the character of Susan, for example, to sustain a complete theme, and the film's structure could be explored extensively. As a repository of film techniques, *Citizen Kane* itself is rich enough for an exhaustive, book-length account.

Paragraph 1 introduces the major topic, the deterioration of Kane's character. Unique to film, credit is given here to the major persons in the production. The thesis sentence indicates the topics to be discussed in the body: character, structure, and film technique.

Paragraph 2 begins the body and carries out a brief analysis of the major character. Paragraphs 3–5 discuss various aspects of the film's structure (the second topic announced in the thesis sentence) as they bear on Kane. In paragraph 3 the unifying importance of the sled and the reporter, Thompson, is explained. Paragraph 4 focuses on the film's use of flashback as a structural technique, while paragraph 5 discusses three of the flashback characters as they either intentionally or unintentionally reveal Kane's flaws.

The topic of paragraphs 6–8 is film technique, the third and last topic of the thesis sentence. Paragraph 6 focuses on light, camera angles, and distortion; paragraph 7 treats visual symbols; paragraph 8 continues the topic of symbols, but extends it to amusing ones.

The final paragraph, 9, restates the central idea, and also relates the theme of deterioration to the larger issue of how great wealth and power affect character. Thus, as a conclusion, this paragraph not only summarizes, but also gives tribute to the film's general implications.

chapter 18

Writing
the Research Theme

Research, as distinguished from pure criticism, refers to using primary and secondary sources for assistance in solving a literary problem. That is, in criticizing a work, pure and simple, you consult only the work in front of you (the primary source), whereas in doing research on the work, you consult not only the work but many other works that were written about it or that may shed light on it (secondary sources). Typical research tasks are to find out more about the historical period in which a story was written or about prevailing opinions of the times or about what modern (or earlier) critics have said about the work. It is obvious that a certain amount of research is always necessary in any critical job or in any theme about a work. Looking up words in a dictionary, for example, is only minimal research; more vigorous research—the type we are considering here—involves introductions, critical articles, encyclopedias, biographies, critical studies, histories, and the like.

It is necessary to put research in perspective. In general, students and scholars do research to uncover some of the accumulated lore of our civilization. This lore—the knowledge that currently exists—may be compared to a large cone that is constantly being filled. At the beginnings of human existence there was little knowledge, and the cone was at its smallest point. As civilization progressed, people learned more, and the cone began to fill. Each time a new piece of information or a new conclusion was recorded, a little more knowledge or lore was in effect poured into the

cone, which became slightly fuller. Though at present our cone of knowledge is quite full, it seems capable of infinite growth. Knowledge keeps
piling up and new disciplines keep developing. It is increasingly difficult
for one person to accumulate more than a small portion of the entirety.
Indeed, historians generally agree that the last person to know virtually
everything about every existing discipline was Aristotle—2400 years ago.

If you grant that you cannot learn everything, you can make a positive
start by recognizing that research provides two things: (1) a systematic
understanding of a portion of the knowledge filling the cone, and (2) an
understanding of, and ability to handle, the methods by which you might
someday be able to make your own contributions.

Thus far we have been speaking broadly about the relevance of research to any discipline. The chemist, the anthropologist, the ecologist,
the marine biologist—all employ research. Our subject here, however, is
literary research, the systematic study of library sources to illuminate a
topic connected with a literary work.

SELECTING A TOPIC

Often an instructor asks for a research theme on a specific topic. However,
if you have only a general research assignment, your first problem is to
make your own selection. It may be helpful to have a general notion of
the kind of research theme you would find most congenial. Here are
some possibilities.

1. A PAPER ON A PARTICULAR WORK.   You might treat character (for
example, "The Character of Smirnov in *The Bear*," or "The Question of
Whether Young Goodman Brown is a Hero or a Dupe"), or tone, point
of view, setting, structure, and the like. A research paper on a single
work is similar to a theme on the same work, except that the research
paper takes into account more views and facts than one without the research. Please see the sample research theme, on Katherine Mansfield's
"Miss Brill," to see how materials may be handled for such an assignment.

2. A PAPER ON A PARTICULAR AUTHOR.   The paper is about an idea
or some facet of style, imagery, setting, or tone of the author, tracing
the origins and development of the topic through a number of different
stories, poems, or plays. An example is "The Idea of Sin and Guilt as
Developed by Hawthorne." This type of paper is suitable for shorter works,
though it is also applicable for a single major work, such as a longer
story, novel, or play.

3. A PAPER BASED ON COMPARISON AND CONTRAST.   There are two types:
   a. *A theme about an idea or artistic quality common to two or more
   authors.* Your intention might be to show points of similarity

or contrast, or else to show that one author's work may be read as a criticism of another's. Representative subjects are "The Use of the Third-Person-Limited Point of View by Hawthorne and Mansfield," and "The Theme of Love and Sexuality in Jackson, Chekhov, and Collier."

b. *Contrasting or opposing critical views of a particular work or body of works*. Sometimes much is to be gained from examining differing critical opinions on topics like "The Meaning of Shirley Jackson's 'The Lottery,' " "The Interpretations of Hawthorne's 'Young Goodman Brown,' " or "The Question of Chekhov's Attitude Toward Women as Seen in *The Bear*." Such a study would attempt to determine the critical opinion and taste to which a work does or does not appeal, and might also determine whether the work was/is in the advance or rear guard of its time.

4. A PAPER SHOWING THE INFLUENCE OF AN IDEA, AUTHOR, PHILOSOPHY, POLITICAL SITUATION, OR ARTISTIC MOVEMENT ON SPECIFIC WORKS OF AN AUTHOR OR AUTHORS. A paper on influences can be direct, as in "Details of Black American Life as Reflected in Hughes's 'Theme for English B,' " or else more abstract and critical, as in "The Influence of Racial Oppression and the Goal of Racial Equality on the Speaker of 'Theme for English B.' "

5. A PAPER ON THE ORIGINS OF A PARTICULAR WORK OR TYPE OF WORK. One avenue of research for such a paper is to examine biography to discover the germination and development of a work—for example, " 'Kubla Khan' as an Outgrowth of Coleridge's Reading." Another way is to relate a work to a particular type or tradition: " 'Theme for English B' and the Harlem Renaissance," or " 'Patterns' and Its Relationship to the Anti-War Literature of World War I."

If you consider these types, an idea of what to write may come to you. Perhaps you have liked one author, or several authors. If so, you might start to think along the lines of types 1, 2, and 3. If you are interested in influences or in origins, then types 4 or 5 may suit you better.

If you still cannot decide on a topic after rereading the works you have liked, then you should carry your search into your school library. Look up your author or authors in the card or computer catalog. Usually works written *by* the authors are included first, followed by works written *about* the authors. Your first goal should be to find a recent book-length critical study published by a university press. Use your judgment here: Look for a title indicating that the book is a general one dealing with the author's major works rather than just one work. Study those chapters relevant to the work you have chosen. Most writers of critical studies describe their purpose and plan in their introductions or first chapters, so begin with the first part. If no separate chapter deals with the primary text, use the index and go to the relevant pages. Reading in this way should soon suggest a topic for further study. Once you have made your decision, you are ready to develop a working bibliography.

SETTING UP A BIBLIOGRAPHY

The best way to develop a working bibliography of books and articles is to begin with major critical studies of the writer or writers. Again, go to the catalog and pick out books published by university presses. These books usually contain selective bibliographies. Be careful to read the chapters on your primary work or works, and look for footnotes and end notes. Often you can save time if you record the names of books and articles listed in these notes; then refer to the bibliographies included at the ends of the books and select likely-looking titles. Now look at the dates of publication of the critical books. Let us suppose that you have been looking at three, published in 1951, 1963, and 1982. The chances are that the bibliography in a book published in 1982 will be complete up through about 1979 or 1980, for the writer usually completes the manuscript two or three years before publication. Then begin gathering a bibliography of works published since 1979; you may assume that writers of the critical works have selected, for your use, the most relevant works published before that time.

Bibliographical Guides

Fortunately for students doing literary research, the Modern Language Association (MLA) of America has been providing a virtually complete bibliography of literary studies for years, not just for English and American literature, but in the literature of most modern foreign languages. The MLA started achieving completeness in the late 1950s, and by 1969 had reached such an advanced state that it divided the bibliography into four parts. Most university and college libraries have a set of these bibliographies readily available on open shelves or tables. There are, of course, many other bibliographies useful for students doing literary research, such as the *Essay and General Literature Index*, the *International Index*, and various specific indexes. There are many more than can be mentioned here meaningfully. For most purposes, however, the *MLA International Bibliography* is more than adequate. Remember that as you progress, the notes and bibliographies in the works you consult will also constitute an unfolding bibliography. For the sample research theme in this chapter, for example, a number of entries were discovered not on the first study of bibliographies, but from a study of the reference lists provided by writers of critical works.

The *MLA International Bibliography* is conveniently organized by period and author. If your author is Katherine Mansfield, look her up under "English Literature X. Twentieth Century," the relevant listing for all twentieth-century English writers. If your author is Hawthorne, refer to "American Literature III. Nineteenth Century, 1800–1870." You will find most books and articles listed under the author's last name. For special help, the MLA has recently developed an exhaustive topics list that is keyed to the bibliographical entries. Using these topics, you may locate important and relevant works that you might not have found with only the authors list. In the MLA bibliographies, journal references are abbreviated, but a lengthy list explaining abbreviations appears at the beginning of the volume. You should begin with the most recent MLA bibliography and then go backward to your stopping point. Be sure to get the complete information, especially volume numbers and years of publication, for each article and book you wish to consult. You are now ready to find your sources and take notes.

TAKING NOTES AND PARAPHRASING MATERIAL

There are many ways of taking notes, but the consensus is that the best method is to use note cards. If you have never used cards before, you might profit from consulting any one of a number of handbooks and special workbooks on research. A lucid and methodical explanation of using cards and taking notes can be found in Lynn Troyka, *Simon & Schuster Handbook for Writers* (Englewood Cliffs: Prentice Hall, 1987), 510–29 and 558–60. The principal virtue of cards, aside from the facts that they stack neatly and do not tear easily, is that they may be classified, numbered, renumbered, shuffled, tried out in one place, rejected, and then used in another (or thrown away), and arranged in order when you start to write.

Taking Notes

WRITE THE SOURCE ON EACH CARD. As you take notes, write the source of your information on each card. This may sound like a lot of bother, but it is easier than going back to the library to find the correct source after you have begun writing your research theme. You can save time by taking the complete data on one card—a master card for that source—and then making an abbreviation for your notes. Here is an example. Observe that the author's last name appears first:

Donovan, Josephine, ed. Feminist Literary Criticism: Explorations in Theory.
Lexington: The University Press of Kentucky, 1975.

DONOVAN

If you plan to write many notes from this book, then the name "Donovan" will serve as a shorthand identification on each card. Be sure not to lose your complete master card, because you will need it in preparing your list of works cited.

RECORD THE PAGE NUMBER FOR EACH NOTE.   It would be hard to guess how much exasperation has been caused by the failure of students to record page numbers. Be sure to write the page number first, *before* you begin to take your note. If the detail you are noting goes from one page to the next in your source, record the exact spot where the page changes, as in this example:

Heilbrun and Stimson, in DONOVAN, pp. 63–64

[63] After the raising of the feminist consciousness it is necessary to develop/
[64] "the growth of moral perception" through anger and the correction of social
inequity.

The reason for such care is that you may wish to use only a part of a
note you have taken, and when there are two pages you will need to be
accurate in locating what goes where.

RECORD ONLY ONE FACT OR OPINION PER CARD.   Record only one thing
on each card—one quotation, one paraphrase, one observation—never
two or more. You might be tempted to fill up the entire card, but such a
try at economy often gets you in trouble because you might want to use
different details recorded on the same card in different places as you write
your research paper.

USE QUOTATION MARKS FOR ALL QUOTED MATERIAL.   A major problem
in taking notes is to distinguish copied material from your own words.
Here you must be extremely cautious. *Always put quotation marks around
every direct quotation you copy verbatim from a source.* Make the quotation
marks immediately, before you forget, so that you will always know that
the words within quotation marks in your notes are the words of another
writer.

Often, as you take a note, you may use some of your own words
and some of the words from your source. It is then even more important
to be cautious. Put quotation marks around *every word* that you take directly
from the source, even if you find yourself with a note that resembles a
picket fence. Later, when you begin writing, your memory of what is
yours and not yours will become dim, and if you use another's words in
your own paper but do not grant recognition, you lay yourself open to
the charge of plagiarism. Statistics are not available, but it is clear that a

great deal of plagiarism has been caused not by deliberate deception but rather by sloppy note-taking habits.

Paraphrasing

When you take notes, it is best to paraphrase the sources. A paraphrase is a restatement in your own words, and because of this it is actually a first step in writing. Chapter 2 in this book describes the way to write a précis or abridgment. Working on this technique will prepare you for the research essay.

A problem in paraphrasing is to capture the idea stated in the source without duplicating the words. The best way to do this is to read and reread the passage you are noting. Turn over the book or journal and write out the idea *in your own words* as accurately as you can. Once you have this note, compare it with the original, and make corrections to improve your thought and emphasis. Add a short quotation if you believe it is needed, but be sure to use quotation marks. If your paraphrase is too close to the original, throw out the note and try again in your own words. It is worth making this effort, because often you can use part or all of your note directly at an appropriate place in your research paper.

To see the problems of paraphrase, let us look at a paragraph of criticism and then see how a student doing research might take notes on it. The paragraph is by Richard F. Peterson, from an essay entitled "The Circle of Truth: The Stories of Katherine Mansfield and Mary Lavin," which was published in *Modern Fiction Studies*, 24 (1978): 383–394. In the passage to be quoted, Peterson is considering the structures of two Mansfield stories, "Bliss" and "Miss Brill":

Peterson 385   structure: negative

"'Bliss' and 'Miss Brill' are flawed stories, but not because the truth they reveal about their protagonists is too brutal or painful for the tastes of the common reader. In each story, the climax of the narrative suggests an arranged reality that leaves a lasting impression, not of life, but of the author's cleverness. This strategy of arrangement for dramatic effect or revelation, unfortunately, is common in Katherine Mansfield's fiction. Too often in her stories a dropped remark at the right or wrong moment, a chance meeting or discovery, an intrusive figure in the shape of a fat man at a ball or in the Café de Madrid, a convenient death of a hired man or a stranger dying aboard a ship, or a deus ex machina in the form of two doves, a dill pickle, or a fly plays too much of a role in / [386] creating a character's dilemma or deciding the outcome of the narrative." 385–386

Because taking notes necessarily forces a shortening of this or any criticism, it also requires selection and interpretation. It therefore also requires discrimination and judgment; good note-taking is no easy task. There are some things to guide you, however, when you go through the many sources you uncover:

THINK OF THE PURPOSE OF YOUR RESEARCH PAPER.   You may not know exactly what you are fishing for when you start to take notes, for you cannot prejudge what your essay will contain. Research is a form of discovery. But soon you will notice patterns or large topics that your sources explore. If you accept one of these as your major topic, or focus of interest, you should use that as your guide.

For example, suppose you take notes on criticism about Katherine Mansfield's "Miss Brill," and after a certain amount of reading you decide to focus on the topic of structure in the story. This decision would prompt you to take a note about Peterson's disapproval of Mansfield's technique of arranging climaxes. In this instance, the following note would be adequate as a brief reminder of the content:

Peterson 385   structure: negative

　　Peterson claims that Mansfield creates climaxes that are too artificial, too unlifelike, giving the impression not of reality but of Mansfield's own "cleverness."

Let us now suppose that you want a fuller note in the expectation that you need not just Peterson's general idea but also some of his supporting detail. Such a note might look like this:

Peterson 385   structure: negative

   Peterson thinks that "Bliss" and "Miss Brill" are "flawed" because they
have contrived endings that give the impression "not of life but of" Mansfield's
"cleverness." She arranges things artificially, according to Peterson, to cause
the endings in many other stories. Some of these things are chance remarks,
discoveries, or meetings, together with other unexpected or chance incidents
and objects. These contrivances make their stories imperfect.   385

When you actually write your essay, you would find any part of this
note useful. The words are almost all the note-taker's own, and the few
quotations are within quotation marks. Note that Peterson, the critic, is
properly recognized as the source of the criticism, so the note could be
adapted readily to a research paper. The key here is that your taking of
notes should be guided by your developing plan for your essay.

TITLE YOUR NOTES.   To help plan and develop the various parts of
your essay, write a title for each of your notes, as in the examples in
this chapter. This practice is a form of outlining. Let us continue discussing
the structure of Mansfield's "Miss Brill," the subject of the sample research
theme (pp. 274–81). As you do your research, you discover that there is
a divergence of critical thought about the ending of the story. Here is a
note about one of the diverging interpretations:

Daly 90   last sentence

> Miss Brill's "complete" "identification" with the shabby fur piece at the very end may cause readers to conclude that she is the one in tears but bravely does not recognize this fact, and also to conclude that she may never use the fur in public again because of her complete defeat. Everything may be for "perhaps the very last time." 90

Notice that the title classifies the topic of the note. If you use such classifications in notes, a number of like-titled cards could underlie a section in your essay about how to understand the concluding sentence of "Miss Brill." In addition, once you decide to explore the last sentence, the topic itself will guide you in further study and note-taking. (Please see the sample research theme, in which paragraphs 19–24 are devoted to this subject.)

WRITE YOUR OWN THOUGHTS AS THEY OCCUR TO YOU. As you take your notes, you will develop many thoughts of your own. Do not let these go, to be remembered later (maybe), but write them down immediately. Often you may notice a detail that your source does not mention, or you may get a hint for an idea that the critic does not develop. Often, too, you may get thoughts which can serve as bridges between details in your notes or as introductions or concluding observations. Be sure to title your comment and also to mark it as your own thought. Here is such a note, which is concerned with the relative lack of action in "Miss Brill" as opposed to the emphasis in the story on the psychological state of the heroine:

My Own   Last Sentence

Mansfield's letter of Jan. 17, 1921, indicates that action as such was less significant in her scheme for the story than the sympathetic evocation of Miss Brill's observations, impressions, and moods. She wanted to reveal character.

Please observe that in paragraph 5 of the sample research theme, the substance of this note, and a good deal of the language, is used to introduce new material once the passage from the Mansfield letter has been quoted.

SORT YOUR CARDS INTO GROUPS. If you have taken your notes well, your essay will have been taking shape in your mind already. The titles of your cards will suggest areas to be developed as you do your planning and prewriting. Once you have assembled a stack of note cards derived from a reasonable number of sources (your instructor may have assigned a minimum number), you can sort them into groups according to the topics and titles. For the sample theme, after some shuffling and retitling, the following groups of cards were distributed:

1. Writing and publication
2. The title: amusement and seriousness
3. General structure
4. Specific structures: season, time of day, levels of cruelty, Miss Brill's own "hierarchies" of unreality
5. The concluding paragraphs, especially the last sentence
6. Concluding remarks

If you look at the major sections of the sample theme, you will see that the topics are adapted with only slight changes from these groups of cards. In other words, the arrangement of the cards is an effective means of outlining and organizing a research essay.

ARRANGE THE CARDS IN EACH GROUP.   There is still much to be done with these individual groups. You cannot use the details as they fall randomly; you need to decide which notes are relevant. You might also need to retitle some cards and use them elsewhere. Of those that remain in the group, you will need to lay them out in an order to be used in the essay.

Once you have your cards in order, you can write whatever comments or transitions are needed to move from detail to detail. Write this material directly on the cards, and be sure to use a different color ink so that you will know what was on the original card and what you added at this stage of your composing process. Here is an example of such a "developed" note card:

Magalaner 39   Structure, general

Speaking of Mansfield's sense of form, and referring to "Miss Brill" as an example, Magalaner states that Mansfield has power to put together stories from "a myriad of threads into a rigidly patterned whole."   39

Some of these "threads" are the fall season, the time of day, examples of unkindness, the park bench sitters from the cupboards, and Miss Brill's stages of unreality (see Thorpe 661). Each of these is separate, but all work together to unify the story.

By adding such commentary to your note cards, you will facilitate the actual writing of the first draft. In many instances, the note and the comment may be moved directly into the paper with minor adjustments (some of the content of this note appears in paragraph 6 of the sample theme, and almost all the topics introduced here are developed in paragraphs 9–14).

BE CREATIVE AND ORIGINAL IN RESEARCH PAPERS.   You cannot always move your note cards directly into your essay. The major trap to avoid in a research paper is allowing your sources to become ends in themselves, thereby substituting them for your own thinking and writing. Too often students introduce details in a research paper the way a master of ceremonies introduces performers in a variety show. This is unfortunate because it is the student whose essay will be judged, even though the sources, like the performers, do all the work. Thus, it is important to be creative and original in a research essay, and do your own thinking and writing, even though you are relying heavily on sources. Here are four ways in which research essays may be original:

1. *Selection.* In each major section you include a number of details from your sources. To be creative, you should select different but related details and avoid overlapping or repetition. The essay will be judged on the thoroughness with which you make your point with different details (which in turn represent the completeness of your research). Even though you are relying on published materials and cannot be original on that score, your selection is original because you are bringing the materials together for the first time.

2. *Development.* A closely related way of being original is your development of various points. Your arrangement is an obvious area of originality: One detail seems naturally to precede another, and certain conclusions stem from certain details. As you present the details, conclusions, and arguments from your sources, you may add your own original stamp by using supporting details that differ from those in your sources. You may also wish to add your own emphasis to particular points—an emphasis that you do not find in your sources.

Naturally, the words you use are original with you. Your topic sentences, for example, are all your own. As you introduce details and conclusions, you will need to write bridges to get yourself from point to point. These may be introductory remarks or transitions. In other words, as you write, you are not just stringing things out, but are actively tying thoughts together in a variety of creative ways. Your success in these efforts constitutes the area of your greatest originality.

3. *Explanation of controversial views.* Also closely related to selection is the fact that in your research you may have found conflicting or differing views on a topic. It is original for you, as you describe and distinguish these views, to explain the reasons for the differences. In other words, as you explain a conflict or difference, you are writing an original analysis. To see how differing views may be handled, see paragraphs 19–21 of the sample theme.

4. *Creation of your own insights and positions.* There are three possibilities here, all related to how well you have learned the primary texts on which your research in secondary sources is based.

a. *Your own interpretations and ideas.* Remember that an important part of taking notes is to make your own points precisely when they occur to you. Often you can expand these as truly original parts of your essay. Your originality does not need to be extensive; it may consist of no more than a single insight. Here is such a card, written during research on the structure of "Miss Brill":

My Own   Miss Brill's unreality

> It is ironic that the boy and girl sit down on the bench next to Miss Brill just when she is at the height of her fancies. By allowing her to overhear their insults, they introduce objective reality to her. The result is that she is plunged instantly from the height of rapture to the depth of pain.

The originality here is built around the contrast between Miss Brill's exhilaration and her rapid and cruel deflation. The observation is not unusual or startling, but it nevertheless represents an attempt at original thought. When modified and adapted, the material of the note supplies much of paragraph 18 of the sample theme. You can see here that the development of a "my own" note card is an important part of the prewriting stage for a research essay.

    b. *Gaps in the sources.* As you read your secondary sources it may dawn on you that a certain obvious conclusion is not made, or that a certain detail is not stressed. Here is an area that you can develop on your own. Your conclusions may involve a particular interpretation or major point of comparison, or they may rest on a particularly important but understressed word or fact. For example, paragraphs 21–24 form an argument based on observations that critics have overlooked, or neglected to mention, about the conclusion of the story. In your research, whenever you find such a critical "vacuum" (assuming that you cannot read all the articles about some of your topics, where your discovery may already have been made a number of times), it is right to move in with whatever is necessary to fill it. A great deal of scholarship is created in this way.

    c. *Disputes with the sources.* You may also find that your sources present certain arguments that you wish to dispute. As you develop your disagreement, you argue originally, for you use details in a different way from that of the critic or critics whom you are disputing, and your conclusions will be your own. This area of originality is similar to the laying out of controversial critical views, except that you furnish one of the opposing views yourself. The approach is limited, because it is difficult to find many substantive points of interpretation on which there are not already clearly delineated opposing views. Paragraph 13 of the sample research theme (about the woman with the ermine toque) shows how a disagreement can lead to a different if not original interpretation.

WRITING THE RESEARCH THEME

Introduction

In planning, keep in mind that for a research theme, the introduction may be expanded beyond the length of an ordinary essay because of the need to relate the research to your topic. You may bring in relevant historical or biographical information (see, for example, the introduction of the sample theme). You might also wish to summarize critical opinion or describe critical problems as they pertain to your subject. The idea is to introduce interesting and significant materials that you have found during your research. Obviously, you should plan to include your usual guides—your central idea and your thesis sentence.

Because of the greater length of most research themes, some instructors require a topic outline, which is in effect a brief table of contents. This pattern is observed in the sample essay. Inasmuch as the inclusion of any outline is a matter of choice with various instructors, be sure that you understand whether your instructor requires it.

Body and Conclusion

Your development both for the body and the conclusion will be governed by your choice of subject. Please consult the relevant chapters in this book about what to include for whatever approach or approaches you select (setting, point of view, character, tone, or any other).

In length, the research theme may be anywhere from five to fifteen or more pages. It seems reasonable that a theme on only one work will be shorter than one on two or more works. If you narrow your topic, as suggested in the approaches described above, you can readily keep your paper within the assigned length. The sample research theme, for example, illustrates the first approach by being limited to the structural aspects of one story. Were you to write on characteristic structures in a number of other stories by Mansfield or any other writer (the second approach), you could limit your total number of pages by stressing comparative treatments and by avoiding excessive detail about problems pertaining to each and every story. In short, you will decide to include or exclude materials by compromising between the importance of the materials and the limits of your assignment.

Although you limit your topic yourself in consultation with your instructor, you may encounter problems because you deal not with one text alone but with many. Naturally, the sources will provide you with details and also with many of your ideas. The problem is to handle the many strands without piling on too many details, and also without being led into digressions. It is important, therefore, to keep your central idea foremost, for stressing your central idea helps you both in selecting relevant materials and rejecting irrelevant ones.

Because of the sources, there is a problem about authority, and that problem is to quote, paraphrase, and otherwise adapt the materials of others without plagiarism. Your reader will automatically assume that everything you write is your own unless you indicate otherwise. You leave yourself open to a charge of plagiarism, however, if you give no recognition to details, interpretations, or specific language that you clearly derive from a source. To handle this problem, you must be especially careful in the use of quotation marks and in the granting of recognition. Most commonly, if you are simply presenting details and facts, you can write straightforwardly and let parenthetical references suffice as your authority, as the following sentence from the sample essay will show:

> Because Katherine Mansfield's "Miss Brill"—one of the eighty-eight short stories and fragments she wrote in her brief life (Magalaner 5)—succeeds so well as a portrait of the protagonist's inner life, it has become well known and frequently anthologized (Gargano).

Here the parenthetical references to secondary texts adequately recognize the authority beyond your own (the Gargano reference, incidentally, contains no page number because it is an unpaginated one-page article).

If you are using an interpretation that is unique to a particular writer or writers, however, or if you are relying on a significant quotation from your source, you should grant recognition and use quotation marks as an essential part of your discussion, as in this sentence:

> While Cherry Hankin suggests that the structuring is perhaps more "instinctive" than deliberate (474), Marvin Magalaner, using "Miss Brill" as an example, speaks of Mansfield's power to weave "a myriad of threads into a rigidly patterned whole" (39).

Here there can be no question about plagiarism, for the names of the authorities are acknowledged in full, the page numbers are specific, and the quotation marks clearly show the important word and phrase that are introduced from the sources. If you grant recognition as recommended here, no confusion can possibly result about the authority underlying your essay.

Sample Research Essay

The Structure of Mansfield's "Miss Brill"[*]

I. Introduction

A. The Writing of "Miss Brill"

Because Katherine Mansfield's "Miss Brill"—one of the eighty-eight short stories and fragments she wrote in her brief life (Magalaner 5)—succeeds so well as a portrait of the protagonist's inner life, it has become well known and frequently anthologized (Gargano). She apparently wrote it on the evening of November 11, 1920, when she was staying at Isola Bella, an island retreat in north Italy where she had gone in her desperate search to overcome tuberculosis. In her own words, she describes the night of composition:

> Last night I walked about and saw the new moon with the old moon in her arms and the lights in the water and the hollow pools filled with stars—and lamented there was no God. But I came in and wrote Miss Brill instead; which is my insect Magnificat now and always (Letters 594).

[1] Her husband, J. Middleton Murry, who had remained in London, published the story in the November 26, 1920 issue of the journal Athenaeum, which he was then editing. In 1922, Mansfield included "Miss Brill" in her collection entitled *The Garden Party and Other Stories* (Daly 134).

[2] She was particularly productive at the time of "Miss Brill" despite her illness, for she wrote a number of superb stories then. The others, as reported by her biographer Antony Alpers, were "The Lady's Maid," "The Young Girl," "The Daughters of the Late Colonel," and "The Life of Ma Parker" (304–305). All these stories share the common bond of "love and pity" rather than the "harshness or satire" that typifies many of her earlier stories (Alpers 305).

---

[*] For the text of this story, please see Appendix C, pp. 320–23. The type of documentation used here is that recommended in the second edition of the *MLA Handbook for Writers of Research Papers*. See Appendix B, pp. 299–300.

B. The Choice of the Name "Brill"

"Miss Brill," however, does contain at least a minor element of humor. James W. Gargano notes that the title character, Miss Brill, is named after a lowly flatfish, the brill. This fish, with notoriously poor vision, is related to the turbot and the whiting (it is the whiting that the rude girl compares to Miss Brill's fur piece). The Oxford English Dictionary records that the brill is "inferior in flavour" (sic) to the turbot. One may conclude that Mansfield, in choosing the name, wanted to minimize her heroine.

[3]

While Mansfield's use of the name suggests a small trick on poor Miss Brill, the story is anything but amusing. Miss Brill is not mocked as an "alienated city character" symbolizing contemporary decay, but rather is a model of a genuine human being, a person to pity and with whom to identify (Kaplan 165). She is a part of the "feminine world" (Maurois 337), and for this reason is one of those who have been excluded from "public history" (Gubar 31). Her main concerns are not power and greatness but the privacy of personal moments (Gubar 38) which may be upset by no more than a contemptuous giggle. The poignancy of the story stems from everyday callousness and "inhumanity," to quote Sydney Kaplan in specific reference to "Miss Brill," and also from the close identification, in the presentation, of the speaker and the main character (165). The story's power may be explained as a result of the feeling with which Mansfield renders the "inarticulate longings and the tumultuous feelings that lie beneath the surface of daily life" (McLaughlin 381). A mark of skill here is the way in which Mansfield has entered the soul of her heroine and turned it "outward, for her reader to see and understand" (Magill 710). Her friend (but not firm supporter) Virginia Woolf noticed a want of "richness and depth" (75) in Mansfield's work. But Mansfield's own description of her method in composing and revising "Miss Brill" contradicts Woolf, for it demonstrates, in this story at least, how deeply she considered the inner life of her major character:

[4]

> In Miss Brill I choose not only the length of every sentence, but even the sound of every sentence. I choose the rise and fall of every paragraph to fit her, and to fit her on that day at that very moment. After I'd written it I read it aloud—numbers of times—just as one would play over a musical composition—trying to get it nearer to the expression of Miss Brill—until it fitted her. (Letter to Richard Murry of January 17, 1921, qtd. in Sewell, 5–6).

C. The Nature of the Story's Structure

Mansfield's description strongly indicates that action in the story was less significant in her scheme than the sympathetic evocation of Miss Brill's moods and impressions—in other words, the depths of her character. Such a design might lead readers to conclude that the story is not so much formed as forming, a free rather than planned development. In reference to Mansfield's talent generally, Edward Wagenknecht reflects that the stories, including "Miss Brill," are "hardly even episodes or anecdotes. They offer reflections [instead] of some aspect of experience or express a mood" (163). In many ways, Wagenknecht's observation is true of "Miss Brill." The story seems to be built up from within the character, and it leaves the impression of an individual who experiences a "crisis in miniature," a "deep cut into time" in which life changes and all hopes and expectations are reversed (Hankin 465).

[5]

[6]
It therefore follows that Mansfield's achievement in "Miss Brill" is to fashion a credible character in a pathetic and shattering moment of life, and the story embodies an intricate set of structures that simultaneously complement the movement downward.° Mansfield's control over form is strong. While Cherry Hankin suggests that the structuring is perhaps more "instinctive" than deliberate (474), Marvin Magalaner, using "Miss Brill" as an example, speaks of Mansfield's power to weave "a myriad of threads into a rigidly patterned whole" (39). These complementary threads, stages, or "levels" of "unequal length" (Harmat uses the terms "niveaux" and "longueur inégale," 49, 51) are the fall season, the time of day, insensitive or cruel actions, Miss Brill's own unreal perceptions, and the final section or denouement.□

II. The Seasonal Setting as Structure

[7]
The first aspect of structure, on the level of setting, is the autumnal, seasonal backdrop, which is integral to the deteriorating circumstances of Miss Brill. In the very first paragraph we learn that there is a "faint chill" in the air (is the word "chill" chosen to rhyme with "Brill"?), and this phrase is repeated in paragraph 10. Thus the author establishes autumn and the approaching end of the year as the beginning of the movement toward dashed hopes. This seasonal reference is also carried out when we read that "yellow leaves" are "down drooping" in the local Jardins Publiques (paragraph 6) and that leaves are drifting "now and again" from almost "nowhere, from the sky" (paragraph 1). It is of course the autumn cold that has caused Miss Brill to take out her bedraggled fur piece at which the young girl later is so amused. Thus the chill, together with the fur, forms a structural setting integrated both with the action and mood of the story. In a real way, the story begins and ends with the fur (Sewell 25), which is almost literally the direct cause of Miss Brill's deep hurt at the end.

III. The Time of Day as Structure

[8]
Like this seasonal structuring, the times of day parallel the darkening existence of Miss Brill. At the beginning, the day is "brilliantly fine—the blue sky powdered with gold," and the light is "like white wine." This metaphorical language suggests the brightness and crispness of full sunlight. In paragraph 6, where we also learn of the yellow leaves, "the blue sky with gold-veined clouds" indicates that time has been passing as clouds drift in during late afternoon. By the end of the story, Miss Brill has returned to her "little dark room" (paragraph 18). In other words, the time moves from day to evening, from light to darkness, as an accompaniment to the psychological pain of Miss Brill.

IV. Insensitive or Cruel Actions as Structure

What seems to be Mansfield's most significant structural device, which is nevertheless not emphasized by critics, is the introduction of insensitive or cruel actions. It is as though the hurt experienced by Miss Brill on the bright Sunday afternoon in the Public Gardens is also being experienced by many others. Because she is the spectator who is closely related to Mansfield's narrative voice, Miss Brill is the filter through whom these negative examples reach the reader. Considering the patterns that emerge, one may conclude

° Central idea
□ Thesis sentence

[9]   that Mansfield intends the beauty of the day and the joyousness of the band as an ironic contrast to the pettiness and insensitivity of people in the park.

    The first characters are the silent couple on Miss Brill's bench (paragraph 3), and the incompatible couple of the week before (paragraph 4). Because these seem no more than ordinary, they are not at first perceived as a part

[10] of the story's pattern of cruelty and rejection. But the incompatibility suggested by their silence and one-way complaining establishes a structural parallel with the young and insensitive couple who insult Miss Brill. Thus the first two couples prepare the way for the third, and all exhibit behavior of increasing insensitivity.

    Almost unnoticed as a second level of negative life is the vast group of "odd, silent, nearly all old" people filling "the benches and green chairs" (paragraph 5). These people are nevertheless significant structurally because the

[11] "dark little rooms—or even cupboards" that Miss Brill associates with them describe her circumstances at the story's end (paragraph 18). The reader may conclude from Miss Brill's silent, eavesdropping behavior that she herself is one of these nameless and faceless ones.

    Once Mansfield has set these levels for her heroine, she introduces examples of more active rejection and cruelty. The beautiful woman of paragraph

[12] 8, who throws down the bunch of violets, is the first of these. The causes of her scorn are not made clear, and Miss Brill does not know what to make of the incident, but the woman's actions indicate that she has been involved in a relationship that has ended bitterly.

    Perhaps the major figure involved in rejection, who is so important that she may be considered a structural double of Miss Brill, is the woman wearing the ermine toque (paragraph 8). She does her best to please the "gentleman in grey," but this man insults her by blowing smoke in her face as he leaves. It could be, as Peter Thorpe observes, that the woman is "obviously a prostitute" (661). More likely, however, from the content of their conversation overheard

[13] by Miss Brill, is that the toque-wearing woman has had a broken relationship with the gentleman. Being familiar with his Sunday habits, she deliberately comes to the park to meet him, as though by accident, in order to attempt a reconciliation. After her rejection, her hurrying off to meet someone "much nicer" (there is no such person, for Mansfield uses the phrase "as though" to introduce the ermine toque's departure) is her way of masking her hurt. Regardless of the precise situation, however, Mansfield makes plain that the encounter is characterized by vulnerability, unkindness, and pathos.

    Once Mansfield has established this major incident, she introduces two additional examples of insensitivity. At the end of paragraph 8, the hobbling

[14] old man "with long whiskers" is nearly knocked over by the troupe of four girls—arrogance if not contempt. The final examples involve Miss Brill herself. These are the apparent indifference of her students, together with the old invalid gentleman "who habitually sleeps" when Miss Brill reads to him.

    Although "Miss Brill" is a brief story, Mansfield creates a surprisingly large number of structural parallels to the sudden climax brought about by the insulting young couple. The boy and girl do not appear until the very end, in other words (paragraphs 11–14), but actions like theirs have been anticipated structur-

[15] ally throughout the entire narrative. The story does not take us to the homes of the other victims as we follow Miss Brill, but readers may conclude that the silent couple, the complaining wife and long-suffering husband, the unseen man rejected by the beautiful young woman, the ermine toque, and the funny gentleman, not to mention the many silent and withdrawn people sitting in the park, all return to similar loneliness and personal pain.

V. Miss Brill's "Hierarchy of Unrealities" as Structure

[16]

The intricacy of the structure of "Miss Brill" does not end here. Of great importance is the structural development of the heroine herself. Peter Thorpe notes a "hierarchy of unrealities" which govern the reader's increasing awareness of her plight (661). By this measure, the story's actions progressively bring out Miss Brill's failures of perception and understanding—failures which in this respect make her like her namesake fish, the brill (Gargano).

[17]

These unrealities begin with Miss Brill's fanciful but harmless imaginings about her shabby fur piece. This beginning sets up the pattern of her pathetic inner life. When she imagines that the park band is a "single, responsive, and very sensitive creature" (Thorpe 661), we are to realize that she is simply making a great deal out of nothing more than an ordinary band. Though she cannot interpret the actions of the beautiful young woman with the violets, she does see the encounter between the ermine toque and the gentleman in grey as an instance of rejection. Her response is certainly correct, but then her belief that the band's drumbeats are sounding out "The Brute! The Brute!" indicates her vivid overdramatization of the incident. The "top of the hierarchy of unrealities" (Thorpe 661) is her fancy that she is an actor with a vital part in a gigantic drama played by all the people in the park. The most poignant aspect of this daydream is her imagining that someone would miss her if she were absent, for this fancy shows how far she is from reality.

[18]

With regard to this structure or hierarchy of unrealities, it is ironic that the boy and girl sit down next to her just when she is at the height of her fancy about her own importance in life. By allowing her to overhear their insults, the couple introduces objective reality to her with a vengeance, and she is plunged from rapture to pain. The following, and final, two paragraphs hence form a rapid denouement which reflects her loneliness and despair.

VI. The Story's Conclusion

[19]

Of unique importance in the structure of the story are the final two paragraphs—the conclusion or denouement—in which Miss Brill returns to her miserable little room. This conclusion may easily be understood as a total, final defeat. For example, Saralyn Daly, referring to Miss Brill as one of Mansfield's "isolatoes"—that is, solitary persons cut off from normal human contacts (88)—fears that the couple's callous insults have caused Miss Brill to face the outside world with her fur piece "perhaps for the very last time" (90). Eudora Welty points out that Miss Brill is "defenseless and on the losing side" and that her defeat may be for "always" (87). Miss Brill has experienced a pattern described by Zinman as common in Mansfield's stories, in which the old are destroyed "by loneliness and sickness, by fear of death, by the thoughtless energy of the younger world around them" (457). With this disaster for the major character, the story may be fitted to the structuring of Mansfield stories observed by André Maurois: "moments of beauty suddenly broken by contact with ugliness, cruelty, or death" (342–343).

[20]

Because some critics have stated that Miss Brill's downfall is illogically sudden, they have criticized the conclusion. Peterson, for example, complains that the ending is artificial and contrived because of the improbability that the young couple would appear at just that moment to make their insults (385). On much the same ground, Berkman declares that the ending is excessive, mechanical, and obvious (162, 175).

Cherry Hankin, however, suggests another way in which the conclusion may be taken, a way which makes the story seem both ironic and grimly humorous. In describing patterns to be found in Mansfield's stories, Hankin notes the following situation that may account for the ending of "Miss Brill":

> . . . an impending disillusionment or change in expectations may be deflected by the central character's transmutation of the experience into something positive (466).

[21] There is no question that Mansfield's ending indicates that Miss Brill has been totally shattered. Her long, silent, dejected sitting on the bed testifies to the extent of her deflation.

Mansfield's last sentence, however, may be interpreted as a way of indicating that Miss Brill is going back to her earlier habit of making reality over to fit her own needs:

> But when she put the lid on she thought she heard something crying (paragraph 18).

It is hard to read this last sentence without finding irony and pathos. By hearing "something crying," Miss Brill may likely be imagining that the fur piece, and not she, has been hurt. One might remember that the thoughtless young girl

[22] has laughed at the fur because it resembles a "fried whiting" (paragraph 14). The irony here is that Miss Brill, like the Boss in another Mansfield story, "The Fly," is forgetting about the pain of remembrance and slipping back into customary defensive behavior.

This pattern of evasion is totally in keeping with Miss Brill's character. Despite her poverty and loneliness, she has been holding a job (as a teacher of English, presumably to French pupils), and has also been regularly performing her voluntary task of reading to the infirm old man. She has clearly not had a life filled with pleasure, but her Sunday afternoons of eavesdropping have

[23] enabled her to share in the lives of many other people. This vicarious sociability is established by Mansfield as Miss Brill's major way of coming to grips with life. Her method may make her seem strange as well as pathetic, but nevertheless Miss Brill has been getting along; she is presented as a person who is able to function. Within such a framework, the deflating insults of paragraphs 13 and 14, hurtful as they are, may be seen as another incentive for her to adjust by strengthening her flights of fancy, not abandoning them.

This is not to interpret the story's conclusion as an indication that Miss Brill has shaken off the couple's insults. She is first and foremost a "victim" (Zinman 457), if not of others, then of her own reality-modifying imagination. But she is presented as a character who has positive qualities. Indeed, Mansfield herself expressed her own personal liking of Miss Brill (despite the name "brill"). Her husband, J. Middleton Murry, shortly after receiving the story from her for publication, sent her a letter in which he expressed his fondness for

[24] the heroine. In a return letter to him of November 21, 1920, Mansfield wrote that she shared this fondness. She went on in the same letter to say:

> One writes (one reason why is) because one does care so passionately that one must show it—one must declare one's love (qtd. in Magalaner 17).

Surely the author could love her creation out of pity alone, but if she had added an element of strength, such as the brave even if sad ability to cope

[24] and adjust to "impossible and intolerable conditions" in life (Zinman 457), then her love would have an additional cause. Therefore it seems plausible to understand the last sentence of "Miss Brill" as the resumption of the heroine's ways of surviving despite her obvious pain.

VII. Conclusion

[25] "Miss Brill" is a compact story intricately built up from a number of coexisting structures. It is alive, so much so that it justifies the tribute of Antony Alpers that it is a "minor masterpiece" (305). The structural contrast between the heroine and the world around her is derived from a deeply felt dichotomy about life attributed to Mansfield herself, a sense that the human soul is beautiful, on the one hand, but that people are often vile, on the other (Moore 245). It is the vileness from which Miss Brill seems to be escaping at the end.

[26] The greater structure of "Miss Brill" is therefore a hard, disillusioned view of life itself, in which the lonely, closed out, and hurt are wounded even more. This pattern of exclusion affects not only the restricted lives of the lonely, but it also reaches directly into their minds and souls. Miss Brill's response is to retreat further and further into an inner world of unreality, but also to continue life, even at an almost totally subdued level, within these confines. It is Mansfield's "almost uncanny psychological insight" (Hankin 467) into the operation of this characteristic response that gives "Miss Brill" its structure and also accounts for its excellence as a story.

A List of References Consulted

Alpers, Antony. Katherine Mansfield, A Biography. New York: Knopf, 1953.

Berkman, Sylvia. Katherine Mansfield, A Critical Study. New Haven: Yale U. P. (for Wellesley College), 1951.

Daly, Saralyn R. Katherine Mansfield. New York: Twayne, 1965.

Gargano, James W. "Mansfield's MISS BRILL." Explicator 19, No. 2 (Nov., 1960): item 10 (one page, unpaginated).

Gubar, Susan. "The Birth of the Artist as Heroine: (Re)production, the Kunstler-roman Tradition, and the Fiction of Katherine Mansfield," The Representation of Women in Fiction. Eds. Carolyn Heilbrun and Margaret R. Higonnet, Selected Papers from the English Institute, 1981 (Baltimore: Johns Hopkins U.P.,1983)19–59.

Hankin, Cherry. "Fantasy and the Sense of an Ending in the Work of Katherine Mansfield."ModernFictionStudies24(1978):465–474.

Harmat, Andrée-Marie. "Essai D'Analyse Structurale D'Une Nouvelle Lyrique Anglaise: 'Miss Brill' de Katherine Mansfield." Les Cahiers de la Nouvelle 1 (1983):49–74.

Heiney, Donald W. Essentials of Contemporary Literature. Great Neck: Barron's, 1954.

Kaplan, Sydney Janet. " 'A Gigantic Mother': Katherine Mansfield's London." Women Writers and the City: Essays in Feminist Literary Criticism. Knoxville: U. of Tennessee P., 1984. 161–175.

Magalaner, Marvin. The Fiction of Katherine Mansfield. Carbondale: Southern Illinois U. P., 1971.

Magill, Frank N., ed. English Literature: Romanticism to 1945. Pasadena: Salem Softbacks, 1981.

Mansfield, Katherine. Katherine Mansfield's Letters to John Middleton Murry, 1913–1922. Ed. John Middleton Murry. New York: Knopf, 1951. Cited as "Letters."

————. The Short Stories of Katherine Mansfield. New York: Knopf, 1967.

Maurois, André. Points of View from Kipling to Graham Greene. New York: Ungar, 1935, rpt. 1968.

McLaughlin, Ann L. "The Same Job: The Shared Writing Aims of Katherine Mansfield and Virginia Woolf." Modern Fiction Studies 24 (1978): 369–382.

Moore, Virginia. Distinguished Women Writers. Port Washington: Kennikat, 1934, rpt. 1962.

Peterson, Richard F. "The Circle of Truth: The Stories of Katherine Mansfield and Mary Lavin." Modern Fiction Studies 24 (1978): 383–394.

Sewell, Arthur. Katherine Mansfield: A Critical Essay. Auckland: Unicorn, 1936.

Thorpe, Peter. "Teaching 'Miss Brill.' " College English 23 (1962): 661–663.

Wagenknecht, Edward. A Preface to Literature. New York: Holt, 1954.

Welty, Eudora. The Eye of the Story: Selected Essays and Reviews. New York: Random House, 1977. 85–106.

Woolf, Virginia. "A Terribly Sensitive Mind." Granite and Rainbow. New York: Harcourt Brace, 1958. 73–75.

Zimman, Toby Silverman. "The Snail under the Leaf: Katherine Mansfield's Imagery." Modern Fiction Studies 24 (1978): 457–464.

COMMENTARY ON THE THEME

This theme fulfills an assignment of 2500–3000 words, with 15–25 sources. The bibliography was developed from a college library card catalog, together with lists of references in some of the critical books (Magalaner, Daly, Berkman), the *MLA International Bibliography*, and the *Essay and General Literature Index*. The sources were contained in a college library with selective, not exhaustive, holdings, supplemented by the use of a local public library. There is only one rare source, an article (Harmat) which was obtained in Xerox through Interlibrary Loan from one of only two United States libraries holding the journal in which it appears. For most quarterly or semester-long classes, you will likely not have the time to extend your sources by this method, but the article in question refers specifically to "Miss Brill," and it was therefore desirable to examine it.

The sources for the sample essay consist of a mixture of books, articles, and chapters or portions of books. Although a reference is made to an entry in the *Oxford English Dictionary*, it is not necessary to list this work in the sources. One article (Sewell) is published as a separate short monograph. Also a part of the sources is the story "Miss Brill" itself, from Appendix C (with locations made by paragraph number), together with editions of Mansfield's letters and stories. The sources are used in the theme for facts, interpretations, reinforcement of conclusions, and general guidance and authority. The essay also contains passages taking issue with some specific matters in certain of the sources. All necessary thematic devices, including overall organization and transitions, are unique to the sample theme. Additional particulars about the handling of sources and developing a research theme are included in the discussion of note-taking and related matters in the previous part of this appendix.

The introduction to the sample essay contains essential details about the writing of the story and the title, and it also contains a pointed summary of critical appraisals of the story itself. The idea explored here is that the story dramatizes the heroine's emotional responses first to exhilarating and then to deflating experiences. The central idea (paragraph 6) is built out of this idea, explaining that the movement of emotions is accompanied by an intricate and complementary set of structures. The thesis sentence, at the end of paragraph 6, presents the topics to be developed in the body.

Sections II–VI examine various elements of the story for their structural relationship to Miss Brill's emotions. Sections II and III detail the structural uses of the settings of autumn and daylight-darkness, pointing out how they parallel the experiences of Miss Brill. The longest section in the body is part IV (paragraphs 9–18), which is based on an idea not found in the sources. The aspect of the central idea stressed here is that the story is filled with persons going through disappointments that are similar to those of Miss Brill. Paragraph 10 cites the three couples of the story; paragraph 11 the silent old people; and paragraph 12 the woman with violets. The major figure parallel to Miss Brill, the woman wearing the ermine toque, is discussed in paragraph 13. A part of the analysis of the "ermine toque" exemplifies how an original point may be made through the presentation of a view differing from that in a source. Paragraph 14 contains brief descriptions of additional examples of insensitivity, two of them involving Miss Brill herself. Paragraph 15 both concludes and summarizes the instances of insensitivity and cruelty, emphasizing again the "structural parallels" to the situation of the heroine.

Section V (paragraphs 16–18) is based on ideas of the story's structure found in one of the sources (Thorpe). It hence is more derivative than the previous section. Section VI (paragraphs 19–24) is devoted to the denouement of the story. Paragraphs 19 and 20 consider critical disparagements and interpretations of the ending. In paragraph 21, however, a hint found in a source (Hankin) is used to interpret the story's final sentence. An argument in support of this reading is developed in paragraphs 22–

24, concluding with a reference to the author's own personal approval of the main character.

Section VII, the conclusion of the sample theme (paragraphs 25, 26), relates the central idea to further biographical information and also to Mansfield's achievement in the story. Of the three sources used here, two are used earlier in the essay, and one (Moore) is new.

The list of works cited is the basis of all references in the text of the essay, in accord with the *MLA Handbook for Writers of Research Papers*, 2nd ed. By locating the parenthetical references, a reader might readily examine, verify, and further study any of the ideas and details drawn from the sources and developed in the theme.

appendix a

Taking Examinations
on Literature

Taking an examination on literature is not difficult if you prepare correctly.
Preparing means (1) studying the material assigned, studying the comments
made in class by your instructor and by fellow students in discussion,
and studying your own thoughts; (2) anticipating the questions by writing
some of your own on the material to be tested and by writing practice
answers to these questions; and (3) understanding the precise function
of the test in your education.

   You should realize that the test is not designed to plague you or to
hold down your grade. The grade you receive is a reflection of your achievement at a given point in the course. If your grades are low, you can
probably improve them by studying in a coherent and systematic way.
Those students who can easily do satisfactory work might do superior
work if they improve their method of preparation. From whatever level
you begin, you can increase your achievement by improving your method
of study.

   Your instructor has three major concerns in evaluating your tests
(assuming literate English): (1) to see the extent of your command over
the subject material of the course ("How good is your retention?"); (2) to
see how well you are able to think about the material ("How well are
you educating yourself?"); and (3) to see how well you can actually respond
to a question or address yourself to an issue.

   There are many elements that go into writing good answers on tests, but this last point, about responsiveness, is perhaps the most important. A major cause of low exam grades is that students really do not *answer* the questions asked. Does that seem surprising? The problem is that some students do no more than retell the story, never confronting the issues in the question. This is the common problem that has been treated throughout this book. Therefore, if you are asked, "Why does . . . ," be sure to emphasize the *why*, and use the *does* only to exemplify the *why*. If the question is about organization, focus on that. If a problem has been raised, deal with the problem. In short, always *respond* directly to the question or instruction. Let us compare two answers to the same question:

Q. How does the setting of Jackson's "The Lottery" figure in the development of the story?

A

The setting of Jackson's "The Lottery" is a major element in the development of the story. The scene is laid in the village square, between the bank and post office. There are many flowers blooming, and the grass is green. A pile of stones is set up in the square. Into this place, just before ten o'clock in the morning, come the villagers to hold their annual lottery. There are 300 of them—children, men, and housewives. In the center of the square the black lottery box is set up on a three-legged stool. This box has been around for years, and looks broken and shabby. The setting requires that the villagers gather around the box, and that the male head representing each village family draw a slip of paper for that family. Once they have all drawn, it is discovered that Bill Hutchinson is the "winner." He is not a lucky winner, however, because his family of five has to draw again individually. Bill's wife Tessie draws the black spot that Bill had drawn for the family. Then all the villagers in the square fall upon her to stone her to death, because that is the fate of the "winner." The setting here is therefore all important in the development of the story.

B

The setting of Jackson's "The Lottery" is a major element in the development of the story. As a setting for all the action, the town square of the unnamed village is large enough to contain all 300 villagers, piles of stones which they can pick up and hurl, and the black box on a three-legged stool. As a setting in time, the entire action takes place within a two-hour period between ten in the morning and noon. As a seasonal setting, the date of June 27, specifically mentioned as the day of the action, suggests an anachronistic and mindless but nevertheless cruel early summer ritual. As a setting in character and society, the homey, simple life-style of the people indicates inertia and gullibility, not sophistication and innovativeness. It is *likely* that such people would preserve cruel and meaningless customs without thinking about their horrible effects. In all respects, then, the setting in place, time, season, and culture is all important in the development of the story.

While column A introduces the important elements of the story's setting, it does not stress the importance of these elements in the story itself. It is also cluttered with details that have no bearing on the question. On the other hand, column B, focusing directly on the connection, stresses how four aspects of setting relate to the story. Because of this emphasis, B is shorter than A. That is, with the focus directly on the issue, there is no need for irrelevant narrative details. Thus, A is unresponsive and unnecessarily long, while B is responsive and includes only enough detail to exemplify the major points.

PREPARATION

Your problem is how best to prepare yourself to have a knowledgeable and ready mind at examination time. If you simply cram facts into your head for the examination in hopes that you will be able to adjust to whatever questions are asked, you will likely flounder.

Read and Reread

Above all, keep in mind that your preparation should begin not on the night before the exam, but as soon as the course begins. When each assignment is given, you should complete it by the date due, for you will understand your instructor's lecture and the classroom discussion only if you know the material being discussed. Then, about a week before the exam, you should review each assignment, preferably rereading everything completely. With this preparation, your study on the night before the exam will be fruitful, for it might be viewed as a climax of preparation, not the entire preparation itself.

Make Your Own Questions: Go on the Attack

Just to read or reread is too passive to give you the masterly preparation you want for an exam. You should instead go on the attack by trying to anticipate the specific conditions of the test. The best way to reach this goal is to compose and answer your own practice questions. Do not waste your time trying to guess the questions you think your instructor might ask. That might happen—and wouldn't you be happy if it did?—but do not turn your study into a game of chance. What is of greatest importance is to arrange the subject matter by asking yourself questions that help you get things straight.

How can you make your own questions? It is not as hard as you might think. Your instructor may have announced certain topics or ideas to be tested on the exam. You might develop questions from these. Or you might apply general questions to the specifics of your assignments, as in the following examples:

1. About a character: What sort of character is A? How does A grow or change in the work? What does A learn, or not learn, that brings about the conclusion? To what degree is A the representative of any particular type?
2. About the interactions of characters: How does B influence A? Does a change in C bring about any corresponding change in A?
3. About events or situations: What relationship does episode A have to situation B? Does C's thinking about situation D have any influence on the outcome of event E?
4. About a problem: Why is character A or situation X this way and not that way? Is the conclusion justified by the ideas and events leading up to it?

Adapt Your Notes to Make Questions

Perhaps the best way to construct questions is to adapt your classroom notes, for notes are the fullest record you have about your instructor's views of the subject material. As you work with your notes, you should refer to passages from the text that were studied by the class or mentioned by your instructor. If there is time, try to memorize as many important phrases or lines as you can; plan to incorporate these into your answers as evidence to support the points you make. Remember that it is good to work not only with main ideas from your notes, but also with matters such as style, imagery, and organization.

Obviously, you cannot make questions from all your notes, and you will therefore need to select from those that seem most important. As an example, here is a short but significant note from a class about John Dryden's poem *Absalom and Achitophel* (1681): "A political poem—unintelligible unless one learns about the politics of the time." It is not difficult to use this note to make two practice questions:

1. Why is *Absalom and Achitophel* unintelligible unless one learns about the politics of the time?
2. What knowledge of the politics of the time is needed to make *Absalom and Achitophel* intelligible?

The first question consists of the simple adaptation of the word *why* to the phrasing of the note. For the second, the word *what* has been adapted. Either question would force pointed study. The first would require an explanation of how various parts of Dryden's poem become clear only when they are related to aspects of the politics of 1681. The second would emphasize the politics, with less reference to the poem. If you spent fifteen or twenty minutes writing practice answers to these questions, you could be confident in taking an examination on the material. It is likely that you could adapt your preparation to any question related to the politics of the poem.

Work with Questions Even When Time is Short

Whatever your subject, it is important that you spend as much study time as possible making and answering your own questions. You will have limited time and will not be able to write extensive answers indefinitely. Even so, do not give up on the question method. If time is too short for full practice answers, write out the main heads, or topics, of an answer. When the press of time (or the need for sleep) no longer permits you to make even such a brief outline answer, keep thinking of questions, and think about the answers on the way to the exam. Try never to read passively or unresponsively, but always with a creative, question-and-answer goal. Think of studying as a writing experience.

The time you spend in this way will be valuable, for as you practice, you will develop control and therefore confidence. If you have ever known anyone who has had difficulty with tests, or who has claimed a phobia about them, you may find that a major cause has been passive rather than active preparation. A passively prepared student finds that test questions compel thought, arrangement, and responsiveness; but the student is not ready for this challenge and therefore writes answers that are both unresponsive and filled with summary. The grade, needless to say, is low, and the student's fear of tests is reinforced. It seems clear that active, creative study is the best way to break any such long-standing patterns of fear or uncertainty, because it is the best form of preparation. There is no moral case to make against practice question-and-answer study, either, for everyone has the right and obligation to prepare—and all of this is preparation—in the best way possible.

Study with a Fellow Student

Often the thoughts of another person can help you understand the material to be tested. Try to find a fellow student with whom you can work, for both of you can help each other. In view of the need for steady preparation throughout a course, regular conversations are a good idea. Also, you might make your joint study systematic, and thus might set aside a specific evening or afternoon for work sessions. Make the effort; working with someone else can be stimulating and rewarding.

TWO BASIC TYPES OF QUESTIONS
ABOUT LITERATURE

There are two types of questions you will find on any examination about literature. Keep them in mind as you prepare. The first type is *factual*, or *mainly objective*, and the second is *general, comprehensive, broad*, or *mainly subjective*. In a literature course very few questions are purely objective, except multiple-choice questions.

Factual Questions

MULTIPLE-CHOICE QUESTIONS. These are the most factual questions. In a literature course, your instructor will most likely reserve them for short quizzes, usually on days when an assignment is due, to make sure that you are keeping up with the reading. Multiple choice can test your knowledge of facts, and it also can test your ingenuity in perceiving subtleties of phrasing, but on a literature exam this type of question is rare.

IDENTIFICATION QUESTIONS. These questions are decidedly of more interest. They test not only your factual knowledge but also your ability to relate this knowledge to your understanding of the work assigned. This type of question will frequently be used as a check on the depth and scope of your reading. In fact, an entire exam could be composed of only identification questions, each demanding perhaps five minutes to write. Typical examples of what you might be asked to identify are:

1. A *character*, for example, Nora in O'Connor's "First Confession." It is necessary to describe briefly the character's position and main activity (i.e., she is Jackie's older sister who gets him in trouble at home and who takes him to his confession). You should then emphasize the character's importance (i.e., her values help keep Jackie confused throughout most of the story, but by the end it is clear that O'Connor shows that it is really she who is confused).

2. *Incidents or situations*, which may be illustrated as follows: "A woman mourns the death of her husband." After giving the location of the situation or incident (Mrs. Popov in Chekhov's play *The Bear*), try to demonstrate its significance in the work. (That is, Mrs. Popov is mourning the death of her husband when the play opens, and in the course of the play Chekhov uses her feelings to show amusingly that life with real emotion is stronger than devotion or duty to the dead.)

3. *Things, places, and dates*. Your instructor may ask you to identify a bottle of poison (Collier's "The Chaser"), a village square (Jackson's "The Lottery"), or the dates of Mansfield's "Miss Brill" (1920) or Amy Lowell's "Patterns" (1916). For dates, you may be given a leeway of five or ten years if you must guess. What is important

about a date is not so much exactness as historical and intellectual perspective. The date of "Patterns," for example, was the third year of World War I, and the poem consequently reflects a reaction against the protracted and senseless loss of life that war was producing. Thus, to claim "World War I" as the date of the poem would likely be acceptable as an answer, provided that you could not remember the exact date.

4. *Quotations.* Theoretically, you should remember enough of the text to identify a passage taken from it, or at least to make an informed guess. Generally, you should try to locate the quotation, if you remember it, or else to describe the probable location, and to show the ways in which the quotation is typical of the work you have read, with regard to both content and style. You can often salvage much from a momentary lapse of memory by writing a reasoned and careful explanation of your guess, even if the guess is wrong.

TECHNICAL AND ANALYTICAL QUESTIONS AND PROBLEMS. In a scale of ascending importance, the third and most difficult type of factual question is on those matters with which this book has been concerned: technique, analysis, and problems. You might be asked to discuss the *setting, images, point of view,* or *principal idea* of a work; you might be asked about a *specific problem*; you might be asked to analyze a poem that may or may not be duplicated for your benefit (if it is not duplicated, woe to students who have not studied their assignments). Questions like these are difficult, because they assume that you have technical knowledge, while they also ask you to examine the text within the limitations imposed by the terms.

Obviously, technical questions occur more frequently in advanced courses than in elementary ones, and the questions become more subtle as the courses become more advanced. Instructors of elementary courses may use main-idea or special-problem questions, but will probably not use many of the others unless they state their intentions to do so in advance, or unless technical terms have been studied in class.

Questions of this type are fairly long, perhaps with from fifteen to twenty-five minutes allowed for each. If you have two or more of these questions, try to space your time sensibly; do not devote 80 percent of your time to one question and leave only 20 percent for the rest.

Basis of Judging Factual Questions

IDENTIFICATION QUESTIONS. In all factual questions, your instructor is testing (1) your factual command, and (2) your quickness in relating a part to the whole. Thus, suppose you are identifying the incident "A man kills a canary." It is correct to say that Susan Glaspell's *Trifles* is the location of the incident, that the dead farmer Wright was the killer, and that the canary belonged to his wife. Knowledge of these details clearly establishes that you know the facts. But a strong answer must go further. Even in the brief time you have for short answers, you should always aim to connect the facts to (1) major causation in the work, (2) an important idea or ideas, (3) the development of the work, and (4) for a quotation, the style. Time is short and you must be selective, but if you can make your answer move from facts to significance, you will always fashion superior responses. Along these lines, let us look at an answer identifying the action from *Trifles*:

> The action is from Glaspell's *Trifles*. The man who kills the bird is Mr. Wright, and the owner is Mrs. Wright. The killing is important because it is shown as the final indignity in Mrs. Wright's long-developing rage, which prompts her to strangle Wright in his sleep. It is thus the cause not only of murder but also of the investigation bringing the officers and their wives on stage. In fact, the wringing of the bird's neck makes the play possible because it is the wives who discover the dead bird, and it is the means by which Glaspell highlights them as the major characters in the play. Because the husband's brutal act shows how bleak the life of Mrs. Wright actually was, it dramatizes the lonely plight of women generally in a male-dominated way of life like that on the Wright farm. The discovery also raises the issue of legality and morality, because the two wives decide to band together and hide the evidence, therefore protecting Mrs. Wright from conviction and punishment.

Any of the points in this answer could be developed as a separate essay, but the paragraph is successful as a short answer because it goes beyond fact to deal with significance. Clearly, such answers are possible at the time of an exam only if you have devoted considerable thought to the various exam works beforehand. The more thinking and practicing you do before the exam, the better your answers will be. You may remember this advice as a virtual axiom: *A really superior answer cannot be written if your thinking originates entirely at the time you first see the question.* By studying well, you will be able to reduce surprise on an exam to an absolute minimum.

LONGER FACTUAL QUESTIONS.   More-extended factual questions also require more thoroughly developed organization. Remember that here your knowledge of essay writing is important, for the quality of your composition will determine a major share of your instructor's evaluation of your answers. It is therefore best to take several minutes to gather your thoughts together before you begin to write, because a ten-minute planned answer is preferable to a twenty-five minute unplanned answer. You do not need to write every possible fact on each particular question. Of greater significance is the use to which you put the facts you know and the organization of your answer. When the questions are before you, use a sheet of scratch paper to jot down the facts you remember and your ideas about them in relation to the question. Then put them together, phrase a thesis sentence, and use your facts to illustrate or prove your thesis.

It is always necessary to begin your answer pointedly, using key words or phrases from the question or direction if possible, so that your answer will have thematic shape. You should never begin an answer with "Because" and then go on from there without referring again to the question. To be most responsive during the short time available for writing an exam, you should use the question as your guide for your answer. Let us suppose that you have the following question on your test: "How does Glaspell use details in *Trifles* to reveal the character of Mrs. Wright?" The most common way to go astray on such a question, and the easiest thing to do also, is to concentrate on Mrs. Wright's character rather than on how Glaspell uses detail to bring out her character. The word *how* makes a vast difference in the nature of the final answer, and hence a good method on the exam is to duplicate key phrases in the question to ensure that you make your major points clear. Here is an opening sentence that uses the key words and phrases (underlined here) from the question to direct thought and provide focus:

> Glaspell uses details of setting, marital relationships, and personal habits to reveal the character of Mrs. Wright as a person of great but unfulfilled potential whom anger has finally overcome.

Because this sentence repeats the key phrases from the question, and also because it promises to show *how* the details are to be focused on the character, it suggests that the answer to follow will be totally responsive.

General or Comprehensive Questions

General or comprehensive questions are particularly important on final examinations, when your instructor is interested in testing your total comprehension of the course material. Considerable time is usually allowed for answering this type of question, which may be phrased in a number of ways:

1. A direct question asking about philosophy, underlying attitudes, main ideas, characteristics of style, backgrounds, and so on. Here are some possible questions in this category: "What use do _____, _____, and _____ make of the topic of _____?" "Define and characterize the short story as a genre of literature." "Explain the use of dialogue by Jackson, Collier, and De Maupassant." "Contrast the technique of point of view as used by _____, _____, and _____."

2. A "comment" question, often based on an extensive quotation, borrowed from a critic or written by your instructor for the occasion,

about a broad class of writers, or about a literary movement, or the like. Your instructor may ask you to treat this question broadly (taking in many writers) or else to apply the quotation to a specific writer.

3. A "suppose" question, such as "What advice might Mrs. Wright of *Trifles* give the speakers of Lowell's "Patterns" and Keats's "Bright Star," or "What might the speaker of Rossetti's poem 'Echo' say if she learned that her dead lover was Alan Austin of Collier's 'The Chaser' "? Although suppose questions might seem whimsical at first sight, they have a serious design and should prompt original and radical thinking. The first question, for example, should cause a test writer to bring out, from Mrs. Wright's perspective, that the love of both speakers was/is potential, not actual. She would likely sympathize with the speaker's loss in "Patterns," but might also say the lost married life might not have been as totally happy as the speaker assumes. For the speaker of "Bright Star," a male, Mrs. Wright might say that the steadfast love sought by him should also be linked to kindness and toleration as well as passion. Although such questions, and answers, are speculative, the need to respond to them causes a detailed consideration of the works involved, and in this respect the suppose question is a salutary means of learning. Needless to say, it is difficult to prepare for a suppose question, which you may therefore regard as a test not only of your knowledge, but also of your inventiveness.

Basis of Judging General Questions

When answering broad, general questions, you are in fact dealing with an unstructured situation, and you must not only supply an *answer* but—equally important—you must also create a *structure* within which your answer can have meaning. You might say that you make up your own specific question out of the original general question. If you were asked to "Consider the role of women as seen in Lowell, Mansfield, and Glaspell," for example, you would do well to structure the question by focusing a number of clearly defined topics. A possible way to begin answering such a question might be this:

Lowell, Mansfield, and Glaspell present a view of female resilience by demonstrating inner control, power of adaptation, and endurance.

With this sort of focus you would be able to proceed point by point, introducing supporting data as you form your answer.

As a general rule, the best method for answering a comprehensive question is comparison-contrast (see also Chapter 12, pp. 143–57). The reason is that in dealing with, say, a general question on Rossetti, Chekhov, and Keats, it is too easy to write *three* separate essays rather than *one*. Thus, you should try to create a topic like "The treatment of real or idealized love," or "The difficulties in male-female relationships," and then develop your answer point by point rather than writer by writer. By creating your answer in this way, you can bring in references to each or all of the writers as they become relevant to your main idea. But if you were to treat each writer separately, your comprehensive answer would lose focus and effectiveness, and it would be needlessly repetitive.

Remember these things, then: In judging your response to a general question, your instructor is interested in seeing: (1) how intelligently you select material, (2) how well you organize your material, (3) how adequate and intelligent are the generalizations you make about the material, and (4) how relevant are the facts you select for illustration.

Bear in mind that in answering comprehensive questions, though you are ostensibly free, the freedom you have been extended has been that of creating your own structure. The underlying idea of the comprehensive, general question is that you possess special knowledge and insights that cannot be discovered by more factual questions. You must therefore try to formulate your own responses to the material and introduce evidence that reflects your own particular insights and command of information.

A final word, always: Good luck.

appendix b

A Note on Documentation

In any writing not derived purely from your own mind, you must document your facts. In writing about literature, you must base your conclusions on material in particular literary works and must document this material. If you refer to secondary sources, you must be especially careful to document your facts. To document properly, you must use illustrative material in your discussion and mention your sources either in your discussion or in footnotes to it.

INTEGRATION AND MECHANICS
OF QUOTATIONS

DISTINGUISH YOUR THOUGHTS FROM THOSE OF YOUR AUTHOR.   Ideally, your themes should reflect your own thought as it is prompted and illustrated by an author's work. Sometimes a problem arises, however, because it is hard for your reader to know when *your* ideas have stopped and your *author's* have begun. You must therefore arrange things to make the distinction clear, but you must also create a constant blending of materials that will make your themes easy to follow. You will be moving from paraphrase, to general interpretation, to observation, to independent application of everything you choose to discuss. It is not always easy to keep these various elements integrated. Let us see an example in which the writer moves from reference to an author's ideas—really paraphrase—to an independent application of the idea:

> [1] In the "Preface to the Lyrical Ballads," Wordsworth states that the language of poetry should be the same as that of prose. [2] That is, poetic diction should not be artificial or contrived in any sense, but should consist of the words normally used by people in their everyday lives (pp. 791–793). [3] If one follows this principle in poetry, then it would be improper to refer to the sun as anything but *the sun*. [4] To call it a *heavenly orb* or the *source of golden gleams* would be inadmissible because these phrases are not used in common speech.

Here the first two sentences present a paraphrase of Wordsworth's ideas about poetic diction, the second going so far as to locate a particular spot where the idea is developed. The third and fourth sentences apply Wordsworth's idea to examples chosen by the writer. Here the blending is provided by the transitional clause, "If one follows this principle," and the reader is thus not confused about who is saying what.

INTEGRATE MATERIAL BY USING QUOTATION MARKS.   Sometimes you will use short quotations from your author to illustrate your ideas and interpretations. Here the problem of distinguishing your thoughts from the author's is solved by quotation marks. In this sort of internal quotation you may treat prose and poetry in the same way. If a poetic quotation extends from the end of one line to the beginning of another, however, indicate the line break with a virgule (/) and use a capital letter to begin the next line, as in the following:

> Wordsworth states that in his boyhood all of nature seemed like his own personal property. Rocks, mountains, and woods were almost like food to him, and he claimed that "the sounding cataract / Haunted . . . [him] like a passion" (76–80).

BLEND QUOTATIONS INTO YOUR OWN SENTENCES.   Making internal quotations still creates the problem of blending materials, however, for quotations should never be brought in unless you prepare your reader for them in some way. Do not, for example, bring in quotations in the following manner:

> The sky is darkened by thick clouds, bringing a feeling of gloom that is associated with the same feeling that can be sensed at a funeral. "See gloomy clouds obscure the cheerful day."

This abrupt quotation throws the reader off balance. It is better to prepare the reader to move from the discourse to the quotation, as in the following revision:

> The scene is marked by sorrow and depression, as though the spectator, who is asked to "See gloomy clouds obscure the cheerful day," is present at a funeral.

Here the quotation is made an actual part of the sentence. This sort of blending is satisfactory, provided the quotation is brief.

SET OFF AND INDENT LONG QUOTATIONS.   The standard for how to place quotations should be not to quote within a sentence any passage longer than twenty or twenty-five words. Quotations of greater length demand so much separate attention that they interfere with your own sentence. When your quotation is long, you should set it off separately, remembering to introduce it in some way. It is possible but not desirable to have one of your sentences conclude with a quotation, but you should never make an extensive quotation in the middle of a sentence. By the time you finish such an unwieldy sentence, your reader will have lost sight of how it began.

The physical layout of extensive quotations should be as follows: Leave three blank lines between your own discourse and the quotation. Single-space the quotation and make a special indention for it to set it off from the rest of your theme. After the quotation leave a three-line space again and resume your own discourse. Here is a specimen, from a theme about John Gay's "Trivia," an early eighteenth-century poem:

> In keeping with this general examination of the anti-heroic side of life, Gay takes his description into the street, where constant disturbance and even terror were normal conditions after dark. A person trying to sleep was awakened by midnight drunkards, and the person walking late at night could be attacked by gangs of thieves and cutthroats who waited in dark corners. The reality must have been worse than Gay implies in his description of these sinister inhabitants of the darkened streets:
>
>> Now is the time that rakes their revels keep;
>> Kindlers of riot, enemies of sleep.
>> His scattered pence the flying Nicker flings,
>> And with the copper shower the casement rings.
>> Who has not heard the Scourer's midnight fame?
>> Who has not trembled at the Mohock's name?
>> —lines 321–326
>
> Gay mentions only those who have "trembled" at the Mohocks, not those who have experienced their brutality.

This same layout applies also when you are quoting prose passages. When quoting lines of poetry, always remember to quote them *as lines*. Do not run them together. When you set off the quotation by itself, as in the example above, you do *not* need quotation marks.

USE THREE SPACED PERIODS (AN ELLIPSIS) TO SHOW OMISSIONS.   Whether your quotation is long or short, you will often need to change some of the material in it to conform to your own thematic requirements. You might wish to omit something from the quotation that is not essential to your point. Indicate such omissions with three spaced periods (. . .). If your quotation is very brief, however, do not use spaced periods, as they might be more of a hindrance than a help. See, for example, the absurdity of an ellipsis in the following:

> Keats asserts that "a thing of beauty . . ." always gives joy.

USE SQUARE BRACKETS FOR YOUR OWN WORDS WITHIN QUOTATIONS.   If you add words of your own to integrate the quotation into your own train of discourse or to explain words that may seem obscure, put square brackets around these words, as in the following passage:

> In the "Tintern Abbey Lines," Wordsworth refers to a trance-like state of illumination, in which the "affections gently lead . . . [him] on." He is unquestionably describing a state of extreme relaxation, for he mentions that the "motion of . . . human blood [was] / Almost suspended [his pulse slowed]" and that in these states he became virtually "a living soul" (lines 42–49).

DO NOT CHANGE YOUR SOURCE.   Always reproduce your source exactly. Because most freshman anthologies and texts modernize the spelling in works that are old, you may never see any old-spelling editions. But if you use an unmodernized text, as in many advanced courses, duplicate everything exactly as you find it, even if this means spelling words like *achieve* as *atchieve* or *joke* as *joak*. A student once spelled the word *an* as "and" in the construction "an I were" in an Elizabethan text. The result was unnecessary, because *an* really meant *if* (or *and if*) and not *and*. Difficulties like this one are rare, but you will avoid them if you reproduce the text as you find it. Should you think that something is either misspelled or confusing as it stands, you may do one of two things:

1. Within brackets, clarify or correct the confusing word or phrase, as in the following:

    In 1714, fencing was considered a "Gentlemany [i.e., gentlemanly] subject."

2. Use the word *sic* [Latin for *thus*, meaning "It is this way in the text"] immediately after the problematic word or obvious mistake:

    He was just "finning [sic] his way back to health" when the next disaster struck.

DO NOT OVERQUOTE.   A word of caution: Do not use too many quotations. You will be judged on your own thought and on the continuity and development of your own theme. It is tempting to use many quotations on the theory that you need to use examples from the text to support and illustrate your ideas. Naturally, it is important to use illustrative examples, but please remember that too many quotations can disturb the flow of *your own* thought. If you have a theme composed of many illustrations linked together by no more than your introductory sentences, how much thinking have you actually shown? Try, therefore, to create your own discussion, using examples appropriately to connect your thought to the text or texts you are analyzing.

DOCUMENTATION: NOTES AND PARENTHETICAL REFERENCES

It is essential to acknowledge—to document—all sources from which you have quoted *or* paraphrased factual and interpretive information. If you do not grant recognition, you run the risk of being challenged for representing as your own the results of others' work; this is plagiarism. As the means of documentation, there are many reference systems, some using parenthetical references and others using footnotes or end notes. Whatever the system, they have in common a carefully prepared bibliography or list of works cited.

The first system, which uses parenthetical references within the theme itself, is described in detail in Joseph Gibaldi and Walter S. Achtert, *MLA Handbook for Writers of Research Papers*, 2nd ed., 1984, which should be in the hands of all students. The second system, which features footnotes or end notes, is still widely used. Because this system was the commonly accepted MLA system until 1984, it is appropriate to review it here also.

LIST OF WORKS CITED

The key to any reference system is a carefully prepared "List of Works Cited" that is included at the end of the essay. "Works Cited" means exactly that; the list should contain just those books and articles which you have actually *used* within your theme. If, on the other hand, your instructor has required that you use footnotes or end notes, you may extend your concluding list to be a complete bibliography of works both cited and also consulted but not actually used. Check your instructor's preference.

For the Works Cited list, you should include all the following information in each entry:

For a Book

1. The author's name, last name first, period.
2. Title, underlined, period.
3. City of publication (not state), colon; publisher (easily recognized abbreviations may be used), comma; date, period.

For an Article

1. The author's name, last name first, period.
2. Title of article in quotation marks, period.
3. Name of journal or periodical, underlined, followed by volume number in Arabic (not Roman) numbers with no punctuation, followed by the year of publication within parentheses (including month and day of weekly or daily issues), colon. Inclusive page numbers, period (without any preceding "pp.").

The list of works consulted should be arranged alphabetically by author, with unsigned articles being listed by title. Bibliographical lists are begun at the left margin, with subsequent lines being indented, so that the key locating word—usually the author's last name—may be easily seen. The many complex combinations possible in the compilation of a bibliographical list, including ways to describe works of art, musical or other performances, and films, are detailed extensively in the *MLA Handbook* (75–135). Here are two model entries:

> BOOK: Alpers, Antony. Katherine Mansfield, A Biography. New York: Knopf, 1953.

> ARTICLE: Hankin, Cherry. "Fantasy and the Sense of an Ending in the Work of Katherine Mansfield." Modern Fiction Studies 24 (1978): 465–474.

PARENTHETICAL REFERENCES TO THE LIST OF WORKS CITED

Within the text of the essay, you may refer parenthetically to the list of works cited. The parenthetical reference system recommended in the *MLA Handbook* (137–158) involves the insertion of the author's last name and the relevant page number or numbers into the body of the essay. If the author's name is mentioned in the discussion, only the page number or numbers are given in parentheses. Here are two examples:

> Mansfield shaped the story "Miss Brill" as a development from pleasant daydreams to wakefulness, accompanied by the downfall of hope and imagination (Hankin 472).

> Cherry Hankin points out that Mansfield shaped the story "Miss Brill" as a development from daydreams to wakefulness, accompanied by the downfall of hope and imagination (472).

For a full discussion of the types of in-text references and the format to use, see the *MLA Handbook*.

FOOTNOTES AND END NOTES

The most formal system of documentation still most widely used is that of footnotes (references at the bottom of each page) or end notes (references listed numerically at the end of the essay). If your instructor wants you to use one of these formats, do the following: The first time you quote or refer to the source, makes a note with the details in this order:

For a Book

1. The author's name, first name or initials first, comma.
2. The title: underlined for a book, no punctuation. If you are referring to a story found in a collection, use quotation marks for that, but underline the title of the book. (Use a comma after the title if an editor, translator, or edition follows.)
3. The name of the editor or translator, if relevant. Abbreviate "editor" or "edited by" as *ed.*; "editors" as *eds.* Use *trans.* for "translator" or "translated by."
4. The edition (if indicated), abbreviated thus: *2nd ed., 3rd ed.*, and so on.
5. The publication facts should be given in parentheses, without any preceding or following punctuation, in the following order:
   a. City (but *not* the state) of publication, colon.
   b. Publisher (clear abbreviations are acceptable), comma.
   c. Year of publication.
6. The page number(s), for example, 65, 65 f., 6–10. If you are referring to longer works, such as novels or longer stories that may have division or chapter numbers, include these numbers for readers who may be using an edition different from yours.

For an Article

1. The author, first name or initials first, comma.
2. The title of the article, in quotation marks, comma.
3. The name of the journal, underlined, no punctuation.
4. The volume number, in Arabic numbers, no punctuation.
5. The year of publication in parentheses, colon.
6. The page number(s); for example, 65, 65 f., 6–10.

For later notes to the same work, use the last name of the author as the reference unless you are referring to two or more works by the same author. Thus, if you refer to only one work by, say, Joseph Conrad, the name "Conrad" will be enough for all later references. Should you be referring to other works by Conrad, however, you will also need to make a short reference to the specific works to distinguish them, such as "Conrad, 'Youth,' " and "Conrad, 'The Secret Sharer.' "

Footnotes are placed at the bottom of each page, separated from your essay by a line; end notes are included at the end of the essay in a list keyed to the end-note numbers in the essay. Ask your instructor about the practice you should adopt.

The first lines of both footnotes and end notes should be paragraph indented, and continuing lines should be flush with the left margin. Footnote numbers are positioned slightly above the line (as superior numbers), like this (^{12}). Generally, you may single-space such notes, but be sure to ask your instructor about which method to follow.

SAMPLE FOOTNOTES.   In the examples below, book titles and periodicals, which are usually italicized in print, are shown underlined, as they would be in your typewritten or carefully handwritten essay.

[1] André Maurois, Points of View from Kipling to Graham Greene (New York: Ungar, 1968) 342.

[2] Susan Gubar, "The Birth of the Artist as Heroine: (Re)production, the Kunstlerroman Tradition, and the Fiction of Katherine Mansfield," in The Representation of Women in Fiction, eds. Carolyn G. Heilbrun and Margaret R. Higonnet, Selected Papers from the English Institute, 1981 (Baltimore: Johns Hopkins U.P., 1983), 25.

[3] Ann L. McLaughlin, "The Same Job: The Shared Writing Aims of Katherine Mansfield and Virginia Woolf," Modern Fiction Studies 24 (1978): 375.

[4] Gubar 55.

[5] Maurois 344.

[6] McLaughlin 381.

As a general principle, you do not need to repeat in a note any material you have already included in your essay. For example, if you mention the author and title of your source in the essay, then the note should merely give no more than the data about publication. Here is an example:

In *The Fiction of Katherine Mansfield*, Marvin Magalaner points out that Mansfield was as skillful in the development of epiphanies (that is, the use of highly significant though perhaps unobtrusive actions or statements to reveal the depths of a particular character) as Joyce himself, the "inventor" of the technique.[9]

---

[9] (Carbondale: Southern Illinois U.P., 1971) 130.

THE REFERENCE METHOD OF THE AMERICAN PSYCHOLOGICAL ASSOCIATION (APA)

A system of references quite similar to the recent recommendations in the *MLA Handbook* is detailed in the *Publication Manual of the American Psychological Association*, 2nd ed. (Washington: American Psychological Association, 1974, with "Change Sheets" dated 1975 and 1977). The method, used in all the APA journals and in many other publications in the social and natural sciences, is the "author-date method of citation." By this method, the last name of the author or authors, together with the date of publication, is included within the article itself, with the pages not included. Like the MLA method, the APA recommends a concluding list of references cited. The MLA system is a little more analytical and friendly, permitting both page number and first names of authors being cited.

FINAL WORDS

As long as all you want from a reference is the page number of a quotation or a paraphrase, the parenthetical system is suitable and easy. It saves your reader the trouble of searching the bottom of the page or of thumbing through pages to find a reference in a long list of notes. However, you may wish to use footnotes or end notes if you need to add more details or refer your readers to other materials that you are not using in your essay.

Whatever method you use, there is an unchanging need to grant recognition to sources. Remember that whenever you begin to write and make references, you might forget a number of specific details about documentation, and you will certainly discover that you have many questions. Be sure then to ask your instructor, who is your final authority.

appendix c

Works Used for Sample Themes and References

Nathaniel Hawthorne (1804–1864)

Young Goodman Brown   1835

Young Goodman Brown came forth at sunset, into the street of Salem village,° but put his head back, after crossing the threshold, to exchange a parting kiss with his young wife. And Faith, as the wife was aptly named, thrust her own pretty head into the street, letting the wind play with the pink ribbons of her cap, while she called to Goodman Brown.

"Dearest heart," whispered she, softly and rather sadly, when her lips were close to his ear, "prithee, put off your journey until sunrise, and sleep in your own bed to-night. A lone woman is troubled with such dreams and such thoughts, that she's afeard of herself, sometimes. Pray, tarry with me this night, dear husband, of all nights in the year!"

"My love and my Faith," replied young Goodman Brown, "of all nights in the year, this one night must I tarry away from thee. My journey, as thou callest it, forth and back again, must needs be done 'twixt now and sunrise. What, my sweet, pretty wife, dost thou doubt me already, and we but three months married!"

Salem village: in Massachusetts, about 15 miles north of Boston.

"Then God bless you!" said Faith with the pink ribbons, "and may you find all well, when you come back."

"Amen!" cried Goodman Brown. "Say thy prayers, dear Faith, and go to   5
bed at dusk, and no harm will come to thee."

So they parted; and the young man pursued his way, until, being about to turn the corner by the meeting-house, he looked back and saw the head of Faith still peeping after him, with a melancholy air, in spite of her pink ribbons.

"Poor little Faith!" thought he, for his heart smote him. "What a wretch am I, to leave her on such an errand! She talks of dreams, too. Methought, as she spoke, there was trouble in her face, as if a dream had warned her what work is to be done to-night. But no, no! 't would kill her to think it. Well; she's a blessed angel on earth; and after this one night, I'll cling to her skirts and follow her to Heaven."

With this excellent resolve for the future, Goodman Brown felt himself justified in making more haste on his present evil purpose. He had taken a dreary road, darkened by all the gloomiest trees of the forest, which barely stood aside to let the narrow path creep through, and closed immediately behind. It was all as lonely as could be; and there is this peculiarity in such a solitude, that the traveller knows not who may be concealed by the innumerable trunks and the thick boughs overhead; so that, with lonely footsteps, he may yet be passing through an unseen multitude.

"There may be a devilish Indian behind every tree," said Goodman Brown to himself; and he glanced fearfully behind him, as he added, "What if the devil himself should be at my very elbow!"

His head being turned back, he passed a crook of the road, and looking   10
forward again, beheld the figure of a man, in grave and decent attire, seated at the foot of an old tree. He arose at Goodman Brown's approach, and walked onward, side by side with him.

"You are late, Goodman Brown," said he. "The clock of the Old South° was striking, as I came through Boston; and that is full fifteen minutes agone."

"Faith kept me back awhile," replied the young man, with a tremor in his voice, caused by the sudden appearance of his companion, though not wholly unexpected.

It was now deep dusk in the forest, and deepest in that part of it where these two were journeying. As nearly as could be discerned, the second traveller was about fifty years old, apparently in the same rank of life as Goodman Brown, and bearing a considerable resemblance to him, though perhaps more in expression than features. Still, they might have been taken for father and son. And yet, though the elder person was as simply clad as the younger, and as simple in manner too, he had an indescribable air of one who knew the world, and would not have felt abashed at the governor's dinner-table, or in King William's° court, were it possible that his affairs should call him thither. But the only thing about him that could be fixed upon as remarkable, was his staff, which bore the likeness of a great black snake, so curiously wrought, that it might almost be seen to

Old South: The Old South Church, in Boston, is still there.
King William: William IV, King of England from 1830 to 1837.

twist and wriggle itself like a living serpent. This, of course, must have been an ocular deception, assisted by the uncertain light.

"Come, Goodman Brown!" cried his fellow-traveller, "this is a dull pace for the beginning of a journey. Take my staff, if you are so soon weary."

15 "Friend," said the other, exchanging his slow pace for a full stop, "having kept covenant by meeting thee here, it is my purpose now to return whence I came. I have scruples, touching the matter thou wot'st of."

"Sayest thou so?" replied he of the serpent, smiling apart. 'Let us walk on, nevertheless, reasoning as we go, and if I convince thee not, thou shalt turn back. We are but a little way in the forest, yet."

"Too far, too far!" exclaimed the goodman, unconsciously resuming his walk. "My father never went into the woods on such an errand, nor his father before him. We have been a race of honest men and good Christians, since the days of the martyrs.° And shall I be the first of the name of Brown that ever took this path and kept—"

"Such company, thou wouldst say," observed the elder person, interrupting his pause. "Well said, Goodman Brown! I have been as well acquainted with your family as with ever a one among the Puritans; and that's no trifle to say. I helped your grandfather, the constable, when he lashed the Quaker woman so smartly through the streets of Salem. And it was I that brought your father a pitch-pine knot, kindled at my own hearth, to set fire to an Indian village, in King Philip's war.° They were my good friends, both; and many a pleasant walk have we had along this path, and returned merrily after midnight. I would fain be friends with you, for their sake."

"If it be as thou sayest," replied Goodman Brown, "I marvel they never spoke of these matters. Or, verily, I marvel not, seeing that the least rumor of the sort would have driven them from New England. We are a people of prayer, and good works to boot, and abide no such wickedness."

20 "Wickedness or not," said the traveller with twisted staff, "I have a very general acquaintance here in New England. The deacons of many a church have drunk the communion wine with me; the selectmen, of divers towns, make me their chairman; and a majority of the Great and General Court are firm supporters of my interest. The governor and I, too—but these are state secrets."

"Can this be so!" cried Goodman Brown, with a stare of amazement at his undisturbed companion. "Howbeit, I have nothing to do with the governor and council; they have their own ways, and are no rule for a simple husbandman like me. But, were I to go on with thee, how should I meet the eye of that good old man, our minister, at Salem village? Oh, his voice would make me tremble, both Sabbath-day and lecture-day!"

Thus far, the elder traveller had listened with due gravity, but now burst into a fit of irrepressible mirth, shaking himself so violently, that his snakelike staff actually seemed to wriggle in sympathy.

---

days of the martyrs: The martyrdoms of Protestants in England during the reign of Queen Mary (1553–1558).
King Philip's War (1675–1676): It resulted in the suppression of Indian tribal life in New England and prepared the way for unlimited settlement of the area by European immigrants. "Philip" was the English name of Chief Metacomet of the Wampanoag Indian Tribe.

"Ha! ha! ha!" shouted he, again and again; then composing himself, "Well, go on, Goodman Brown, go on; but, prithee, don't kill me with laughing!"

"Well, then, to end the matter at once," said Goodman Brown, considerably nettled, "there is my wife, Faith. It would break her dear little heart; and I'd rather break my own!"

"Nay, if that be the case," answered the other, "e'en go thy ways, Goodman 25
Brown. I would not, for twenty old women like the one hobbling before us, that Faith should come to any harm."

As he spoke, he pointed his staff at a female figure on the path, in whom Goodman Brown recognized a very pious and exemplary dame, who had taught him his catechism in youth, and was still his moral and spiritual adviser, jointly with the minister and Deacon Gookin.

"A marvel, truly, that Goody° Cloyse should be so far in the wilderness, at nightfall!" said he. "But, with your leave, friend, I shall take a cut through the woods, until we have left this Christian woman behind. Being a stranger to you, she might ask whom I was consorting with, and whither I was going."

"Be it so," said his fellow-traveller. "Betake you to the woods, and let me keep the path."

Accordingly, the young man turned aside, but took care to watch his companion, who advanced softly along the road, until he had come within a staff's length of the old dame. She, meanwhile, was making the best of her way, with singular speed for so aged a woman, and mumbling some indistinct words, a prayer, doubtless, as she went. The traveller put forth his staff, and touched her withered neck with what seemed the serpent's tail.

"The devil!" screamed the pious old lady. 30

"Then Goody Cloyse knows her old friend?" observed the traveller, confronting her, and leaning on his writhing stick.

"Ah, forsooth, and is it your worship, indeed?" cried the good dame. "Yea, truly is it, and in the very image of my old gossip,° Goodman Brown, the grandfather of the silly fellow that now is. But, would your worship believe it? My broomstick hath strangely disappeared, stolen, as I suspect, by that unhanged witch, Goody Cory," and that, too, when I was all anointed with the juice of smallage and cinquefoil and wolf's-bane—"

"Mingled with fine wheat and the fat of a new-born babe," said the shape of old Goodman Brown.

"Ah, your worship knows the recipe," cried the old lady, cackling aloud. "So, as I was saying, being all ready for the meeting, and no horse to ride on, I made up my mind to foot it; for they tell me there is a nice young man to be taken into communion to-night. But now your good worship will lend me your arm, and we shall be there in a twinkling."

"That can hardly be," answered her friend. "I will not spare you my arm, 35
Goody Cloyse, but here is my staff, if you will."

Goody: a shortened form of "goodwife," a respectful name for a married woman of low rank. A "Goody Cloyse" was one of the women sentenced to execution by Hawthorne's great grandfather, Judge John Hathorne.
gossip: from "good sib" or "good relative."
Goody Cory: the name of a woman who was also sent to execution by Judge Hathorne.

So saying, he threw it down at her feet, where, perhaps, it assumed life, being one of the rods which its owner had formerly lent to the Egyptian Magi.° Of this fact, however, Goodman Brown could not take cognizance. He had cast up his eyes in astonishment, and looking down again, beheld neither Goody Cloyse nor the serpentine staff, but his fellow-traveller alone, who waited for him as calmly as if nothing had happened.

"That old woman taught me my catechism!" said the young man; and there was a world of meaning in this simple comment.

They continued to walk onward, while the elder traveller exhorted his companion to make good speed and persevere in the path, discoursing so aptly, that his arguments seemed rather to spring up in the bosom of his auditor, than to be suggested by himself. As they went he plucked a branch of maple, to serve for a walking-stick, and began to strip it of the twigs and little boughs, which were wet with evening dew. The moment his fingers touched them, they became strangely withered and dried up, as with a week's sunshine. Thus the pair proceeded, at a good free pace, until suddenly, in a gloomy hollow of the road, Goodman Brown sat himself down on the stump of a tree, and refused to go any farther.

"Friend," said he, stubbornly, "my mind is made up. Not another step will I budge on this errand. What if a wretched old woman do choose to go to the devil, when I thought she was going to Heaven! Is that any reason why I should quit my dear Faith, and go after her?"

40   "You will think better of this by and by," said his acquaintance, composedly. "Sit here and rest yourself a while; and when you feel like moving again, there is my staff to help you along."

Without more words, he threw his companion the maple stick, and was as speedily out of sight as if he had vanished into the deepening gloom. The young man sat a few moments by the roadside, applauding himself greatly, and thinking with how clear a conscience he should meet the minister, in his morning walk, nor shrink from the eye of good old Deacon Gookin. And what calm sleep would be his, that very night, which was to have been spent so wickedly, but purely and sweetly now, in the arms of Faith! Amidst these pleasant and praiseworthy meditations, Goodman Brown heard the tramp of horses along the road, and deemed it advisable to conceal himself within the verge of the forest, conscious of the guilty purpose that had brought him thither, though now so happily turned from it.

On came the hoof-tramps and the voices of the riders, two grave old voices, conversing soberly as they drew near. These mingled sounds appeared to pass along the road, within a few yards of the young man's hiding-place; but owing, doubtless, to the depth of the gloom, at that particular spot, neither the travellers nor their steeds were visible. Though their figures brushed the small boughs by the wayside, it could not be seen that they intercepted, even for a moment, the faint gleam from the strip of bright sky, athwart which they must have passed. Goodman Brown alternately crouched and stood on tiptoe, pulling aside the branches, and thrusting forth his head as far as he durst, without discerning so

lent to the Egyptian Magi: See Exodus 7:10–12.

much as a shadow. It vexed him the more, because he could have sworn, were such a thing possible, that he recognized the voices of the minister and Deacon Gookin, jogging° along quietly, as they were wont to do, when bound to some ordination or ecclesiastical council. While yet within hearing, one of the riders stopped to pluck a switch.

"Of the two, reverend Sir," said the voice like the deacon's, "I had rather miss an ordination dinner than to-night's meeting. They tell me that some of our community are to be here from Falmouth and beyond, and others from Connecticut and Rhode Island; besides several of the Indian powwows,° who, after their fashion, know almost as much deviltry as the best of us. Moreover, there is a goodly young woman to be taken into communion."

"Mighty well, Deacon Gookin!" replied the solemn old tones of the minister. "Spur up, or we shall be late. Nothing can be done, you know, until I get on the ground."

The hoofs clattered again, and the voices, talking so strangely in the empty   45
air, passed on through the forest, where no church had ever been gathered, nor solitary Christian prayed. Whither, then, could these holy men be journeying, so deep into the heathen wilderness? Young Goodman Brown caught hold of a tree, for support, being ready to sink down on the ground, faint and over-burthened with the heavy sickness of his heart. He looked up to the sky, doubting whether there really was a Heaven above him. Yet, there was the blue arch, and the stars brightening in it.

"With Heaven above, and Faith below, I will yet stand firm against the devil!" cried Goodman Brown.

While he still gazed upward, into the deep arch of the firmament, and had lifted his hands to pray, a cloud, though no wind was stirring, hurried across the zenith, and hid the brightening stars. The blue sky was still visible, except directly overhead, where this black mass of cloud was sweeping swiftly northward. Aloft in the air, as if from the depths of the cloud, came a confused and doubtful sound of voices. Once, the listener fancied that he could distinguish the accents of town's-people of his own, men and women, both pious and ungodly, many of whom he had met at the communion-table, and had seen others rioting at the tavern. The next moment, so indistinct were the sounds, he doubted whether he had heard aught but the murmur of the old forest, whispering without a wind. Then came a stronger swell of those familiar tones, heard daily in the sunshine, at Salem village, but never, until now, from a cloud at night. There was one voice, of a young woman, uttering lamentations, yet with an uncertain sorrow, and entreating for some favor, which, perhaps, it would grieve her to obtain. And all the unseen multitude, both saints and sinners, seemed to encourage her onward.

"Faith!" shouted Goodman Brown, in a voice of agony and desperation; and the echoes of the forest mocked him, crying—"Faith! Faith!" as if bewildered wretches were seeking her, all through the wilderness.

---

jogging: riding a horse at a slow trot.
powwow: a Narragansett Indian word describing a ritual ceremony of dancing, incantation, and magic.

The cry of grief, rage, and terror was yet piercing the night, when the unhappy husband held his breath for a response. There was a scream, drowned immediately in a louder murmur of voices fading into far-off laughter, as the dark cloud swept away, leaving the clear and silent sky above Goodman Brown. But something fluttered lightly down through the air, and caught on the branch of a tree. The young man seized it and beheld a pink ribbon.

50   "My Faith is gone!" cried he, after one stupefied moment. "There is no good on earth, and sin is but a name. Come, devil! for to thee is this world given."

And maddened with despair, so that he laughed loud and long, did Goodman Brown grasp his staff and set forth again, at such a rate, that he seemed to fly along the forest path, rather than to walk or run. The road grew wilder and drearier, and more faintly traced, and vanished at length, leaving him in the heart of the dark wilderness, still rushing onward, with the instinct that guides mortal man to evil. The whole forest was peopled with frightful sounds; the creaking of the trees, the howling of wild beasts, and the yell of Indians; while, sometimes, the wind tolled like a distant church bell, and sometimes gave a broad roar around the traveller, as if all Nature were laughing him to scorn. But he was himself the chief horror of the scene, and shrank not from its other horrors.

"Ha! ha! ha!" roared Goodman Brown, when the wind laughed at him. "Let us hear which will laugh loudest! Think not to frighten me with your deviltry! Come witch, come wizard, come Indian powwow, come devil himself! and here comes Goodman Brown. You may as well fear him as he fear you!"

In truth, all through the haunted forest, there could be nothing more frightful than the figure of Goodman Brown. On he flew, among the black pines, brandishing his staff with frenzied gestures, now giving vent to an inspiration of horrid blasphemy, and now shouting forth such laughter, as set all the echoes of the forest laughing like demons around him. The fiend in his own shape is less hideous, than when he rages in the breast of man. Thus sped the demoniac on his course, until, quivering among the trees, he saw a red light before him, as when the felled trunks and branches of a clearing have been set on fire, and throw up their lurid blaze against the sky, at the hour of midnight. He paused, in a lull of the tempest that had driven him onward, and heard the swell of what seemed a hymn, rolling solemnly from a distance, with the weight of many voices. He knew the tune. It was a familiar one in the choir of the village meeting-house. The verse died heavily away, and was lengthened by a chorus, not of human voices, but of all the sounds of the benighted wilderness, pealing in awful harmony together. Goodman Brown cried out; and his cry was lost to his own ear, by its unison with the cry of the desert.

In the interval of silence, he stole forward, until the light glared full upon his eyes. At one extremity of an open space, hemmed in by the dark wall of the forest, arose a rock, bearing some rude, natural resemblance either to an altar or a pulpit, and surrounded by four blazing pines, their tops aflame, their stems untouched, like candles at an evening meeting. The mass of foliage, that had overgrown the summit of the rock, was all on fire, blazing high into the night, and fitfully illuminating the whole field. Each pendent twig and leafy festoon was in a blaze. As the red light arose and fell, a numerous congregation alternately shone forth, then disappeared in shadow, and again grew, as it were, out of the darkness, peopling the heart of the solitary woods at once.

"A grave and dark-clad company!" quoth Goodman Brown.   55

In truth, they were such. Among them, quivering to-and-fro, between gloom and splendor, appeared faces that would be seen, next day, at the council-board of the province, and others which, Sabbath after Sabbath, looked devoutly heavenward, and benignantly over the crowded pews, from the holiest pulpits in the land. Some affirm that the lady of the governor was there. At least, there were high dames well known to her, and wives of honored husbands, and widows a great multitude, and ancient maidens, all of excellent repute, and fair young girls, who trembled lest their mothers should espy them. Either the sudden gleams of light, flashing over the obscure field, bedazzled Goodman Brown, or he recognized a score of the church members of Salem village, famous for their especial sanctity. Good old Deacon Gookin had arrived, and waited at the skirts of that venerable saint, his reverend pastor. But, irreverently consorting with these grave, reputable, and pious people, these elders of the church, these chaste dames and dewy virgins, there were men of dissolute lives and women of spotted fame, wretches given over to all mean and filthy vice, and suspected even of horrid crimes. It was strange to see, that the good shrank not from the wicked, nor were the sinners abashed by the saints. Scattered, also, among their pale-faced enemies, were the Indian priests, or powwows, who had often scared their native forest with more hideous incantations than any known to English witchcraft.

"But, where is Faith?" thought Goodman Brown; and, as hope came into his heart, he trembled.

Another verse of the hymn arose, a slow and mournful strain, such as the pious love, but joined to words which expressed all that our nature can conceive of sin, and darkly hinted at far more. Unfathomable to mere mortals is the lore of fiends. Verse after verse was sung, and still the chorus of the desert swelled between, like the deepest tone of a mighty organ. And, with the final peal of that dreadful anthem, there came a sound, as if the roaring wind, the rushing streams, the howling beasts, and every other voice of the unconverted wilderness were mingling and according with the voice of guilty man, in homage to the prince of all. The four blazing pines threw up a loftier flame, and obscurely discovered shapes and visages of horror on the smoke-wreaths, above the impious assembly. At the same moment, the fire on the rock shot redly forth, and formed a glowing arch above its base, where now appeared a figure. With reverence be it spoken, the apparition bore no slight similitude, both in garb and manner, to some grave divine of the New England churches.

"Bring forth the converts!" cried a voice, that echoed through the field and rolled into the forest.

At the word, Goodman Brown stepped forth from the shadow of the trees,   60
and approached the congregation, with whom he felt a loathful brotherhood, by the sympathy of all that was wicked in his heart. He could have well-nigh sworn, that the shape of his own dead father beckoned him to advance, looking downward from a smoke-wreath, while a woman, with dim features of despair, threw out her hand to warn him back. Was it his mother? But he had no power to retreat one step, nor to resist, even in thought, when the minister and good old Deacon Gookin seized his arms, and led him to the blazing rock. Thither came also the

slender form of a veiled female, led between Goody Cloyse, that pious teacher of the catechism, and Martha Carrier, who had received the devil's promise to be queen of hell. A rampant hag was she! And there stood the proselytes, beneath the canopy of fire.

"Welcome, my children," said the dark figure, "to the communion of your race! Ye have found, thus young, your nature and your destiny. My children, look behind you!"

They turned; and flashing forth, as it were, in a sheet of flame, the fiend-worshippers were seen; the smile of welcome gleamed darkly on every visage.

"There," resumed the sable form, "are all whom ye have reverenced from youth. Ye deemed them holier than yourselves, and shrank from your own sin, contrasting it with their lives of righteousness and prayerful aspirations heavenward. Yet, here are they all, in my worshipping assembly! This night it shall be granted you to know their secret deeds; how hoary-bearded elders of the church have whispered wanton words to the young maids of their households; how many a woman, eager for widow's weeds, has given her husband a drink at bedtime, and let him sleep his last sleep in her bosom; how beardless youths have made haste to inherit their father's wealth; and how fair damsels—blush not, sweet ones!—have dug little graves in the garden, and bidden me, the sole guest, to an infant's funeral. By the sympathy of your human hearts for sin, ye shall scent out all the places—whether in church, bed-chamber, street, field, or forest—where crime has been committed, and shall exult to behold the whole earth one stain of guilt, one mighty blood-spot. Far more than this! It shall be yours to penetrate, in every bosom, the deep mystery of sin, the fountain of all wicked arts, and which inexhaustibly supplies more evil impulses than human power—than my power, at its utmost!—can make manifest in deeds. And now, my children, look upon each other."

They did so; and, by the blaze of the hell-kindled torches, the wretched man beheld his Faith, and the wife her husband, trembling before that unhallowed altar.

65   "Lo! there ye stand, my children," said the figure, in a deep and solemn tone, almost sad, with its despairing awfulness, as if his once angelic nature could yet mourn for our miserable race. "Depending upon one another's hearts, ye had still hoped that virtue were not all a dream! Now are ye undeceived!—Evil is the nature of mankind. Evil must be your only happiness. Welcome, again, my children, to the communion of your race!"

"Welcome!" repeated the fiend-worshippers, in one cry of despair and triumph.

And there they stood, the only pair, as it seemed, who were yet hesitating on the verge of wickedness, in this dark world. A basin was hollowed, naturally, in the rock. Did it contain water, reddened by the lurid light? or was it blood? or, perchance, a liquid flame? Herein did the Shape of Evil dip his hand, and prepare to lay the mark of baptism upon their foreheads, that they might be partakers of the mystery of sin, more conscious of the secret guilt of others, both in deed and thought, than they could now be of their own. The husband cast one look at his pale wife, and Faith at him. What polluted wretches would the next glance show them to each other, shuddering alike at what they disclosed and what they saw!

"Faith! Faith!" cried the husband. "Look up to Heaven, and resist the Wicked One!"

Whether Faith obeyed, he knew not. Hardly had he spoken, when he found himself amid calm night and solitude, listening to a roar of the wind, which died heavily away through the forest. He staggered against the rock, and felt it chill and damp, while a hanging twig, that had been all on fire, besprinkled his cheek with the coldest dew.

The next morning, young Goodman Brown came slowly into the street of Salem village staring around him like a bewildered man. The good old minister was taking a walk along the grave-yard, to get an appetite for breakfast and meditate his sermon, and bestowed a blessing, as he passed, on Goodman Brown. He shrank from the venerable saint, as if to avoid an anathema. Old Deacon Gookin was at domestic worship, and the holy words of his prayer were heard through the open window. "What God doth the wizard pray to?" quoth Goodman Brown. Goody Cloyse, that excellent old Christian, stood in the early sunshine, at her own lattice, catechising a little girl, who had brought her a pint of morning's milk. Goodman Brown snatched away the child, as from the grasp of the fiend himself. Turning the corner by the meetinghouse, he spied the head of Faith, with the pink ribbons, gazing anxiously forth, and bursting into such joy at sight of him that she skipt along the street, and almost kissed her husband before the whole village. But Goodman Brown looked sternly and sadly into her face, and passed on without a greeting.

Had Goodman Brown fallen asleep in the forest, and only dreamed a wild dream of a witch-meeting?

Be it so, if you will. But, alas! it was a dream of evil omen for young Goodman Brown. A stern, a sad, a darkly meditative, a distrustful, if not a desperate man did he become, from the night of that fearful dream. On the Sabbath day, when the congregation were singing a holy psalm, he could not listen, because an anthem of sin rushed loudly upon his ear, and drowned all the blessed strain. When the minister spoke from the pulpit, with power and fervid eloquence, and with his hand on the open Bible, of the sacred truths of our religion, and of saint-like lives and triumphant deaths, and of future bliss or misery unutterable, then did Goodman Brown turn pale, dreading lest the roof should thunder down upon the gray blasphemer and his hearers. Often, awaking suddenly at midnight, he shrank from the bosom of Faith, and at morning or eventide, when the family knelt down at prayer, he scowled, and muttered to himself, and gazed sternly at his wife, and turned away. And when he had lived long, and was borne to his grave, a hoary corpse, followed by Faith, an aged woman, and children and grand-children, a goodly procession, besides neighbors not a few, they carved no hopeful verse upon his tombstone; for his dying hour was gloom.

70

Guy De Maupassant (1850–1893)

The Necklace   1884

She was one of those pretty and charming women, born, as if by an error of destiny, into a family of clerks and copyists. She had no dowry, no prospects, no way of getting known, courted, loved, married by a rich and distinguished man. She finally settled for a marriage with a minor clerk in the Ministry of Education.

She was a simple person, without the money to dress well, but she was as unhappy as if she had gone through bankruptcy, for women have neither rank nor race. In place of high birth or important family connections, they can rely only on their beauty, their grace, and their charm. Their inborn finesse, their elegant taste, their engaging personalities, which are their only power, make working-class women the equals of the grandest duchesses.

She suffered constantly, feeling herself destined for all delicacies and luxuries. She suffered because of her grim apartment with its drab walls, threadbare furniture, ugly curtains. All such things, which most other women in her situation would not even have noticed, tortured her and filled her with despair. The sight of the young country girl who did her simple housework awakened in her only a sense of desolation and lost hopes. She daydreamed of large, silent anterooms, decorated with oriental tapestries and lighted by high bronze floor lamps, with two elegant valets in short culottes dozing in large armchairs under the effects of forced-air heaters. She visualized large drawing rooms draped in the most expensive silks, with fine end tables on which were placed knickknacks of inestimable value. She dreamed of the perfume of dainty private rooms, which were designed only for intimate tête-à-têtes with the closest friends, who because of their achievements and fame would make her the envy of all other women.

When she sat down to dinner at her round little table covered with a cloth that had not been washed for three days, in front of her husband who opened the kettle while declaring ecstatically, "Oh boy, beef stew, my favorite," she dreamed of expensive banquets with shining placesettings, and wall hangings depicting ancient heroes and exotic birds in an enchanted forest. She imagined a gourmet-prepared main course carried on the most exquisite trays and served on the most beautiful dishes, with whispered gallantries which she would hear with a sphinxlike smile as she dined on the pink meat of a trout or the delicate wing of a quail.

5   She had no decent dresses, no jewels, nothing. And she loved nothing but these; she believed herself born only for these. She burned with the desire to please, to be envied, to be attractive and sought after.

She had a rich friend, a comrade from convent days, whom she did not want to see anymore because she suffered so much when she returned home.

Translated by Edgar V. Roberts

She would weep for the entire day afterward with sorrow, regret, despair, and misery.

Well, one evening, her husband came home glowing and carrying a large envelope.

"Here," he said, "this is something for you."

She quickly tore open the envelope and took out a card engraved with these words:

> *The Chancellor of Education and Mrs. George Ramponneau request that Mr. and Mrs. Loisel do them the honor of coming to dinner at the Ministry of Education on the evening of January 8.*

Instead of being delighted, as her husband had hoped, she threw the invitation spitefully on the table while muttering: 10

"What do you expect me to do with this?"

"But Honey, I thought you'd be glad. You never get to go out, and this is a special occasion! I had a lot of trouble getting the invitation. Everyone wants one; the demand is high and not many clerks get invited. Everyone important will be there."

She looked at him angrily and stated impatiently:

"What do you want me to wear to go there?"

He had not thought of that. He stammered: 15

"But your theatre dress. That seems nice to me . . ."

He stopped, amazed and bewildered, as his wife began to cry. Large tears fell slowly from the corners of her eyes to her mouth. He said falteringly:

"What's wrong? What's wrong?"

But with a strong effort she had recovered, and she answered calmly as she wiped her damp cheeks:

"Nothing, except that I have nothing to wear and therefore can't go to the   20
party. Give your invitation to someone else at the office whose wife will have nicer clothes than mine."

Distressed, he responded:

"Well, okay, Mathilde. How much would a new dress cost, something you could use at other times, but not anything fancy?"

She thought for a few moments, adding things up and thinking also of an amount that she could ask without getting an immediate refusal and a frightened outcry from the frugal clerk.

Finally she responded tentatively: 25

"I don't know exactly, but it seems to me that I could get by on four hundred francs."

He blanched slightly at this, because he had set aside just that amount to buy a shotgun and go with a few friends to Nanterre on Sundays the next summer to shoot larks.

However, he said:

"Okay, you've got four hundred francs, but make it a pretty dress."

As the day of the party drew near, Mrs. Loisel seemed sad, uneasy, anxious, even though her dress was all ready. One evening her husband said to her:

30 "What's up? You've been acting strange for several days."

She answered:

"It's awful, but I don't have any jewels, not a single stone, nothing for matching jewelry. I'm going to look poor, and cheap. I'd almost rather not go to the party."

He responded:

"You can wear a corsage of cut flowers. This year that's really the *in* thing. For no more than ten francs you can get two or three gorgeous roses."

35 She was not convinced.

"No . . . there's nothing more humiliating than to look ragged in the middle of rich women."

But her husband exclaimed:

"God, but you're silly! Go to your friend Mrs. Forrestier, and ask her to lend you some jewelry. You know her well enough to do that."

She uttered a cry of joy:

40 "That's right. I hadn't thought of that."

The next day she went to her friend's house and described her problem.

Mrs. Forrestier went to her glass-plated wardrobe, took out a large jewel box, opened it, and said to Mrs. Loisel:

"Choose, my dear."

She saw bracelets, then a pearl necklace, then a Venetian cross of finely worked gold and gems. She tried on the jewelry in front of a mirror, and hesitated, unable to make up her mind about which ones to give back. She kept asking:

45 "Do you have anything else?"

"Certainly. Look to your heart's content. I don't know what will please you most."

Suddenly she found, in a black satin box, a superb diamond necklace, and her heart throbbed with desire for it. Her hands shook as she took it up. She fastened it around her neck, watched it gleam at her throat, and looked at herself ecstatically.

Then she asked, haltingly and anxiously:

"Could you lend me this, nothing but this?"

50 "Why yes, certainly."

She jumped up, hugged her friend joyfully, then hurried away with her treasure.

The day of the party came, Mrs. Loisel was a success. She was prettier than anyone else, stylish, graceful, smiling, and wild with joy. All the men saw her, asked her name, and sought to be introduced. All the important administrators stood in line to waltz with her. The Chancellor himself eyed her.

She danced joyfully, passionately, intoxicated with pleasure, thinking of nothing but the moment, in the triumph of her beauty, in the glory of her success, in a cloud-nine of happiness made up of all the admiration, of all the aroused desire, of this victory so complete and so sweet to the heart of any woman.

She did not leave until four o'clock in the morning. Her husband, since midnight, had been sleeping in a little empty room with three other men whose wives had also been enjoying themselves.

55 He threw over her shoulders the shawl that he had brought for the trip home, modest clothing from everyday life, the poverty of which contrasted sharply

with the elegance of the party dress. She felt it and hurried away to avoid being noticed by the other women who luxuriated in rich furs.

Loisel tried to hold her back:

"Wait a while. You'll catch cold outdoors. I'll call a cab."

But she paid no attention and hurried down the stairs. When they reached the street they found no carriages. They began to look for one, shouting at cabmen passing by at a distance.

They walked toward the Seine, desperate, shivering. Finally, on a quay, they found one of those old night-going buggies that are seen in Paris only after dark, as if they were ashamed of their wretched appearance in daylight.

It took them to their door, on the Street of Martyrs, and they sadly climbed   60
the stairs to their flat. For her, it was finished. As for him, he could think only that he had to begin work at the Ministry of Education at ten o'clock.

She took the shawl off her shoulders, in front of the mirror, to see herself once more in her glory. But suddenly she cried out. The necklace was no longer around her neck!

Her husband, already half undressed, asked:

"What's wrong with you?"

She turned toward him frantically:

"I . . . I . . . I no longer have Mrs. Forrestier's necklace."   65

He stood up, bewildered·

"What! . . . How! . . . It's not possible!"

And they looked in the folds of the dress, in the creases of the shawl, in the pockets, everywhere. They found nothing.

He asked:

"You're sure you still had it when you left the party?"   70

"Yes. I checked it in the vestibule of the Ministry."

"But if you had lost it in the street, we would have heard it fall. It must be in the cab."

"Yes, probably. Did you notice the number?"

"No. Did you see it?"

"No."   75

Overwhelmed, they looked at each other. Finally, Loisel got dressed again:

"I'm going out to retrace all our steps," he said, "to see if I can find the necklace that way."

And he went out. She stayed in her evening dress, without the energy to get ready for bed, prostrated in a chair, drained of strength and thought.

Her husband came back at about seven o'clock. He had found nothing.

He went to Police Headquarters and to the newspapers to announce a reward.   80
He went to the small cab companies, and finally he followed up even the slightest hopeful lead.

She waited the entire day, in the same enervated state, in the face of this frightful disaster.

Loisel came back in the evening, his face pale and haggard. He had found nothing.

"You'll have to write to your friend," he said, "that you broke a fastening on her necklace and that you will have it fixed. That will give us time to look around."

She wrote as he dictated.

85   At the end of a week they had lost all hope.

And Loisel, seemingly five years older, declared:

"We'll have to see about replacing the jewels."

The next day, they took the case which had contained the necklace, and went to the jeweler whose name was inside. He looked at his books:

"I wasn't the one, Madam, who sold the necklace. I only made the case."

90   Then they went from jeweler to jeweler, searching for a necklace like the other one, racking their memories, both of them sick with worry and anguish.

In a shop in the Palais-Royal, they found a string of diamonds that seemed to them exactly like the one they were seeking. It was priced at forty thousand francs. They could buy it for thirty-six thousand.

They got the jeweler to promise not to sell it for three days. And they made an agreement that he would buy it back for thirty-four thousand francs if the original was recovered before the end of February.

Loisel had saved eighteen thousand francs that his father had left him. He would have to borrow the rest.

He borrowed, asking a thousand francs from one, five hundred from another, five louis° here, three louis here. He made promissory notes, undertook ruinous obligations, did business with finance companies and the whole tribe of loan sharks. He compromised himself for the remainder of his days, risked his signature without knowing whether he would be able to honor it, and, terrified by anguish over the future, by the black misery that was about to descend on him, by the prospect of all kinds of physical deprivations and moral tortures, he went to get the new necklace, and put down thirty-six thousand francs on the jeweler's counter.

95   Mrs. Loisel took the necklace back to Mrs. Forrestier, who said with an offended tone:

"You should have brought it back sooner, because I might have needed it."

She did not open the case, as her friend feared she might. If she had noticed the substitution, what would she have thought? What would she have said? Would she not have taken her for a thief?

Mrs. Loisel soon discovered the horrible life of the needy. She did her share, however, completely, heroically. That horrifying debt had to be paid. She would pay. They dismissed the maid; they changed their address; they rented an attic flat.

She learned to do heavy housework, dirty kitchen jobs. She washed the dishes, wearing away her manicured fingernails on greasy pots and encrusted baking dishes. She handwashed dirty linen, shirts, and dish towels that she hung out on the line to dry. Each morning, she took the garbage down to the street, and she carried up water, stopping at each floor to catch her breath. And, dressed in cheap house dresses, she went to the fruit dealer, the grocer, the butchers, with her basket under her arms, haggling, insulting, defending her measly cash penny by penny.

100   They had to make installment payments every month, and, to buy more time, to refinance loans.

louis: a twenty-franc coin.

The husband worked evenings to make fair copies of tradesmen's accounts, and late into the night he made copies at five cents a page.

And this life lasted ten years.

At the end of ten years, they had paid back everything—everything—including the extra charges imposed by loan sharks and the accumulation of compound interest.

Mrs. Loisel seemed old now. She had become the strong, hard, and rude woman of poor households. Her hair unkempt, with uneven skirts and rough, red hands, she spoke loudly, washed floors with large buckets of water. But sometimes, when her husband was at work, she sat down near the window, and she dreamed of that evening so long ago, of that party, where she had been so beautiful and so admired.

What would life have been like if she had not lost that necklace? Who knows?   *105* Who knows? Life is so peculiar, so uncertain. How little a thing it takes to destroy you or to save you!

Well, one Sunday, as she had gone on a stroll along the Champs-Elysées to relax from the cares of the week, she suddenly noticed a woman walking with a child. It was Mrs. Forrestier, always youthful, always beautiful, always attractive.

Mrs. Loisel felt moved. Would she speak to her? Yes, certainly. And now that she had paid, she could tell all. Why not?

She walked closer.

"Hello, Jeanne."

The other did not recognize her at all, being astonished to be addressed so   *110* intimately by this working woman. She stammered:

"But . . . Madam! . . . I don't know. . . . You must have made a mistake."

"No. I'm Mathilde Loisel."

Her friend cried out:

"Oh! . . . My poor Mathilde, you've changed so much."

"Yes. I've had some hard times since I saw you last; in fact, miseries . . .   *115* and all this because of you! . . ."

"Of me . . . how so?"

"You remember the diamond necklace that you lent me to go to the party at the Ministry of Education?"

"Yes. What then?"

"Well, I lost it."

"How, since you gave it back to me?"   *120*

"I brought back another exactly like it. And for ten years we've been paying for it. You understand that this wasn't easy for us, who have nothing. . . . Finally it's over, and I'm mighty damned glad."

Mrs. Forrestier stopped her.

"You say that you bought a diamond necklace to replace mine?"

"Yes, you didn't notice it, eh? They were exactly like yours."

And she smiled with proud and childish joy.   *125*

Mrs. Forrestier, deeply moved, took both her hands.

"Oh, my poor Mathilde! But mine was false. At the most, it was worth five hundred francs! . . ."

Katherine Mansfield (1888–1923)

Miss Brill   1920

Although it was so brilliantly fine—the blue sky powdered with gold and great spots of light like white wine splashed over the Jardins Publiques° —Miss Brill was glad that she had decided on her fur. The air was motionless, but when you opened your mouth there was just a faint chill, like a chill from a glass of iced water before you sip, and now and again a leaf came drifting—from nowhere, from the sky. Miss Brill put up her hand and touched her fur. Dear little thing! It was nice to feel it again. She had taken it out of its box that afternoon, shaken out the moth-powder, given it a good brush, and rubbed the life back into the dim little eyes. "What has been happening to me?" said the sad little eyes. Oh, how sweet it was to see them snap at her again from the red eiderdown! . . . But the nose, which was of some black composition, wasn't at all firm. It must have had a knock, somehow. Never mind—a little dab of black sealing-wax when the time came—when it was absolutely necessary. . . . Little rogue! Yes, she really felt like that about it. Little rogue biting its tail just by her left ear. She could have taken it off and laid it on her lap and stroked it. She felt a tingling in her hands and arms, but that came from walking, she supposed. And when she breathed, something light and sad—no, not sad, exactly—something gentle seemed to move in her bosom.

There were a number of people out this afternoon, far more than last Sunday. And the band sounded louder and gayer. That was because the Season had begun. For although the band played all the year round on Sundays, out of season it was never the same. It was like some one playing with only the family to listen; it didn't care how it played if there weren't any strangers present. Wasn't the conductor wearing a new coat, too? She was sure it was new. He scraped with his foot and flapped his arms like a rooster about to crow, and the bandsmen sitting in the green rotunda blew out their cheeks and glared at the music. Now there came a little "flutey" bit—very pretty!—a little chain of bright drops. She was sure it would be repeated. It was; she lifted her head and smiled.

Only two people shared her "special" seat: a fine old man in a velvet coat, his hands clasped over a huge carved walking-stick, and a big old woman, sitting upright, with a roll of knitting on her embroidered apron. They did not speak. This was disappointing, for Miss Brill always looked forward to the conversation. She had become really quite expert, she thought, at listening as though she didn't listen, at sitting in other people's lives just for a minute while they talked round her.

Jardins Publiques: public gardens, or public park. The setting of the story is a seaside town in France.

She glanced, sideways, at the old couple. Perhaps they would go soon. Last Sunday, too, hadn't been as interesting as usual. An Englishman and his wife, he wearing a dreadful Panama hat and she button boots. And she'd gone on the whole time about how she ought to wear spectacles; she knew she needed them; but that it was no good getting any; they'd be sure to break and they'd never keep on. And he'd been so patient. He'd suggested everything—gold rims, the kind that curved round your ears, little pads inside the bridge. No, nothing would please her. "They'll always be sliding down my nose!" Miss Brill had wanted to shake her.

The old people sat on the bench, still as statues. Never mind, there was   5
always the crowd to watch. To and fro, in front of the flower-beds and the band rotunda, the couples and groups paraded, stopped to talk, to greet, to buy a handful of flowers from the old beggar who had his tray fixed to the railings. Little children ran among them, swooping and laughing; little boys with big white silk bows under their chins, little girls, little French dolls, dressed up in velvet and lace. And sometimes a tiny staggerer came suddenly rocking into the open from under the trees, stopped, stared, as suddenly sat down "flop," until its small high-stepping mother, like a young hen, rushed scolding to its rescue. Other people sat on the benches and green chairs, but they were nearly always the same, Sunday after Sunday, and—Miss Brill had often noticed—there was something funny about nearly all of them. They were odd, silent, nearly all old, and from the way they stared they looked as though they'd just come from dark little rooms or even—even cupboards!

Behind the rotunda the slender trees with yellow leaves down drooping, and through them just a line of sea, and beyond the blue sky with gold-veined clouds.

Tum-tum-tum tiddle-um! tiddle-um! tum tiddley-um tum ta! blew the band.

Two young girls in red came by and two young soldiers in blue met them, and they laughed and paired and went off arm-in-arm. Two peasant women with funny straw hats passed, gravely, leading beautiful smoke-coloured donkeys. A cold, pale nun hurried by. A beautiful woman came along and dropped her bunch of violets, and a little boy ran after to hand them to her, and she took them and threw them away as if they'd been poisoned. Dear me! Miss Brill didn't know whether to admire that or not! And now an ermine toque° and a gentleman in grey met just in front of her. He was tall, stiff, dignified, and she was wearing the ermine toque she'd bought when her hair was yellow. Now everything, her hair, her face, even her eyes, was the same colour as the shabby ermine, and her hand, in its cleaned glove, lifted to dab her lips, was a tiny yellowish paw. Oh, she was so pleased to see him—delighted! She rather thought they were going to meet that afternoon. She described where she'd been—everywhere, here, there, along by the sea. The day was so charming—didn't he agree? And wouldn't he, perhaps? . . . But he shook his head, lighted a cigarette, slowly breathed a great deep puff into her face, and, even while she was still talking and laughing, flicked the match away and walked on. The ermine toque was alone; she smiled more brightly than ever. But even the band seemed to know what she was feeling

toque: a hat. The phrase "ermine toque" refers to a woman wearing a hat made of the fur of a weasel.

and played more softly, played tenderly, and the drum beat, "The Brute! The Brute!" over and over. What would she do? What was going to happen now? But as Miss Brill wondered, the ermine toque turned, raised her hand as though she'd seen some one else, much nicer, just over there, and pattered away. And the band changed again and played more quickly, more gaily than ever, and the old couple on Miss Brill's seat got up and marched away, and such a funny old man with long whiskers hobbled along in time to the music and was nearly knocked over by four girls walking abreast.

Oh, how fascinating it was! How she enjoyed it! How she loved sitting here, watching it all! It was like a play. It was exactly like a play. Who could believe the sky at the back wasn't painted? But it wasn't till a little brown dog trotted on solemn and then slowly trotted off, like a little "theatre" dog, a little dog that had been drugged, that Miss Brill discovered what it was that made it so exciting. They were all on the stage. They weren't only the audience, not only looking on; they were acting. Even she had a part and came every Sunday. No doubt somebody would have noticed if she hadn't been there; she was part of the performance after all. How strange she'd never thought of it like that before! And yet it explained why she made such a point of starting from home at just the same time each week—so as not to be late for the performance—and it also explained why she had quite a queer, shy feeling at telling her English pupils how she spent her Sunday afternoons. No wonder! Miss Brill nearly laughed out loud. She was on the stage. She thought of the old invalid gentleman to whom she read the newspaper four afternoons a week while he slept in the garden. She had got quite used to the frail head on the cotton pillow, the hollowed eyes, the open mouth and the high pinched nose. If he'd been dead she mightn't have noticed for weeks; she wouldn't have minded. But suddenly he knew he was having the paper read to him by an actress! "An actress!" The old head lifted; two points of light quivered in the old eyes. "An actress—are ye?" And Miss Brill smoothed the newspaper as though it were the manuscript of her part and said gently: "Yes, I have been an actress for a long time."

10   The band had been having a rest. Now they started again. And what they played was warm, sunny, yet there was just a faint chill—a something, what was it?—not sadness—no, not sadness—a something that made you want to sing. The tune lifted, lifted, the light shone; and it seemed to Miss Brill that in another moment all of them, all the whole company, would begin singing. The young ones, the laughing ones who were moving together, they would begin, and the men's voices, very resolute and brave, would join them. And then she too, she too, and the others on the benches—they would come in with a kind of accompaniment—something low, that scarcely rose or fell, something so beautiful—moving. . . . And Miss Brill's eyes filled with tears and she looked smiling at all the other members of the company. Yes, we understand, we understand, she thought—though what they understood she didn't know.

Just at that moment a boy and a girl came and sat down where the old couple had been. They were beautifully dressed; they were in love. The hero and heroine, of course, just arrived from his father's yacht. And still soundlessly singing, still with that trembling smile, Miss Brill prepared to listen.

"No, not now," said the girl. "Not here, I can't."

"But why? Because of that stupid old thing at the end there?" asked the boy. "Why does she come here at all—who wants her? Why doesn't she keep her silly old mug at home?"

"It's her fu-fur which is so funny," giggled the girl. "It's exactly like a fried whiting."

"Ah, be off with you!" said the boy in an angry whisper. Then: "Tell me,   *15*
ma petite chérie—"

"No, not here," said the girl. "Not *yet*."

On her way home she usually bought a slice of honeycake at the baker's. It was her Sunday treat. Sometimes there was an almond in her slice, sometimes not. It made a great difference. If there was an almond it was like carrying home a tiny present—a surprise—something that might very well not have been there. She hurried on the almond Sundays and struck the match for the kettle in quite a dashing way.

But to-day she passed the baker's by, climbed the stairs, went into the little dark room—her room like a cupboard—and sat down on the red eiderdown. She sat there for a long time. The box that the fur came out of was on the bed. She unclasped the necklet quickly; quickly, without looking, laid it inside. But when she put the lid on she thought she heard something crying.

John Collier (1901–1980)

The Chaser   1940

Alan Austen, as nervous as a kitten, went up certain dark and creaky stairs in the neighborhood of Pell Street, and peered about for a long time on the dim landing before he found the name he wanted written obscurely on one of the doors.

He pushed open this door, as he had been told to do, and found himself in a tiny room, which contained no furniture but a plain kitchen table, a rocking-chair, and an ordinary chair. On one of the dirty buff-coloured walls were a couple of shelves, containing in all perhaps a dozen bottles and jars.

An old man sat in the rocking-chair, reading a newspaper. Alan, without a word, handed him the card he had been given. "Sit down, Mr. Austen," said the old man very politely. "I am glad to make your acquaintance."

"Is it true," asked Alan, "that you have a certain mixture that has—er—quite extraordinary effects?"

"My dear sir," replied the old man, "my stock in trade is not very large—I   *5*
don't deal in laxatives and teething mixtures—but such as it is, it is varied. I think nothing I sell has effects which could be precisely described as ordinary."

"Well, the fact is . . ." began Alan.

"Here, for example," interrupted the old man, reaching for a bottle from the shelf. "Here is a liquid as colourless as water, almost tasteless, quite imperceptible in coffee, wine, or any other beverage. It is also quite imperceptible to any known method of autopsy."

"Do you mean it is a poison?" cried Alan, very much horrified.

"Call it a glove-cleaner if you like," said the old man indifferently. "Maybe it will clean gloves. I have never tried. One might call it a life-cleaner. Lives need cleaning sometimes."

10   "I want nothing of that sort," said Alan.

"Probably it is just as well," said the old man. "Do you know the price of this? For one teaspoonful, which is sufficient, I ask five thousand dollars. Never less. Not a penny less."

"I hope all your mixtures are not as expensive," said Alan apprehensively.

"Oh dear, no," said the old man. "It would be no good charging that sort of price for a love potion, for example. Young people who need a love potion very seldom have five thousand dollars. Otherwise they would not need a love potion."

"I am glad to hear that," said Alan.

15   "I look at it like this," said the old man. "Please a customer with one article, and he will come back when he needs another. Even if it *is* more costly. He will save up for it, if necessary."

"So," said Alan, "you really do sell love potions?"

"If I did not sell love potions," said the old man, reaching for another bottle, "I should not have mentioned the other matter to you. It is only when one is in a position to oblige that one can afford to be so confidential."

"And these potions," said Alan. "They are not just—just—er—"

"Oh, no," said the old man. "Their effects are permanent, and extend far beyond the mere casual impulse. But they include it. Oh, yes, they include it. Bountifully, insistently. Everlastingly."

20   "Dear me!" said Alan, attempting a look of scientific detachment. "How very interesting!"

"But consider the spiritual side," said the old man.

"I do, indeed," said Alan.

"For indifference," said the old man, "they substitute devotion. For scorn, adoration. Give one tiny measure of this to the young lady—its flavour is imperceptible in orange juice, soup, or cocktails—and however gay and giddy she is, she will change altogether. She will want nothing but solitude and you."

"I can hardly believe it," said Alan. "She is so fond of parties."

25   "She will not like them any more," said the old man. "She will be afraid of the pretty girls you may meet."

"She will actually be jealous?" cried Alan in a rapture. "Of me?"

"Yes, she will want to be everything to you."

"She is, already. Only she doesn't care about it."

"She will, when she has taken this. She will care intensely. You will be her sole interest in life."

30   "Wonderful!" cried Alan.

"She will want to know all you do," said the old man. "All that has happened

to you during the day. Every word of it. She will want to know what you are
thinking about, why you smile suddenly, why you are looking sad."

"That is love!" cried Alan.

"Yes," said the old man. "How carefully she will look after you! She will
never allow you to be tired, to sit in a draught, to neglect your food. If you are
an hour late, she will be terrified. She will think you are killed, or that some
siren has caught you."

"I can hardly imagine Diana like that!" cried Alan, overwhelmed with joy.

"You will not have to use your imagination," said the old man. "And, by   *35*
the way, since there are always sirens, if by any chance you *should*, later on, slip
a little, you need not worry. She will forgive you, in the end. She will be terribly
hurt, of course, but she will forgive you—in the end."

"That will not happen," said Alan fervently.

"Of course not," said the old man. "But, if it did, you need not worry.
She would never divorce you. Oh, no! And, of course, she will never give you
the least, the very least, grounds for—uneasiness."

"And how much," said Alan, "is this wonderful mixture?"

"It is not as dear," said the old man, "as the glove-cleaner, or life-cleaner,
as I sometimes call it. No. That is five thousand dollars, never a penny less. One
has to be older than you are, to indulge in that sort of thing. One has to save up
for it."

"But the love potion?" said Alan.   *40*

"Oh, that," said the old man, opening the drawer in the kitchen table,
and taking out a tiny, rather dirty-looking phial. "That is just a dollar."

"I can't tell you how grateful I am," said Alan, watching him fill it.

"I like to oblige," said the old man. "Then customers come back, later in
life, when they are better off, and want more expensive things. Here you are.
You will find it very effective."

"Thank you again," said Alan. "Good-bye."

"Au revoir," said the old man.   *45*

Frank O'Connor (1903–1966)

First Confession   1951

All the trouble began when my grandfather died and my grandmother—my father's
mother—came to live with us. Relations in the one house are a strain at the best
of times, but, to make matters worse, my grandmother was a real old country-
woman and quite unsuited to the life in town. She had a fat, wrinkled old face,

and, to Mother's great indignation, went round the house in bare feet—the boots had her crippled, she said. For dinner she had a jug of porter° and a pot of potatoes with—sometimes—a bit of salt fish, and she poured out the potatoes on the table and ate them slowly, with great relish, using her fingers by way of a fork.

Now, girls are supposed to be fastidious, but I was the one who suffered most from this. Nora, my sister, just sucked up to the old woman for the penny she got every Friday out of the old-age pension, a thing I could not do. I was too honest, that was my trouble; and when I was playing with Bill Connell, the sergeant-major's son, and saw my grandmother steering up the path with the jug of porter sticking out from beneath her shawl I was mortified. I made excuses not to let him come into the house, because I could never be sure what she would be up to when we went in.

When Mother was at work and my grandmother made the dinner I wouldn't touch it. Nora once tried to make me, but I hid under the table from her and took the bread-knife with me for protection. Nora let on to be very indignant (she wasn't, of course, but she knew Mother saw through her, so she sided with Gran) and came after me. I lashed out at her with the bread-knife, and after that she left me alone. I stayed there till Mother came in from work and made my dinner, but when Father came in later Nora said in a shocked voice: "Oh, Dadda, do you know what Jackie did at dinnertime?" Then, of course, it all came out; Father gave me a flaking; Mother interfered, and for days after that he didn't speak to me and Mother barely spoke to Nora. And all because of that old woman! God knows, I was heart-scalded.

Then, to crown my misfortune, I had to make my first confession and communion. It was an old woman called Ryan who prepared us for these. She was about the one age with Gran; she was well-to-do, lived in a big house on Montenotte, wore a black cloak and bonnet, and came every day to school at three o'clock when we should have been going home, and talked to us of hell. She may have mentioned the other place as well, but that could only have been by accident, for hell had the first place in her heart.

5   She lit a candle, took out a new half-crown, and offered it to the first boy who would hold one finger—only one finger!—in the flame for five minutes by the school clock. Being always very ambitious I was tempted to volunteer, but I thought it might look greedy. Then she asked were we afraid of holding one finger—only one finger!—in a little candle flame for five minutes and not afraid of burning all over in roasting hot furnaces for all eternity. "All eternity! Just think of that! A whole lifetime goes by and it's nothing, not even a drop in the ocean of your sufferings." The woman was really interesting about hell, but my attention was all fixed on the half-crown. At the end of the lesson she put it back in her purse. It was a great disappointment; a religious woman like that, you wouldn't think she'd bother about a thing like a half-crown.

Another day she said she knew a priest who woke one night to find a fellow he didn't recognize leaning over the end of his bed. The priest was a bit frightened—naturally enough—but he asked the fellow what he wanted, and the fellow said in a deep, husky voice that he wanted to go to confession. The priest

---

porter: beer.

said it was an awkward time and wouldn't it do in the morning, but the fellow said that last time he went to confession, there was one sin he kept back, being ashamed to mention it, and now it was always on his mind. Then the priest knew it was a bad case, because the fellow was after making a bad confession and committing a mortal sin. He got up to dress, and just then the cock crew in the yard outside, and—lo and behold!—when the priest looked round there was no sign of the fellow, only a smell of burning timber, and when the priest looked at his bed didn't he see the print of two hands burned in it? That was because the fellow had made a bad confession. This story made a shocking impression on me.

But the worst of all was when she showed us how to examine our conscience. Did we take the name of the Lord, our God, in vain? Did we honour our father and our mother? (I asked her did this include grandmothers and she said it did.) Did we love our neighbours as ourselves? Did we covet our neighbour's goods? (I thought of the way I felt about the penny that Nora got every Friday.) I decided that, between one thing and another, I must have broken the whole ten command-ments, all on account of that old woman, and so far as I could see, so long as she remained in the house I had no hope of ever doing anything else.

I was scared to death of confession. The day the whole class went I let on to have a toothache, hoping my absence wouldn't be noticed; but at three o'clock, just as I was feeling safe, along comes a chap with a message from Mrs. Ryan that I was to go to confession myself on Saturday and be at the chapel for communion with the rest. To make it worse, Mother couldn't come with me and sent Nora instead.

Now, that girl had ways of tormenting me that Mother never knew of. She held my hand as we went down the hill, smiling sadly and saying how sorry she was for me, as if she were bringing me to the hospital for an operation.

"Oh, God help us!" she moaned. "Isn't it a terrible pity you weren't a   10
good boy? Oh, Jackie, my heart bleeds for you! How will you ever think of all your sins? Don't forget you have to tell him about the time you kicked Gran on the shin."

"Lemme go!" I said, trying to drag myself free of her. "I don't want to go to confession at all."

"But sure, you'll have to go to confession, Jackie," she replied in the same regretful tone. "Sure, if you didn't, the parish priest would be up to the house, looking for you. 'Tisn't, God knows, that I'm not sorry for you. Do you remember the time you tried to kill me with the bread-knife under the table? And the language you used to me? I don't know what he'll do with you at all, Jackie. He might have to send you up to the bishop."

I remember thinking bitterly that she didn't know the half of what I had to tell—if I told it. I knew I couldn't tell it, and understood perfectly why the fellow in Mrs. Ryan's story made a bad confession; it seemed to me a great shame that people wouldn't stop criticizing him. I remember that steep hill down to the church, and the sunlit hillsides beyond the valley of the river, which I saw in the gaps between the houses like Adam's last glimpse of Paradise.°

Then, when she had manœuvered me down the long flight of steps to the

Adam's last glimpse of Paradise: Genesis 3:23–24.

chapel yard, Nora suddenly changed her tone. She became the raging malicious devil she really was.

"There you are!" she said with a yelp of triumph, hurling me through the church door. "And I hope he'll give you the penitential psalms, you dirty little caffler."

I knew then I was lost, given up to eternal justice. The door with the coloured-glass panels swung shut behind me, the sunlight went out and gave place to deep shadow, and the wind whistled outside so that the silence within seemed to crackle like ice under my feet. Nora sat in front of me by the confession box. There were a couple of old woman ahead of her, and then a miserable-looking poor devil came and wedged me in at the other side, so that I couldn't escape even if I had the courage. He joined his hands and rolled his eyes in the direction of the roof, muttering aspirations in an anguished tone, and I wondered had he a grandmother too. Only a grandmother could account for a fellow behaving in that heartbroken way, but he was better off than I, for he at least could go and confess his sins; while I would make a bad confession and then die in the night and be continually coming back and burning people's furniture.

Nora's turn came, and I heard the sound of something slamming, and then her voice as if butter wouldn't melt in her mouth, and then another slam, and out she came. God, the hypocrisy of women! Her eyes were lowered, her head was bowed, and her hands were joined very low down on her stomach, and she walked up the aisle to the side altar looking like a saint. You never saw such an exhibition of devotion, and I remembered the devilish malice with which she had tormented me all the way from our door, and wondered were all religious people like that, really. It was my turn now. With the fear of damnation in my soul I went in, and the confessional door closed of itself behind me.

It was pitch-dark and I couldn't see priest or anything else. Then I really began to be frightened. In the darkness it was a matter between God and me, and He had all the odds. He knew what my intentions were before I even started; I had no chance. All I had ever been told about confession got mixed up in my mind, and I knelt to one wall and said: "Bless me, father, for I have sinned; this is my first confession." I waited for a few minutes, but nothing happened, so I tried it on the other wall. Nothing happened there either. He had me spotted all right.

It must have been then that I noticed the shelf at about one height with my head. It was really a place for grown-up people to rest their elbows, but in my distracted state I thought it was probably the place you were supposed to kneel. Of course, it was on the high side and not very deep, but I was always good at climbing and managed to get up all right. Staying up was the trouble. There was room only for my knees, and nothing you could get a grip on but a sort of wooden moulding, a bit above it. I held on to the moulding and repeated the words a little louder, and this time something happened all right. A slide was slammed back; a little light entered the box, and a man's voice said: "Who's there?"

"'Tis me, father," I said for fear he mightn't see me and go away again. I couldn't see him at all. The place the voice came from was under the moulding, about level with my knees, so I took a good grip of the moulding and swung myself down till I saw the astonished face of a young priest looking up at me.

He had to put his head on one side to see me, and I had to put mine on one side to see him, so we were more or less talking to one another upside-down. It struck me as a queer way of hearing confessions, but I didn't feel it my place to criticize.

"Bless me, father, for I have sinned; this is my first confession." I rattled off all in one breath, and swung myself down the least shade more to make it easier for him.

"What are you doing up there?" he shouted in an angry voice, and the strain the politeness was putting on my hold of the moulding, and the shock of being addressed in such an uncivil tone, were too much for me. I lost my grip, tumbled, and hit the door an unmerciful wallop before I found myself flat on my back in the middle of the aisle. The people who had been waiting stood up with their mouths open. The priest opened the door of the middle box and came out, pushing his biretta back from his forehead; he looked something terrible. Then Nora came scampering down the aisle.

"Oh, you dirty little caffler!" she said. "I might have known you'd do it. I might have known you'd disgrace me. I can't leave you out of my sight for one minute."

Before I could even get to my feet to defend myself she bent down and gave me a clip across the ear. This reminded me that I was so stunned I had even forgotten to cry, so that people might think I wasn't hurt at all, when in fact I was probably maimed for life. I gave a roar out of me.

"What's all this about?" the priest hissed, getting angrier than ever and   *25*
pushing Nora off me. "How dare you hit the child like that, you little vixen?"

"But I can't do my penance with him, father," Nora cried, cocking an outraged eye up to him.

"Well, go and do it, or I'll give you some more to do," he said, giving me a hand up. "Was it coming to confession you were, my poor man?" he asked me.

" 'Twas, father," said I with a sob.

"Oh," he said respectfully, "a big hefty fellow like you must have terrible sins. Is this your first?"

" 'Tis, father," said I.   *30*

"Worse and worse," he said gloomily. "The crimes of a lifetime. I don't know will I get rid of you at all today. You'd better wait now till I'm finished with these old ones. You can see by the looks of them they haven't much to tell."

"I will, father," I said with something approaching joy.

The relief of it was really enormous. Nora stuck out her tongue at me from behind his back, but I couldn't even be bothered retorting. I knew from the very moment that man opened his mouth that he was intelligent above the ordinary. When I had time to think, I saw how right I was. It only stood to reason that a fellow confessing after seven years would have more to tell than people that went every week. The crimes of a lifetime, exactly as he said. It was only what he expected, and the rest was the cackle of old women and girls with their talk of hell, the bishop, and the penitential psalms. That was all they knew. I started to make my examination of conscience, and barring the one bad business of my grandmother it didn't seem so bad.

The next time, the priest steered me into the confession box himself and left the shutter back the way I could see him get in and sit down at the further side of the grille from me.

35   "Well, now," he said, "what do they call you?"

"Jackie, father," said I.

"And what's a-trouble to you, Jackie?"

"Father," I said, feeling I might as well get it over while I had him in good humour," I had it all arranged to kill my grandmother."

He seemed a bit shaken by that, all right, because he said nothing for quite a while.

40   "My goodness," he said at last, "that'd be a shocking thing to do. What put that into your head?"

"Father," I said, feeling very sorry for myself, "she's an awful woman."

"Is she?" he asked. "What way is she awful?"

"She takes porter, father," I said, knowing well from the way Mother talked of it that this was a mortal sin, and hoping it would make the priest take a more favourable view of my case.

"Oh, my!" he said, and I could see he was impressed.

45   "And snuff, father," said I.

"That's a bad case, sure enough, Jackie," he said.

"And she goes round in her bare feet, father," I went on in a rush of self-pity, "and she knows I don't like her, and she gives pennies to Nora and none to me, and my da sides with her and flakes me, and one night I was so heart-scalded I made up my mind I'd have to kill her."

"And what would you do with the body?" he asked with great interest.

"I was thinking I could chop that up and carry it away in a barrow I have," I said.

50   "Begor, Jackie," he said, "do you know you're a terrible child?"

"I know, father," I said, for I was just thinking the same thing myself. "I tried to kill Nora too with a bread-knife under the table, only I missed her."

"Is that the little girl that was beating you just now?" he asked.

"'Tis, father."

"Someone will go for her with a bread-knife one day, and he won't miss her," he said rather cryptically. "You must have great courage. Between ourselves, there's a lot of people I'd like to do the same to but I'd never have the nerve. Hanging is an awful death."

55   "Is it, father?" I asked with the deepest interest—I was always very keen on hanging. "Did you ever see a fellow hanged?"

"Dozens of them," he said solemnly. "And they all died roaring."

"Jay!" I said.

"Oh, a horrible death!" he said with great satisfaction. "Lots of the fellows I saw killed their grandmothers too, but they all said 'twas never worth it."

He had me there for a full ten minutes talking, and then walked out the chapel yard with me. I was genuinely sorry to part with him, because he was the most entertaining character I'd ever met in the religious line. Outside, after the shadow of the church, the sunlight was like the roaring of waves on a beach; it dazzled me; and when the frozen silence melted and I heard the screech of trams on the road my heart soared. I knew now I wouldn't die in the night and

come back, leaving marks on my mother's furniture. It would be a great worry
to her, and the poor soul had enough.

Nora was sitting on the railing, waiting for me, and she put on a very sour   60
puss when she saw the priest with me. She was made jealous because a priest
had never come out of the church with her.

"Well," she asked coldly, after he left me, "what did he give you?"

"Three Hail Marys," I said.

"Three Hail Marys," she repeated incredulously. "You mustn't have told
him anything."

"I told him everything," I said confidently.

"About Gran and all?"   65

"About Gran and all."

(All she wanted was to be able to go home and say I'd made a bad confession.)

"Did you tell him you went for me with the bread-knife?" she asked with
a frown.

"I did to be sure."

"And he only gave you three Hail Marys?"   70

"That's all."

She slowly got down from the railing with a baffled air. Clearly, this was
beyond her. As we mounted the steps back to the main road she looked at me
suspiciously.

"What are you sucking?" she asked.

"Bullseyes."

"Was it the priest gave them to you?"   75

"'Twas."

"Lord God," she wailed bitterly, "some people have all the luck! 'Tis no
advantage to anybody trying to be good. I might just as well be a sinner like
you."

Eudora Welty (b. 1909)

A Worn Path   1941

It was December—a bright frozen day in the early morning. Far out in the country
there was an old Negro woman with her head tied in a red rag, coming along a
path through the pinewoods. Her name was Phoenix Jackson. She was very old
and small and she walked slowly in the dark pine shadows, moving a little from
side to side in her steps, with the balanced heaviness and lightness of a pendulum
in a grandfather clock. She carried a thin, small cane made from an umbrella,

and with this she kept tapping the frozen earth in front of her. This made a grave and persistent noise in the still air, that seemed meditative like the chirping of a solitary little bird.

She wore a dark striped dress reaching down to her shoe tops, and an equally long apron of bleached sugar sacks, with a full pocket: all neat and tidy, but every time she took a step she might have fallen over her shoelaces, which dragged from her unlaced shoes. She looked straight ahead. Her eyes were blue with age. Her skin had a pattern all its own of numberless branching wrinkles and as though a whole little tree stood in the middle of her forehead, but a golden color ran underneath, and the two knobs of her cheeks were illumined by a yellow burning under the dark. Under the rag her hair came down on her neck in the frailest of ringlets, still black, and with an odor like copper.

Now and then there was a quivering in the thicket. Old Phoenix said, "Out of my way, all you foxes, owls, beetles, jack rabbits, coons and wild animals! . . . Keep out from under these feet, little bob-whites. . . . Keep the big wild hogs out of my path. Don't let none of those come running my direction. I got a long way." Under her small black-freckled hand her cane, limber as a buggy whip, would switch at the brush as if to rouse up any hiding things.

On she went. The woods were deep and still. The sun made the pine needles almost too bright to look at, up where the wind rocked. The cones dropped as light as feathers. Down in the hollow was the mourning dove—it was not too late for him.

5   The path ran up a hill. "Seem like there is chains about my feet, time I get this far," she said, in the voice of argument old people keep to use with themselves. "Something always take a hold of me on this hill—pleads I should stay."

After she got to the top she turned and gave a full, severe look behind her where she had come. "Up through pines," she said at length. "Now down through oaks."

Her eyes opened their widest, and she started down gently. But before she got to the bottom of the hill a bush caught her dress.

Her fingers were busy and intent, but her skirts were full and long, so that before she could pull them free in one place they were caught in another. It was not possible to allow the dress to tear. "I in the thorny bush," she said. "Thorns, you doing your appointed work. Never want to let folks pass, no sir. Old eyes thought you was a pretty little *green* bush."

Finally, trembling all over, she stood free, and after a moment dared to stoop for her cane.

10   "Sun so high!" she cried, leaning back and looking, while the thick tears went over her eyes. "The time getting all gone here."

At the foot of this hill was a place where a log was laid across the creek.

"Now comes the trial," said Phoenix.

Putting her right foot out, she mounted the log and shut her eyes. Lifting her skirt, leveling her cane fiercely before her, like a festival figure in some parade, she began to march across. Then she opened her eyes and she was safe on the other side.

"I wasn't as old as I thought," she said.

15   But she sat down to rest. She spread her skirts on the bank around her and folded her hands over her knees. Up above her was a tree in a pearly cloud

of mistletoe. She did not dare to close her eyes, and when a little boy brought her a plate with a slice of marble-cake on it she spoke to him. "That would be acceptable," she said. But when she went to take it there was just her own hand in the air.

So she left that tree, and had to go through a barbed-wire fence. There she had to creep and crawl, speading her knees and stretching her fingers like a baby trying to climb the steps. But she talked loudly to herself: she could not let her dress be torn now, so late in the day, and she could not pay for having her arm or her leg sawed off if she got caught fast where she was.

At last she was safe through the fence and risen up out in the clearing. Big dead trees, like black men with one arm, were standing in the purple stalks of the withered cotton field. There sat a buzzard.

"Who you watching?"

In the furrow she made her way along.

"Glad this not the season for bulls," she said, looking sideways, "and the   20
good Lord made his snakes to curl up and sleep in the winter. A pleasure I don't see no two-headed snake coming around that tree, where it come once. It took a while to get by him, back in the summer."

She passed through the old cotton and went into a field of dead corn. It whispered and shook and was taller than her head. "Through the maze now," she said, for there was no path.

Then there was something tall, black, and skinny there, moving before her.

At first she took it for a man. It could have been a man dancing in the field. But she stood still and listened, and it did not make a sound. It was as silent as a ghost.

"Ghost," she said sharply, "who be you the ghost of? For I have heard of nary death close by."

But there was no answer—only the ragged dancing in the wind.   25

She shut her eyes, reached out her hand, and touched a sleeve. She found a coat and inside that an emptiness, cold as ice.

"You scarecrow," she said. Her face lighted. "I ought to be shut up for good," she said with laughter. "My senses is gone. I too old. I the oldest people I ever know. Dance, old scarecrow," she said, "while I dancing with you."

She kicked her foot over the furrow, and with mouth drawn down, shook her head once or twice in a little strutting way. Some husks blew down and whirled in streamers about her skirts.

Then she went on, parting her way from side to side with the cane, through the whispering field. At last she came to the end, to a wagon track where the silver grass blew between the red ruts. The quail were walking around like pullets, seeming all dainty and unseen.

"Walk pretty," she said. "This is the easy place. This the easy going."   30

She followed the track, swaying through the quiet bare fields, through the little strings of trees silver in their dead leaves, past cabins silver from weather, with the doors and windows boarded shut, all like old women under a spell sitting there. "I walking in their sleep," she said, nodding her head vigorously.

In a ravine she went where a spring was silently flowing through a hollow log. Old Phoenix bent and drank. "Sweet-gum makes the water sweet," she said, and drank more. "Nobody know who made this well, for it was here when I was born."

The track crossed a swampy part where the moss hung as white as lace from every limb. "Sleep on, alligators, and blow your bubbles." Then the track went into the road.

Deep, deep the road went down between the high green-colored banks. Overhead the live-oaks met, and it was as dark as a cave.

35   A black dog with a lolling tongue came up out of the weeds by the ditch. She was meditating, and not ready, and when he came at her she only hit him a little with her cane. Over she went in the ditch, like a little puff of milkweed.

Down there, her senses drifted away. A dream visited her, and she reached her hand up, but nothing reached down and gave her a pull. So she lay there and presently went to talking. "Old woman," she said to herself, "that black dog come up out of the weeds to stall you off, and now there he sitting on his fine tail smiling at you."

A white man finally came along and found her—a hunter, a young man, with his dog on a chain.

"Well, Granny!" he laughed. "What are you doing there?"

"Lying on my back like a June-bug waiting to be turned over, mister," she said, reaching up her hand.

40   He lifted her up, gave her a swing in the air, and set her down. "Anything broken, Granny?"

"No sir, them old dead weeds is springy enough," said Phoenix, when she had got her breath. "I thank you for your trouble."

"Where do you live, Granny?" he asked, while the two dogs were growling at each other.

"Away back yonder, sir, behind the ridge. You can't even see it from here."

"On your way home?"

45   "No sir, I going to town."

"Why, that's too far! That's as far as I walk when I come out myself, and I get something for my trouble." He patted the stuffed bag he carried, and there hung down a little closed claw. It was one of the bob-whites, with its beak hooked bitterly to show it was dead. "Now you go on home, Granny!"

"I bound to go to town, mister," said Phoenix. "The time come around."

He gave another laugh, filling the whole landscape. "I know you old colored people! Wouldn't miss going to town to see Santa Claus!"

But something held old Phoenix very still. The deep lines in her face went into a fierce and different radiation. Without warning, she had seen with her own eyes a flashing nickel fall out of the man's pocket onto the ground.

50   "How old are you, Granny?" he was saying.

"There is no telling, mister," she said, "no telling."

Then she gave a little cry and clapped her hands and said, "Git on away from here, dog! Look! Look at that dog!" She laughed as if in admiration. "He ain't scared of nobody. He a big black dog." She whispered, "Sic him!"

"Watch me get rid of that cur," said the man. "Sic him, Pete! Sic him!"

Phoenix heard the dogs fighting, and heard the man running and throwing sticks. She even heard a gunshot. But she was slowly bending forward by that time, further and further forward, the lids stretched down over her eyes, as if she were doing this in her sleep. Her chin was lowered almost to her knees. The yellow palm of her hand came out from the fold of her apron. Her fingers slid down and along the ground under the piece of money with the grace and care they would have in lifting an egg from under a setting hen. Then she slowly straightened up, she stood erect, and the nickel was in her apron pocket. A bird flew by. Her lips moved. "God watching me the whole time. I come to stealing."

The man came back, and his own dog panted about them. "Well, I scared   55
him off that time," he said, and then he laughed and lifted his gun and pointed it at Phoenix.

She stood straight and faced him.

"Doesn't the gun scare you?" he said, still pointing it.

"No, sir, I seen plenty go off closer by, in my day, and for less than what I done," she said, holding utterly still.

He smiled, and shouldered the gun. "Well, Granny," he said, "you must be a hundred years old, and scared of nothing. I'd give you a dime if I had any money with me. But you take my advice and stay home, and nothing will happen to you."

"I bound to go on my way, mister," said Phoenix. She inclined her head   60
in the red rag. Then they went in different directions, but she could hear the gun shooting again and again over the hill.

She walked on. The shadows hung from the oak trees to the road like curtains. Then she smelled wood-smoke, and smelled the river, and she saw a steeple and the cabins on their steep steps. Dozens of little black children whirled around her. There ahead was Natchez shining. Bells were ringing. She walked on.

In the paved city it was Christmas time. There were red and green electric lights strung and crisscrossed everywhere, and all turned on in the daytime. Old Phoenix would have been lost if she had not distrusted her eyesight and depended on her feet to know where to take her.

She paused quietly on the sidewalk where people were passing by. A lady came along in the crowd, carrying an armful of red-, green- and silver-wrapped presents; she gave off perfume like the red roses in hot summer, and Phoenix stopped her.

"Please, missy, will you lace up my shoe?" She held up her foot.

"What do you want, Grandma?"   65

"See my shoe," said Phoenix. "Do all right for out in the country, but wouldn't look right to go in a big building."

"Stand still then, Grandma," said the lady. She put her packages down on the sidewalk beside her and laced and tied both shoes tightly.

"Can't lace 'em with a cane," said Phoenix. "Thank you, missy. I doesn't mind asking a nice lady to tie up my shoe, when I gets out on the street."

Moving slowly and from side to side, she went into the big building, and into a tower of steps, where she walked up and around and around until her feet knew to stop.

She entered a door, and there she saw nailed up on the wall the document   70
that had been stamped with the gold seal and framed in the gold frame, which matched the dream that was hung up in her head.

"Here I be," she said. There was a fixed and ceremonial stiffness over her body.

"A charity case, I suppose," said an attendant who sat at the desk before her.

But Phoenix only looked above her head. There was sweat on her face, the wrinkles in her skin shone like a bright net.

"Speak up, Grandma," the woman said. "What's your name? We must have your history, you know. Have you been here before? What seems to be the trouble with you?"

75   Old Phoenix only gave a twitch to her face as if a fly were bothering her.

"Are you deaf?" cried the attendant.

But then the nurse came in.

"Oh, that's just old Aunt Phoenix," she said. "She doesn't come for herself— she has a little grandson. She makes these trips just as regular as clockwork. She lives away back off the Old Natchez Trace." She bent down. "Well, Aunt Phoenix, why don't you just take a seat? We won't keep you standing after your long trip." She pointed.

The old woman sat down, bolt upright in the chair.

80   "Now, how is the boy?" asked the nurse.

Old Phoenix did not speak.

"I said, how is the boy?"

But Phoenix only waited and stared straight ahead, her face very solemn and withdrawn into rigidity.

"Is his throat any better?" asked the nurse. "Aunt Phoenix, don't you hear me? Is your grandson's throat any better since the last time you came for the medicine?"

85   With her hands on her knees, the old woman waited, silent, erect and motion-less, just as if she were in armor.

"You mustn't take up our time this way, Aunt Phoenix," the nurse said. "Tell us quickly about your grandson, and get it over. He isn't dead, is he?"

At last there came a flicker and then a flame of comprehension across her face, and she spoke.

"My grandson. It was my memory had left me. There I sat and forgot why I made my long trip."

"Forgot?" the nurse frowned. "After you came so far?"

90   Then Phoenix was like an old woman begging a dignified forgiveness for waking up frightened in the night. "I never did go to school, I was too old at the Surrender," she said in a soft voice. "I'm an old woman without an education. It was my memory fail me. My little grandson, he is just the same, and I forgot it in the coming."

"Throat never heals, does it?" said the nurse, speaking in a loud, sure voice to old Phoenix. By now she had a card with something written on it, a little list. "Yes. Swallowed lye. When was it—January—two, three years ago—"

Phoenix spoke unasked now. "No, missy, he not dead, he just the same. Every little while his throat begin to close up again, and he not able to swallow. He not get his breath. He not able to help himself. So the time come around, and I go on another trip for the soothing medicine."

"All right. The doctor said as long as you came to get it, you could have it," said the nurse. "But it's an obstinate case."

"My little grandson, he sit up there in the house all wrapped up, waiting by himself," Phoenix went on. "We is the only two left in the world. He suffer and it don't seem to put him back at all. He got a sweet look. He going to last. He wear a little patch quilt and peep out holding his mouth open like a little bird. I remembers so plain now. I not going to forget him again, no, the whole enduring time. I could tell him from all the others in creation."

"All right." The nurse was trying to hush her now. She brought her a 95
bottle of medicine. "Charity," she said, making a check mark in a book.

Old Phoenix held the bottle close to her eyes, and then carefully put it into her pocket.

"I thank you," she said.

"It's Christmas time, Grandma," said the attendant. "Could I give you a few pennies out of my purse?"

"Five pennies is a nickel," said Phoenix stiffly.

"Here's a nickel," said the attendant. 100

Phoenix rose carefully and held out her hand. She received the nickel and then fished the other nickel out of her pocket and laid it beside the new one. She stared at her palm closely, with her head on one side.

Then she gave a tap with her cane on the floor.

"This is what come to me to do," she said. "I going to the store and buy my child a little windmill they sells, made out of paper. He going to find it hard to believe there such a thing in the world. I'll march myself back where he waiting, holding it straight up in this hand."

She lifted her free hand, gave a little nod, turned around, and walked out of the doctor's office. Then her slow step began on the stairs, going down.

Shirley Jackson (1919–1965)

The Lottery 1948

The morning of June 27th was clear and sunny, with the fresh warmth of a full-summer day; the flowers were blossoming profusely and the grass was richly green. The people of the village began to gather in the square, between the post office and the bank, around ten o'clock; in some towns there were so many people that the lottery took two days and had to be started on June 26th, but in this village, where there were only about three hundred people, the whole lottery took less than two hours, so it could begin at ten o'clock in the morning and still be through in time to allow the villagers to get home for noon dinner.

The children assembled first, of course. School was recently over for the summer, and the feeling of liberty sat uneasily on most of them; they tended to gather together quietly for a while before they broke into boisterous play, and their talk was still of the classroom and the teacher, of books and reprimands. Bobby Martin had already stuffed his pockets full of stones, and the other boys soon followed his example, selecting the smoothest and roundest stones; Bobby and Harry Jones and Dickie Delacroix—the villagers pronounced this name "Della-croy"—eventually made a great pile of stones in one corner of the square and guarded it against the raids of the other boys. The girls stood aside, talking among themselves, looking over their shoulders at the boys, and the very small children rolled in the dust or clung to the hands of their older brothers or sisters.

Soon the men began to gather, surveying their own children, speaking of planting and rain, tractors and taxes. They stood together, away from the pile of stones in the corner, and their jokes were quiet and they smiled rather than laughed. The women, wearing faded house dresses and sweaters, came shortly after their menfolk. They greeted one another and exchanged bits of gossip as they went to join their husbands. Soon the women, standing by their husbands, began to call to their children, and the children came reluctantly, having to be called four or five times. Bobby Martin ducked under his mother's grasping hand and ran, laughing, back to the pile of stones. His father spoke up sharply, and Bobby came quickly and took his place between his father and his oldest brother.

The lottery was conducted—as were the square dances, the teen-age club, the Halloween program—by Mr. Summers, who had time and energy to devote to civic activities. He was a round-faced, jovial man and he ran the coal business, and people were sorry for him, because he had no children and his wife was a scold. When he arrived in the square, carrying the black wooden box, there was a murmur of conversation among the villagers, and he waved and called, "Little late today, folks." The postmaster, Mr. Graves, followed him, carrying a three-legged stool, and the stool was put in the center of the square and Mr. Summers set the black box down on it. The villagers kept their distance, leaving a space between themselves and the stool, and when Mr. Summers said, "Some of you fellows want to give me a hand?" there was a hesitation before two men, Mr. Martin and his oldest son, Baxter, came forward to hold the box steady on the stool while Mr. Summers stirred up the papers inside it.

5   The original paraphernalia for the lottery had been lost long ago, and the black box now resting on the stool had been put into use even before Old Man Warner, the oldest man in town, was born. Mr. Summers spoke frequently to the villagers about making a new box, but no one liked to upset even as much tradition as was represented by the black box. There was a story that the present box had been made with some pieces of the box that had preceded it, the one that had been constructed when the first people settled down to make a village here. Every year, after the lottery, Mr. Summers began talking again about a new box, but every year the subject was allowed to fade off without anything's being done. The black box grew shabbier each year; by now it was no longer completely black but splintered badly along one side to show the original wood color, and in some places faded or stained.

Mr. Martin and his oldest son, Baxter, held the black box securely on the stool until Mr. Summers had stirred the papers thoroughly with his hand. Because so much of the ritual had been forgotten or discarded, Mr. Summers had been successful in having slips of paper substituted for the chips of wood that had been used for generations. Chips of wood, Mr. Summers had argued, had been all very well when the village was tiny, but now that the population was more than three hundred and likely to keep on growing, it was necessary to use something that would fit more easily into the black box. The night before the lottery, Mr. Summers and Mr. Graves made up the slips of paper and put them in the box, and it was then taken to the safe of Mr. Summers' coal company and locked up until Mr. Summers was ready to take it to the square next morning. The rest of the year, the box was put away, sometimes one place, sometimes another; it had spent one year in Mr. Graves' barn and another year underfoot in the post office, and sometimes it was set on a shelf in the Martin grocery and left there.

There was a great deal of fussing to be done before Mr. Summers declared the lottery open. There were the lists to make up—of heads of families, heads of households in each family, members of each household in each family. There was the proper swearing-in of Mr. Summers by the postmaster, as the official of the lottery; at one time, some people remembered, there had been a recital of some sort, performed by the official of the lottery, a perfunctory, tuneless chant that had been rattled off duly each year; some people believed that the official of the lottery used to stand just so when he said or sang it, others believed that he was supposed to walk among the people, but years and years ago this part of the ritual had been allowed to lapse. There had been, also, a ritual salute, which the official of the lottery had had to use in addressing each person who came up to draw from the box, but this also had changed with time, until now it was felt necessary only for the official to speak to each person approaching. Mr. Summers was very good at all this; in his clean white shirt and blue jeans, with one hand resting carelessly on the black box, he seemed very proper and important as he talked interminably to Mr. Graves and the Martins.

Just as Mr. Summers finally left off talking and turned to the assembled villagers, Mrs. Hutchinson came hurriedly along the path to the square, her sweater thrown over her shoulders, and slid into place in the back of the crowd. "Clean forgot what day it was," she said to Mrs. Delacroix, who stood next to her, and they both laughed softly. "Thought my old man was out back stacking wood," Mrs. Hutchinson went on, "and then I looked out the window and the kids was gone, and then I remembered it was the twenty-seventh and came a-running." She dried her hands on her apron, and Mrs. Delacroix said, "You're in time, though. They're still talking away up there."

Mrs. Hutchinson craned her neck to see through the crowd and found her husband and children standing near the front. She tapped Mrs. Delacroix on the arm as a farewell and began to make her way through the crowd. The people separated good-humoredly to let her through; two or three people said, in voices just loud enough to be heard across the crowd. "Here comes your Missus, Hutchinson," and "Bill, she made it after all." Mrs. Hutchinson reached her husband, and Mr. Summers, who had been waiting, said cheerfully, "Thought we were going to have to get on without you, Tessie." Mrs. Hutchinson said, grinning,

"Wouldn't have me leave m'dishes in the sink, now, would you, Joe?," and soft laughter ran through the crowd as the people stirred back into position after Mrs. Hutchinson's arrival.

10   "Well, now," Mr. Summers said soberly, "guess we better get started, get this over with, so's we can go back to work. Anybody ain't here?"

"Dunbar," several people said. "Dunbar, Dunbar."

Mr. Summers consulted his list. "Clyde Dunbar," he said. "That's right. He's broke his leg, hasn't he? Who's drawing for him?"

"Me, I guess," a woman said, and Mr. Summers turned to look at her. "Wife draws for her husband," Mr. Summers said. "Don't you have a grown boy to do it for you, Janey?" Although Mr. Summers and everyone else in the village knew the answer perfectly well, it was the business of the official of the lottery to ask such questions formally. Mr. Summers waited with an expression of polite interest while Mrs. Dunbar answered.

"Horace's not but sixteen yet," Mrs. Dunbar said regretfully. "Guess I gotta fill in for the old man this year."

15   "Right," Mr. Summers said. He made a note on the list he was holding. Then he asked, "Watson boy drawing this year?"

A tall boy in the crowd raised his hand. "Here," he said. "I'm drawing for m'mother and me." He blinked his eyes nervously and ducked his head as several voices in the crowd said things like "Good fellow, Jack," and "Glad to see your mother's got a man to do it."

"Well," Mr. Summers said, "guess that's everyone. Old Man Warner make it?"

"Here," a voice said, and Mr. Summers nodded.

A sudden hush fell on the crowd as Mr. Summers cleared his throat and looked at the list. "All ready?" he called. "Now, I'll read the names—heads of families first—and the men come up and take a paper out of the box. Keep the paper folded in your hand without looking at it until everyone has had a turn. Everything clear?"

20   The people had done it so many times that they only half listened to the directions; most of them were quiet, wetting their lips, not looking around. Then Mr. Summers raised one hand high and said, "Adams." A man disengaged himself from the crowd and came forward. "Hi, Steve," Mr. Summers said, and Mr. Adams said, "Hi, Joe." They grinned at one another humorlessly and nervously. Then Mr. Adams reached into the black box and took out a folded paper. He held it firmly by one corner as he turned and went hastily back to his place in the crowd, where he stood a little apart from his family, not looking down at his hand.

"Allen," Mr. Summers said. "Anderson. . . . Bentham."

"Seems like there's no time at all between lotteries any more," Mrs. Delacroix said to Mrs. Graves in the back row. "Seems like we got through with the last one only last week."

"Time sure goes fast," Mrs. Graves said.

"Clark. . . . Delacroix."

25   "There goes my old man," Mrs. Delacroix said. She held her breath while her husband went forward.

"Dunbar," Mr. Summers said, and Mrs. Dunbar went steadily to the box while one of the women said, "Go on, Janey," and another said, "There she goes."

"We're next," Mrs. Graves said. She watched while Mr. Graves came around from the side of the box, greeted Mr. Summers gravely, and selected a slip of paper from the box. By now, all through the crowd there were men holding the small folded papers in their large hands, turning them over and over nervously. Mrs. Dunbar and her two sons stood together, Mrs. Dunbar holding the slip of paper.

"Harburt. . . . Hutchinson."

"Get up there, Bill," Mrs. Hutchinson said, and the people near her laughed.

"Jones."   30

"They do say," Mr. Adams said to Old Man Warner, who stood next to him, "that over in the north village they're talking of giving up the lottery."

Old Man Warner snorted. "Pack of crazy fools," he said. "Listening to the young folks, nothing's good enough for *them*. Next thing you know, they'll be wanting to go back to living in caves, nobody work any more, live *that* way for a while. Used to be a saying about 'Lottery in June, corn be heavy soon.' First thing you know, we'd all be eating stewed chickweed and acorns. There's *always* been a lottery," he added petulantly. "Bad enough to see young Joe Summers up there joking with everybody."

"Some places have already quit lotteries," Mrs. Adams said.

"Nothing but trouble in *that*," Old Man Warner said stoutly. "Pack of young fools."

"Martin." And Bobby Martin watched his father go forward. "Overdyke.   35
. . . Percy."

"I wish they'd hurry," Mrs. Dunbar said to her older son. "I wish they'd hurry."

"They're almost through," her son said.

"You get ready to run tell Dad," Mrs. Dunbar said.

Mr. Summers called his own name and then stepped forward precisely and selected a slip from the box. Then he called, "Warner."

"Seventy-seventh year I been in the lottery," Old Man Warner said as he   40
went through the crowd. "Seventy-seventh time."

"Watson." The tall boy came awkwardly through the crowd. Someone said, "Don't be nervous, Jack," and Mr. Summers said, "Take your time, son."

"Zanini."

After that, there was a long pause, a breathless pause, until Mr. Summers, holding his slip of paper in the air, said, "All right, fellows." For a minute, no one moved, and then all the slips of paper were opened. Suddenly, all the women began to speak at once, saying, "Who is it?" "Who's got it?" "Is it the Dunbars?" "Is it the Watsons?" Then the voices began to say, "It's Hutchinson. It's Bill," "Bill Hutchinson's got it."

"Go tell your father," Mrs. Dunbar said to her older son.

People began to look around to see the Hutchinsons. Bill Hutchinson was standing quiet, staring down at the paper in his hand. Suddenly, Tessie Hutchinson shouted to Mr. Summers. "You didn't give him time enough to take any paper he wanted. I saw you. It wasn't fair!"

"Be a good sport, Tessie," Mrs. Delacroix called, and Mrs. Graves said, "All of us took the same chance."

"Shut up, Tessie," Bill Hutchinson said.

"Well, everyone," Mr. Summers said, "that was done pretty fast, and now we've got to be hurrying a little more to get done in time." He consulted his next list. "Bill," he said, "you draw for the Hutchinson family. You got any other households in the Hutchinsons?"

"There's Don and Eva," Mrs. Hutchinson yelled. "Make *them* take their chance!"

"Daughters draw with their husbands' families, Tessie," Mr. Summers said gently. "You know that as well as anyone else."

"It wasn't *fair*," Tessie said.

"I guess not, Joe," Bill Hutchinson said regretfully. "My daughter draws with her husband's family, that's only fair. And I've got no other family except the kids."

"Then, as far as drawing for families is concerned, it's you," Mr. Summers said in explanation, "and as far as drawing for households is concerned, that's you, too. Right?"

"Right," Bill Hutchinson said.

"How many kids, Bill?" Mr. Summers asked formally.

"Three," Bill Hutchinson said. "There's Bill, Jr., and Nancy, and little Dave. And Tessie and me."

"All right, then," Mr. Summers said. "Harry, you got their tickets back?"

Mr. Graves nodded and held up the slips of paper. "Put them in the box, then," Mr. Summers directed. "Take Bill's and put it in."

"I think we ought to start over," Mrs. Hutchinson said, as quietly as she could. "I tell you it wasn't *fair*. You didn't give him time enough to choose. *Every*-body saw that."

Mr. Graves had selected the five slips and put them in the box, and he dropped all the papers but those onto the ground, where the breeze caught them and lifted them off.

"Listen, everybody," Mrs. Hutchinson was saying to the people around her.

"Ready, Bill?" Mr. Summers asked, and Bill Hutchinson, with one quick glance around at his wife and children, nodded.

"Remember," Mr. Summers said, "take the slips and keep them folded until each person has taken one. Harry, you help little Dave." Mr. Graves took the hand of the little boy, who came willingly with him up to the box. "Take a paper out of the box, Davy," Mr. Summers said. Davy put his hand into the box and laughed. "Take just *one* paper," Mr. Summers said. "Harry, you hold it for him." Mr. Graves took the child's hand and removed the folded paper from the tight fist and held it while little Dave stood next to him and looked up at him wonderingly.

"Nancy next," Mr. Summers said. Nancy was twelve, and her school friends breathed heavily as she went forward, switching her skirt, and took a slip daintily from the box. "Bill, Jr.," Mr. Summers said, and Billy, his face red and his feet over-large, nearly knocked the box over as he got a paper out. "Tessie," Mr. Summers said. She hesitated for a minute, looking around defiantly, and then set her lips and went up to the box. She snatched a paper out and held it behind her.

"Bill," Mr. Summers said, and Bill Hutchinson reached into the box and felt around, bringing his hand out at last with the slip of paper in it.

The crowd was quiet. A girl whispered, "I hope it's not Nancy," and the sound of the whisper reached the edges of the crowd.   65

"It's not the way it used to be," Old Man Warner said clearly. "People ain't the way they used to be."

"All right," Mr. Summers said. "Open the papers. Harry, you open little Dave's."

Mr. Graves opened the slip of paper and there was a general sigh through the crowd as he held it up and everyone could see that it was blank. Nancy and Bill, Jr., opened theirs at the same time, and both beamed and laughed, turning around to the crowd and holding their slips of paper above their heads.

"Tessie," Mr. Summers said. There was a pause, and then Mr. Summers looked at Bill Hutchinson, and Bill unfolded his paper and showed it. It was blank.

"It's Tessie," Mr. Summers said, and his voice was hushed. "Show us her paper, Bill."   70

Bill Hutchinson went over to his wife and forced the slip of paper out of her hand. It had a black spot on it, the black spot Mr. Summers had made the night before with the heavy pencil in the coal-company office. Bill Hutchinson held it up, and there was a stir in the crowd.

"All right, folks," Mr. Summers said. "Let's finish quickly."

Although the villagers had forgotten the ritual and lost the original black box, they still remembered to use stones. The pile of stones the boys had made earlier was ready; there were stones on the ground with the blowing scraps of paper that had come out of the box. Mrs. Delacroix selected a stone so large she had to pick it up with both hands and turned to Mrs. Dunbar. "Come on," she said. "Hurry up."

Mrs. Dunbar had small stones in both hands, and she said, gasping for breath, "I can't run at all. You'll have to go ahead and I'll catch up with you."

The children had stones already, and someone gave little Davy Hutchinson a few pebbles.   75

Tessie Hutchinson was in the center of a cleared space by now, and she held her hands out desperately as the villagers moved in on her. "It isn't fair," she said. A stone hit her on the side of the head.

Old Man Warner was saying, "Come on, come on, everyone." Steve Adams was in the front of the crowd of villagers with Mrs. Graves beside him.

"It isn't fair, it isn't right," Mrs. Hutchinson screamed, and then they were upon her.

William Shakespeare (1564–1616)

Sonnet 73: That Time
of Year Thou Mayest
in Me Behold

1609

That time of year thou mayest in me behold,
When yellow leaves, or none, or few do hang
Upon those boughs which shake against the cold,
Bare ruined choirs, where late the sweet birds sang.
In me thou seest the twilight of such day,
As after Sunset fadeth in the West,
Which by and by black night doth take away,
Death's second self that seals up all in rest.
In me thou seest the glowing of such fire,
That on the ashes of his youth doth lie,
As the death bed, whereon it must expire,
Consumed with that which it was nourished by.
    This thou perceiv'st, which makes thy love more strong.
    To love that well, which thou must leave ere long.

Sonnet 116: Let Me Not
to the Marriage
of True Minds

1609

Let me not to the marriage of true minds
Admit impediments; love is not love
Which alters when it alteration finds,
Or bends with the remover to remove.
O no, it is an ever fixed mark
That looks on tempests and is never shaken;
It is the star to every wandering bark
Whose worth's unknown, although his height be taken.
Love's not Time's fool, though rosy lips and cheeks
Within his bending sickle's compass come;
Love alters not with his brief hours and weeks.
But bears it out even to the edge of doom:
    If this be error and upon me proved,
    I never writ, nor no man ever loved.

Sonnet 130: My Mistress' Eyes Are Nothing Like the Sun

1609

My Mistress' eyes are nothing like the Sun,
Coral is far more red, than her lips' red,
If snow be white, why then her breasts are dun:
If hairs be wires, black wires grow on her head:
I have seen Roses damasked, red and white,   5
But no such Roses see I in her cheeks,
And in some perfumes is there more delight,
Than in the breath that from my Mistress reeks.
I love to hear her speak, yet well I know,
That Music hath a far more pleasing sound: 10
I grant I never saw a goddess go,
My Mistress when she walks treads on the ground.
　　And yet by heaven I think my love as rare,
　　As any she belied with false compare.

John Donne (1572–1631)

A Valediction: Forbidding Mourning   1633

As virtuous men pass mildly away,
　　And whisper to their souls to go,
Whilst some of their sad friends do say
　　The breath goes now, and some say, No;

So let us melt, and make no noise,   5
　　No tear-floods, nor sigh-tempests move,
'Twere profanation° of our joys
　　To tell the laity° our love.

---

profanation, laity: as though the two lovers are priests of love, while ordinary people are ignorant of their relationship.

Moving of th'earth brings harms and fears,
10   Men reckon what it did and meant;
But trepidation° of the spheres,
    Though greater far, is innocent.°

Dull sublunary lovers' love
    (Whose soul is sense°) cannot admit
15 Absence, because it doth remove
    Those things which elemented it.

But we by a love so much refined
    That our selves know not what it is,
Inter-assured of the mind,
20   Care less, eyes, lips, and hands to miss.

Our two souls therefore, which are one,
    Though I must go, endure not yet
A breach, but an expansion,
    Like gold to airy thinness beat.°

25 If they be two, they are two so
    As stiff twin compasses° are two;
Thy soul, the fixt foot, makes no show
    To move, but doth, if th'other do.

And though it in the center sit,
30   Yet when the other far doth roam,
It leans and harkens after it,
    And grows erect, as that comes home.

Such wilt thou be to me, who must
    Like th'other foot, obliquely run;
35 Thy firmness draws my circle just,°
    And makes me end where I begun.

trepidation: Before Sir Isaac Newton explained the precession of the equinoxes, it was assumed that the positions of heavenly bodies should be constant and perfectly circular. The clearly observable irregularities (caused by the slow wobbling of the earth's axis) were explained by the concept of *trepidation*, or a trembling or oscillation that occurred in the outermost of the spheres surrounding the earth.
innocent: harmless.
soul is sense: lovers whose attraction is totally physical.
gold to airy thinness beat: a reference to the malleability of gold.
compasses: a compass used for drawing circles.
just: perfectly round

Edmund Waller (1606–1687)

Go, Lovely Rose   1645

Go, lovely rose,
Tell her that wastes her time and me
  That now she knows,
When I resemble° her to thee,
How sweet and fair she seems to be.   *5*

Tell her that's young,
And shuns to have her graces spied,
  That hadst thou sprung
In deserts, where no men abide,
Thou must have uncommended died.   *10*

Small is the worth
Of beauty from the light retired;
  Bid her come forth,
Suffer herself to be desired,
And not blush so to be admired.   *15*

Then die, that she
The common fate of all things rare
  May read in thee:
How small a part of time they share
That are so wondrous sweet and fair.   *20*

resemble: compare

Robert Burns (1759–1796)

O My Luve's Like a Red, Red Rose   1796

O my Luve's like a red, red rose,
  That's newly sprung in June:
O my Luve's like the melodie
  That's sweetly play'd in tune.

5
> As fair art thou, my bonnie lass,
>> So deep in luve am I;
> And I will luve thee still, my Dear,
>> Till a'° the seas gang° dry.

> Till a' the seas gang dry, my Dear,
10
>> And the rocks melt wi'° the sun:
> And I will luve thee still, my Dear,
>> While the sands o'° life shall run.

> And fare thee weel, my only Luve!
>> And fare thee weel, awhile!
15
> And I will come again, my Luve,
>> Tho' it were ten thousand mile!

a': all   *gang*: go   *wi'*: with   *o'*: of

Samuel Taylor Coleridge (1772–1834)

Kubla Khan   1816

> In Xanadu did Kubla Khan
> A stately pleasure dome decree:
> Where Alph, the sacred river, ran
> Through caverns measureless to man
5
>> Down to a sunless sea.
> So twice five miles of fertile ground
> With walls and towers were girdled round:
> And there were gardens bright with sinuous rills,
> Where blossomed many an incense-bearing tree;
10
> And here were forests ancient as the hills,
> Enfolding sunny spots of greenery.

> But oh! that deep romantic chasm which slanted
> Down the green hill athwart a cedarn cover!
> A savage place! as holy and enchanted
15
> As e'er beneath a waning moon was haunted
> By woman wailing for her demon lover!
> And from this chasm, with ceaseless turmoil seething,
> As if this earth in fast thick pants were breathing,
> A mighty fountain momently was forced:
20
> Amid whose swift half-intermitted burst
> Huge fragments vaulted like rebounding hail,

Or chaffy grain beneath the thresher's flail:
And 'mid these dancing rocks at once and ever
It flung up momently the sacred river.
Five miles meandering with a mazy motion   25
Through wood and dale the sacred river ran,
Then reached the caverns measureless to man,
And sank in tumult to a lifeless ocean:
And 'mid this tumult Kubla heard from far
Ancestral voices prophesying war!   30
   The shadow of the dome of pleasure
   Floated midway on the waves;
   Where was heard the mingled measure
   From the fountain and the caves.
It was a miracle of rare device,   35
A sunny pleasure dome with caves of ice!

   A damsel with a dulcimer
   In a vision once I saw:
   It was an Abyssinian maid,
   And on her dulcimer she played,   40
   Singing of Mount Abora.
Could I revive within me
Her symphony and song,
To such a deep delight 'twould win me,
That with music loud and long,   45
I would build that dome in air,
That sunny dome! those caves of ice!
And all who heard should see them there,
And all should cry. Beware! Beware!
His flashing eyes, his floating hair!   50
Weave a circle round him thrice,
And close your eyes with holy dread,
For he on honeydew hath fed,
And drunk the milk of Paradise.

John Keats (1795–1821)

On First Looking into Chapman's Homer   1816

Much have I travell'd in the realms of gold,
  And many goodly states and kingdoms seen;
  Round many western islands have I been

Which bards in fealty to Apollo hold.
Oft of one wide expanse had I been told
   That deep-brow'd Homer ruled as his demesne;
   Yet did I never breathe its pure serene
Till I heard Chapman speak out loud and bold:
Then felt I like some watcher of the skies
   When a new planet swims into his ken:
Or like stout Cortez when with eagle eyes
   He star'd at the Pacific—and all his men
Look'd at each other with a wild surmise—
   Silent, upon a peak in Darien.

Matthew Arnold (1822–1888)

Dover Beach

The sea is calm to-night.
The tide is full, the moon lies fair
Upon the straits:—on the French coast the light
Gleams and is gone; the cliffs of England stand,
Glimmering and vast, out in the tranquil bay.
Come to the window, sweet is the night air!
Only, from the long line of spray
Where the sea meets the moon-blanched land,
Listen! you hear the grating roar
Of pebbles which the waves draw back, and fling,
At their return, up the high strand,
Begin, and cease, and then again begin,
With tremulous cadence slow, and bring
The eternal note of sadness in.

Sophocles long ago
Heard it on the Ægean, and it brought
Into his mind the turbid ebb and flow
Of human misery; we
Find also in the sound a thought,
Hearing it by this distant northern sea.
The Sea of Faith
Was once, too, at the full, and round earth's shore
Lay like the folds of a bright girdle furled.
But now I only hear
Its melancholy, long, withdrawing roar,

Retreating, to the breath
Of the night wind, down the vast edges drear
And naked shingles of the world.

Ah, love, let us be true
To one another! for the world, which seems   *30*
To lie before us like a land of dreams,
So various, so beautiful, so new,
Hath really neither joy, nor love, nor light,
Nor certitude, nor peace, nor help for pain;
And we are here as on a darkling plain   *35*
Swept with confused alarms of struggle and flight
Where ignorant armies clash by night.

Emily Dickinson (1830–1886)

After Great Pain, a Formal Feeling Comes

1929 (ca. 1862)

After great pain, a formal feeling comes—
The Nerves sit ceremonious, like Tombs—
The stiff Heart questions was it He, that bore,
And Yesterday, or Centuries before?

The Feet, mechanical, go round—   5
Of Ground, or Air, or Ought° —
A Wooden way
Regardless grown,
A Quartz contentment, like a stone—

This is the Hour of Lead—   10
Remembered, if outlived,
As Freezing persons, recollect the Snow—
First—Chill—then Stupor—then the letting go—

Ought: anything, nothing

Thomas Hardy (1840–1928)

Channel Firing   1914

That night your great guns unawares,
Shook all our coffins as we lay,
And broke the chancel window squares.
We thought it was the Judgment-day

5   And sat upright. While drearisome
Arose the howl of wakened hounds:
The mouse let fall the altar-crumb,
The worms drew back into the mounds,

The glebe cow drooled. Till God called, "No;
10   It's gunnery practice out at sea
Just as before you went below;
The world is as it used to be:

"All nations striving strong to make
Red war yet redder. Mad as hatters
15   They do no more for Christés sake
Than you who are helpless in such matters.

"That this is not the judgment-hour
For some of them's a blessed thing,
For if it were they'd have to scour
20   Hell's floor for so much threatening . . .

"Ha, ha. It will be warmer when
I blow the trumpet (if indeed
I ever do; for you are men,
And rest eternal sorely need)."

25   So down we lay again. "I wonder,
Will the world ever saner be,"
Said one, "than when He sent us under
In our indifferent century!"

And many a skeleton shook his head.
30   "Instead of preaching forty year,"
My neighbor Parson Thirdly said,
"I wish I had stuck to pipes and beer."

Again the guns disturbed the hour,
Roaring their readiness to avenge,
35   As far inland as Stourton Tower,
And Camelot, and starlit Stonehenge.

Amy Lowell (1874–1925)

Patterns   1916

I walk down the garden paths,
And all the daffodils
Are blowing, and the bright blue squills.
I walk down the patterned garden-paths
In my stiff, brocaded gown.   *5*
With my powdered hair and jewelled fan,
I too am a rare
Pattern. As I wander down
The garden paths.

My dress is richly figured,   *10*
And the train
Makes a pink and silver stain
On the gravel, and the thrift
Of the borders.
Just a plate of current fashion   *15*
Tripping by in high-heeled, ribboned shoes.
Not a softness anywhere about me,
Only whalebone° and brocade.
And I sink on a seat in the shade

Of a lime tree. For my passion   *20*
Wars against the stiff brocade.
The daffodils and squills
Flutter in the breeze
As they please.
And I weep;   *25*
For the lime-tree is in blossom
And one small flower has dropped upon my bosom.

And the plashing of waterdrops
In the marble fountain
Comes down the garden-paths.   *30*
The dripping never stops.
Underneath my stiffened gown
Is the softness of a woman bathing in a marble basin,
A basin in the midst of hedges grown
So thick, she cannot see her lover hiding.   *35*

whalebone: Used as a stiffener in tightly laced corsets.

But she guesses he is near,
And the sliding of the water
Seems the stroking of a dear
Hand upon her.
40   What is Summer in a fine brocaded gown!
I should like to see it lying in a heap upon the ground.
All the pink and silver crumpled up on the ground.

I would be the pink and silver as I ran along the paths,
And he would stumble after,
45   Bewildered by my laughter.
I should see the sun flashing from his sword-hilt and buckles on his shoes.
I would choose
To lead him in a maze along the patterned paths,
A bright and laughing maze for my heavy-booted lover.
50   Till he caught me in the shade,
And the buttons of his waistcoat bruised my body as he clasped me,
Aching, melting, unafraid.
With the shadows of the leaves and the sundrops,
And the plopping of the waterdrops,
55   All about us in the open afternoon—
I am very like to swoon
With the weight of this brocade,
For the sun sifts through the shade.

Underneath the fallen blossom
60   In my bosom,
Is a letter I have hid.
It was brought to me this morning by a rider from the Duke.
Madam, we regret to inform you that Lord Hartwell
Died in action Thursday se'nnight.°
65   As I read it in the white, morning sunlight,
The letters squirmed like snakes.
"Any answer, Madam," said my footman.
"No," I told him.
"See that the messenger takes some refreshment.

70   No, no answer."
And I walked into the garden,
Up and down the patterned paths,
In my stiff, correct brocade.
The blue and yellow flowers stood up proudly in the sun,
75   Each one.
I stood upright too,
Held rigid to the pattern
By the stiffness of my gown.
Up and down I walked.
80   Up and down.

---

se'nnight: i.e. a week ago (seven nights) last Thursday

In a month he would have been my husband.
In a month, here, underneath this lime,
We would have broken the pattern;
He for me, and I for him,
He as Colonel, I as Lady,   85
On this shady seat.
He had a whim
That sunlight carried blessing.
And I answered, "It shall be as you have said."
Now he is dead.   90

In Summer and in Winter I shall walk
Up and down
The patterned garden-paths
In my stiff, brocaded gown.
The squills and daffodils   95
Will give place to pillared roses, and to asters, and to snow.
I shall go
Up and down,
In my gown.
Gorgeously arrayed,   100
Boned and stayed.
And the softness of my body will be guarded from embrace
By each button, hook, and lace.
For the man who should loose me is dead,
Fighting with the Duke in Flanders,°   105
In a pattern called a war.
Christ! What are patterns for?

Flanders: In western Belgium, an area of fierce fighting in 1914 and 1915. The second Battle of Ypres, in the spring of 1915, caused the losses of thousands of British officers and men (chlorine gas was used in the German attacks).

Robert Frost (1875–1963)

Desert Places   1936

Snow falling and night falling fast, oh, fast
In a field I looked into going past,
And the ground almost covered smooth in snow,
But a few weeds and stubble showing last.

5   The woods around it have it—it is theirs.
     All animals are smothered in their lairs.
     I am too absent-spirited to count;
     The loneliness includes me unawares.

     And lonely as it is that loneliness
10   Will be more lonely ere it will be less—
     A blanker whiteness of benighted snow
     With no expression, nothing to express.

     They cannot scare me with their empty spaces
     Between stars—on stars where no human race is.
15   I have it in me so much nearer home
     To scare myself with my own desert places.

John Masefield (1878–1967)

Cargoes   1902

     Quinquereme° of Nineveh° from distant Ophir,°
     Rowing home to haven in sunny Palestine,
     With a cargo of ivory,
     And apes and peacocks,°
5   Sandalwood, cedarwood,° and sweet white wine.

     Stately Spanish galleon coming from the Isthmus,°
     Dipping through the Tropics by the palm-green shores,
     With a cargo of diamonds,
     Emeralds, amethysts,
10   Topazes, and cinnamon, and gold moidores.°

     Dirty British coaster with a salt-caked smoke-stack,
     Butting through the Channel in the mad March days,
     With a cargo of Tyne coal,°
     Road-rails, pig-lead,
15   Firewood, iron-ware, and cheap tin trays.

Quinquereme: an ancient large ship with five tiers of oars.
Nineveh: "an exceeding great city," Jonah 3:3.
Ophir: Ophir probably was in Africa, and was known for its gold, I Kings 10:11; I Chron. 29:4.
apes and peacocks: I Kings 10:22, and 2 Chron. 9:21. These goods were brought to King Solomon.
cedarwood: I Kings 9:11.
Isthmus: the Isthmus of Panama.
moidores: Coin in use in Portugal and Brazil during the early times of exploration.
Tyne coal: Newcastle upon Tyne, a coal-producing area in north England.

    Reprinted with permission of Macmillan Publishing Company from *Poems* (1953) by John Masefield.

Wilfred Owen (1893–1918)

Anthem for Doomed Youth 1920

What passing-bells for these who die as cattle?
Only the monstrous anger of the guns.
Only the stuttering rifles' rapid rattle
Can patter out their hasty orisons.
No mockeries for them from prayers or bells, 5
Nor any voice of mourning save the choirs—
The shrill, demented choirs of wailing shells;
And bugles calling for them from sad shires.

What candles may be held to speed them all?
Not in the hands of boys, but in their eyes 10
Shall shine the holy glimmers of good-byes.
The pallor of girls' brows shall be their pall;
Their flowers the tenderness of patient minds,
And each slow dusk a drawing-down of blinds.

Langston Hughes (1902–1967)

Theme for English B (1951)

The instructor said,

Go home and write
a page tonight. 5
And let that page come out of you—
Then, it will be true.

I wonder if it's that simple?

I am twenty-two, colored, born in Winston-Salem.
I went to school there, then Durham, then here
to this college on the hill above Harlem.
10   I am the only colored student in my class.
The steps from the hill lead down to Harlem,
through a park, then I cross St. Nicholas,
Eighth Avenue, Seventh, and I come to the Y,
the Harlem Branch Y, where I take the elevator
15   up to my room, sit down, and write this page:

It's not easy to know what is true for you or me
at twenty-two, my age. But I guess I'm what
I feel and see and hear. Harlem, I hear you:
hear you, hear me—we two—you, me talk on this page.
20   (I hear New York, too.) Me—who?

Well, I like to eat, sleep, drink, and be in love.
I like to work, read, learn, and understand life.
I like a pipe for a Christmas present,
or records—Bessie, bop, or Bach.

25   I guess being colored doesn't make me not like
the same things other folks like who are other races.
So will my page be colored that I write?
Being me, it will not be white.
But it will be
30   a part of you, instructor.
You are white—
yet a part of me, as I am a part of you.
That's American.
35   Sometimes perhaps you don't want to be a part of me.
Nor do I often want to be a part of you.
But we are, that's true!
As I learn from you,
I guess you learn from me—
although you're older—and white—
40   and somewhat more free.

This is my page for English B.

Anton Chekhov (1860–1904)

The Bear:
A Joke in One Act

CAST OF CHARACTERS

Mrs. Popov. *A widow of seven months, Mrs. Popov is small and pretty, with dimples. She is a landowner. At the start of the play, she is pining away in memory of her dead husband.*

Grigory Stepanovich Smirnov. *Easily angered and loud,* Smirnov *is older. He is a landowner, too, and a gentleman farmer of some substance.*

Luka. Luka *is* Mrs. Popov's *footman (a servant whose main tasks were to wait table and attend the carriages, in addition to general duties.) He is old enough to feel secure in telling* Mrs. Popov *what he thinks.*

Gardener, Coachman, Workmen, *who enter at the end.*

The drawing room of Mrs. Popov's *country home.*

(Mrs. Popov, *in deep mourning, does not remove her eyes from a photograph.*)

Luka.   It isn't right madam   you're only destroying yourself. . . . The chambermaid and the cook have gone off berry picking; every living being is rejoicing; even the cat knows how to be content, walking around the yard catching birds, and you sit in your room all day as if it were a convent, and you don't take pleasure in anything. Yes, really! Almost a year has passed since you've gone out of the house!

Mrs. Popov.   And I shall never go out. . . . What for? My life is already ended. *He* lies in his grave; I have buried myself in these four walls . . . we are both dead.

Luka.   There you go again! Your husband is dead, that's as it was meant to be, it's the will of God, may he rest in peace. . . . You've done your mourning and that will do. You can't go on weeping and mourning forever. My wife died when her time came, too. . . . Well? I grieved, I wept for a month, and that was enough for her; the old lady wasn't worth a second more. (*Sighs.*) You've forgotten all your neighbors. You don't go anywhere or accept any calls. We live, so to speak, like spiders. We never see the light. The mice have eaten my uniform. It isn't as if there weren't any nice neighbors—the district is full of them . . . there's a regiment stationed at Riblov, such officers—they're like candy— you'll never get your fill of them! And in the barracks, never a Friday goes by without a dance; and, if you please, the military band plays music every day. . . . Yes, madam, my dear lady: you're young, beautiful, in the full bloom of youth—if only you took a little pleasure in life . . . beauty doesn't last forever,

Slightly altered from the Bantam Press edition of *Ten Great One-Act Plays*, Morris Sweetkind, ed. (1968).

you know! In ten years' time, you'll be wanting to wave your fanny in front of the officers—and it will be too late.

MRS. POPOV (*determined*).   I must ask you never to talk to me like that! You know that when Mr. Popov died, life lost all its salt for me. It may seem to you that I am alive, but that's only conjecture! I vowed to wear mourning to my grave and not to see the light of day. . . . Do you hear me? May his departed spirit see how much I love him. . . . Yes, I know, it's no mystery to you that he was often mean to me, cruel . . . and even unfaithful, but I shall remain true to the grave and show him I know how to love. There, beyond the grave, he will see me as I was before his death. . . .

5   LUKA.   Instead of talking like that, you should be taking a walk in the garden or have Toby or Giant harnessed and go visit some of the neighbors . . .

MRS. POPOV.   Ai! (*She weeps.*)

LUKA.   Madam! Dear lady! What's the matter with you! Christ be with you!

MRS. POPOV.   Oh, how he loved Toby! He always used to ride on him to visit the Korchagins or the Vlasovs. How wonderfully he rode! How graceful he was when he pulled at the reins with all his strength! Do you remember? Toby, Toby! Tell them to give him an extra bag of oats today.

LUKA.   Yes, madam.

(*Sound of loud ringing.*)

10   MRS POPOV (*shudders*).   Who's that? Tell them I'm not at home!

LUKA.   Of course, madam. (*He exits.*)

MRS. POPOV (*alone. Looks at the photograph*).   You will see, Nicholas, how much I can love and forgive . . . my love will die only when I do, when my poor heart stops beating. (*Laughing through her tears.*) Have you no shame? I'm a good girl, a virtuous little wife. I've locked myself in and I'll be true to you to the grave, and you . . . aren't you ashamed, you chubby cheeks? You deceived me, you made scenes, for weeks on end you left me alone . . .

LUKA (*enters, alarmed*).   Madam, somebody is asking for you. He wants to see you. . . .

MRS. POPOV.   But didn't you tell them that since the death of my husband, I don't see anybody?

15   LUKA.   I did, but he didn't want to listen; he spoke about some very important business.

MRS. POPOV.   I am *not at home*!

LUKA.   That's what I told him . . . but . . . the devil . . . he cursed and pushed past me right into the room . . . he's in the dining room right now.

MRS. POPOV (*losing her temper*).   Very well, let him come in . . . such manners! (LUKA *goes out.*) How difficult these people are! What does he want from me? Why should he disturb my peace? (*Sighs.*) But it's obvious I'll have to go live in a convent. . . . (*Thoughtfully.*) Yes, a convent. . . .

SMIRNOV (*to* LUKA).   You idiot, you talk too much. . . . Ass! (*Sees* MRS. POPOV *and changes to dignified speech.*) Madam, may I introduce myself: retired lieutenant of the artillery and landowner, Grigory Stepanovich Smirnov! I feel the necessity of troubling you about a highly important matter. . . .

20   MRS. POPOV (*refusing her hand*).   What do you want?

SMIRNOV. Your late husband, whom I had the pleasure of knowing, has remained in my debt for two twelve-hundred-ruble notes. Since I must pay the interest at the agricultural bank tomorrow, I have come to ask you, madam, to pay me the money today.

MRS. POPOV. One thousand two hundred. . . . And why was my husband in debt to you?

SMIRNOV. He used to buy oats from me.

MRS. POPOV (*sighing, to* LUKA). So, Luka, don't you forget to tell them to give Toby an extra bag of oats.

(LUKA *goes out.*)

(*To* SMIRNOV). If Nikolai, my husband, was in debt to you, then it goes without saying that I'll pay; but please excuse me today. I haven't any spare cash. The day after tomorrow, my steward will be back from town and I will give him instructions to pay you what is owed; until then I cannot comply with your wishes. . . . Besides, today is the anniversary— exactly seven months ago my husband died, and I'm in such a mood that I'm not quite disposed to occupy myself with money matters.

SMIRNOV. And I'm in such a mood that if I don't pay the interest tomorrow, 25 I'll be owing so much that my troubles will drown me. They'll take away my estate!

MRS. POPOV. You'll receive your money the day after tomorrow.

SMIRNOV. I don't want the money the day after tomorrow. I want it today.

MRS. POPOV. You must excuse me. I can't pay you today.

SMIRNOV. And I can't wait until after tomorrow.

MRS. POPOV. What can I do, if I don't have it now? 30

SMIRNOV. You mean to say you can't pay?

MRS. POPOV. I can't pay. . . .

SMIRNOV. Hm! Is that your last word?

MRS. POPOV. That is my last word.

SMIRNOV. Positively the last? 35

MRS. POPOV. Positively.

SMIRNOV. Thank you very much. We'll make a note of that. (*Shrugs his shoulders.*) And people want me to be calm and collected! Just now, on the way here, I met a tax officer and he asked me: why are you always so angry, Grigory Stepanovich? Goodness' sake, how can I be anything but angry? I need money desperately . . . I rode out yesterday early in the morning, at daybreak, and went to see all my debtors; and if only one of them had paid his debt . . . I was dog-tired, spent the night God knows where—a Jewish tavern beside a barrel of vodka. . . . Finally I got here, fifty miles from home, hoping to be paid, and you treat me to a "mood." How can I help being angry?

MRS. POPOV. It seems to me that I clearly said: My steward will return from the country and then you will be paid.

SMIRNOV. I didn't come to your steward, but to you! What the hell, if you'll pardon the expression, would I do with your steward?

MRS. POPOV. Excuse me, my dear sir, I am not accustomed to such un- 40 usual expressions nor to such a tone. I'm not listening to you any more. (*Goes out quickly.*)

SMIRNOV (*alone*).   Well, how do you like that? "A mood.". . . "Husband died seven months ago"! Must I pay the interest or mustn't I? I ask you: Must I pay, or must I not? So, your husband's dead, and you're in a mood and all that finicky stuff . . . and your steward's away somewhere; may he drop dead. What do you want me to do? Do you think I can fly away from my creditors in a balloon or something? Or should I run and bash my head against the wall? I go to Gruzdev—and he's not at home; Yaroshevich is hiding, with Kuritsin it's a quarrel to the death and I almost throw him out the window; Mazutov has diarrhea, and this one is in a "mood." Not one of these swine wants to pay me! And all because I'm too nice to them. I'm a sniveling idiot, I'm spineless, I'm an old lady! I'm too delicate with them! So, just you wait! You'll find out what I'm like! I won't let you play around with me, you devils! I'll stay and stick it out until she pays. Rrr! . . . How furious I am today, how furious! I'm shaking inside from rage and I can hardly catch my breath. . . . Damn it! My God, I even feel sick! (*He shouts.*) Hey, you!

LUKA (*enters*).   What do you want?

SMIRNOV.   Give me some beer or some water! (LUKA *exits.*) What logic is there in this! A man needs money desperately, it's like a noose around his neck— and she won't pay because, you see, she's not disposed to occupy herself with money matters! . . . That's the logic of a woman! That's why I never did like and do not like to talk to women. I'd rather sit on a keg of gunpowder than talk to a woman. Brr! . . . I even have goose pimples, this broad has put me in such a rage! All I have to do is see one of those spoiled bitches from a distance, and I get so angry it gives me a cramp in the leg. I just want to shout for help.

LUKA (*entering with water*).   Madam is sick and won't see anyone.

45   SMIRNOV.   Get out! (LUKA *goes.*) Sick and won't see anyone! No need to see me . . . I'll stay and sit here until you give me the money. You can stay sick for a week, and I'll stay for a week . . . if you're sick for a year, I'll stay a year. . . . I'll get my own back, dear lady! You can't impress me with your widow's weeds and your dimpled cheeks . . . we know all about those dimples! (*Shouts through the window.*) Semyon, unharness the horses! We're not going away quite yet! I'm staying here! Tell them in the stable to give the horses some oats! You brute, you let the horse on the left side get all tangled up in the reins again! (*Teasing.*) "Never mind" . . . I'll give you a never mind! (*Goes away from the window.*) Shit! The heat is unbearable and nobody pays up. I slept badly last night and on top of everything else this broad in mourning is "in a mood" . . . my head aches . . . (*Drinks, and grimaces.*) Shit! This is water! What I need is a drink! (*Shouts.*) Hey, you!

LUKA (*enters*).   What is it?

SMIRNOV.   Give me a glass of vodka. (LUKA *goes out.*) Oof! (*Sits down and examines himself.*) Nobody would say I was looking well! Dusty all over, boots dirty, unwashed, unkempt, straw on my waistcoat. . . . The dear lady probably took me for a robber. (*Yawns.*) It's not very polite to present myself in a drawing room looking like this; oh well, who cares? . . . I'm not here as a visitor but as a creditor, and there's no official costume for creditors. . . .

LUKA (*enters with vodka*).   You're taking liberties, my good man. . . .

SMIRNOV (*angrily*).   What?

LUKA.   I . . . nothing . . . I only . . .   50
SMIRNOV.   Who are you talking to? Shut up!
LUKA (*aside*).   The devil sent this leech. An ill wind brought him. . . . (LUKA *goes out.*)
SMIRNOV.   Oh how furious I am! I'm so mad I could crush the whole world into a powder! I even feel faint! (*Shouts.*) Hey, you!
MRS. POPOV (*enters, eyes downcast*).   My dear sir, in my solitude, I have long ago grown unaccustomed to the masculine voice and I cannot bear shouting. I must request you not to disturb my peace and quiet!
SMIRNOV.   Pay me my money and I'll go.
MRS. POPOV.   I told you in plain language: I haven't any spare cash now;   55
wait until the day after tomorrow.
SMIRNOV.   And I also told you respectfully, in plain language: I don't need the money the day after tomorrow, but today. If you don't pay me today, then tomorrow I'll have to hang myself.
MRS. POPOV.   But what can I do if I don't have the money? You're so strange!
SMIRNOV.   Then you won't pay me now? No?
MRS. POPOV.   I can't. . . .   60
SMIRNOV.   In that case, I can stay here and wait until you pay. . . . (*Sits down.*) You'll pay the day after tomorrow? Excellent! In that case I'll stay here until the day after tomorrow. I'll sit here all that time . . . (*Jumps up.*) I ask you: Have I got to pay the interest tomorrow, or not? Or do you think I'm joking?
MRS. POPOV.   My dear sir, I ask you not to shout! This isn't a stable!
SMIRNOV.   I wasn't asking you about a stable but about this: Do I have to pay the interest tomorrow or not?
MRS. POPOV.   You don't know how to behave in the company of a lady!
SMIRNOV.   No, I don't know how to behave in the company of a lady!   65
MRS. POPOV.   No, you don't! You are an ill-bred, rude man! Respectable people don't talk to a woman like that!
SMIRNOV.   Ach, it's astonishing! How would you like me to talk to you? In French, perhaps? (*Lisps in anger.*) Madam, je vous prie° . . . how happy I am that you're not paying me the money. . . . Ah, pardon, I've made you uneasy! Such lovely weather we're having today! And you look so becoming in your mourning dress. (*Bows and scrapes.*)
MRS. POPOV.   That's rude and not very clever!
SMIRNOV (*teasing*).   Rude and not very clever! I don't know how to behave in the company of ladies. Madam, in my time I've seen far more women than you've seen sparrows. Three times I've fought duels over women; I've jilted twelve women, nine have jilted me! Yes! There was a time when I played the fool; I became sentimental over women, used honeyed words, fawned on them, bowed and scraped. . . . I loved, suffered, sighed at the moon; I became limp, melted, shivered . . . I loved passionately, madly, every which way, devil take me, I chattered away like a magpie about the emancipation of women, ran through half my fortune as a result of my tender feelings; but now, if you will excuse me, I'm on to your ways! I've had enough! Dark eyes, passionate eyes, ruby

Madam, je vous prie: Madam, I beg you.

lips, dimpled cheeks; the moon, whispers, bated breath—for all that I wouldn't give a good goddamn. Present company excepted, of course, but all women, young and old alike, are affected clowns, gossips, hateful, consummate liars to the marrow of their bones, vain, trivial, ruthless, outrageously illogical, and as far as this is concerned (*taps on his forehead*), well, excuse my frankness, any sparrow could give pointers to a philosopher in petticoats! Look at one of those romantic creatures: muslin, ethereal demigoddess, a thousand raptures, and you look into her soul—a common crocodile! (*Grips the back of a chair; the chair cracks and breaks.*) But the most revolting part of it all is that this crocodile imagines that she has, above everything, her own privilege, a monopoly on tender feelings. The hell with it—you can hang me upside down by that nail if a woman is capable of loving anything besides a lapdog. All she can do when she's in love is slobber! While the man suffers and sacrifices, all her love is expressed in playing with her skirt and trying to lead him around firmly by the nose. You have the misfortune of being a woman, you know yourself what the nature of a woman is like. Tell me honestly; Have you ever in your life seen a woman who is sincere, faithful, and constant? You never have! Only old and ugly ladies are faithful and constant! You're more liable to meet a horned cat or a white woodcock than a faithful woman!

70   Mrs. Popov.   Pardon me, but in your opinion, who is faithful and constant in love? The man?

Smirnov.   Yes, the man!

Mrs. Popov.   The man! (*Malicious laugh.*) Men are faithful and constant in love! That's news! (*Heatedly*) What right have you to say that? Men are faithful and constant! For that matter, as far as I know, of all the men I have known and now know, my late husband was the best. . . . I loved him passionately, with all my being, as only a young intellectual woman can love; I gave him my youth, my happiness, my life, my fortune; he was my life's breath; I worshipped him as if I were a heathen, and . . . and, what good did it do—this best of men himself deceived me shamelessly at every step of the way. After his death, I found his desk full of love letters; and when he was alive—it's terrible to remember— he used to leave me alone for weeks at a time, and before my very eyes he flirted with other women and deceived me. He squandered my money, made a mockery of my feelings . . . and, in spite of all that, I loved him and was true to him . . . and besides, now that he is dead, I am still faithful and constant. I have shut myself up in these four walls forever and I won't remove these widow's weeds until my dying day. . . .

Smirnov (*laughs contemptuously*).   Widow's weeds! . . . I don't know what you take me for! As if I didn't know why you wear that black outfit and bury yourself in these four walls! Well, well! It's no secret, so romantic! When some fool of a poet passes by this country house, he'll look up at your window and think: "Here lives the mysterious Tamara, who, for the love of her husband, buried herself in these four walls." We know these tricks!

Mrs. Popov (*flaring*).   What? How dare you say that to me?

75   Smirnov.   You may have buried yourself alive, but you haven't forgotten to powder yourself!

Mrs. Popov.   How dare you use such expressions with me?

SMIRNOV.   Please don't shout. I'm not your steward! You must allow me to call a spade a spade. I'm not a woman and I'm used to saying what's on my mind! Don't you shout at me!

MRS. POPOV.   I'm not shouting, you are! Please leave me in peace!

SMIRNOV.   Pay me my money and I'll go.

MRS. POPOV.   I won't give you any money!   *80*

SMIRNOV.   Yes, you will.

MRS. POPOV.   To spite you, I won't pay you anything. You can leave me in peace!

SMIRNOV.   I don't have the pleasure of being either your husband or your fiancé, so please don't make scenes! (*Sits down.*) I don't like it.

MRS. POPOV (*choking with rage*).   You're sitting down?

SMIRNOV.   Yes, I am.

MRS. POPOV.   I ask you to get out!   *85*

SMIRNOV.   Give me my money . . . (*Aside.*) Oh, I'm so furious! Furious!

MRS. POPOV.   I don't want to talk to impudent people! Get out of here! (*Pause.*) You're not going? No?

SMIRNOV.   No.

MRS. POPOV.   No?

SMIRNOV.   No!   *90*

MRS. POPOV.   We'll see about that. (*Rings.*)

(LUKA *enters.*)

Luka, show the gentleman out!

LUKA (*goes up to* SMIRNOV).   Sir, will you please leave, as you have been asked. You mustn't . . .

SMIRNOV (*jumping up*).   Shut up! Who do you think you're talking to? I'll make mincemeat out of you!

LUKA (*his hand to his heart*).   Oh my God! Saints above! (*Falls into chair.*)   *95* Oh, I feel ill! I feel ill! I can't catch my breath!

MRS. POPOV.   Where's Dasha? Dasha! (*She shouts.*) Dasha! Pelagea! Dasha! (*She rings.*)

LUKA.   Oh! They've all gone berry picking . . . there's nobody at home . . . I'm ill! Water!

MRS. POPOV.   Will you please get out!

SMIRNOV.   Will you please be more polite?

MRS. POPOV (*clenches her fist and stamps her feet*).   You're nothing but a crude   *100* bear! A brute! A monster!

SMIRNOV.   What? What did you say?

MRS. POPOV.   I said that you were a bear, a monster!

SMIRNOV (*advancing toward her*).   Excuse me, but what right do you have to insult me?

MRS. POPOV.   Yes, I am insulting you . . . so what? Do you think I'm afraid of you?

SMIRNOV.   And do you think just because you're one of those romantic cre   *105* ations, that you have the right to insult me with impunity? Yes? I challenge you!

LUKA.   Lord in Heaven! Saints above! . . . Water!

SMIRNOV.   Pistols!

MRS. POPOV.   Do you think just because you have big fists and you can bellow like a bull, that I'm afraid of you? You're such a bully!

SMIRNOV.   I challenge you! I'm not going to let anybody insult me, and I don't care if you are a woman, a delicate creature!

110   MRS. POPOV (*trying to get a word in edgewise*).   Bear! Bear! Bear!

SMIRNOV.   It's about time we got rid of the prejudice that only men must pay for their insults! Devil take it, if women want to be equal, they should behave as equals! Let's fight!

MRS. POPOV.   You want to fight! By all means!

SMIRNOV.   This minute!

MRS. POPOV.   This minute! My husband had some pistols . . . I'll go and get them right away. (*Goes hurriedly and then returns.*) What pleasure I'll have putting a bullet through that thick head of yours! The hell with you! (*She goes out.*)

115   SMIRNOV.   I'll shoot her down like a chicken! I'm not a little boy or a sentimental puppy. I don't care if she is delicate and fragile.

LUKA.   Kind sir! Holy father! (*Kneels.*) Have pity on a poor old man and go away from here! You've frightened her to death and now you're going to shoot her?

SMIRNOV (*not listening to him*).   If she fights, then it means she believes in equality of rights and emancipation of women. Here the sexes are equal! I'll shoot her like a chicken! But what a woman! (*Imitates her.*) "The hell with you! . . . I'll put a bullet through that thick head of yours! . . ." What a woman! How she blushed, her eyes shone . . . she accepted the challenge! To tell the truth, it was the first time in my life I've seen a woman like that. . . .

LUKA.   Dear sir, please go away! I'll pray to God on your behalf as long as I live!

SMIRNOV.   That's a woman for you! A woman like that I can understand! A real woman! Not a sour-faced nincompoop but fiery, gundpowder! Fireworks! I'm even sorry to have to kill her!

120   LUKA (*weeps.*)   Dear sir . . . go away!

SMIRNOV.   I positively like her! Positively! Even though she has dimpled cheeks, I like her! I'm almost ready to forget about the debt. . . . My fury has diminished. Wonderful woman!

MRS. POPOV (*enters with pistols*).   Here they are, the pistols. Before we fight, you must show me how to fire. . . . I've never had a pistol in my hands before . . .

LUKA.   Oh dear Lord, for pity's sake. . . . I'll go and find the gardener and the coachman. . . . What did we do to deserve such trouble? (*Exit.*)

SMIRNOV (*examining the pistols*).   You see, there are several sorts of pistols . . . there are special dueling pistols, the Mortimer with primers. Then there are Smith and Wesson revolvers, triple action with extractors . . . excellent pistols! . . . they cost a minimum of ninety rubles a pair. . . . You must hold the revolver like this . . . (*Aside.*) What eyes, what eyes! A woman to set you on fire!

125   MRS. POPOV.   Like this?

SMIRNOV.   Yes, like this . . . then you cock the pistol . . . take aim . . . put your head back a little . . . stretch your arm out all the way . . . that's right . . . then with this finger press on this little piece of goods . . . and that's all there is to do . . . but the most important thing is not to get excited and aim without hurrying . . . try to keep your arm from shaking.

MRS. POPOV.   Good . . . it's not comfortable to shoot indoors. Let's go into the garden.

SMIRNOV.   Let's go. But I'm giving you advance notice that I'm going to fire into the air.

MRS. POPOV.   That's the last straw! Why? 130

SMIRNOV.   Why? . . . Why . . . because it's my business, that's why.

MRS. POPOV.   Are you afraid? Yes? Aahhh! No, sir. You're not going to get out of it that easily! Be so good as to follow me! I will not rest until I've put a hole through your forehead . . . that forehead I hate so much! Are you afraid?

SMIRNOV.   Yes, I'm afraid.

MRS. POPOV.   You're lying! Why don't you want to fight?

SMIRNOV.   Because . . . because you . . . because I like you.

MRS. POPOV (*laughs angrily*).   He likes me! He dares say that he likes me! 135
(*Points to the door.*) Out!

SMIRNOV (*loads the revolver in silence, takes cap and goes; at the door, stops for half a minute while they look at each other in silence; then he approaches* MRS. POPOV *hesitantly*). Listen. . . . Are you still angry? I'm extremely irritated, but, do you understand me, how can I express it . . . the fact is, that, you see, strictly speaking . . . (*He shouts.*) Is it my fault, really, for liking you? (*Grabs the back of a chair, which cracks and breaks.*) Why the hell do you have such fragile furniture! I like you! Do you understand? I . . . I'm almost in love with you!

MRS. POPOV.   Get away from me—I hate you!

SMIRNOV.   God, what a woman! I've never in my life seen anything like her! I'm lost! I'm done for! I'm caught like a mouse in a trap!

MRS. POPOV.   Stand back or I'll shoot!

SMIRNOV.   Shoot! You could never understand what happiness it would be 140
to die under the gaze of those wonderful eyes, to be shot by a revolver which was held by those little velvet hands. . . . I've gone out of my mind! Think about it and decide right away, because if I leave here, then we'll never see each other again! Decide . . . I'm a nobleman, a respectable gentleman, of good family. I have an income of ten thousand a year. . . . I can put a bullet through a coin tossed in the air . . . I have some fine horses. . . . Will you be my wife?

MRS. POPOV (*indignantly brandishes her revolver*).   Let's fight! I challenge you!

SMIRNOV.   I'm out of my mind . . . I don't understand anything . . . (*Shouts.*) Hey, you, water!

MRS. POPOV (*shouts*).   Let's fight!

SMIRNOV.   I've gone out of my mind. I'm in love like a boy, like an idiot! (*He grabs her hand, she screams with pain.*) I love you! (*Kneels.*) I love you as I've never loved before! I've jilted twelve women, nine women have jilted me, but I've never loved one of them as I love you. . . . I'm weak, I'm a limp rag. . . . I'm on my knees like a fool, offering you my hand. . . . Shame, shame! I haven't been in love for five years, I vowed I wouldn't; and suddenly I'm in love, like a fish out of water. I'm offering my hand in marriage. Yes or no? You don't want to? You don't need to! (*Gets up and quickly goes to the door.*)

MRS. POPOV.   Wait! 145

SMIRNOV (*stops*).   Well?

MRS. POPOV.   Nothing . . . you can go . . . go away . . . wait. . . . No, get out, get out! I hate you! But—don't go! Oh, if you only knew how furious I am, how angry! (*Throws revolver on table.*) My fingers are swollen from that nasty thing. . . . (*Tears her handkerchief furiously.*) What are you waiting for? Get out!

SMIRNOV.   Farewell!

MRS. POPOV.   Yes, yes, go away! (*Shouts.*) Where are you going? Stop. . . . Oh, go away! Oh, how furious I am! Don't come near me! Don't come near me!

150   SMIRNOV (*approaching her*).   How angry I am with myself! I'm in love like a student. I've been on my knees. . . . It gives me the shivers. (*Rudely.*) I love you! A lot of good it will do me to fall in love with you! Tomorrow I've got to pay the interest, begin the mowing of the hay. (*Puts his arm around her waist.*) I'll never forgive myself for this. . . .

MRS. POPOV.   Get away from me! Get your hands away! I . . . hate you! I . . . challenge you!

(*Prolonged kiss.* LUKA *enters with an ax, the* GARDENER *with a rake, the* COACHMAN *with a pitchfork, and* WORKMAN *with cudgels.*)

LUKA (*catches sight of the pair kissing*).   Lord in heaven! (*Pause.*)

MRS. POPOV (*lowering her eyes*).   Luka, tell them in the stable not to give Toby any oats today.

CURTAIN

Susan Glaspell (1882–1948)

Trifles   1916

CAST OF CHARACTERS

George Henderson, *county attorney*
Henry Peters, *sheriff*
Lewis Hale, *a neighboring farmer*
Mrs. Peters
Mrs. Hale

Scene. *The kitchen in the now abandoned farmhouse of John Wright, a gloomy kitchen, and left without having been put in order—unwashed pans under the sink, a loaf of bread outside the breadbox, a dish towel on the table—other signs of incompleted work. At the rear the outer door opens and the Sheriff comes in followed by the County Attorney and*

Reprinted by permission of Sirius C. Cook.

Hale. *The Sheriff and Hale are men in middle life, the County Attorney is a young man; all are much bundled up and go at once to the stove. They are followed by two women— the Sheriff's wife first; she is a slight wiry woman, a thin nervous face. Mrs. Hale is larger and would ordinarily be called more comfortable looking, but she is disturbed now and looks fearfully about as she enters. The women have come in slowly, and stand close together near the door.*

COUNTY ATTORNEY. (*Rubbing his hands.*)   This feels good. Come up to the fire, ladies.

MRS. PETERS. (*After taking a step forward.*)   I'm not—cold.

SHERIFF. (*Unbuttoning his overcoat and stepping away from the stove as if to mark the beginning of official business.*)   Now, Mr. Hale, before we move things about, you explain to Mr. Henderson just what you saw when you came here yesterday morning.

COUNTY ATTORNEY.   By the way, has anything been moved? Are things just as you left them yesterday?

SHERIFF. (*Looking about.*)   It's just the same. When it dropped below zero   5
last night I thought I'd better send Frank out this morning to make a fire for us—no use getting pneumonia with a big case on, but I told him not to touch anything except the stove—and you know Frank.

COUNTY ATTORNEY.   Somebody should have been left here yesterday.

SHERIFF.   Oh—yesterday. When I had to send Frank to Morris Center for that man who went crazy—I want you to know I had my hands full yesterday, I knew you could get back from Omaha by today and as long as I went over everything here myself—

COUNTY ATTORNEY.   Well, Mr. Hale, tell just what happened when you came here yesterday morning.

HALE.   Harry and I had started to town with a load of potatoes. We came along the road from my place and as I got here I said, "I'm going to see if I can't get John Wright to go in with me on a party telephone." I spoke to Wright about it once before and he put me off, saying folks talked too much anyway, and all he asked was peace and quiet—I guess you know about how much he talked himself; but I thought maybe if I went to the house and talked about it before his wife, though I said to Harry that I didn't know as what his wife wanted made much difference to John—

COUNTY ATTORNEY.   Let's talk about that later, Mr. Hale. I do want to talk   10
about that, but tell now just what happened when you got to the house.

HALE.   I didn't hear or see anything; I knocked at the door, and still it was all quiet inside. I knew they must be up, it was past eight o'clock. So I knocked again, and I thought I heard somebody say, "Come in." I wasn't sure, I'm not sure yet, but I opened the door—this door (*Indicating the door by which the two women are still standing*) and there in that rocker—(*Pointing to it*) sat Mrs. Wright.

(*They all look at the rocker.*)

COUNTY ATTORNEY.   What—was she doing?

HALE.   She was rockin' back and forth. She had her apron in her hand and was kind of—pleating it.

Country Attorney.   And how did she—look?

15   Hale.   Well, she looked queer.

Country Attorney.   How do you mean—queer?

Hale.   Well, as if she didn't know what she was going to do next. And kind of done up.

Country Attorney.   How did she seem to feel about your coming?

Hale.   Why, I don't think she minded—one way or other. She didn't pay much attention. I said, "How do, Mrs. Wright, it's cold, ain't it?" She she said, "Is it?"—and went on kind of pleating at her apron. Well, I was surprised; she didn't ask me to come up to the stove, or to set down, but just sat there, not even looking at me, so I said, "I want to see John." And then she—laughed. I guess you would call it a laugh. I thought of Harry and the team outside, so I said a little sharp: "Can't I see John?" "No," she says, kind o' dull like. "Ain't he home?" says I. "Yes," says she, "he's home." "Then why can't I see him?" I asked her, out of patience. " 'Cause he's dead," says she. "*Dead*?" says I. She just nodded her head, not getting a bit excited, but rockin' back and forth. "Why—where is he?" says I, not knowing what to say. She just pointed upstairs—like that (*Himself pointing to the room above*). I got up, with the idea of going up there. I walked from there to here—then I says, "Why, what did he die of?" "He died of a rope round his neck," says she, and just went on pleatin' at her apron. Well, I went out and called Harry. I thought I might—need help. We went upstairs and there he was lyin'—

20   Country Attorney.   I think I'd rather have you go into that upstairs, where you can point it all out. Just go on now with the rest of the story.

Hale.   Well, my first thought was to get that rope off. It looked . . . (*Stops, his face twitches*) . . . but Harry, he went up to him, and he said, "No, he's dead all right, and we'd better not touch anything." So we went back down stairs. She was still sitting that same way. "Has anybody been notified?" I asked. "No," says she, unconcerned. "Who did this, Mrs. Wright?" said Harry. He said it businesslike—and she stopped pleatin' of her apron. "I don't know," she says. "You don't *know*?" says Harry. "No," says she. "Weren't you sleepin' in the bed with him?" says Harry. "Yes," says she, "but I was on the inside." "Somebody slipped a rope round his neck and strangled him and you didn't wake up?" says Harry. "I didn't wake up," she said after him. We must 'a looked as if we didn't see how that could be, for after a minute she said, "I sleep sound." Harry was going to ask her more questions but I said maybe we ought to let her tell her story first to the coroner, or the sheriff, so Harry went fast as he could to Rivers' place, where there's a telephone.

Country Attorney.   And what did Mrs. Wright do when she knew that you had gone for the coroner?

Hale.   She moved from that chair to this one over here (*Pointing to a small chair in the coroner*) and just sat there with her hands held together and looking down. I got a feeling that I ought to make some conversation, so I said I had come in to see if John wanted to put in a telephone, and at that she started to laugh, and then she stopped and looked at me—scared. (*The County Attorney, who has had his notebook out, makes a note.*) I dunno, maybe it wasn't scared. I wouldn't like to say it was. Soon Harry got back, and then Dr. Lloyd came, and you, Mr. Peters, and so I guess that's all I know that you don't.

COUNTY ATTORNEY. (*Looking around.*) I guess we'll go upstairs first—and then out to the barn and around there. (*To the Sheriff*) You're convinced that there was nothing important here—nothing that would point to any motive.

SHERIFF. Nothing here but kitchen things. 25

(*The County Attorney, after again looking around the kitchen, opens the door of a cupboard closet. He gets up on a chair and looks on a shelf. Pulls his hand away, sticky.*)

COUNTY ATTORNEY. Here's a nice mess.

(*The women draw nearer.*)

MRS. PETERS. (*To the other woman.*) Oh, her fruit; it did freeze. (*To the County Attorney*) She worried about that when it turned so cold. She said the fire'd go out and her jars would break.

SHERIFF. Well, can you beat the women! Held for murder and worryin' about her preserves.

COUNTY ATTORNEY. I guess before we're through she may have something more serious than preserves to worry about.

HALE. Well, women are used to worrying over trifles. 30

(*The two women move a little closer together.*)

COUNTY ATTORNEY. (*With the gallantry of a young politician.*) And yet, for all their worries, what would we do without the ladies? (*The women do not unbend. He goes to the sink, takes a dipperful of water from the pail and pouring it into a basin, washes his hands. Starts to wipe them on the roller towel, turns it for a cleaner place.*) Dirty towels! (*Kicks his foot against the pans under the sink.*) Not much of a housekeeper, would you say, ladies?

MRS. HALE. (*Stiffly.*) There's a great deal of work to be done on a farm.

COUNTY ATTORNEY. To be sure. And yet (*With a little bow to her*) I know there are some Dickson county farmhouses which do not have such roller towels.

(*He gives it a pull to expose its full length again.*)

MRS. HALE. Those towels get dirty awful quick. Men's hands aren't always as clean as they might be.

COUNTY ATTORNEY. Ah, loyal to your sex, I see. But you and Mrs. Wright 35 were neighbors. I suppose you were friends, too.

MRS. HALE. (*Shaking her head.*) I've not seen much of her of late years. I've not been in this house—it's more than a year.

COUNTY ATTORNEY. And why was that? You didn't like her?

MRS. HALE. I liked her all well enough. Farmers' wives have their hands full, Mr. Henderson. And then—

COUNTY ATTORNEY. Yes—?

MRS. HALE. (*Looking about.*) It never seemed a very cheerful place. 40

COUNTY ATTORNEY. No—it's not cheerful. I shouldn't say she had the home-making instinct.

MRS. HALE. Well, I don't know as Wright had, either.

COUNTY ATTORNEY. You mean that they didn't get on very well?

MRS. HALE. No, I don't mean anything. But I don't think a place'd be any cheerfuller for John Wright's being in it.

45   COUNTY ATTORNEY.   I'd like to talk more of that a little later. I want to get the lay of things upstairs now.

(*He goes to the left, where three steps lead to a stair door.*)

        SHERIFF.   I suppose anything Mrs. Peter does'll be all right. She was to take in some clothes for her, you know, and a few little things. We left in such a hurry yesterday.
        COUNTY ATTORNEY.   Yes, but I would like to see what you take, Mrs. Peters, and keep an eye out for anything that might be of use to us.
        MRS. PETERS.   Yes, Mr. Henderson.

(*The women listen to the men's steps on the stairs, then look about the kitchen.*)

        MRS. HALE.   I'd hate to have men coming into my kitchen, snooping around and criticising.

(*She arranges the pans under the sink which the County Attorney had shoved out of place.*)

50   MRS. PETERS.   Of course it's no more than their duty.
        MRS. HALE.   Duty's all right, but I guess that deputy sheriff that came out to make the fire might have got a little of this on. (*Gives the roller towel a pull.*) Wish I'd thought of that sooner. Seems mean to talk about her for not having things slicked up when she had to come away in such a hurry.
        MRS. PETERS. (*Who has gone to a small table in the left rear corner of the room, and lifted one end of a towel that covers a pan.*) She had bread set.

(*Stands still.*)

        MRS. HALE. (*Eyes fixed on a loaf of bread beside the breadbox, which is on a low shelf at the other side of the room. Moves slowly toward it.*)   She was going to put this in there. (*Picks up loaf, then abruptly drops it. In a manner of returning to familiar things.*) It's a shame about her fruit. I wonder if it's all gone. (*Gets up on the chair and looks.*) I think there's some here that's all right, Mrs. Peters. Yes—here; (*Holding it toward the window*) this is cherries, too. (*Looking again.*) I declare I believe that's the only one. (*Gets down, bottle in her hand. Goes to the sink and wipes it off on the outside.*) She'll feel awful bad after all her hard work in the hot weather. I remember the afternoon I put up my cherries last summer.

(*She puts the bottle on the big kitchen table, center of the room. With a sigh, is about to sit down in the rocking-chair. Before she is seated realizes what chair it is; with a slow look at it, steps back. The chair which she has touched rocks back and forth.*)

        MRS. PETERS.   Well, I must get those things from the front room closet. (*She goes to the door at the right, but after looking into the other room, steps back.*) You coming with me, Mrs. Hale? You could help me carry them.

(*They go. in the other room; reappear, Mrs. Peters carrying a dress and skirt, Mrs. Hale following with a pair of shoes.*)

55   MRS. PETERS.   My, it's cold in there.

(*She puts the clothes on the big table, and hurries to the stove.*)

Mrs. Hale. (*Examining her skirt*). Wright was close. I think maybe that's why she kept so much to herself. She didn't even belong to the Ladies Aid. I suppose she felt she couldn't do her part, and then you don't enjoy things when you feel shabby. She used to wear pretty clothes and be lively, when she was Minnie Foster, one of the town girls singing in the choir. But that—oh, that was thirty years ago. This all you was to take in?

Mrs. Peters. She said she wanted an apron. Funny thing to want, for there isn't much to get you dirty in jail, goodness knows. But I suppose just to make her feel more natural. She said they was in the top drawer in this cupboard. Yes, here. And then her little shawl that always hung behind the door. (*Opens stair door and looks.*) Yes, here it is.

(*Quickly shuts door leading upstairs.*)

Mrs. Hale. (*Abruptly moving toward her.*) Mrs. Peters?
Mrs. Peters. Yes, Mrs. Hale?
Mrs. Hale. Do you think she did it?   60
Mrs. Peters. (*In a frightened voice.*) Oh, I don't know.
Mrs. Hale. Well, I don't think she did. Asking for an apron and her little shawl. Worrying about her fruit.
Mrs. Peters. (*Starts to speak, glances up, where footsteps are heard in the room above. In a low voice.*) Mr. Peters says it looks bad for her. Mr. Henderson is awful sarcastic in a speech and he'll make fun of her sayin' she didn't wake up.
Mrs. Hale. Well, I guess John Wright didn't wake when they was slipping that rope under his neck.
Mrs. Peters. No, it's strange. It must have been done awful crafty and   65
still. They say it was such a—funny way to kill a man, rigging it all up like that.
Mrs. Hale. That's just what Mr. Hale said. There was a gun in the house. He says that's what he can't understand.
Mrs. Peters. Mr. Henderson said coming out that what was needed for the case was a motive; something to show anger, or—sudden feeling.
Mrs. Hale. (*Who is standing by the table.*) Well, I don't see any signs of anger around here. (*She puts her hand on the dish towel which lies on the table, stands looking down at table, one half of which is clean, the other half messy.*) It's wiped to here. (*Makes a move as if to finish work, then turns and looks at loaf of bread outside the breadbox. Drops towel. In that voice of coming back to familiar things.*) Wonder how they are finding things upstairs. I hope she had it a little more red-up° up there. You know, it seems kind of *sneaking*. Locking her up in town and then coming out here and trying to get her own house to turn against her!
Mrs. Peters. But Mrs. Hale, the law is the law.   70
Mrs. Hale. I s'pose 'tis. (*Unbuttoning her coat.*) Better loosen up your things, Mrs. Peters. You won't feel them when you go out.

(*Mrs. Peters takes off her fur tippet, goes to hang it on hook at back of room, stands looking at the under part of the small corner table.*)

Mrs. Peters. She was piecing a quilt.

---

red-up: neat, arranged in order

(*She brings the large sewing basket and they look at the bright pieces.*)

MRS. HALE.   It's log cabin pattern. Pretty, isn't it? I wonder if she was goin' to quilt it or just knot it?

(*Footsteps have been heard coming down the stairs. The Sheriff enters followed by Hale and the County Attorney.*)

SHERIFF.   They wonder if she was going to quilt it or just knot it!

(*The men laugh; the women look abashed.*)

COUNTY ATTORNEY. (*Rubbing his hands over the stove.*)   Frank's fire didn't do much up there, did it? Well, let's go out to the barn and get that cleared up.

(*The men go outside.*)

75   MRS. HALE. (*Resentfully.*)   I don't know as there's anything so strange, our takin' up our time with little things while we're waiting for them to get the evidence. (*She sits down at the big table smoothing out a block with decision.*) I don't see as it's anything to laugh about.
MRS. PETERS.   (*Apologetically.*)   Of course they've got awful important things on their minds.

(*Pulls up a chair and joins Mrs. Hale at the table.*)

MRS. HALE. (*Examining another block.*)   Mrs. Peters, look at this one. Here, this is the one she was working on, and look at the sewing! All the rest of it has been so nice and even. And look at this! It's all over the place! Why, it looks as if she didn't know what she was about!

(*After she has said this they look at each other, then start to glance back at the door. After an instant Mrs. Hale has pulled at a knot and ripped the sewing.*)

MRS. PETERS.   Oh, what are you doing, Mrs. Hale?
MRS. HALE. (*Mildly.*)   Just pulling out a stitch or two that's not sewed very good. (*Threading a needle.*) Bad sewing always made me fidgety.
80   MRS. PETERS. (*Nervously.*)   I don't think we ought to touch things.
MRS. HALE.   I'll just finish up this end. (*Suddenly stopping and leaning forward.*) Mrs. Peters?
MRS. PETERS.   Yes, Mrs. Hale?
MRS. HALE.   What do you suppose she was so nervous about?
MRS. PETERS.   Oh—I don't know. I don't know as she was nervous. I sometimes sew awful queer when I'm just tired. (*Mrs. Hale starts to say something, looks at Mrs. Peters, then goes on sewing.*) Well, I must get these things wrapped up. They may be through sooner than we think. (*Putting apron and other things together.*) I wonder where I can find a piece of paper, and string.
85   MRS. HALE.   In that cupboard, maybe.
MRS. PETERS. (*Looking in cupboard.*)   Why, here's a birdcage. (*Holds it up.*) Did she have a bird, Mrs. Hale?
MRS. HALE.   Why, I don't know whether she did or not—I've not been here for so long. There was a man around last year selling canaries cheap, but I don't know as she took one; maybe she did. She used to sing real pretty herself.

Mrs. Peters. (*Glancing around.*)   Seems funny to think of a bird here. But she must have had one, or why would she have a cage? I wonder what happened to it.

Mrs. Hale.   I s'pose maybe the cat got it.

Mrs. Peters.   No, she didn't have a cat. She's got that feeling some people   90
have about cats—being afraid of them. My cat got in her room and she was real upset and asked me to take it out.

Mrs. Hale.   My sister Bessie was like that. Queer, ain't it?

Mrs. Peters. (*Examining the cage.*)   Why, look at this door, It's broke. One hinge is pulled apart.

Mrs. Hale. (*Looking too.*)   Looks as if someone must have been rough with it.

Mrs. Peters.   Why, yes.

(*She brings the cage forward and puts it on the table.*)

Mrs. Hale.   I wish if they're going to find any evidence they'd be about   95
it. I don't like this place.

Mrs. Peters.   But I'm awful glad you came with me, Mrs. Hale. It would be lonesome for me sitting here alone.

Mrs. Hale.   It would, wouldn't it? (*Dropping her sewing.*) But I tell you what I do wish, Mrs. Peters. I wish I had come over sometimes when *she* was here. I—(*Looking around the room*)—wish I had.

Mrs. Peters.   But of course you were awful busy, Mrs. Hale—your house and your children.

Mrs. Hale.   I could've come. I stayed away because it weren't cheerful— and maybe that's why I ought to have come. I—I've never liked this place. Maybe because it's down in a hollow and you don't see the road. I dunno what it is but it's a lonesome place and always was. I wish I had come over to see Minnie Foster sometimes. I can see now—

(*Shakes her head.*)

Mrs. Peters.   Well, you mustn't reproach yourself, Mrs. Hale. Somehow   100
we just don't see how it is with other folks until—something comes up.

Mrs. Hale.   Not having children makes less work—but it makes a quiet house, and Wright out to work all day, and no company when he did come in. Did you know John Wright, Mrs. Peters?

Mrs. Peters.   Not to know him; I've seen him in town. They say he was a good man.

Mrs. Hale.   Yes—good; he didn't drink, and kept his word as well as most, I guess, and paid his debts. But he was a hard man, Mrs. Peters. Just to pass the time of day with him—(*Shivers.*) Like a raw wind that gets to the bone. (*Pauses, her eye falling on the cage.*) I should think she would 'a wanted a bird. But what do you suppose went with it?

Mrs. Peters.   I don't know, unless it got sick and died.

(*She reaches over and swings the broken door, swings it again. Both women watch it.*)

Mrs. Hale.   You weren't raised round here, were you? (*Mrs. Peters shakes*   105
her head.) You didn't know—her?

Mrs. Peters.   Not till they brought her yesterday.

Mrs. Hale.   She—come to think of it, she was kind of like a bird herself—real sweet and pretty, but kind of timid and—fluttery. How—she—did—change. (*Silence; then as if struck by a happy thought and relieved to get back to everyday things.*) Tell you what, Mrs. Peters, why don't you take the quilt in with you? It might take up her mind.

Mrs. Peters.   Why, I think that's a real nice idea, Mrs. Hale. There couldn't possibly be any objection to it, could there? Now, just what would I take? I wonder if her patches are in here—and her things.

(*They look in the sewing basket.*)

Mrs. Hale.   Here's some red. I expect this has got sewing things in it. (*Brings out a fancy box.*) What a pretty box. Looks like something somebody would give you. Maybe her scissors are in here. (*Opens box. Suddenly puts her hand to her nose.*) Why—(*Mrs. Peters bends nearer, then turns her face away.*) There's something wrapped up in this piece of silk.

110   Mrs. Peters.   Why, this isn't her scissors.

Mrs. Hale. (*Lifting the silk.*)   Oh, Mrs. Peters—it's—

(*Mrs. Peters bends closer.*)

Mrs. Peters.   It's the bird.

Mrs. Hale. (*Jumping up.*)   But, Mrs. Peters—look at it! Its neck! Look at its neck! It's all—other side *to*.

Mrs. Peters.   Somebody—wrung—its—neck.

(*Their eyes meet. A look of growing comprehension, of horror. Steps are heard outside. Mrs. Hale slips box under quilt pieces, and sinks into her chair. Enter Sheriff and County Attorney. Mrs. Peters rises.*)

115   County Attorney. (*As one turning from serious things to little pleasantries.*)   Well, ladies, have you decided whether she was going to quilt it or knot it?

Mrs. Peters.   We think she was going to—knot it.

County Attorney.   Well, that's interesting, I'm sure. (*Seeing the birdcage.*) Has the bird flown?

Mrs. Hale. (*Putting more quilt pieces over the box.*)   We think the—cat got it.

County Attorney. (*Preoccupied.*)   Is there a cat?

(*Mrs. Hale glances in a quick covert way at Mrs. Peters.*)

120   Mrs. Peters.   Well, not *now*. They're superstitious, you know. They leave.

County Attorney. (*To Sheriff Peters, continuing an interrupted conversation.*)   No sign at all of anyone having come from the outside. Their own rope. Now let's go up again and go over it piece by piece. (*They start upstairs.*) It would have to have been someone who knew just the—

(*Mrs. Peters sits down. The two women sit there not looking at one another, but as if peering into something and at the same time holding back. When they talk now it is in the manner of feeling their way over strange ground, as if afraid of what they are saying, but as if they can not help saying it.*)

MRS. HALE.   She like the bird. She was going to bury it in that pretty box.

MRS. PETERS.   (*In a whisper.*)   When I was a girl—my kitten—there was a boy took a hatchet, and before my eyes—and before I could get there—(*Covers her face an instant*) If they hadn't held me back I would have—(*Catches herself, looks upstairs where steps are heard, falters weakly*)—hurt him.

MRS. HALE. (*With a slow look around her.*)   I wonder how it would seem never to have had any children around. (*Pause.*) No, Wright wouldn't like the bird—a thing that sang. She used to sing. He killed that, too.

MRS. PETERS. (*Moving uneasily.*)   We don't know who killed the bird.   125

MRS. HALE.   I knew John Wright.

MRS. PETERS.   It was an awful thing was done in this house that night, Mrs. Hale. Killing a man while he slept, slipping a rope around his neck that choked the life out of him.

MRS. HALE.   His neck. Choked the life out of him.

(Her hand goes out and rests on the birdcage.)

MRS. PETERS. (*With rising voice.*)   We don't know who killed him. We don't know.

MRS. HALE. (*Her own feeling not interrupted.*)   If there'd been years and years   130 of nothing, then a bird to sing to you, it would be awful—still, after the bird was still.

MRS. PETERS. (*Something within her speaking.*)   I know what stillness is. When we homesteaded in Dakota, and my first baby died—after he was two years old, and me with no other then—

MRS. HALE. (*Moving.*)   How soon do you suppose they'll be through, looking for the evidence?

MRS. PETRES.   I know what stillness is. (*Pulling herself back.*) The law has got to punish crime, Mrs. Hale.

MRS. HALE. (*Not as if answering that.*)   I wish you'd seen Minnie Foster when she wore a white dress with blue ribbons and stood up there in the choir and sang. (*A look around the room.*) Oh, I *wish* I'd come over here once in a while! That was a crime! That was a crime! Who's going to punish that?

MRS. PETERS. (*Looking upstairs.*)   We mustn't—take on.   135

MRS. HALE.   I might have known she needed help! I know how things can be—for women. I tell you, it's queer, Mrs. Peters. We live close together and we live far apart. We all go through the same things—it's all just a different kind of the same thing. (*Brushes her eyes; noticing the bottle of fruit, reaches out for it.*) If I was you I wouldn't tell her her fruit was gone. Tell her it *ain't*. Tell her it's all right. Take this in to prove it to her. She—she may never know whether it was broke or not.

MRS. PETERS. (*Takes the bottle, looks about for something to wrap it in; takes petticoat from the clothes brought from the other room, very nervously begins winding this around the bottle. In a false voice.*)   My, it's a good thing the men couldn't hear us. Wouldn't they just laugh! Getting all stirred up over a little thing like a—dead canary. As if that could have anything to do with—with—wouldn't they *laugh*!

(The men are heard coming down stairs.)

MRS. HALE. (*Under her breath.*)   Maybe they would—maybe they wouldn't.

COUNTY ATTORNEY.   No, Peters, it's all perfectly clear except a reason for doing it. But you know juries when it comes to women. If there was some definite thing. Something to show—something to make a story about—a thing that would connect up with this strange way of doing it—

(*The women's eyes meet for an instant. Enter Hale from outer door.*)

140   HALE.   Well, I've got the team around. Pretty cold out there.

COUNTY ATTORNEY.   I'm going to stay here a while by myself. (*To the Sheriff.*) You can send Frank out for me, can't you? I want to go over everything. I'm not satisfied that we can't do better.

SHERIFF.   Do you want to see what Mrs. Peters is going to take in?

(*The County Attorney goes to the table, picks up the apron, laughs.*)

COUNTY ATTORNEY.   Oh, I guess they're not very dangerous things the ladies have picked out. (*Moves a few things about, disturbing the quilt pieces which cover the box. Steps back.*) No, Mrs. Peters doesn't need supervising. For that matter, a sheriff's wife is married to the law. Ever think of it that way, Mrs. Peters?

MRS. PETERS.   Not—just that way.

145   SHERIFF. (*Chuckling*)   Married to the law. (*Moves toward the other room.*) I just want you to come in here a minute, George. We ought to take a look at these windows.

COUNTY ATTORNEY. (*Scoffingly.*)   Oh, windows!

SHERIFF.   We'll be right out, Mr. Hale.

(*Hale goes outside. The Sheriff follows the County Attorney into the other room. Then Mrs. Hale rises, hands tight together, looking intensely at Mrs. Peters, whose eyes make a slow turn, finally meeting Mrs. Hale's. A moment Mrs. Hale holds her, then her own eyes point the way to where the box is concealed. Suddenly Mrs. Peters throws back quilt pieces and tries to put the box in the bag she is wearing. It is too big. She opens box, starts to take bird out, cannot touch it, goes to pieces, stands there helpless. Sound of a knob turning in the other room. Mrs. Hale snatches the box and puts it in the pocket of her big coat. Enter County Attorney and Sheriff.*)

COUNTY ATTORNEY. (*Facetiously.*)   Well, Henry, at least we found out that she was not going to quilt it. She was going to—what is it you call it, ladies?

MRS. HALE. (*Her hand against her pocket.*)   We call it—knot it, Mr. Henderson.

CURTAIN

Glossary and Index

Abstract diction   Language far removed from reality, and therefore applicable to many things rather than to one or a few. *232–33*

Accent   See *Stress.*

Accentual, strong stress, or "sprung" rhythm   Lines relying not on traditional meters but rather on strong stresses. *190–91*

Accumulation   See *Cumulatio.*

ACHTERT   See *MLA Handbook.*

Actions, or Incidents   The events or occurrences in a work. *41*

AESOP, *The Fox and the Grapes. 136*

Allegory   A complete narrative that also may be applied to a parallel set of situations. *134 ff.* Ch. 11, Writing About Symbolism and Allegory. *132–42*

ALLEN, WOODY (film director), *Stardust Memories. 250*

Alliteration   The repetition of identical consonant sounds in different words in close proximity. *202*

American Psychological Association (APA), *Publication Manual. 303*

Amphibrach   A three-syllable foot consisting of a light, heavy, and light stress. *189*

Amphimacer, or Cretic   A three-syllable metrical foot consisting of a heavy, light, and heavy stress. *189*

Anapaest   A three-syllable foot consisting of two light stresses followed by a heavy stress. *188*

Antagonist(s), antagonism   The character or characters opposing the protagonist. A conflict between a protagonist and opposing forces is *antagonism. 47, 66*

Anticipation   See *Procatalepsis.*

Antimetabole   See *Chiasmus.*

ARNOLD, MATTHEW, "Dover Beach." *105.* Text, *350.* Sample theme, *154–57*

Article   A composition presenting facts and drawing conclusions; an essay. *6*

Assertion   A complete sentence putting an idea (the subject) into operation (the predicate); necessary for both expressing and understanding the idea. *102.*

Assonance   The repetition of identical vowel sounds in different words in close proximity. *202*

Atmosphere, or Mood   The emotional aura evoked by a work. *95*

Audience, or Mythical reader   See *Mythical Reader.*

Auditory images   Language describing sounds. *114*

Authorial voice   The voice or speaker used by authors when seemingly speaking for themselves. *79*

Bacchius, or Bacchic   A three-syllable metrical foot consisting of a light stress followed by two heavy stresses. *190*

Ballad, or Common measure   Quatrains in which lines of iambic tetrameter alternate with iambic trimeter, rhyming X-B-X-B. *5, 214*

Beast fable   See *Fable.*

Bellerophon (ancient myth). *135*

BENET, WILLIAM ROSE, *The Reader's Encyclopedia. 137*

Beowulf (Old English Poem). *135*

BERGMAN, INGMAR (film director), *The Virgin Spring. 250*

BLAKE, WILLIAM, "To Mrs. Anna Flaxman." *192*

Blank verse   Unrhymed iambic pentameter. *192*

Body (of a theme)   The middle and most extensive part of a theme, in which the major sub-points are developed. *18*

Brainstorming   The exploration and discovery of details to be used in composition. *14–15*

Crisis (Turning point) A point of uncertainty and tension that results from decisions and efforts made to resolve the conflict of a work; the crisis leads to the climax (q.v.). *47*

Cruden's Complete Biblical Concordance. 137

Cultural or universal symbols Symbols recognized and shared as a result of a common social and cultural heritage. *133*

Cumulatio, or Accumulation The parallel building up of much detail; a short way of introducing a considerable amount of material. *237*

Dactyl A three-syllable foot consisting of a heavy stress followed by two lights. *188*

DE MAUPASSANT, GUY, "The Necklace." *10, 35–38, 56–63, 70, 83, 84, 94, 104, 105, 140, 147, 160, 236.* Text, *314–19.* Sample themes, *38–39, 61–62*

Denotation The standard dictionary meaning of a word. *233–34*

Denouement (releasing, untying), or Resolution The actions following the climax, in which the work is brought to a conclusion. *48*

Device A rhetorical figure, or a verbal strategy. *121*

Dialogue The speech of two or more characters in a story, play, or poem. *5*

DICKINSON, EMILY, "After Great Pain a Formal Feeling Comes." *81, 161.* Text, *351*

Diction Word choice, types of words, and the level of language. *230–34*
  Formal Proper, elevated, elaborate, and often polysyllabic language. *230–31*
  Informal or Low Relaxed, conversational, and colloquial language, sometimes employing slang and grammatical mistakes. *230–32*
  Middle or Neutral Correct language characterized by directness and simplicity. *230–31*

Digraph Two letters spelling one segment of a sound, as in the word *digraph,* where *ph* spells the sound *f. 200*

Dilemma Two choices facing a protagonist, with either one being unacceptable or damaging; a cause of internal and also external conflicts. *42*

Dimeter A line consisting of two metrical feet. *185*

Diphthong A vowel produced by movement from one vowel position to another, as in *fly* and *cow. 200*

Dipody or Syzygy The submergence of two normal feet, usually iambs or trochees, under a stronger beat, so that a "galloping" or "rollicking" rhythm results. *190–91*

DISNEY, WALT *136*

Documentation Appendix B: A Note on Documentation, *295–303*

DONNE, JOHN, "Batter My Heart." *203.* "The Canonization." *214.* First Holy Sonnet. *222.* "A Valediction: Forbidding Mourning." *127, 129.* Text, *345–46*

Double Entendre Deliberate ambiguity, often sexual. *171–72*

DOYLE, SIR ARTHUR CONAN. Sherlock Holmes and point of view. *81*

Drama An individual play; also plays considered as a group. *5–6*

Dramatic Irony A special kind of situational irony in which a character perceives his or her plight in a limited way while the audience and one or more of the other characters understand it entirely. *172–73*

Dramatic Monologue A poem in which the speaker is presumed to be addressing a listener; hence the reader is like a witness or an eavesdropper. *5*

Dramatic, or Third-person objective point of view A third person narration reporting speech and action, but rigorously excluding commentary. *82–83, 85*

Dynamic character A character with the capacity to adapt, change, and grow (opposed to *static character*). *66*

Echoic words Words echoing the actions they describe, such as *buzz, bump,* and *slap,* important in the device of *onomatopoeia. 203*

Editing, or Montage (film). See *Montage.*

ELIOT, T. S., "Macavity, the Mystery Cat." *190*

Enclosing, or Framing use of setting See *Framing.*

End-stopped line A line ending in a full pause, usually indicated with a period or semicolon. *192*

Enjambement, or Run-on lines A line having no end punctuation but running over to the next line. *192*

Ephesians 2:8. *137.*

Epic A long narrative poem elevating human character, speech, and action. *4, 5*

Essay, or theme A short discourse unified by a dominating or central idea. *6, 10,* and *passim.*

Studying. *6–8*

Style   The manipulation of language, the placement of words in the service of content. *228*. Ch. 16 II: Writing About the Style of a Passage. *228–42*

Substitution   *Formal Substitution* is the use of a variant foot within a line. *Rhetorical Substitution* is the manipulation of the caesura to create the *effect* of a differing rhythm from the prevailing one. *192–94*

Swift, Jonathan, *Gulliver's Travels.* *105*

Syllable   A separately pronounced part of a word, or, in some cases, a complete word. *184*

Symbol, Symbolism   A specific thing that may stand for ideas, values, persons, or ways of life. *132*. Ch. 11, Writing About Symbolism and Allegory. *132–42*

Tactile image   Language describing touch. *114–15*

Tennyson, Alfred, Lord, "Locksley Hall." *189. The Passing of Arthur. 194.* Sample theme, *206–9*

Tension   The product of doubt or suspense; the major cause of interest in literature. *42*

Terza Rima   A three-line stanza form with the pattern A-B-A, B-C-B, etc. *215*

Tetrameter   A line consisting of four metrical feet. *185*

Theme   (a) The major or central idea of a work. *101–02* (b) A complete but short composition, with all paragraphs related systematically to a central idea. *10 ff*

Thesis sentence   An introductory sentence which names the topics to be developed in the body. *17–18*

Third-person objective point of view   See *Dramatic point of view.*

Third-person point of view   A method of narration in which all things are described in the third person (i.e., she, he, it, they, them, etc.) and in which the narrator is not introduced as an identifiable persona. *82–83, 85*

Tone   The methods used by writers to control attitudes. Ch. 14, Writing About Tone, *167–80*

Topic sentence   The sentence naming the subject of a paragraph. *18–19*

Tracking (film)   A cinematic technique in which the camera follows a moving subject *248*

Traditional poetry   Poetry using regular metrical and stanzaic patterns. *183*

Tragedy   A dramatic form in which a worthy protagonist meets a fate that is in excess of what he/she deserves. *6*

Trait   A typical mode of behavior. *65*

Trimeter   A line consisting of three metrical feet. *185*

Trochee   A two-syllable metrical foot containing a heavy accent followed by a light accent. *186–87*

Troyka, Lynn, *261*

Twain, Mark, "Luck." *237*

Understatement   The deliberate underplaying or undervaluing of a thing to create emphasis. *171*

Universal symbols   See *Cultural symbols.*

Value   Ideas that embody important concerns, loves, and objectives. *103*

Vangelis Papathanassiou (film composer); also simply *Vangelis. Chariots of Fire. 250*

Verbal irony   Language stating the opposite of what is meant. *171*

Verisimilitude (i.e., "like truth") or Probability   Adherence to reality, so that a work may be believable even if it is fictional. *70*

Visual images   Language describing visible objects. *114*

Visuals (film)   Unspoken action and movement in a film. *6, 248–50*

Voice   The speaker or persona; the point of view. *77*

Voiced consonant   A consonant produced with the vibration of the vocal chords, as in *z, v, d,* and *b. 201*

Voiceless consonant   A consonant produced without the vibration of the vocal chords, as in *s, f, t,* and *p;* whispered consonants. *201*

Vowel   A sound produced by the resonation of the voice in the space between the tongue and the top of the mouth, such as the *ee* in *feel,* the *eh* in *bet,* and the *ah* in *abroad. 200–201*

Waller, Edmund, "Go, Lovely Rose." *124*

Welles, Orson (film director), *Citizen Kane. 244, 247, 250.* Sample theme, *252–56*

Welty, Eudora, "A Worn Path." *44, 48, 51, 69, 70, 93, 102, 134, 137–38, 140, 145.* Sample themes, *45–46, 52–53, 154–57*